D1669770

TIGERS
IN THE MUD

22.12.03

0 11557 02911 6

TIGERS
IN THE MUD

The Combat Career of German Panzer
Commander Otto Carius

Otto Carius
Translated by Robert J. Edwards

STACKPOLE
BOOKS

First published in paperback in 2003 by
STACKPOLE BOOKS
5067 Ritter Road
Mechanicsburg, PA 17055
www.stackpolebooks.com

www.jjfpub.mb.ca

Printed in the United States of America

10 9 8 7 6 5 4 3 2 1

FIRST EDITION

Library of Congress Cataloging-in-Publication Data

Carius, Otto.
   Tigers in the mud : the combat career of German Panzer commander Otto Carius / by Otto Carius ; translated by Robert J. Edwards.— 1st ed.
       p. cm. — (Stackpole Military history series)
   ISBN 0-8117-2911-7 (pbk.)
   1. Carius, Otto. 2. World War, 1939–1945—Personal narratives, German. 3. World War, 1939–1945—Tank warfare. 4. Germany. Heer—Officers—Biography. 5. Tiger (Tank) I. Title. II. Series.
D811.C27735A3 2003
940.54'1343'092—dc21

                                                           2003008243

Table of Contents

Publisher's Acknowledgments ix

Foreword to the English-Language Edition xi

Dedication xiii

Foreword to the German Edition xv

The Fatherland Calls 1

In Napoleon's Wake 5

The First T34s 10

Back With the Old Gang 12

A Catastrophe 14

In Brittany 19

Portrait of the "Tiger" 21

On an Express Train to the Leningrad Front 25

Defensive Battle at Newel 33

Retreat to the Narwa 44

"Old Fritz" 53

The Front Held at Narwa 61

Calm Before the Storm 73

Ivan Attacks 84

Mutiny in the Bunker 97

"Operation Strachwitz" 100

The Night Was Hell 109

Fact or Fiction? 112

In Praise of the "Tiger" 117

Failure and Farewell 120

Knight's Cross at the Hospital 137

The German Fighters Didn't Show 146

"Report immediately to the unit" 151

Refusal to Obey Orders 153

Defensive Fighting at Dünaburg 162

The Ambush 166

A Fateful Difference of Opinion 174

Knocking on Death's Door! 180

Rapid Recovery in the Hospital 189

A Visit with Heinrich Himmler 194

The Catastrophe Looms 203

The Ruhr Pocket 206

The Chaos Grows 212

A Strange City Commandant 216

Approaching the End 222

The Heathens are Often the Better Christians 226

In Closing 228

Afterword to the English-Language Edition 229

    Glossary 232

    Documents:

        Notes to First Six Documents 238

        Document 1: After-Action Report 239

        Document 2: Technical After-Action Report 248

Document 3: After-Action Report for the Period
from March 17 to 21, 1944 256

Document 4: Secret 260

Document 5: After-Action Report on the Employment of
the staff, 2nd Company, and 3rd Company
of the 502nd Heavy Panzer Battalion in
the Area of the 18th Army in the Period
from June 24 to 30, 1944 263

Document 6: After-Action Report on the Employment
of the 502nd Heavy Panzer Battalion
in the 16th Army Sector from July 4
to August 17, 1944 275

Appendix 310

Index 361

Maps:

Map 1 32

Map 2 62

Map 3: Attack against the "Judennase" 138

Publisher's Acknowledgments

(For original English translation)

I wish to thank the following individuals who have contributed to the original publishing of this book in English.

Robert J. Edwards—Translation

George Rugenius—Proofreading

Brian Molloy—Cover Art

Brian Molloy—Signing Box

I also wish to thank you the reader for purchasing this book and all those of you who have written to me with your kind words of praise and encouragement. It gives me the impetus to continue to publish translations of the best German books available. More excellent books are either being prepared or negotiated, thanks to your helpful proposals. These will be announced as they near completion.

The photos in this book come from the personal photo album of Mr. Otto Carius. I am forever grateful to Mr. Carius for allowing me to use these photos [most never published before] in this book. I am also grateful, and very moved, that he agreed to have J. J. Fedorowicz Publishing bring out his book in English.

John Fedorowicz

Foreword to the English-Language Edition

We soldiers of the former German Wehrmacht are thankful to Fedorowicz Publishing for the English-language editions of German books concerning World War II. Through these publications, the defamation of the German soldier in film, television, and the press has been countered, and the picture of the Wehrmacht has become a more objective one by means of the help offered by many sources.

We are especially grateful when we think of our fallen comrades who, together with volunteers from all countries of Western Europe, fought to be saved from communism and whose memory has been stained by defamation.

Unfortunately, we have had to experience firsthand how war memorials have been destroyed and desecrated in our own country while "memorials in honor of the unknown deserter" have been ceremoniously dedicated in Bremen, Hamburg, and Bonn. This despicable behavior is probably unthinkable in any other country.

(It must be noted: Up until December 31, 1944, there were 1,408 deserters registered in the Wehrmacht out of approximately seven million members of the Wehrmacht during five years of war!)

No other people had been so audaciously and (which embarrasses me) so successfully lied to as the German people after 1945. Despite the latest sources, the historical picture has not been corrected. With the help of a lot of former propaganda people of the Third Reich, the "reeducation" was a complete success. Tradition is smiled at; the achievements of the Wehrmacht and of our entire people in World War II are recognized, at best, by our former opponents. In some cases, they are even admired.

Given the attitude of the public, it can be understood why the "citizen in uniform" usually only performs his military service in order to avoid the possibility of the longer and more unpleasant civil service. Politicians, church leaders, and other personalities from public life characterize soldiers of the Bundeswehr as "potential murderers" and go unpunished by the courts. Even Minister Blüm (the Minister of Labor) can declare in a speech in Poland that for him there was no difference between a soldier and a guard in a concentration camp.

Thus it amazes me that the "western community" was surprised by the reaction of the German public to the war in the Gulf. If soldierly virtues and any type of idealism have been trampled on and ridiculed for decades, then nothing else can be expected. If everyone just watches out for himself, then idealism simply cannot be pulled out of a drawer when it is needed!

Each soldier has to do his duty "as the law prescribes." The enemy is never determined by him, but rather for him by the politicians. *"Mourir au feu ou sur la route, c'est le metier du soldat"* (To die under fire or on the march, that is the lot of the soldier.) This saying of Napoleon continues to apply to all soldiers. The common experience binds the combat soldiers of all nations, as is seen in many get-togethers.

Since 1945, there hasn't been a week without war somewhere in the world. In the delirium following victory after both of the world wars, the Allies have twice lost world peace in the 20th century. Let us hope in the future that politicians are in charge who always keep the political goals in sight during the most brilliantly fought battles and in the heady aftermath of victory.

All people want to live in peace and freedom. But we shouldn't just always talk about human rights; we should also point out human obligations.

Let us hope that the young generation creates a peaceful order that is lasting. The prerequisite for that will be the readiness to compromise on the part of all nations.

In any case, we former combat troops know from bitter experience and, in memory of our fallen comrades, wish to pass on this reminder: War is the worst alternative in politics!

                                   Otto Carius

Dedication

Dedicated to my comrades-in-arms of the 2nd Company of the 502nd Heavy Panzer Battalion to remember in honor those who fell and to serve to remind those living of our undying and unforgettable fellowship.

Foreword to the German Edition

When I first wrote down my experiences at the front, it was intended solely for the members of the 502nd Tiger Tank Battalion.

When that finally evolved into this book, it was done as an attempt to vindicate the German frontline soldier. The defamation of the German soldier has been openly and systematically carried on either intentionally or unintentionally since 1945, both in Germany and abroad. The public, however, has the right to know what the war and the common German soldier were really like!

Above all, however, this book is geared to my fellow former tankers. For them, it is intended as a reminder of those difficult times. We did exactly what our fellow soldiers in all the other branches of the service did—our duty!

I have been able to portray the events that make up the main point of the narrative, the operations between February 24 and March 22, 1944, because I managed to save the respective combat reports of the division and the corps after the war. They were presented to me back then, and I sent them home. In addition to my memory, the usual official documents were at my disposal for all of the other events.

Otto Carius

The Fatherland Calls

"What they want with that little runt . . . that's what I'd like to know, too," said one of the card players. They were hunched together, a suitcase over their knees, attempting to make their departure a little easier by passing the time playing cards.

"What they want with that little runt . . ." applied to me. I stood at the compartment window and gazed back at the Haardt Mountains while the train rattled eastward through the flatlands of the Rhine. It seemed as if a ship were leaving the safety of its port, sailing into the unknown. I still had to convince myself occasionally that my draft notice was actually in my pocket: Posen, 104th Infantry Replacement Battalion, Infantry, the Queen of Battle!

I was the odd man out in this group, and I couldn't really blame everyone else for not taking me seriously. It certainly hadn't been meant seriously. In fact, it was quite understandable. I had already been turned down twice after being called up: "Not fit for service at present under-weight!" Twice I had to swallow hard and furtively dry the tears. My God, they don't ask one about his weight out there at the front!

Our armies had already cut through Poland in an unprecedented race to victory. Only a few days before, France had also begun to feel the first numbing blows of our weapons. My father was there. At the begin-ning of the war, he had donned the uniform again. This meant that my mother would now only have a small household to manage whenever she was allowed back into our home at the border. And I had to spend my eighteenth birthday in Posen on my own for the first time. Only then did I realize how much I owed my parents for my happy youth! When and how would I be able to return home again, to sit down at the piano or to pick up my cello or the violin. Up until a few months before, I had wanted to devote my future studies to music. Then I changed my mind and began to take a fancy to mechanical engineering. For that reason, I had also volunteered for the Tank Destroyer branch. But in the spring of 1940, they didn't need any volunteers. I was supposed to become an infantryman. But that was OK, too. The main thing was that I was in!

1

After a while, it became quiet in our compartment. No doubt everyone had a lot of things to think over for themselves. The long hours of our trip certainly allowed ample opportunity for that. By the time we had debarked in Posen with our stiff legs and sore backs, we were actually quite happy that the time for introspection was being taken away from us.

A group from the 104th Infantry Replacement Battalion received us, told us to get in step, and took us to the post. The enlisted barracks were certainly no thing of beauty. Room was scarce, and I found myself with forty other men in an open barracks room. There wasn't a lot of free time left over to contemplate the exalted duties of a defender of the Fatherland; a battle for survival began against the old-timers. They considered us troublesome "foreigners." My situation was practically hopeless: I still had peach fuzz! Since only a heavy beard was clearly a sign of real manhood, I was on the defensive from the very beginning. The jealousy of the others over the fact that I got away with just one shave a week only made matters worse.

Our training was well suited for getting on my nerves. I often thought about my high school, the Maximilianeum, whenever drill and ceremonies were practiced to the point of no return or whenever we rolled around in the mud of the training area during terrain drills. Not until later did I learn the value of such fundamental training. I was able to use the knowledge I gained in Posen more than once to get out of dangerous situations. A few hours later and all of the misery had been forgotten. The rage we had experienced against the service, our superiors, and our own stupidities in the course of training soon blew over. Basically, we were all convinced that what we were doing had a purpose.

Every nation can consider itself lucky when it has a young generation that gives all for country and so selflessly fights as did the Germans in both world wars. No one has the right to reproach us, as we were after the war, even if the ideals that filled us were misused. Let us hope that the present generation is spared the same disappointment as that which was handed to us. It would be even better if a time were to come when a country didn't need any soldiers because of permanent peace.

My dream in Posen was to finish my basic infantry course smelling like a rose. That dream ended in a disappointment mostly because of the foot marches. They started at fifteen kilometers, increased by five each week and ended at fifty. It was an unwritten rule that all the college prep grads had to carry the machine gun. Apparently, they wanted to put me, the smallest guy in the lot, to the test and see what were the limits of my stubborn will to succeed. It was no wonder then that I returned to the post one day with tendonitis and a festering blister the size of a small egg. I wasn't able to put on any more demonstrations of my infantry prowess in Posen. We were transferred to Darmstadt. The closeness to home suddenly made life in the billets easier to take, and the prospect of a weekend pass provided additional incentive.

I suppose I was feeling pretty cocky one day when the company commander was looking for twelve volunteers for the Panzer corps. Only auto mechanics were supposed to apply, but with a sympathetic smile I was allowed to join the ranks of the dozen volunteers. The old man was probably happy to get rid of this half pint. I didn't have a completely clear conscience with my decision, however. My father had given me permission to join any branch, even aviation, but categorically forbade the Panzer corps. In his mind's eye, he probably already saw me burning and suffering horribly. And despite all that, I found myself in the black Panzer uniform! I've never regretted this step, however, and if I ever had to become a soldier again, there would be no question about it, the Panzer corps would be my only choice.

I became a recruit again when I got to the 7th Panzer Replacement Battalion in Vaihingen. My tank commander was Unteroffizier August Dehler, a tremendous person and a good soldier. I was the loader, and we were all bursting with pride when we received our Czechoslovakian Panzer 38t's. We felt practically invincible with our 37-mm cannon and two Czech machine guns. We were enthusiastic about the armor protection and didn't realize until later that it would only serve as moral protection for us. If necessary, it would stop small arms fire.

We learned the fundamentals of tank warfare at Putlos in Holstein, where we went for live firing at the training area. In October 1940, the 21st Panzer Regiment was formed in Vaihingen. Shortly before the beginning of the Russian campaign, it was integrated into the 20th Panzer Division while at the training area in Ohrdurf. Our advanced training consisted of joint exercises with infantry units.

When we were given our basic allotment of emergency rations in June 1941, we knew that something was about to happen. It was anybody's guess as to where we were going to be committed, until we found ourselves en route to East Prussia. Although the East Prussian farmers whispered this and that to us, we still believed that we had been sent to the border to pull security. This assumption was an illusion formed by our training in Putlos, where we worked with submergible tanks. These tanks drove under the water up to the coast and then surfaced. We were inclined to think that England would be our opponent. Now we were in East Prussia, but our uncertainties wouldn't torture us much longer.

We moved to the border on June 21. After receiving a situation report, we finally knew what our upcoming role would be. Everyone displayed an icy calm demeanor, although inside we were all extremely excited. The tension became almost unbearable during the night. Our hearts were practically pounding out of our chests when we heard the bomber and Stuka squadrons thundering eastward over the division. We were positioned on the edge of a woods south of Kalwarya. Our commander had placed a civilian radio on his tank. It officially proclaimed the start of the Russian campaign five minutes before X-hour. Except for a few officers and NCOs, none of us had seen action yet. The only live rounds we had heard were on a range. We had trust in the old hands. They already had their Iron Crosses and assault badges, and they gave an impression of unshakable calm. For everyone else, stomachs and bladders became restless. We believed the Russians would open fire any minute. But everything remained quiet and, to our relief, we received the attack order.

In Napoleon's Wake

We broke through the border positions southwest of Kalwarya. As we reached Olita in the evening, after a 120-kilometer road march, we felt almost like old veterans. Even so, we were happy when we halted, as our senses had been strained to the utmost on the march during the day. We had kept our weapons at the ready; every man was at his post.

As the loader, I had the worst position. Not only could I not see anything, I also never got to stick my nose out into the fresh air. The scorching heat in our crate was almost unbearable. Every barn we approached caused some excitement, but not a single one was occupied. With enormous curiosity, I waited for the descriptions from our tank commander. I thought it was terribly exciting, when he reported seeing his first dead Russian. With both anticipation and anxiety, we waited for our first contact with the Russians. But nothing of the sort happened. Since we weren't the point battalion, we could only count on contact if the advance was held up.

And so we reached the first objective of the day, the airfield at Olita, without incident. We happily peeled out of our dust-encrusted uniforms and were glad to finally find some water for a proper cleaning up.

"I never imagined the war running just like the training schedule," said our gunner, who showed no limit to his desire to clean up.

"Pretty nice war here," chortled our tank commander, Unteroffizier Dehler. This was after he finally pulled his head out of a wash bucket in what appeared to be a never-ending procedure. He had been in France the year before. That thought had bolstered my confidence as I rode into action for the first time, excited, but also somewhat fearful.

We literally had to dig our weapons out of the dirt. In case of the real thing, none of them would have functioned. We got everything spic and span and looked forward to the evening meal.

"Those flyboys really went to town here," our radio operator said while cleaning weapons. He was looking over to the edge of the woods where the Russian aircraft had been caught on the ground during the first strikes by the Luftwaffe.

We had taken off our uniforms and felt as good as gold. Thoughts of those cigarette album pictures we had collected so passionately years before popped involuntarily into my mind: "Bivouac in Enemy Territory."

Suddenly, it started buzzing around our heads. "Damn it to hell!" our commander cursed. He lay next to me in the muck. But he wasn't cursing the enemy fire, only my clumsiness: I was lying on his crust of Army bread. It was a rather unromantic baptism of fire.

The Russians were still in the woods around the airfield. They had pulled themselves together after the initial shock of the day and began shooting at us. Before we really knew what was happening, we were back in our tanks. And then we drove into our first night action, as if we had never done anything else for years on end. I was surprised at how quiet we had all become once we knew that what we were doing was in deadly earnest.

We almost felt like old-timers the next day when we helped out at the tank battle at Olita. We helped force the crossing over the Njemen. We were somehow tickled to know that our tanks were the equal of the Russians, despite a few friendly losses.

The advance continued smoothly. Following the capture of the Pilsudski tract, it continued toward Wilna. After Wilna had been captured on June 24, we were proud and perhaps somewhat arrogant. We believed we had really been a part of something. We scarcely noticed how dog tired the exertions of the march had made us. Only when we halted, did we drop where we stood and sleep like dead men.

We gave little thought to what was going on. Who could stop this advance? A few had perhaps considered the fact that we were marching along the same path as that taken by the great French Emperor Napoleon. On the same day and at the same hour 129 years before, he had also given the very same attack order to another group of soldiers accustomed to victory. Was this strange coincidence really just chance? Or did Hitler want to prove that he wouldn't make the same mistakes as the great Corsican. At any rate, we soldiers believed in our abilities and in our luck. And it was good that we couldn't see into the future. Instead, we possessed only the will to storm ahead and end the war as quickly as possible.

We were greeted enthusiastically everywhere by the Lithuanian population. They saw us as their liberators. We were quite shocked that Jewish businesses had been plundered and demolished just about everywhere prior to our arrival. We thought that such things could only be possible during a "Kristallnacht" in Germany. This vexed us, and we condemned the rage of the mob. But we didn't have a lot of time for pursuing these thoughts. The advance continued without a break.

Until the beginning of July, we were caught up in the exploitation and pursuit to the Düna River. Our orders were: move on and on and on again, day and night, around the clock. The impossible was demanded of drivers. Soon even I was sitting in the driver's seat in order to relieve our exhausted comrade for a few hours. If only there hadn't been that unbearable dust! We wrapped cloth around our noses and mouths in order to breathe through the clouds of dust, which hung over the roads. We had long since dropped the vision blocks in the armor so we could at least see something. Like flour, the fine dust penetrated everything. Our clothes, drenched in sweat, clung to our bodies, and a thick coating of dust covered us from head to toe.

With a sufficient amount of something potable, everything would have been more bearable, but that was not to be. Drinking was against orders, because the wells could be poisoned. We would jump out of our crates at halts, looking for a puddle. Pushing aside the green layer on the top, we would then moisten our lips. That kept us going a little while longer.

Our advance pointed toward Minsk. We were involved in the fighting north of the city. The first big encirclement was formed, the Beresina crossed, and the advance continued to Witebsk. The tempo of the march continued unabated. Even supply now had trouble keeping up. The ground troops couldn't follow at all of course, no matter how hard they marched. Nobody was worried about the area on either side of the Rollbahn.

The partisans, whom we would get to know later, hid out there. Our field bakeries were also soon hopelessly held up in the rear. Army bread became a rare delicacy. Although the poultry supplied us with meat in spades, this monotonous menu soon became boring. Our mouths started to water when we thought about bread and potatoes. But soldiers who are advancing and hearing the trumpets and fanfares of special victory announcements on the radio don't take anything too seriously.

On July 8, we got hit. I had to bail out for the first time.

We were in the lead. It was at Ulla, a village that was completely burned down. Our engineers had built a pontoon bridge next to the one blown up over the Düna. It was there that we penetrated the positions along the Düna. They put us out of commission just this side of the wood line on the other side of the river. It happened like greased lightning. A hit against our tank, a metallic crack, the scream of a comrade, and that was all there was! A large piece of armor plating had been penetrated next to the radio operator's seat. No one had to tell us to get out. Not until I had run my hand across my face while crawling in the ditch next to the road did I discover that they had also got me. Our radio operator had lost his left arm. We cursed the brittle and inelastic Czech steel that gave the Russian 47-mm AT gun so little trouble. The pieces of our own armor plating and assembly bolts caused considerably more damage than the shrapnel of the round itself.

My smashed teeth soon found their way into the trash can at the aid station. The shrapnel embedded in my face remained there until it saw the light of day all by itself—as had been correctly predicted.

I hitchhiked my way back to the front. The burning villages pointed the way until I met up with the company just before Witebsk. The burning city painted the nighttime sky a bloody red. After we had taken Witebsk the next day, we started to feel that the war was only just beginning.

Advancing, defending, eliminating resistance, pursuing; all these alternated with one another. The events of three weeks were noted with only a few lines in my diary.

> *7/11 to 7/16: Advance via Demidow–Duchowschtschina toward Jarzewo (Smolensk–Moscow Highway) to encircle enemy forces in the Witebsk–Smolensk area. Fighting for the Dnieper crossings at Ratschino.*
>
> *7/17 to 7/24: Defensive fighting for Jarzewo and at the Wop River. Defensive fighting in the Wop–Wotrja position. Fighting to eliminate the encircled enemy forces in the Smolesk pocket.*
>
> *7/25 to 7/26: Pursuit along the Upper Düna.*
>
> *7/27 to 8/4: Defensive battle at Jelnja and Smolensk. Defensive fighting at the Wop and before Bjeloj.*

Beyond this sober recapitulation of facts are hidden the hardships, which can only be fathomed by those who were there. To those who weren't, their description would only bring to mind thoughts of exaggeration. It will certainly be permitted then that I do not make more explicit comments, particularly since I experienced everything from the perspective of a loader. A loader is not in the position of being able to give an overview of the operations conducted.

Each of us exerted himself and took all the unpleasantness in stride. We were convinced there could only be success when everyone gave his utmost.

Despite this, we sometimes blew our tops when certain individuals didn't recognize their duties and responsibilities. After one hot day of fighting during which our parched throats had waited in vain for some water, we cursed a blue streak when the news seeped through that our battalion commander had ordered himself a bath prepared with our coffee water. This unbelievable behavior on the part of a superior went beyond comprehension. But the thought of our bathing superior gave us so much opportunity for jokes and coarse soldierly humor, that the matter was soon only seen from its humorous side.

The First T34s

Another event hit us like a ton of bricks: The Russians showed up for the first time with their T34s! The surprise was complete. How was it possible that those at the "top" hadn't known about the existence of this superior tank?

The T34 with its good armor, ideal shape, and magnificent 76.2-mm long-barreled cannon was universally feared and a threat to every German tank up until the end of the war. What were we supposed to do to these monstrosities that were being committed in quantity against us? We could only "knock at the door" with our cannons; inside, the Russians were able to play an undisturbed hand of cards. At that time, the 37-mm Pak was still our strongest armor defeating weapon. If lucky, we could hit the T34 on the turret ring and jam it. With a whole lot more luck, it became combat ineffective. Certainly not a very positive situation!

Our only salvation was the 88-mm Flak. Even this new Russian tank could be effectively engaged with it. We thus started paying the utmost respect to the Flak troops who previously had sometimes received a condescending smile from us.

As if Ivan perceived our predicament, he started attacking in our sector for the first time with his "Urraaaay! Urraaaay!" At first we thought that our infantry were attacking with their own "Hurrah!" However, we soon knew otherwise. Because Moscow was now almost within our grasp—in our opinion—the feeling began to sneak up on us that it was no longer possible to count upon a quick end to the campaign.

I therefore had mixed feelings as I received marching orders to Erlangen and the 25th Panzer Replacement Battalion on August 4, 1941. Three days prior to that I had put Unteroffizier braid on the shoulder straps of my uniform.

We tested for our truck and tank driver licenses in Erlangen. Right after that, we arrived in Wünsdorf near Berlin to attend Officer Candidate Course Number 8.

On February 2, 1942, I was informed that I had not met the standards of the course. Just like Gert Meyer and Klaus Waldenmeier from our platoon, I clearly had not taken the whole affair seriously enough. Besides, there was one question I really shouldn't have asked. I thought I had occasion to confide my doubts to the blackboard. But my superiors didn't find the question "Are reserve officers also human?" at all funny. Thus we were still noncommissioned officers and officer candidates when we departed the course. Actually, we weren't too upset about it.

The freshly baked lieutenants, after all, had to pull duty in the replacement units, while we were immediately transferred back to our old regiment. We were released with words of encouragement. Our tactical officer, whom we were all crazy about because he was a true character and led his charges with real feeling, said in departure that he was certain we would soon obtain our goal at the front. There we could more easily prove our suitability to become officers. We wanted to prove him right.

Even today I still think of him. I silently congratulated the Bundeswehr in its luck when I discovered that Oberst Philipp was the commander of the training regiment in Andernach.

Back With the Old Gang

We found the 21st Regiment in its winter positions at Gshatsk. It was horribly decimated: Only one company was still equipped with tanks. All other vehicles had been lost in the fighting during the withdrawal of the infamous winter of 1941–42.

"We've been waiting for you," came the greeting from our comrades. "Now show us what you've learned!" They smirked in a conspiratorial manner, and we sensed something was up. We received the mission to take over the snow shovel details.

These had to clear the way through the terrain in front of the tanks during engagements in order to prevent their getting stuck. In the snow, in our black uniforms, in front of the tanks—what a great deal! Contrary to all expectations, everything went well. Besides, we were certainly better off than the comrades who, in their Panzer uniforms, were employed as infantry.

Full of jealousy, we repeatedly saw how well Ivan was equipped in contrast to us. We were really happy when a few replacement tanks finally reached us from the home front. The 10th Company was completely resupplied with vehicles, and I could finally take over my platoon. From March until the end of June 1942, we slugged it out in defensive fighting with the Russians around our winter positions at Gshatsk and east of Wjasma. We were then transferred to the area around Ssytschewka where we joined in the offensive fighting east of Bjeloj.

I was put in for a promotion during this fighting, and a few days after the promotion something happened where I almost had to take my new shoulder straps off again.

My platoon was positioned along a wooded trail. "Nice area!" my driver said, and he was right. There was no visibility in front of or behind us, everywhere just trees and bushes. No-man's-land began on the other side of the trail. There was a Pak next to us, somewhat offset. The few infantrymen were divided among us.

The drivers and loaders of my four tanks had just gone to fetch the meal. My thoughts were already drifting to chow when the fireworks went off and the Russians attacked. Half of the crews were missing; no tank was ready for combat. I panicked at that point, slid into the driver's seat and backed out of the woods. The other tanks in my platoon followed me in the belief that radio communications had failed. They were following the order to do exactly what the platoon leader's tank did whenever something like that occurred.

After we had driven a few hundred meters, it was clear to me what kind of a mess I had engineered. The Pak crew and the handful of infantrymen had probably lost their nerves when they saw me bug out. I quickly turned around and returned to the old position. Those great guys in the foxholes had held their nerves and had already repulsed the attack. "Man, what a bunch of heroes," the Pak commander said. "If that's all you can handle, then you'd be better off not even coming to the front!" I stood there with my tail between my legs and could only assure him that something like that would never happen again.

That experience still weighed heavily on my mind for many days afterwards. How easy it is to make such a hasty decision; how badly it could have ended! I should have stayed there of course, even if we weren't quite combat ready. That had become clear to me after a few minutes, but the mistake had already been made when we cranked up.

This episode was a damned good lesson for me, and I always reminded myself of it, especially when I had to pass judgment on subordinates. I was happy that I had the opportunity to wipe the slate clean before our unit's transfer to the area north of Orel. By doing that, I could at least wait for my promotion with a clearer conscience.

Before I received my promotion, however, I was destined to get acquainted with a special area of operations. I became the leader of the engineer platoon in the headquarters company for a short time.

A Catastrophe

We were in our bunkers far behind the front. One morning, the commander called to me excitedly, "Hey, Carius, take a look—just like in the movies! How is such a thing possible?!" A newly equipped Luftwaffe field division advanced past our quarters on the way to the front. It took my breath away: Just like a fairy tale! From the bread bags to the cannons, everything was new. We saw weapons we had only heard rumors about: the MG42, the 75-mm long-barreled Pak, and other amazing things. Certainly nothing could happen here. We wanted to believe that we would finally be able to completely refit our units as well. Everything that was rolling toward the front was a guarantee for a peaceful winter in this sector.

Naturally our company commander was itching to be able to see all the nice things up close. So we drove to the front lines to recon the situation. A dignified atmosphere prevailed. We thought we were in a training area. The noncommissioned officers wore their elegant visor caps; the troops were clueless and a bit bored in their positions.

There were absolutely no signs of battle. Because of that, they had also packed away the MG42s, so nothing would get into them. The comrades simply couldn't be convinced to demonstrate these previously unknown wonder weapons to us just once. An uncomfortable feeling crept over us. What would happen if Ivan were to attack there? Before these weapons were combat ready, the Russians would have already overrun the positions.

Our fears would soon be justified. A dull rolling from the northeast woke us one morning. We strained our ears for a few minutes, then nothing could keep us in our bunkers anymore. Outside, an icy snow storm practically took our breath away and almost blew us over. That was ideal attack weather for the Russians. Without waiting for the alarm, we woke up the company. Our suspicions were confirmed. The report soon came that the Russians had broken through.

We found the commander of the Luftwaffe division in a state of complete despair at his command post. He didn't know where his units were. The Russian tanks had rolled over everything before the Pak guns had fired a shot. Ivan had captured the brand new material, and the division had scattered to the four winds. Fortunately, the enemy stood fast after his quick initial victory. He feared a trap. Thus, with some effort, our regiment was able to seal off the breakthrough. It was a complete madhouse!

When one infantry unit marched up to a village, men in Luftwaffe uniforms waved to it. Shortly afterwards, they opened fire with devastating effectiveness. The Russians were wearing the captured winter clothing.

We thus received the order to shoot at every Luftwaffe uniform, since only Russians could be lurking in them. Unfortunately, a few of our own isolated assault groups also fell victim to this order. Whenever we heard a MG42 hammer away in the next few days and weeks, we could bet our lives on it that the Russians were firing it. We still hadn't used one in action, and our foot soldiers usually had to be contented with captured Russian weapons.

We all became enraged whenever we thought about the failure of those responsible. They put the best weapons into the hands of completely inexperienced, poorly trained troops and threw them straight to the front.

How well we could have used men and materiel—intelligently employed—in the following weeks in the offensive and defensive fighting south of Bjeloj–Koselsk–Sschinitschie!

I survived a particularly nasty action as a newly baked lieutenant and engineer platoon leader. We had the mission to clear the mines ahead of the tanks. I was amazed that I got away with only a superficial flesh wound on the hand. I then started to appreciate the work that was demanded from our engineers.

I was happy when I was transferred back to our old 1st Company. I saw August Dehler again, my old tank commander. He had become a Feldwebel in the meantime, and, naturally, we rode together in the same platoon. The operations we jointly participated in brought about the greatest losses to our battalion since the beginning of the campaign.

The Russians employed great quantities of AT rifles, which penetrated our tanks with ease. Our losses were very high. Many of our comrades were mortally wounded in their tanks or could only be evacuated with serious wounds.

We were completely helpless in night engagements. The Russians let us approach quite close. By the time we recognized them, it was much too late to defend ourselves, especially since an exact laying of the tank sights was impossible at night.

The feeling of being practically defenseless got to us. Fortunately, the first 75-mm long-barreled Mark IVs and the more heavily armored, 50-mm long-barreled Mark IIIs started to arrive in small quantities from the home front. That was the silver lining on the horizon, a lining which so often let our hopes be revived in Russia.

After practically giving up hope and losing all confidence in our own vehicles, we again gathered some courage and made it through the last unsuccessful attack through Ploskaja on Beljajewa.

In the meantime, it had become January 1943. I was supposed to take my home-front leave before the upcoming leave cancellations.

On the evening before my departure, August Dehler motioned his tank out of its "box." It had been dug into the earth to ward against the enormous cold. Dehler slipped on the smooth, sloped ramp with his felt boots and slid in front of the left track of the vehicle. It grabbed him without his driver noticing it. The tank was immediately brought to a stop when the remainder of the crew yelled, but the track had already rolled up to Dehler's upper thigh. He was killed immediately, without ever having uttered a sound. I had lost one of my best friends.

I was then really ready for leave and looked forward to home and my parents' house. But it seemed as if I were not supposed to enjoy my time there. A telegram soon arrived announcing my transfer to the 500th Replacement Battalion. Disappointed, I kept on guessing why I could not return to my old company.

I reached Putlos with mixed feelings and with the certain expectation of having to go through another gunnery course. I would much rather have returned to my old gang at the front. Not until I reported to headquarters did I discover that officers with front-line experience and a few companies from the Eastern Front were supposed to be trained there on a new type of tank, the "Tiger." The news spread like wildfire, and yet no one knew anything specific about it. We got to view a few of its precursors from development, but we didn't like them very much.

Hauptmann von Lüttichau was supposed to lead the training. I knew him from Russia and didn't think it was very nice of him that he saddled me with the job of running the officers' club. There was probably no more junior officer to be found. Therefore, I couldn't change anything—nitschewo! That this job would bring me luck was something I didn't discover until later.

We went to Paderborn, the home of the 500th Replacement and Training Battalion, which was later responsible for all units with "Tigers."

As the club officer, I met Hauptmann Schober. He had come from Russia with his company for retraining. Von Lüttichau had given me strict orders to accommodate Schober's every wish concerning the allocation of alcoholic drinks. They were both close friends. Schober liked to drink a drop or two now and then.

He showed up at my location almost daily, since I had to control the scarce supplies. We thus came to know and respect one another. I had the feeling that he liked me, and not only because of his special allotment of French vermouth.

We often sat together with the men of his company as well. I was especially happy when he asked me one day,

"Carius, how would you like it, if you were to come to my company?"

"Yes, sir—right away, sir!" I could scarcely believe my luck. Only two companies were initially being organized. At most, only six men were required from the entire group of officers. And I was one of them! On my recommendation, Schober took Oberleutnant von Schiller for his executive officer. I knew him from the 21st Regiment.

I was finally relieved of my post as the club officer soon after my transfer to the new company. Schober had consumed quite a bit. One must also consider that he had also supplied his company with spirits in the process.

When a few bottles were demanded for the reception of some sort of "higher up," I had to "respectfully" report there wasn't a single drop left. Oh, well—my successor didn't need to accept any stock. The transfer was easy!

I could begin to devote myself entirely to the company. When Schober introduced me to them, I couldn't help but recall the comments made by my fellow travelers when I was called up. I will never forget the eyes made by Hauptfeldwebel Rieger and Oberfeldwebel Delzeit. They later confessed their first impressions of me. It could be summed up in the following statement: "Man, Sepp, what kind of a little fart did the old man dredge up?"

Naturally, it was difficult to find trust in a combat company as an outsider. But everything went well. Even before our departure to France where we were supposed to get our "Tigers," I had become very tight with those guys. It was as if I had always been with them.

Unfortunately, Hauptmann Schober was summoned to take over a battalion. His departure speech stayed with me for a long time and became an inspiration to me. He requested the men to show me the same trust as they did to him.

I dedicated myself with heart and soul to my duty. After a few months of training, we had surpassed the other companies in the battalion with regard to our successes. In the process, we had the least number of mechanical failures.

I had not dared to hope for that when Schober handed over the company to Hauptmann Radtke. Hauptmann Oehme led the 3rd Company. The 1st Company had been collecting experience as an experimental company in the northern sector of the Eastern Front since the autumn of 1942. After our activation, we were supposed to follow them into the area around Leningrad.

In Brittany

Initially, however, we headed west, to Ploermel in Brittany. The company was directed to an abandoned and neglected chateau. The company commander and the executive officer lived by themselves in the city. I had preferred to live with the company. We had to get to know one another, if we were supposed to go into action together. The company never forgot what I did. I gladly took all the unpleasantness in stride that I had to accept in the small, musty room of our "castle."

The fun began as soon as we moved in. We had to put the old stables in order, before we could be expected to live there. There was neither a wooden floor nor wooden planks. For the time being, I wanted to get hold of a few bails of straw for my men. But in the neighboring farm, they refused to give me anything without a receipt from the local headquarters. I thus drove to the headquarters in the city, but they had already closed up shop.

I promptly filled out a certificate to the farmer myself, so he could file a complaint with it. Just as promptly came the dressing down from the battalion. If we hadn't departed for the Eastern Front soon thereafter, they would have probably saddled me with proceedings for plundering or something similar. After the war, I often had to think about that, whenever I saw how easily the French occupation troops simply covered their needs through us. . . .

During this period, I also had to add a war crime to my conscience: an execution without trial or judgment. I was the next one up during live firing at the edge of town, when the rooster of a neighboring farm ran straight across the range. More than likely, it had been directed that farm animals were supposed to be penned in during the firing. I had just taken aim when the rooster crossed between me and the target.

The commander yelled something out, but it was too late. I couldn't help myself. I gave up on the target rings to make the rooster a source of amusement for us all. It made a few somersaults, and then it became something scarcely edible. The company commander was already giving me a huge dressing down when the grieving owner of the dearly departed also came running up. Even with money she couldn't be calmed down, since the deceased had plainly been the best rooster far and wide.

Of course, the red wine was a part of our stay in France as well. The Austrians in the company were especially partial to it. There was hardly an evening where I didn't have to get up again and put my Austrians to bed.

The charge of quarters usually wasn't able to impose lights out, since more than half of the company were noncommissioned officers who pulled duty as drivers, gunners, and tank commanders. I almost always had to personally announce closing time. But usually that didn't happen until I had drained the glass offered to me and listened to a Viennese song.

We didn't take the obligatory drill and ceremonies too seriously. We simply went through the motions whenever a superior came into view, so we wouldn't stick out too noticeably. Besides, I was happy to be able to experience a few carefree days before we went back to the front.

Soon the transportation details were formed to fetch the "Tigers" from Germany. One of these details was entrusted to me.

I had a layover in Paris both coming and going. The city and its inhabitants were very interesting to me, although it was difficult to get a conversation going with them. I admired the attitude of the French. God knows, they had really lost the war, but not a word was said against their own soldiers. They also refrained from any type of criticism against us. To dirty one's own name after losing a war seemed to remain a trait of the Germans.

Our troops in Paris acted as if the war had already ended and been won. This behavior was unbelievable to me. I wasn't able to forget that in a few weeks we would be slugging it out with the Russians again.

Portrait of the "Tiger"

Naturally, our thoughts were occupied with the new tank on our return journey. How would the "Tiger" perform? Its outer form was anything but pretty and pleasing. It looked plump; almost all of the flat surfaces were horizontal, and only the front slope was welded obliquely. Thicker armor compensated for the elimination of rounded shapes. The irony isn't lost when one discovers that we had delivered the large hydraulic press to the Russians shortly before the war with which they could manufacture the so elegantly rounded-off surfaces of their T34s and T43s. Our armament experts had placed no value in it. In their opinion, such thick armor would never be needed. As a result, we had to put up with flat surfaces.

Even if our "Tiger" wasn't beautiful, its robustness could fill us with enthusiasm. It really drove just like a car. With two fingers, we could literally shift 700 horsepower, steer 60 tons, drive 45 kilometers an hour on roads, and trek 20 kilometers an hour cross-country. In consideration of the equipment, however, we only drove twenty to twenty-five kilometers on the roads and correspondingly slower cross-country.

Obviously, the greatest responsibility for the readiness of the vehicle fell to the driver. The man *really* had to be top notch. He had to drive using his head and not his "rear end." If he was on his toes, then his "Tiger" never left him in the lurch. The really good tank driver—and no other type was let loose on a "Tiger"—also had to have an instinctive feel for the terrain. He had to move properly cross-country. He always had to keep the tank's best side facing the enemy without the tank commander giving him every move first. Only then was it possible for a tank commander to concentrate completely on the enemy. And only then could a platoon leader or company commander properly direct his vehicles in an operation without having to pay constant attention to the terrain.

The tank driver position also demanded a generous helping of guts. He was, after all, the only man in the vehicle who saw a lot yet had to remain completely passive whenever the tank was under fire and the rest of the crew slugged it out with the enemy. In those instances, he helped by observing and had to rely completely on his comrades in the turret.

The properties of a tank driver described above make it understand-able that not all tank commanders came from the ranks of the gunners, but rather from those of the drivers. For example, Kerscher and Linck—to name only two commanders—had been drivers first. My "old reliable," Karl Baresch, also immediately took over my seat as tank commander after I was wounded in 1944.

The reader must permit me to present some interesting information in order to show how the work was in no way through after the opera-tion. For all of us, especially for the driver, it really only began then, so that we could be in shape the next day.

The fuel tanks held 530 liters. That's twenty-seven canisters of twenty liters or three barrels. With that quantity, we could travel exactly eighty kilometers cross-country.

The maintenance of the batteries was important, especially in winter. They had to be constantly charged up by letting the motor run whenever we didn't drive a lot. Otherwise, the starter didn't turn over the engine any more. If that happened, two of the crew members had to climb out and crank over the engine with an inertial starter similar to those on old aircraft, only at the rear. It doesn't take too much imagination to realize that doing that was no great thrill in the middle of a battle and in view of the enemy. Despite that, it sometimes happened that the batteries were too weak. At the front, we soon found an elegant method to avoid having to climb out.

A neighboring tank was called over. It turned its cannon to the rear and slowly approached the rear of the front tank. The stranded tank was pushed, and the motor usually reported after the first few meters.

The radio equipment, the inner and outer lights, the ventilator, and the electrical ignition for the cannon were dependent upon the batter-ies. It was understandable then that their maintenance was of great importance.

A water radiator with a 120-liter capacity and four fans took care of cooling the engine. The cooling grills on the rear deck, absolutely nec-essary so warm air could be extracted, were often the reason that tanks became disabled by otherwise harmless rounds or shrapnel. They dam-aged the radiators that were underneath.

The motor held twenty-eight liters of oil, the transmission thirty liters, the reduction gears twelve liters, the turret power system five liters, and the ventilation motors seven liters. A pair of large air filters caught the dust. When one considers that on a move of only seven kilometers 170,000 liters of air were sucked into the engine while the dust of almost four acres of land was stirred up—the quantity a person would breathe in ten days if he were to sit on the rear deck in the dustiest spot—then it is understandable that the cleaning of air filters was necessary before every move. With a regularly cleaned filter, everyone could get 5,000 kilometers of operation on a single motor. If the filters were covered with dirt, we couldn't get 500.

Four dual carburetors fed the motor and controlled it through a governor. The sensitivity of the carburetors was the greatest disadvantage of the German gasoline motors in comparison with the robust diesel engines of the Russians. On the other hand, a greater resilience was the advantage of the German tank engine.

The transmission, which functioned semiautomatically, had eight forward and four rear gears. The steering gears enabled the power taken away from the one track in steering to be transferred to the other. In turning in place, one track ran forward and the other backward. This power was negated by steering brakes on the Panzer I through Panzer IV. The "Tiger" driver sat at a steering wheel and could direct the 63 tons as easily as a car. Up to then, a lot of strength had been necessary in steering a tank.

The overlapping suspension had eight axles on each side. Each axle had three road wheels, which ran on the track and supported it at the same time. The lighter types of German tanks, on the other hand, had both road wheels and support rollers. Just imagine how many road wheels on the "Tiger" had to be removed whenever one of the inner ones had to be changed!

The twenty-two-liter motor performed best at 2,600 RPM. At 3,000, it soon became too hot. Before loading the tanks on trains, the cross-country track had to be exchanged with a narrower one. Otherwise, it extended over the sides of the cars and would have endangered oncoming traffic. Special six-axle cars had been constructed for rail transportation. They carried eighty tons and accompanied each battalion into the area of operations. In order not to endanger any railway bridges, at least four other freight cars had to be placed between two "Tigers."

The turret was turned by a hydraulic gearbox. The gunner's feet rested on a tilting platform. If he pressed the tip of his foot toward the front, the turret turned toward the right; if he pressed with his sole to the rear, it turned to the left. The more he pressed in the corresponding direction, the faster the movement. At its slowest, a 360-degree revolution of the weapons in the turret took sixty minutes. At its quickest, it took sixty seconds. Extreme aiming accuracy was thus ensured. The practised gunner didn't need to adjust afterwards with his hand.

Because of the electrical ignition of the cannon, slight pressure by the little finger sufficed to let loose a round. The unavoidable jumping, usually caused when pulling the trigger by mechanical methods, was thus avoided.

Our most dangerous opponents in Russia were the T34 and the T43, which were equipped with long-barreled 76.2-mm cannons. The tanks were dangerous to us from 600 meters in the front, 1,500 meters in the sides, and as far as 1,800 meters in the rear. If we hit these enemy tanks in the right place, we could still destroy them at 900 meters with our 88-mm cannon. The Stalin tank, which we first got to know in 1944, was, at a very minimum, the equal of the "Tiger." It was considerably superior in its shape (just like the T34). I won't describe the KVI, the KV85, the other, less frequently encountered types of enemy tanks, and the assault guns with their large caliber cannons in detail here.

A completely outfitted "Tiger" company had fourteen tanks. Its firepower was thus greater than that of an entire Flak battalion (three batteries with four guns each). The production costs of one "Tiger" ran to not quite one million Reichsmarks. For that reason, only a few heavy tank battalions were organized. To be the commander of such a company meant carrying a considerable responsibility. . . .

On an Express Train
to the Leningrad Front

After we were more or less acquainted with our "Tigers," we were shipped out to the east. The little city of Ploermel was celebrating the Feast of Corpus Christi. Our rail loading time had been announced to the city administration, so the parade of the faithful would already be gone whenever we rolled to the train station with our tanks. But what did the people there care if the German front near Leningrad needed reinforcements and that the troops there were waiting for us expectantly? Cursing all the while, we had to wait nearly three hours before we could load.

Our "Tigers" were being handled very secretively. They covered them with tarpaulins, not allowing a single screw to be seen. Despite that, we always had the hunch that our enemy already knew as much about the new tanks as we did.

It really was an express train, as we soon noticed. We only stopped shortly to change engines. From Metz, I telegrammed home. I doubted that any of my relatives would be able to go from Zweibrücken to Homburg on the Saar in such a short time. But a real soldier's mother can do everything!

As our train pulled in, I was already expected on the platform. Besides that, I had some additional luck; right there was an engine change. I was thus able to introduce my mother to the guys I was riding to the front with. Fortunately, we had no idea what was going to happen to us as we continued to roll through Germany and on to Leningrad. Besides, we had our new vehicles and were approaching the coming events with more calm than before any previous operation.

Occasionally, we looked at the monsters hidden under the tarpaulins with something approaching love. At least we could do something with these! The "Tiger" was the heavyweight of our fighting vehicles.

The runt of the litter was the Panzer I, the "Krupp sports car" as our troops had christened it. It carried a two-man crew, barely weighed six tons, and was equipped with two machine guns. By the time of the Russian campaign, we had already left it home. Three men sat in a Panzer II. It was somewhat heavier than the Panzer I and also had a 20-mm rapid fire cannon. By then, it was only employed for reconnaissance purposes in light platoons.

Five men belonged to the crew of a Panzer III. It weighed exactly twenty tons and had a 50-mm short-barreled cannon (later long) and two machine guns. The Czech tank, the Panzer 38t, roughly corresponded to the Panzer III. Besides having a poorer quality of steel, it also had the disadvantage of only having four men in it. The tank commander had to observe and fire simultaneously.

One found the Panzer IV in the heavy company of every battalion. Five men also rode in it. The weight was between twenty-two and twenty-eight tons. Until the end of 1942, this fighting vehicle was equipped with a short-barreled 75-mm cannon. From then on, it had a long-barreled cannon of the same caliber.

The Panzer V was known as the "Panther." It was a new development that bore the fruit of wartime experience. Serviced by five men, it tipped the scales at forty-two tons and had a 75-mm extra-long cannon, two machine guns, and a turret traversing system like the "Tiger."

Finally, there were also five of us in our "Tiger." An 88-mm cannon, two machine guns, a semiautomatic transmission, and the 700 horsepower engine completed the imposing picture of the sixty-ton vehicle.

The 88-mm cannon was the same one that had proven itself so magnificently in Flak units. It was also used with an even longer barrel in the new antitank guns. Soon we were to put the tank through its acid test.

✠

Our railhead was near Gatschina. We experienced our first bad luck there. The end ramp was missing, and one of the "Tigers" tipped over while offloading "over the side." A promising start!

The after-action reports of the 1st Company were also not exactly encouraging. Our comrades had been dashing about in the area around Leningrad since September 4, 1942. In the first four weeks, they had participated in the first defensive battle south of Lake Ladoga. They were then involved in the positional fighting around Leningrad in the 11th Army sector. From January 12 to May 5, 1943, they took part in the second defensive battle south of Lake Ladoga in the Pogostje pocket and south of Kolpino.

Casualties couldn't be avoided during these operations. It also became quite clear in the marshy operational area that tanks would have to be abandoned by their crews once in a while. While the order had been given that no "Tigers" were to fall into the hands of the Russians under any circumstances, a burned-out tank often had to be left behind with its weapons destroyed by its crew.

The wrecks and the ruins provided the Russians with enough information that we had something new. In the operations that followed, we promptly found superb descriptions by the Russians of our "Tigers." Every Ivan had them in order to become familiarized with our weak points. Since our own leadership still hadn't produced any training manuals, we were able to use the Russian publications for our training. In this manner, we were also made aware of our own vulnerable spots.

Our "Tiger" debut was supposed to begin on July 22, 1943, with daily performances for eight weeks. It was the third battle for Ladoga. With all means available, the Russians were attempting to reopen the land connection with Leningrad for the third time. This would make possible the use of the Stalin Canal and the Wolchow–Leningrad rail line.

We were loaded on the trains on July 21. We were not able to reach the planned destination at all. Only with a great deal of difficulty did we come to Sniigri, a small train station near Mga. By the skin of our teeth, we got our "Tigers" off the cars. The Russian artillery had already shifted its fire to our vicinity, and we had to detrain once again without a ramp.

The 3rd Company had been thrown straight into battle from the ramp. Hauptmann Oehme, the company commander, and Lieutenant Grünewald had already been killed before we arrived with our train.

Ivan had let loose great swarms of fighter planes on us—something we weren't used to. Swirling about and imitating our Stukas, they mowed down everything. Desolate clusters of decimated human and animal corpses and destroyed material were left on the Rollbahn. It was a scene that I only saw repeated in 1945 along the retreat routes in the west.

We were usually only able to drive along the Rollbahn at night. For the slow horse-drawn units, it was practically impossible to move forward.

We too were then thrown into this inferno. We slugged it out with the Russians until the end of September. Neither side could register a success, only losses. Sinjawino, Hill X, the Masurian Road, and Bunker Village—for each survivor, these names once again bring back to life the memory of the severity of the operations. The battles went back and forth, day-in and day-out. Important positions often changed hands several times daily.

Once, we were employed with the company against Bunker Village. I moved from the southeast. After reaching the village, I was supposed to be relieved by an attack from a patch of woods southwest of me.

After reaching our objective, however, we waited in vain for the second group of "Tigers." I never did discover the real reason why the comrades in the other company had left us in the lurch. We had to slug it out by ourselves with the antitank positions.

We also got a glimpse of a few tanks, but soon we didn't even know ourselves where the front and rear were. With a lot of luck, we got out of there but without having shook up the Russians at all. I was as happy as could be to have all my "Tigers" collected together again. Who would have had time in such a mess to follow orders and ensure that no damaged "Tiger" was left behind!

Someone had "thoughtfully" provided every "Tiger" tank commander a demolition charge. It was fastened upright in a holder next to the tank commander's right hand beside the seat in the turret. With it, the gun could be destroyed effortlessly. In addition to the hand grenades laying around the tank commander, these were yet another novelty item.

I could have gladly done without them. If one's tank got a proper dead-on hit, then it was a sure guarantee to the tank commander that it didn't fall into Russian hands. At least not so that it was recognizable any more. I finally used the aforementioned holder to secure a bottle of schnapps. For my five-man crew, it was more soothing than any demo charge!

Sometimes we really believed that only alcohol would help us get through this damned operation. We were disappointed that the successes we had promised ourselves with our new vehicles didn't arrive.

In addition, our battalion changed commanders almost as quickly as the hill near Sinjawino changed hands. Many comrades were killed: the platoon leader of our 3rd platoon, then Unteroffizier Pfannstiel, and also Unteroffizier Kienzle. He was one of my humorous Austrians from the Chateau in Ploermel, a true Viennese in the good, old sense.

The senselessness of many measures taken in the immediate vicinity of the front also spread vexation among us. For example, someone had come up with the idea of reinforcing the roads in the marsh in the area around Tossno. They were to be anchored with wood and have asphalt surfaces. The roadway had already made it as far as Gatschina, and it was then approaching the front. The Russians certainly got a kick out of it when they had such great roads at their disposal for their advance in January 1944.

We had had to put up with corduroy roads for nearly three years.

The corduroy roads were a chapter onto themselves! Anyone who rode on them can tell some stories. Despite the many cutouts, traffic jams could not be avoided. Driving off the roads was impossible, even far behind the front. The low-lying marshy woods started immediately to the right and left.

On one trip over this "traffic network," I once again attracted unfavorable attention to myself. I was coming from a meeting, wanted to get to the front, and was, as usual, in a hurry. Suddenly, someone was honking like crazy behind me.

I was supposed to pull into a cutout and let him pass, because he plainly had a more powerful vehicle and was in even more of a hurry than I was. But if we had pulled into one of those cutouts, we could almost certainly count on checking out of the net. The traffic was continuous, and no one would have stopped to let us blend back in again. Therefore, I drove on, even after I looked around and determined that it was a vehicle with a staff flag.

Finally, one of the usual jams forced us to halt, and the big shot soon had me by the scruff of the neck. It was a Hauptmann on the staff of Lindemann, the commander of the Northern Front. He immediately began to dress me down.

When I explained to him that my presence at the front was just as important as his inspection and that he probably wouldn't even be able to drive around there if not for the men holding the front, he demanded to see my papers. "You will report to the front commander and discover from him what is necessary and what isn't!" he announced to me in an ominous manner.

I then discovered the next day what was necessary and what wasn't. Lindemann received me grinning. While employed at the West Wall, he had become acquainted with my father. Instead of a dressing down, an entertaining conversation took place.

"That guy has nothing but luck," my comrades said when I came back from my meeting with a satisfied grin.

After many weeks, the Russians had finally been brought to a standstill in the sector south of Lake Ladoga. Once again, they were quiet. We were pulled out of the front line and set up our quarters in Tschernowo, near Gatschina. Most of the vehicles were ready for the workshop; the usual teething troubles had to be fixed. Our company commander had been transferred, and Oberleutnant von Schiller, the former executive officer, took over the company. I was to remain the only other officer in the company until summer of the following year.

During our break in action, I received the mission to recon the roads to Leningrad, the ones leading north from Gatschina to the shoreline road, and the connecting roads in between. While doing that, I was to establish contact with the infantry at the front. In addition, all bridges and culverts had to be checked out for their carrying capacity. If necessary, they were then reinforced by the engineers to accommodate the width of a "Tiger" and the roadway was emblazoned with our tactical symbol, a mammoth.

Unfortunately, the Russians became the only beneficiaries of our work there when they attacked in 1944.

During these reconnaissance trips, I had the opportunity to become familiar with the Leningrad Front. From many kilometers away along the Rollbahn, we could see the moving crane of the port. The crane had already caused us a tremendous amount of problems, because it was a fabulous observation post for the Russians.

It simply couldn't be brought down with artillery. Whenever I reached the front line at the final stop of the Leningrad streetcar line and cast a glance into the city from the shot-up trolley cars, I asked myself over and over, Why hadn't we taken it in 1941? Back then, there had scarcely been any resistance worth mentioning.

We discovered from a female medic we had captured that the city had been practically starved out in the winter of 1941–42. The corpses had been stacked like firewood. (As the driver of a colonel, she had let her vehicle run onto a mine. As punishment, she had to accompany assault parties as a medic.) She said that life in Leningrad had practically normalized itself again. The populace went about its work undisturbed. Where and when the Germans would fire was already known.

Besides, she said, we scarcely had any ammunition. When we then discovered from other prisoner statements that there had scarcely been a soldier in the city in 1941 and that Leningrad had practically already been given up by the Russians, it dawned on even the lowliest mess hall driver that this error could never be rectified.

Although the front had run the same course for nearly three years, nothing of substance had been done to hold up the Russian attack, which surely had to come. They had promised the divisional commanders that bulldozers would be sent from the home front in the fall of 1943. They were supposed to dig out antitank ditches behind especially endangered sections of the front line. This was after we had already been there for three years.

By the time that these bulldozers finally arrived, the ground was frozen so solidly that their use could not be considered. The Russians certainly had a better use for them next spring.

With Leningrad as the northern cornerstone of the Eastern Front, we could have wintered over in well-prepared positions. This would have given us a reasonable starting point for a renewed attack in the spring of 1942.

The attack on Moscow was given precedence over the taking of Leningrad. That attack bogged down in the mud when we had the capital of Russia within our grasp in front of us. What then happened in the infamous winter of 41–42 cannot be recounted in oral or written reports. The German soldier had to hold out under inhuman conditions against winter-experienced and extremely well-equipped Russian divisions.

Our regiments—or better yet, that which was still left of them—stood their ground for months that were sheer hell for them—with frozen limbs, half starved and emotionally depressed. It seems incomprehensible that we were ever able to last the entire winter in these primitive holding positions.

Ask the men who were on the Eastern Front during this first winter—or perhaps even one or two more winters—why they had no sympathy for those who were punished severely or landed in a camp for sedition or sabotage or other similar offences during the war. The same people who later were celebrated as heroes or martyrs.

Did the simple soldier at the front hold out simply for the sheer joy of dying? Wasn't it also a matter of luck for the frontline soldier, if he came through it all alive and saw his homeland again? God knows, no one will buy the story that we all held out because Hitler's gaze or Goebbels's voice or Göring's uniform was especially pleasing to us.

How can anyone ever equate the terms "government" and "fatherland?" We held our positions and gave it our best because we were bound by law. And when we couldn't even think of that anymore, because we were half-mad from the hardship, cold, and hunger, then we held out because of fear and instinct.

Yes, we followed our instinct, which let us believe that a great danger from the East was threatening us and all of western society.

Cursing this crappy war, we found ourselves in front of Leningrad. But it went without saying that we fell in whenever the command was given. Perhaps this then is the spirit of the German soldier, which many often attempt to cast in a bad light: to demand performance of oneself, apparently against all better judgment, which contributes to unexpected successes and often transforms almost certain defeats into victories.

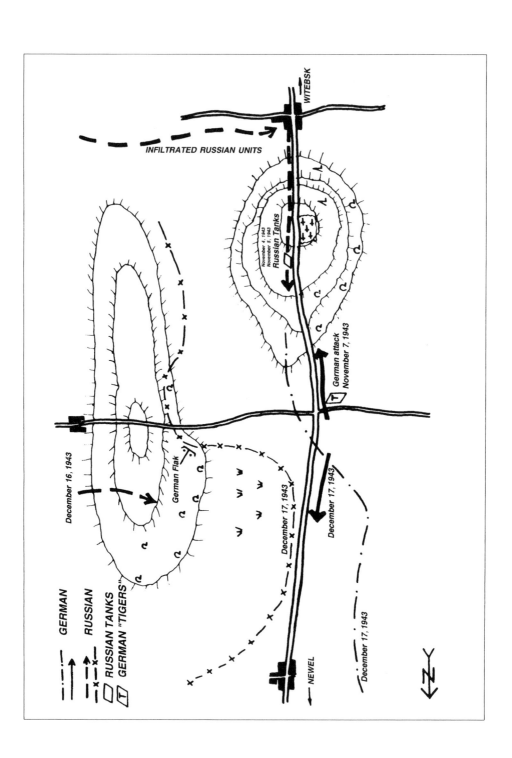

WITEBSK

INFILTRATED RUSSIAN UNITS

November 4, 1943
November 5, 1943
Russian Tanks

German attack
November 7, 1943

December 16, 1943

German Flak

December 17, 1943

December 17, 1943

December 17, 1943

NEWEL

GERMAN
RUSSIAN
RUSSIAN TANKS
GERMAN "TIGERS"

N

Defensive Battle at Newel

The front had quieted down to a certain extent on Lake Ladoga. Yet before we could properly catch our breath, a new march order surprised us. Area of operations: the area around Newel. The Russians had attacked there suddenly and taken Newel. The attack had arrived so unexpectedly that some of our troops were caught at the movies. There was a real panic. As was only right, the commandant of Newel had to answer to a court-martial later for gross negligence in his security measures.

And we were given the mission to hold open the Welikije–Luki–Newel–Witebsk Rollbahn at all costs so that the infantry could occupy the best positions possible east of the road. Ivan was, after all, supposed to be pushed back again.

We soon recognized what type of an opponent we were dealing with through some unforeseen events.

There had been a gap in our front lines south of Newel since the winter of 1941–42. It was considered to be a natural obstacle, because the terrain was an out-and-out marsh. To everyone's surprise after the breakthrough to Newel, it was determined that the Russians had succeeded in slipping smaller units through the marsh to harass the Rollbahn. I was thus sent out ahead as a single tank to provide cover; the rest of the company was supposed to follow. Nothing could be seen of the enemy.

The Rollbahn we had to hold open stretched in front of us from the right to the left. It rose upward toward the right and disappeared behind high ground after about 2,000 meters. The rest of our battalion was supposed to advance to us from that direction and reinforce our line between Lowez and Newel. It was November 4.

We had left our tank. My driver, Unteroffizier Köstler, worked on the damaged left track. We were thus standing in the open and noted with satisfaction that our tanks were rolling toward us on the Rollbahn over the previously mentioned high ground. My radio operator hadn't made any report to the contrary to me, at any rate.

When I identified the first tanks more clearly, I was startled. Infantry was sitting on them. Binoculars out—yes, indeed, the Russians were personally paying their respects. As fast as lightning, everyone was back in his seat. But they didn't even take notice of us. They probably thought we were a knocked-out vehicle and weren't counting on enemy contact.

My driver, Köstler, practically ruined the whole thing; he always saw red whenever tanks showed up. The firing couldn't start fast enough for him. He would have preferred to ram them. He had already started the engine. He repeatedly demanded that we start firing. He couldn't understand our "quiet" at all. My gunner, Unteroffizier Clajus, had been one of those older university students who enjoyed his drinking. Compared to his former superiors, I got along quite well with him. Unfortunately, we soon had to part company, because his request to return to his studies had been approved. I hope that he has his diploma on the wall—despite his liking of the god Bacchus—and that today he holds the position of a chief engineer somewhere. Just as I wanted to call out "open fire," Köstler lost his nerves and attempted to move out. The first Russians were no more than sixty meters away from us. Just in the nick of time, Clajus cleaned their clock with a round between the turret and the hull. The tank turned off into the ditch and smouldered. There were no more signs of life from the crew. The Russian infantry scattered in the countryside next to the Rollbahn.

Clajus was then occupied with the remainder of the enemy tanks. They ran into one another in a wild panic, turned around, and didn't think at all about initiating a fight with us. Only two of the twelve T34s escaped our fire.

In the evening, I was called back to the north. We were supposed to conduct a small operation at Schelkunicha. Flak personnel took over our security duties at the old position. After two days, I had returned. To reinforce me, I received a tank from the 3rd Company. Feldwebel Dittmar was its commander.

We weren't counting on any more Russian tanks after the enemy had suffered such a thrashing. As usual, however, we had underestimated Ivan's stubbornness. He arrived at noontime at the exact same spot as he did two days before. This time though, he had closed his hatches in preparation for combat and turned his turrets halfway to the right.

By all appearances, however, he had only identified the Flak piece and completely overlooked us, the main culprits. The enemy tanks made efforts to detour around their burned-out vehicles. There were five of them. They made the big mistake of all driving at the same time and just observing the high ground.

When they fired—very inaccurately, by the way—they also woke up the Flak crew, which had counted completely on us. We knocked out three tanks; the rudely awakened Flak took care of the rest. Right afterwards, we took a short recon probe to the hill. The Russians had actually brought additional material through the pathless marsh.

In the evening, we returned to our old position. There we received the mission to occupy the village behind that high ground the next morning. We were thus supposed to open the way for an infantry regiment. Two more tanks and three 20-mm quad Flak guns were attached to me at the onset of darkness. The latter proved themselves magnificently in action against ground targets.

It was a moonlit night. I decided to attack as soon as possible. I assumed that the enemy's surprise would compensate somewhat for our numerical inferiority. We formed up so my "Tiger" drove point. The tanks and the quads alternated behind it. Using our black-out lights, we approached quite close to the village.

Amazingly enough, not a shot was fired. Ivan probably assumed we were one of his own march columns. We stopped just before the village and the quads opened fire. Against my orders, a gunner also fired on the houses left of the Rollbahn. The result was that the easterly wind blew the dense smoke over the street and blocked our sight. In the village, we rolled over three Russian AT guns located quietly next to houses.

We dispersed to provide security and established contact with the regiment. It now approached, combed the houses, and, in the morning, was able to continue its way north. The raid succeeded without any losses on our own side. Only two Russian tanks were able to get away. If we had waited until day to move, the enemy would have brought down a lot of fire on us, as we were able to determine from the material we had captured.

Despite all precautions and despite all attempts to seal them off, the Russians had succeeded in continuing to infiltrate our front through the old gap. They had built a long, thin "pipeline" through which they pumped more and more men and materiel. With our weak forces, we were not in position to seal off this penetrated area, cut off the Russians, and eradicate the ensuing pocket. The danger became greater every day that the "pipeline" would burst and that the Russians would encircle us. That was the question that was often asked during the Russian campaign:

"Who is encircling whom?" We were therefore withdrawn to the west in order to prevent any further advances from out of the "pipeline." The terrain was simply not suited for tankers.

Despite the frost and the snow, there were stretches of marsh everywhere, where we could get bogged down. We didn't care for the woods very much either. But compared to conditions in the northern sector of the Eastern Front, we thought we had it quite good there.

On November 10, we made a counterattack at Pugatschina and cut off an outgrowth of the "pipeline." Our route went through about five kilometers of alpine forest where the Russians had recently captured two German long-barreled 88-mm Pak guns. We found these guns, intact and unused. Clearly, Ivan didn't know how to use them.

There was nothing left for us to do but blow those undamaged guns to bits. We didn't want to give the Russians yet another opportunity to test their penetrating capabilities on us. We were somewhat careless when we continued to advance after that, and there was soon the crack of cannon fire coming from some direction.

One of our vehicles was immediately engulfed in flames. Fortunately, the crew could save themselves by getting into another tank. We moved out rapidly to get back to the main road again. In spite of everything, we had determined that the enemy had only advanced with light forces in this area. All in all, however, the situation remained unclear. Even at higher levels, no one could give us information about the exact position of the battle lines.

We had an experience during this time where we didn't know whether to laugh or to cry. A horse-mounted messenger approached us while we were on a security patrol. We drove slowly so as not to make the horse nervous.

But when we were even with them, the young horse began to prance. Unfortunately, it jumped so close in front of the left track that my driver couldn't brake fast enough. The animal was so severely hurt that the rider, who was able to jump off, had to give him the coup de grace. We took him aboard and brought him to his unit. There I said for the record that he was not responsible for the incident in any manner.

When we drove back, the dead horse had disappeared. I found it again at our field mess. My people had hauled it on a tank. Our rather meager rations were enriched by it, especially since the meat could be stored for days due to the cold. The next evening, we had meatballs. Unaware of the incident, our commander ate three pieces and praised the kitchen for its taking care of us. When I blurted out the truth to him, however, the poor man actually had to vomit.

For many days afterwards, until he was certain that the last bit of horsemeat had been consumed, he only ate *meatless* meals.

Trouble began to brew again a few days later. We were pulling security on a slight rise from which we could get a good glimpse of the village of Ssergeizewo. The village itself was in our hands, but behind it were the Russians.

We were supposed to help beat back an expected attack. Toward evening, Ivan actually did move from out of the woods with four tanks and infantry. It was easy to repulse the attack from our elevated position. The tank commanders even stood outside their tanks during the engagement and directed fire. Four T34s went up in flames. At that point, the Russians pulled back into the woods.

The fighting didn't stop until the end of the year. On November 25, we had to support one battalion from the 503rd Infantry Regiment in its attack against some woods to the west of Ssergeizewo. According to the plan, it started at dawn.

Our four tanks had occupied their positions, and we saw—somewhat surprised—that our infantry comrades were rushing upright toward the woodline. We admired their elan but were even more surprised that the Russians allowed it to occur without any interference! After we had advanced about seventy meters, we found the solution to the mystery.

The men who were hurrying to the woods were not our comrades, after all, but Russians who had dug in during the night. They were clearing out prior to our attack. Our foot soldiers were on line with us to the right and left and were waiting for our involvement. Ivan had the incredible good fortune that we had deceived ourselves in the morning twilight.

We then had to slug it out with them in the woods, when we could have finished them off without any problems in the open field. The battalion commander, Hauptmann Johannmeyer, was severely wounded in the evening by a Soviet sniper in the trees. We all feared he wouldn't reach the main aid station alive because he was shot in the lungs. Because of that, I was even happier when I received greetings from him in the hospital in 1944. Just prior to his severe wounding, he had become the 329th soldier to be awarded the Oak Leaves to the Knight's Cross. Because of his wounding, he almost didn't get to participate in his own award ceremony.

On December 2, I was employed with Oberfeldwebel Zwetti at Gor-uschka in order to cut off some more of the "pipeline" via an advance with the infantry. The Russians had dug themselves in extremely well on a small, but commanding rise.

They had always been masters at that. Beyond the hill and to each side of it, they had set up heavy weapons such as AT guns, mortars, and the like. We could not engage them. We had to drive along a trail, which led to a completely impassable bridge.

The Russians had a tremendous line of sight and greeted us with mortar attacks. I could have killed the commander of the engineers, a Hauptmann. While the bridge was certainly not negotiable, he had assured us that we could easily get through the ditch on the right-hand side. Understandably, he didn't want to reinforce the bridge right in the line of sight of the enemy. But I had just as little desire to remain stuck in the ditch and perform an unnecessary recovery in front of the Russians.

The Hauptmann soon appeared and demanded that I immediately initiate the attack. One word led to another, and Ivan accompanied our harsh words with a little "friendly" fire.

When he finally started talking about malingering, cowardice, and so on, I abruptly ripped my Iron Cross from my jacket and tossed it at his feet. I mounted up and drove off. I immediately got bogged down so firmly and deeply, that I could easily reach the ground with a single step from the turret. The Hauptmann had been taught a lesson. He had also "vanished into thin air," as they say. Not that I could blame him, since Ivan, who had observed our senseless undertaking at close range, could have practically fired down our turret hatches.

I waved to Zwetti, and we hooked up the cable. It was really more luck than anything else that nothing else happened. Only a piece of shrapnel from a mortar round disfigured my temple. Like a fool, I let my gunner pull it out after we had got our vehicle free again. It required backing up and a lot of effort. The wound began to bleed like crazy. Apparently, a larger vein had been ripped open, and Zwetti had to apply an expert "pressure dressing." Our "first aid" instruction proved itself well. I now had a fine, white turban on me. It helped serve as wonderful camouflage in the snow-covered landscape. We had already painted the tanks white, as was usual in winter. My head scarcely stuck out at greater distances—a blessing in disguise.

That evening, the engineer captain sent me my award along with a letter. He apologized and also assured me that the bridge would be negotiable by the following morning. We did, in fact, cross the bone of contention in the early morning light without major problems. It swayed a little bit, to be sure, but it still held.

Using luck and skill, we crossed a minefield. I had Zwetti drive in my tracks behind me. We were then right in front of the Russians. We could see into their foxholes on the forward slope. We then gave our infantry a little breathing room. Zwetti quickly finished off the two AT guns that had covered the mines.

The guys to our right then began firing point-blank at us with AT rifles. None of the vision blocks were functioning anymore after a short period of time. Zwetti tried in vain to find one of the riflemen, but those guys always went to other positions and then disappeared again as fast as lightning. We reconned by fire along the entire length of the earthen fortifications. The Russians were so sure of themselves, however, that they even threw hand grenades out from under their cover. When we advanced a little, the first AT round was already hissing past my head. It seemed senseless to move ahead anymore until after the infantry had advanced to us. We thus stood there for a few hours without seeing anything of our comrades. They didn't exit their foxholes at all, because Ivan controlled the entire area from the trees. Even we had to button up, since we feared that the Russians could shoot us from above.

In the afternoon, Zwetti pointed out to me that a puddle was under the rear of my tank. I didn't have a good feeling. The driver started up the motor, and the thermometer immediately climbed to more than 250 degrees.

The Russians had shot a hole in the radiator with their AT rifles and mortars. What could be done? Jumping ship or towing was impossible in our situation. We therefore had to try to get back over the bridge under our own power and without the pistons freezing up.

Misery loves company! Zwetti had forgotten to switch back to receive. That meant that I got splendid reception of the conversation in his tank, something which was of little interest to me at that time. Those are the things that make one realize just how necessary the hated battle drills are. It was beat into a radio operator's head a dozen times a day to switch back to receive immediately after transmitting a radio call. And then, in this situation, it still didn't work!

I began to wave from the hatch with my headphones in order to point out to Zwetti that I wanted to talk to him. There wasn't any time to lose because of the steadily leaking radiator. He finally noticed my waving and rudely awakened his radio operator—something which I could also hear. I directed the driver of my wing man through the mines. He had to drive blind—backwards—but he guided us through. With a great deal of anxiety, we reached the bridge. It had already suffered due to our first crossing. It was sagging in the middle.

We crossed our fingers and were able to do it. After about 100 meters, we were protected from the Russians' sight by low, marshy woods. We never again attempted an attack at that location. It was simply impossible for the infantry. No one could reach that hill alive, even though it was so palpably close in front of us.

On December 12, we were sent to Lowez on the Witebsk–Newel Rollbahn. The Russians were exerting pressure from the east on a broad front against our lines there. During the first couple of days, we only had one mission. We had to drive a few kilometers up and down along the Rollbahn to feign larger Panzer formations to the Russians.

On December 16, using armor support, the enemy attempted to attack over the hill where we had knocked out a Russian antitank gun a few weeks before. We immediately launched a successful counterattack.

Many enemy tanks were knocked out by us in the process. Ivan could have avoided these losses, if he had moved over the hill en masse with his tanks. They felt their way forward, however, somewhat anxiously and one after another. We had an easy time with them.

On the other hand, we had a lot of trouble with the Russian fighters. They "lurched" past us, almost without a break. That's really the way one has to describe that type of flying. My gunner, Unteroffizier Kramer, can take credit for a deed that was probably unparalleled on the Eastern Front. That is, he succeeded in shooting down a Russian fighter with the tank cannon. Of course, he was also helped by chance. This was how it happened. Kramer, upset by the unrelenting nuisance of these guys, elevated his cannon along the approach route. I talked him in. He took a chance and pulled the trigger. On the second attempt, he hit one of the "bees" in its wing. The Russian crashed behind us. On the same day, we received yet another breather; two Russians collided and tore each other apart before crashing.

In the evening, I had a situation briefing with the regimental commander of the infantry. It took longer than expected. I was finally able to start back around two o'clock in the morning. On the way, I found our infantry in front of the Rollbahn.

They were just settling down. Occasionally, the Russians fired over the road with a carbine or a machine gun. Just before the point where I knew my tanks were, I quietly walked along the road leading south, that is, toward "home." The tank crews had shrunk down to two men per vehicle.

They were looking for me. My long absence had upset them. We were very happy to see one another again. Zwetti told me that our front lines had been lost on the stretch of Rollbahn I had walked down. The road was in no man's land.

In the meantime, the enemy was continuously bringing up reinforcements. Only with difficulty could our position be held much longer. Russian troops and materiel were arriving from the east in trucks that had their headlights on. They were unconcerned about our countermeasures. Our artillery fire came sparingly and not until after the enemy columns had already disappeared.

The next day, we once again attacked along the Rollbahn leading north. We wanted to make it possible for our infantry to win back the position vacated the previous day. The Russians were already just to the right of the road.

A Stalin Organ located in the open registered on us. My tank was hit in the front by a rocket. Using the radio, Zwetti asked what had happened. At first, he couldn't recognize anything in the smoke. We had been lucky. We then cleared out quickly from the enemy's line of sight.

Despite repeated attempts, our infantry wasn't able to advance to the east over the Rollbahn. The Russians, on the other hand, began crossing over from the other side. During the process, we were able to admire the composure of a Soviet commissar who stood upright in the midst of the fire and stubbornly waved his men on. The machine guns appeared unable to touch him. We flew into a rage, and Kramer blew him into the air with the 88. The Russians then ran back across the Rollbahn again. Despite that, our attack was called off. A new front line was set up farther west.

When I got back to the regimental command post, the commander was in an uproar. Two Alsatians had disappeared. Actually, at that point in the war, they weren't supposed to be used at the front any more. Because of their dependability, someone had made an exception, and it was feared they had crossed the lines and spilled the beans.

There was another painful incident with two captured Russian T34s. The two "German" tanks were pulling security and came back in the evening twilight. Our Pak elements, which had no idea there were German crews inside them, promptly knocked both of them out. The painted-on Balkan Cross could no longer be recognized in the dusk.

From then on, it was impossible to get any of our men to mount a captured tank.

Our days in the Newel sector were numbered. New and difficult missions were waiting for us south of Leningrad. The front at Newel still hadn't settled down when we quickly withdrew to go to the next railhead. We were needed even more for the withdrawal movements in the Leningrad area. Our objective was the chokepoint of Gatschina on the Leningrad–Narwa road. During our departure from the Newel front, bridges and rail lines were already going up in the air behind us. The front had to be pulled back a good distance again.

✠

At this juncture, I have to sing the praises of a special group: the recovery platoon of our maintenance company. These men performed the impossible. The platoon leader, Lieutenant Ruwiedel, would have much preferred to have stayed with his friends in the tank company, but he was irreplaceable. Such a post could only be filled by an extraordinary person. Not one of us envied him at all. One has to try to imagine what the recovery platoon's mission was.

The men—usually under enemy fire—had to tow immobilized tanks with their eighteen–ton prime movers. On many occasions, the heavy recovery vehicles had to drive up to and in front of the forward most positions at night. There they freed the tanks with winches, attached their cables, and then hauled them out. With normal ground conditions, that would work to a certain extent, as long as the infantry remained quiet and didn't alert the enemy by firing flares.

But our men also had to do their work in snow and ice. Moving a sixty-ton "Tiger" safely with two prime movers in tandem at front demanded a lot of experience and uncommon nerves. Whenever the enemy sat dead on our heels, as was the case in all fighting withdrawals, a mistake usually meant the loss of a valuable vehicle.

✠

Luckily, we reached the train station before its demolition. We loaded up and steamed off in the direction of Gatschina. The great haste didn't bode well. All sorts of things were probably going on up there, and once again we had the mission to be the "fire brigade."

Our misgivings proved correct. The main train station in Gatschina was already under artillery fire when we arrived, so we couldn't unload there anymore. In addition, we received the news that our 1st Company had already been committed and had taken a beating. It had been sent to battle straight from the offload ramp.

The reason was that the Russians had broken through to the west with superior forces between Leningrad and Gatschina. They directed one of their main thrusts along the shoreline road; the other one was in the vicinity of Puschkin, east of Gatschina. The unfortunate incident that I already indicated previously in the text caught up with us.

We had reconnoitered all the bridges between Gatschina and Leningrad so they could be made negotiable for heavy tanks. That had been done in the meantime, but our comrades came too late to blow up the bridges. We had therefore done practically all the work for Ivan. Because of this, he could roll forward at a brisk pace.

When we arrived, we discovered the sad details of the destruction of our 1st Company. It had been surrounded on the Rollbahn by Russian tanks. Lieutenant Meyer's platoon was almost completely annihilated. Meyer himself put his pistol to his head when the Russians tried to take him prisoner. We were crestfallen by this news. In my mind, I faulted the commander for not delaying the employment of the men until all companies were together.

Later I realized that there had been no other way. To a certain extent, every unit drives off into the unknown; no one had an exact orientation on the battlefield situation. Moreover, Major Jähde was the best commander we ever had in the 502nd. He was always an example to us, because he stood up for his men without exception. He always surfaced during critical situations. That was how we knew him and why we will never forget him.

Retreat to the Narwa

Gatschina had to be given up, and Army Group North moved to the rear along the Gatschina–Wolosowo–Narwa Rollbahn.

It was said that terrific positions had been built along the Narwa. The "Panther Line" could be held after an orderly withdrawal. As experienced troops we were skeptical, even though there was talk of solid bunkers and built-up Panzer positions. It would have been great for our infantry comrades to find good bunkers, because it was practically impossible at that time of year to dig in or construct positions. Our skepticism was well founded: the "Panther Line" existed only on paper. No one who was there back then later regretted that those responsible for the blocking positions were called to account!

While the process of being brought back to reality upon reaching the Narwa position was unpleasant, there was once again a bright spot in another area. We formed the rear guard with "Wengler's Infantry," and our working relationship with this regiment was magnificent. Our mission—to cover the retreat of all infantry and artillery units out of the Gatschina–Leningrad area—wasn't easy.

Almost all the units had to be brought back on the single Rollbahn. At the same time, the Russians, always moving between the coast and the Rollbahn, advanced past us and cut the Rollbahn. We then had to move forward to clear the Rollbahn. Ivan was then able to attack the rear guard again. Occasionally, we advanced farther to the north to hold the enemy away from the Rollbahn and prevent his attempts to overtake us.

On one occasion, we had once again advanced in the direction of the coast and set up positions in an unoccupied village. The edge of a woodline extended about a kilometer behind the village, almost halfway between the Rollbahn and the coast.

We therefore set up on the edge of the village. Toward evening, a few infantrymen who had been delayed appeared. Both groups were happy, since we also felt better with infantry support. As it became dark,

I saw a Russian recon patrol come out of the woods, probably to determine whether the village was clear of the enemy.

It moved somewhat boldly toward us. About 500 meters in front of us, the Russians suddenly sprang into the ditch along the path. We then opened fire but were not able to prevent a few of them from disappearing in the woods. That meant that the Russians already had the high ground in front of us in their possession.

The nights stretch out long whenever one pulls security in a tank. The minutes become hours, especially in winter, when the day ends at 3 P.M. and doesn't start again until 9 A.M. I had made it a principle of mine to remain in the turret by myself and not be relieved. I knew how easily one can fall asleep when exhausted, and I didn't want to demand too much of my men. Besides, they had to rest in order to be ready in case of problems.

Of course, I sometimes hit my head on the edge of the turret when I nodded off—that always proved to be very "invigorating." When I was smoking, I often didn't notice that I had nodded off until the lit end of my cigarette singed my fingers. In such a condition, it also happened that I suddenly saw apparitions which moved about.

They were in the form of trucks, tanks, and all sorts of things that revealed themselves in daylight as harmless trees or bushes. Occasionally, a flare was shot off in order to check out the immediate vicinity. But after the flare had extinguished, the night was even darker than before. After we had realized that we only revealed our position and could basically see very little, we avoided these illumination effects as much as possible. That was different of course in battle. One then had to make it possible for the gunner to aim. That simply could not be done if the moon did not provide any shooting assistance.

We had recently received parachute flares, which burned longer. There was a bittersweet incident in my tank with them. I had had the flare pistol handed to me and wanted to cock it. I didn't pull the hammer all the way back, however. It sprang forward, and the thing went off in the tank. It zipped around like a cat on fire. It's unbelievable how long such a flare round burns when one is waiting for it to go out. We were quite lucky that nothing happened to any of us during this accident.

For hours we pulled security outside of the village without anything stirring. Suddenly, around two in the morning, I heard mortar fire. The impacting rounds were actually too short, but there was no doubt at all: They were meant for us.

Soon the village was under extremely heavy fire. The Russians had noticed that it was occupied and wanted to "clean up" the affair before they advanced farther to the west. Their methods showed, however, that they certainly didn't suspect an entire "Tiger" company in the village.

I saw muzzle fire in the woodline. It moved farther to the right from flash to flash. Those had to be tanks moving along the woodline. They wanted to reach the road at the opposite end of the village. Oberfeldwebel Zwetti was in position there.

Behind him was von Schiller's tank. I radioed to Zwetti. With the help of a flare, I could determine that a T34 was moving no more than fifty meters away from Zwetti. Due to the firing, we couldn't hear any motor noises. Because of that, the enemy had already made his way to the village. Zwetti shot his neighbor into flames, but we saw in astonishment a second T34 in the middle of the village street, right next to von Schiller.

It often proved fateful to the Russians that they kept completely buttoned up. Because of that, they could scarcely see anything, especially at night. They also had infantrymen riding on the tank, but even they didn't recognize the situation until too late.

Von Schiller wanted to turn his turret but in the process hit the Russian tank with his cannon. He had to back up first in order to be able to knock it out. I didn't feel confident enough to shoot. One of the craziest situations I ever experienced!

After Zwetti had finished off another three tanks, the Russians pulled back. Apparently, the losses they suffered were enough. We stayed in radio contact for the rest of the night and could hear the Russians quite well on one channel. That meant they couldn't be too far from us.

At the break of day, our infantrymen approached the T34 somewhat carelessly. It still stood directly next to von Schiller. Except for a hole in the hull, it was undamaged. Surprisingly, as they went to open the turret hatch completely, it was closed. Immediately thereafter, a hand grenade flew out of the tank and severely wounded three soldiers.

Von Schiller once again took the enemy under fire. Not until the third shot, however, did the Russian tank commander leave his tank. He then collapsed, severely wounded. The other Russians were dead. We took the Soviet lieutenant to division, but he couldn't be interrogated any more. He succumbed to his injuries along the way.

This incident proved to us how careful we had to be. This Russian had passed on detailed reports to his unit on us. He would only have had to turn his turret slowly in order to knock out von Schiller at point blank

range. I remember how we cursed the stubbornness of this Soviet lieutenant at the time. Nowadays, I have another opinion. . . .

The withdrawal movements of Army Group North were disrupted
considerably by the outflanking maneuvers of the Russians. The withdrawal route become more and more congested by the units pressing
together, especially since our enemy increasingly blocked our route. We
had our hands full trying to keep the route somewhat open.

In the process, we frequently had the opportunity to admire the
exemplary combat discipline of our opponents. On one occasion, we
were able to beat back an attack that was literally executed as if in a training area.

The Russians had attacked a few kilometers west of us with a fully
equipped infantry regiment supported by tanks. They were moving from
north to south toward our retreat route. We approached them from the
east along their left flank.

We then experienced a spectacle, such as is seldom seen in war. Ivan
had left his flanks unprotected—as he often did—and maneuvered in
front of our eyes as if on the drill field. We stopped at the edge of a village and opened fire.

For the time being, the enemy tanks fell victim to our fire. These
losses didn't appear to disturb the Russian infantry at all, and they continued to advance unconcerned. It never once happened that two Russians rushed at the same time next to one another. After three or four
steps, they always disappeared once again into the earth.

They thus reached the Rollbahn without armor support. We then
had to clear it again. The spectacle presented to us proved once again
how valuable proper battle drill is and how low the casualties are when
everyone knows how to maneuver properly.

Whenever we had finished clearing the retreat route to the front, it
immediately began to get hot again at the rear. This wild state of affairs
continued uninterrupted up to the Narwa. One night, the Russians even
succeeded in encircling a division command post.

It wasn't difficult for us to smash them out again, since the Russians
could only execute their flanking maneuvers with fast units, that is, with
motorized infantry, light antitank guns, and light tanks. In the morning,
the staff could continue its move. The general rode on my tank as the
last one out.

We landed in a sticky situation just in front of the junction at Wolosowo. We had the mission to hold a position outside the village of Opolje at all costs until the order to move out came. We were on the southern edge of the Rollbahn.

The village was about 100 meters on the other side of the road. In the morning, everything was still clear of the enemy and the rearward flood of troops rolled on past us. An infantry battalion was covering behind our four "Tigers." Because many units weren't motorized, the withdrawal proceeded in fits and starts. Except for a few stragglers, the Rollbahn was as good as empty in the afternoon. The village in front of us then came to life.

We saw figures run back and forth, and we had to be on our toes. Once again, it promised to be a very pleasant night. At the onset of darkness, the infantry battalion had also departed. I was alone with my four "Tigers" for far and wide. Fortunately, the Russians weren't in the know about our sticky situation. Perhaps they also had too much respect for us. In any case, they twice set up AT guns in positions across from us, but we never let them fire more than a single round. They didn't make a third attempt.

The Russian commander appeared to believe that we would also leave in the morning. In any case, he assumed there were all sorts of infantry with us. Otherwise, he would have probably approached our tanks on foot.

Shortly before midnight, vehicles appeared from the west. We were able to recognize them in time as ours. It was a fusilier battalion, which had missed its linkup and advanced to the Rollbahn late. As I later discovered, the commander sat in the only tank that formed the lead. He was completely drunk. The disaster occurred with great alacrity.

The entire unit had no idea of what was going on and moved in the open into the Russian fields of fire. A terrible panic followed when the machine-gun and mortar fire kicked off. Many soldiers were hit. With no one in charge, everyone ran back on the Rollbahn instead of seeking cover in the area south of it. Any form of comradeship had disappeared. The only thing that counted was: "Every man for himself."

The vehicles drove right over the wounded, and the Rollbahn offered a portrait of horror. The entire disaster would have been preventable had the commander of this mob done his duty and led his men cross-country instead of sitting in his tank and sleeping off his drunk.

After the fire of the Russians had let up, the radio operators and the tank commanders of our "Tigers" climbed out and crawled to the Rollbahn to save at least a few of the severely wounded. We took care of them as well as we could and placed them on the tanks. This effort to save the men was made more difficult by the moonlight.

Ivan could observe all of our movements from the houses while we could only identify the enemy by their muzzle fire. Our position became increasingly precarious. I spoke with the battalion at least every fifteen minutes, but the requested order did not come. The Russians launched very unpleasant mortar barrages at regular intervals without approaching any closer to us. Even so, the damage was serious enough.

Toward morning, Feldwebel Wesely reported to me that his tank's radiator had a hole shot in it. The same report came a half hour later from a second tank. That meant that we had to tow both vehicles with the remaining two tanks. We couldn't afford a complete loss, because we knew how hard it was to get new tanks. The drivers also had a hard time leaving their tanks, just like riders in earlier times had taking leave of their horses.

I reported the new situation to the battalion. After about twenty minutes, the long-awaited order to evacuate arrived. We hooked up the two disabled tanks as best we could and towed them two kilometers to an army food depot, which was already burning brightly.

Naturally, our soldiers who hadn't been able to take everything with them weren't going to bestow it to Ivan either. We then turned off the Rollbahn to the south because, according to the latest reports, the Russians had already reached the Rollbahn farther to the west. Getting through there was impossible. We were still in the light cast by the glowing flames of the food supply depot. We dismounted once again and hooked up the cables properly.

Suddenly, an unnerving explosion shook the air. Because of the air pressure, we were lying on the ground as if we had been mown down. At the same time, the food we had often waited so long for literally came whirling through the air toward us. Among everything else, there were also boards and beams of all sizes, enough so that we could count our luck that we weren't wounded in a somewhat inglorious manner.

The combat engineers who blew up the depot had done a great job. It was just that the place could have gone up a little bit later. The rare opportunity to die a hero's death due to a can of preserves didn't excite us. So we hurried up to get out of there quickly. Thanks to the frost, our route south of the road was completely negotiable.

In the gray of morning, I spotted a Kübel heading for us. We were all happy when we recognized our commander. He didn't hesitate for one minute to drive out to meet us, although no more German soldiers were to be seen far and wide and Ivan could appear any moment. Major Jähde literally hugged me and confessed that he had already written us off.

He was really happy that we had even brought back both disabled vehicles.

Unfortunately, we had a sad incident take place with the infantry-men we had taken along with us on the last leg of the move. The men had taken a place on the rear deck. They were dead tired and scarcely capable of walking anymore. They sat above the cooling vents, where the warm air was expelled from the engine compartment.

They soon fell asleep and suffered carbon monoxide poisoning, because the cooling air was mixed with exhaust fumes. Despite immedi-ate resuscitation efforts, three of them couldn't be saved. At that time we hadn't known any better, but from then on we were able to warn every soldier.

✠

The junction at Wolosowo was supposed to be held with all effort to ensure the return transportation of all army elements to Narwa. Oberst Wengler had set up a blocking position on the eastern edge of Wolosowo with his infantry. The rest of our battalion was incorporated into this line along with all of the Pak units.

The desire to get through to Wolosowo without incident was not real-ized. Major Jähde explained to us that we would have to detour around a large marsh. Because of that, we would have to swing north to the Roll-bahn once again. He was also nice enough not to hide the fact from us that Ivan had already reached the Rollbahn just before Wolosowo.

We just had to box our way through to the west somehow. This seemed to be a practically hopeless operation during the day, and we therefore waited for the evening. Before starting, Major Jähde took a hefty swig and positioned himself at the feet of the loader in my tank. What else could he do anyway, besides "cross his fingers?"

In order to be able to use the firepower of the two towed vehicles, we had turned their turrets backward. These crews could then cover the rear. We were scarcely on the road and turning to the west, when a Russ-ian AT gun started knocking on the turret from the rear. The vehicle in tow, however, soon created some breathing room for us. Despite that, we had to dismount, as the Russians had shot through a tow cable. But even that went well. We only had another three kilometers until the new line. Of course the Russians on both sides of the Rollbahn wanted to finish us off. A few of them jumped onto our tanks but without success. In this instance, our hand grenades did the trick. Whether the cursing of my steadfast driver Köstler also scared away Ivan could not be determined with any certainty. Shortly before our objective, we received Pak fire. Our comrades thought we were the enemy! Not until we shot back with the same caliber did we get any relief. The layman will probably object that we could have identified ourselves with flares. Of course we did that. But who is concerned about flares during such a retreat, when he doesn't know whether they are being used by Ivan or by his own people.

In Wolosowo, we met up with the remainder of the company. Strong forces were ready for the defense. Oberst Wengler's soldiers were already building a defensive line around the place. It left only the road to the west open to Narwa. I was attached to Oberst Wengler with four combat-ready "Tigers." The rest of the battalion had already departed to the railhead, where all heavy weapons were being loaded on trains to avoid further losses. Later, we would be very happy to have the firepower of the super-heavy artillery batteries, which were saved in this manner.

Oberst Wengler was responsible for the defense of Wolosowo. Later, in honor of his infantrymen, it was always called "Wenglerowo." Wengler was the model of a troop leader. He was a reservist and a bank director by profession. He had a personality that inspired complete confidence in his people. They would have gone through hell anytime for their commander. Admirable was his composure, a characteristic that is priceless in critical situations. On one occasion, we had a situation briefing in a little wooden house about a hundred meters behind the front line. The Russians were shooting from three sides, and it was anything but cozy. Wengler was already briefing the situation to us, when an impacting mortar round shattered the window. One officer was grazed on the arm and sought cover under the table. Our Oberst just looked nonchalantly in his direction and said: "Gentlemen, let's not allow ourselves to be driven crazy by this shooting. Let's stay with the subject matter at hand, so we can finish and return quickly to our posts." We had our self-confidence back again in no time. Only *the* leader who has himself under control can demand *everything* from his people.

In Wolosowo, we met members of the IIIrd SS Panzer Corps for the first time. Their greatest claim to fame later on was their holding of the Narwa position. We were excited about meeting them. We had always envied them somewhat because of their better equipment. We were quite pleasantly surprised. Their devil-may-care attitude consistently inspired us, even if their unsparing treatment of men and material alienated us somewhat. Wherever SS-units were used, things were taken care of, but the casualties were often so great that the troops had to be pulled out for reorganization. We couldn't afford that. We had to husband our men and materiel. My goal was always to effect the greatest possible success with the least possible casualties.

The Russians then began exerting pressure with all their strength against "Wenglerowo." We were all happy when the order to withdraw finally came. With its fast motorized forces, the SS covered the withdrawal. Our special railcars had already been spotted at the railhead. We took off with full steam ahead to the west, toward Narwa. While loading, we received some sad news: The commander of the 1st Company, Oberleutnant Diels, had been killed. A Russian tank had taken the Rollbahn under fire, and a piece of shrapnel had penetrated Diels's heart while he was sitting in his Kübel.

"Old Fritz"

We were happy after we had finally reached Narwa. The new position was supposed to be well fortified and strong enough to hold up the Russians. But first we needed a long time to find our support trains. There were no quarters, because all the areas around Narwa were overfilled with retreating troops. We therefore looked for a place to stay with other units in order to warm up a little bit. In the meantime, I set out to find the men of the two disabled tanks. They apparently had also already arrived in Narwa.

Prepared for any eventuality, I carried two canisters of good pea soup with me. I imagined them standing around somewhere, freezing and hungry. Because all of the traffic was flowing against us, getting through to the east was very difficult. We found both of our tanks without any problems at the train station, but none of the people. We literally had to go searching from house to house. And then I didn't believe my eyes: My "hungry" and "freezing" men sat at a table set up as if in peacetime.

They were eating cutlets and other tasty morsels and were being served to no end by the lady of the house. My arrival with the cold peas was greeted with a hello, and, of course, I did not hesitate to partake of the better meal. It was understandable that one desired a long period of rest and a decent bed. The most heartfelt wish was sleep . . . sleep . . . sleep!

As usual, things happened quite differently.

We headed west to our unit on the Rollbahn. It had already become dark, and we had about twenty kilometers behind us when it was suddenly announced:

"Everyone pull over to the right! Oncoming traffic!"

We stopped and recognized a "Tiger," which was passing the oncoming traffic only with great difficulty. When I stopped it, Oberfeldwebel Zwetti climbed out and gave me the good news: I didn't need to drive back to the trains.

He had brought the remainder of the company, and I could mount up immediately. We then proceeded east with our four "Tigers." Bed and sleep were but a pleasant, short dream. Zwetti didn't know any details about our mission; just that we were supposed to report to the commander of the SS-division that had to hold the bridgehead at Narwa.

We tortured ourselves with thoughts all the way to Narwa and drove over the bridge built by our engineers. Excitement was in the air everywhere. In the city we only saw SS vehicles driving back and forth. It was not easy to find the division command post, because the men of the SS PanzerGrenadier Division "Nordland" had mostly come from Nordic countries and barely understood German. But they were practically all strapping, energetic young soldiers.

Their commander was SS-Brigadeführer Fritz von Scholz, whom I immediately dubbed "old Fritz." I finally found him in a unique type of command post, a bus. It was parked next to a house. It was the only divisional command post I saw during the war that was closer to the front than the regimental command posts.

I reported to the operations officer who was located in a second bus: Rank, grade, troop unit—the usual—". . . wishes to see the Herr General."

The Hauptsturmführer then observed me with the interest one would devote to a creature from another planet.

"The Herr General," he finally said, stretching each syllable, "the Herr General. Hmm! We don't have that here! You are with the Waffen-SS, in case you already don't know that. And we don't have either a 'Herr' or a 'General.' There is probably a Brigadeführer here, without the 'Herr,' if you would like to see him. In addition, the title of 'Herr' also disappears from all other rank titles, up to and including the Reichsführer!"

I wasn't prepared for this type of reception but immediately switched gears: "I would like to report to your Brigadeführer!"

The operations officer nodded.

"That already sounds better," he said in a somewhat condescending tone. "Wenger, go and ask the Brigadeführer whether he has time for *Herr* Lieutenant Carius from the 'Tigers'?" He felt compelled to stress the word "Herr" in front of my rank quite distinctly.

In the meantime, an Untersturmführer had stood up from his work place and disappeared with a "Right away, Hauptsturmführer!" Shortly later he appeared again. "The Brigadeführer is expecting you!"

I then went into the other bus and was completely surprised after everything that had preceded this when I met a man who was the personification of sweetness and light. In my entire time at the front, I rarely encountered another divisional commander I could compare with our "old Fritz." He identified completely with his troops and his people deified him.

He was always there and available to anyone.

During our work together, he treated me as a son. It therefore hit all of us hard when we later discovered at Dunabürg that our "old Fritz" had been killed in the Narwa sector. The swords to the Knight's Cross had been awarded to him in August 1944, but what did that mean to those of us who had truly lost a "frontline father?"

When I reported to "old Fritz" on the bus, he immediately patted me on the shoulder in a friendly manner. "Well then, why don't we drink a schnapps to our future work together," he said. He poured two cups full and clinked glasses with me. "Where do you come from?"

After my answer, our conversation continued into personal and family-type matters, during which I also described my initial impression of his troops. When I got to the part about my reception by the operations officer, he laughed.

"Yeah, that's the way it is here," he then said. "At first, I also had to reorient myself somewhat, when I transferred from the Army. In the process, I had very mixed feelings. But now I wouldn't get rid of these guys under any circumstances.

"These men in the Waffen-SS are really fantastic and have a comradeship, such as you'll probably never see anywhere else. But be that as it may, and also for your own personal orientation, I like to hear it when someone addresses me as 'Herr General.' Whenever you come from the old school, such as I do, then such things somehow seem more natural to you. . . ."

We then spoke about the situation. In the process, it was shown that my skepticism about the legendary "Panther" line had only been all too well justified.

"Old Fritz" explained to me: "You see, if you want to be exact about it, this entire line exists only on paper. At this time of year, of course, it is completely impossible for our comrades in the front line to dig in. There are still probably a few bunkers around from the time of our advance, but they are usually not located exactly where you could use them.

"Besides, the Russians have advanced more quickly than anticipated. In addition to all of that, our troops have already got so used to continuous withdrawal that they have already passed the lines to be held. When we then wanted to occupy the front line of the bridgehead indicated on the map, we discovered that Ivan was already sitting in it.

"I then set up a new bridgehead line. It will be your mission to help the men up front in reaching the best positions for their sectors. They then have to be fortified and held. Since the Russians only have weak advance guard forces in the area, it shouldn't be all too difficult to push them back, thus enabling my men to fortify their front line."

My mission was thus clearly outlined. In its execution, the SS men and I were supported by the artillery that we had brought back from Leningrad.

Without this support, the Narwa Front could never have held out for months. Our tanks were near the division command post east of the Narwa. From the south, the front ran up to the edge of the city on the eastern side of the Narwa. There, after a short distance, it jumped over to the west bank of the river where it formed the front line until it emptied into the Baltic.

The relatively quiet times were soon gone. The Russians employed increasingly stronger forces against our bridgehead. Soon they had brought up heavy and super heavy artillery and put on a wild display of fireworks over the city. Thanks to the brave defense of the SS men, they were not successful in making inroads into the bridgehead. Only the bridge caused me worries. The Russians had it under constant artillery fire.

After the railway bridge had been eliminated, it was the last crossing over the Narwa. In case of its destruction, we would have sat in a trap with our tanks and would not have been able to be used in other threatened sectors of the front.

I described the situation to "old Fritz"; he agreed with me to place my tanks on the west bank of the Narwa, on the other side of the bridge. In an emergency, we could always be in position in a few minutes.

I then drove back over the bridge. I was taking a look around for a suitable assembly area for my vehicles, when a Kübel with a corps flag roared on up from the front. It immediately stopped, and I didn't believe my eyes when Feldmarschall Model jumped out. The high command had ordered him—as it always did in hopeless situations—to the Northern Front to restore order. I made the required report and then a storm broke over me, the likes of which one will rarely see! Model's eyebrows were twitching. I had seen this before on the Central Front.

I wasn't allowed an explanation or any answer at all. I mounted up with my people and was on the other side of the Narwa in a flash. The Feldmarschall had given me an order that I will never forget: "I am holding you personally responsible that no Russian tank breaks through. None of your 'Tigers' may be lost due to enemy fire. We need every barrel here!"

With regard to himself, Feldmarschall Model allowed no compromise and was ruthless, but he was indulgent to the men in the front lines who adored him. He demanded nothing for himself. In the Ruhr pocket in 1945, I once heard a characteristic answer from him: "The day has twenty-four hours. Add the night to that and you'll probably get through with your work!"

Unfortunately, our guest performance with the SS Division "Nordland" was soon over. We continued to cover the sector for a few days until the SS men had taken root in their new positions. In the process, we were able to liberate them from four Russian antitank guns. I'll never forget the magnificent men of the "Nordland" Division. They fought like lions.

They were better acquainted with Bolshevism through personal experience than many people of the western world with their thick books.

I discovered later that many members of the Courland Army had got to Sweden under the most trying of circumstances, in the belief that this would save them. Among them were also men of the IIIrd SS Panzer Corps. They were then interned but later handed over to the Russians under Allied pressure. When one considers that even back then the relationship between the western powers and the Soviets wasn't the best and that people in the west knew very well what kind of fate awaited the people who came from the Baltic states, then the decision of the Swedish government becomes even more ignominious, the decision of a country in which the people like to talk so much and so gladly about the "Red Cross."

The Estonians, Lithuanians, and Latvians of the SS went to a certain death or at least to Siberia, just like their parents and grandparents before them. Shocking reports are available of the scenes that took place in the Swedish internment camps when the transfer to the Russians became known. Suicide and self-mutilation are a terrible indictment against a so-called "host country." Men who had only taken up arms against Bolshevism to preserve their homeland, western civilization, and, as part of that, Sweden were delivered to certain death.

Our new assignments awaited us between Narwa and the mouth of the river. The Russians were shifting the main points of their attacks there, after they had suffered a setback at the Narwa bridgehead. They were trying to penetrate across the frozen Narwa and form a bridgehead on the western bank of the river.

The focal point of the attacks was the village of Riigi, located on the western bank of the river halfway between Narwa and the Baltic. Wengler's long-suffering infantrymen were there. They benefitted from an old trench left over from the advance in 1941.

On February 16, I was sent to Oberst Wengler with two tanks to support his people in their defense against the massed attacks of the Russians over the Narwa. Wengler's command post was located about two kilometers behind the front lines, separated from them by marshy woods. The colonel greeted me with outstretched arms.

"Well, here you are again! I'm really happy that it was you that they sent to me, since we're already on the same wavelength. The situation is pretty serious here, but you already know that. Unfortunately, I suffered quite a few casualties in the course of the fighting during the retreat. The combat strength of my regiment on a good day consists of that of a battalion at the most. For the sector I have to hold, I really need at least an entire regiment, if not more.

"For that reason, the front is only thinly held. I've attempted to help myself by constructing it as a series of strongpoints. It's best that we take a personal look at the situation for ourselves as soon as possible; you'll gain a better impression than if I show you the whole mess on the map!"

We immediately took off for an orientation. Such an orientation helped us find our way around at night as well. The level of combat activity was quite high.

When we arrived at the battalion command post, Wengler was told about another Russian penetration. The Russians had suffered terrific losses during their attacks as there was no cover at all while crossing over the ice of the Narwa. But even if only a small group was successful in establishing itself on our side of the Narwa, they stuck to our trench system like leeches and had to be wiped out in immediate counterattacks before the next attack rolled. It was clear to see that the Russians wanted to reach their objective there at all costs and without regard to casualties.

We had to support the infantrymen in rolling up the occupied portions of the trenches. That required a great deal of precision while shooting so our own people didn't fall victim to our fire. We had to approach to within about fifty meters of the trenches, which ran in the normal zigzag pattern. From there, we observed the advance of our own people.

Whenever they took a section, the first man waved. We then shot up the next ten to twenty meter section with our 88-mm cannons until it was ready for assault. As soon as our soldiers' helmets appeared over the edge of the trench, we stopped our fire and our men took the trench. Our teamwork functioned magnificently.

The Russians were not able to chalk up a success despite their heavy casualties. But they also reacted immediately to the appearance of our tanks with artillery. They sent over quite a few very pleasant "greetings" to us. The eastern bank of the Narwa climbed quite steeply, and the edge of a large forested area extended along the high ground. From the woodline, Ivan was able to see quite well into our positions. We thus stuck out like a sore thumb for their artillery, which gave us many problems. As soon as we left our little bit of woods, it didn't take more than three minutes before we saw the first muzzle flashes on the far bank.

Only by driving evasively all the time were we able to avoid a direct hit. I concentrated exclusively on the far bank, while Zwetti supported the infantry with his vehicle. Although I silenced a few Russian pieces during every encounter, we were once again under fire whenever we reappeared.

During one such occasion, I finally taught Lustig, one of the drivers, to dampen his innate daredevil attitude. Normally, this bundle of energy only drove me when my vehicle was disabled, but his tank commander had often told me that he was a wild man who always charged to the front and could hardly be convinced to back up. Certainly a praiseworthy if also dangerous characteristic! Lustig was a blacksmith by trade, a guy built like a fireplug. Once when a lit cigar stump had fallen between his shirt and his skin, instead of opening up the different layers of clothing that we wore in winter and taking it out, he simply extinguished it on his bare skin from the outside. When he shook hands with me, I felt like a horse had kicked me. That was our man Lustig, a man whose heart was in the right place. He always drove to the front and was unstoppable in front of the enemy.

But one day, as I said, he also learned to control his impetuosity. We were about 500 meters in front of our little woods when the Russians opened fire. The first salvo landed too short; the second behind us. I didn't want to wait for the third, since we could then count on a hit. I called out to Lustig: "Back up!"

But he didn't react. So we stayed there, and the Russians fired off their third salvo. The impacting rounds began to land all around us, and a 28-cm colossus landed directly in front of us on the trail. It didn't explode.

Like a large mouse, it skittered along as a dud toward us. It slid along the snow underneath our vehicle. We were later able to see it in front of the woods on our move back. After this incident, even our friend Lustig was convinced there was no more time to be lost whenever I gave him the command to back up.

Again and again, we admired the quality of the steel on our tanks. It was hard without being brittle. Despite its hardness, it was also elastic. If an AT round didn't hit the armor dead on, it slid off on its side and left behind a gouge as if you had run your finger over a soft piece of butter.

At night we couldn't help our long-suffering comrades very much. We would have endangered them by shooting. We just fired up the ice-covered surface of the Narwa whenever a new Russian attack started. By doing that, we could steal some of Ivan's thunder. They often attempted to cross as many as a dozen times during the night. They even employed sleds. Despite their enormous casualties, they wanted to force the river. Whenever they did it, we called it "stubbornness." Of course when we did it, it was "bravery."

We were forced to become thoroughly familiar with the reversed application of such terms after the war. The soldier who had performed his duty for his country to the very end was suddenly a "militarist" and a "warmonger," in short, an "evil Nazi."

After it had finally become somewhat quieter in the Riigi sector, we received new marching orders. I took leave of Oberst Wengler, and, as we wished one another continued good luck, he hesitantly revealed to me that he probably had the hardest and longest battle of his life in front of him. He intended to get married.

The occasion that allowed his wedding was the awarding of the Oak Leaves to the Knight's Cross, for which he was returning to Germany. He was the 404th soldier to receive this high award. Unfortunately, his young marriage came to an all-too-early end. Wengler was killed as a General-major in 1945 in the west, after he had been awarded the Swords to his Knight's Cross. He was the 123rd soldier of the Wehrmacht to receive it.

The Front Held at Narwa

To make the following operations understandable, I have to discuss the layout of the defensive positions along the Narwa as it was known to the battalion staff on February 24, 1944. The river presented itself as a defensive position. If one follows it upstream, it initially runs about ten kilometers in a southeasterly direction from its mouth in the Bay of Finland. It flows past Riigi and Siivertsi and toward the city of Narwa before turning south. After one or two kilometers, it curves to the west. This leg—where the Narwa flows for almost ten kilometers from east to west—will be important for the following narrative. Following this section, one then reaches the northeast corner of Lake Peipus after about forty-five kilometers in a south–southeasterly direction.

When we were withdrawn from Riigi, the front ran from the Bay of Narwa—from Hungerburg, to be exact—along the western bank of the river. It went via Riigi to just before Narwa. It then jumped over to the eastern bank, where the bridgehead had been formed in front of the city. This bridgehead was necessary for holding the city.

The front line met the Narwa again where it made its bend. It had been intended to continue the line on the eastern bank. It had even been planned to build a bridgehead in the middle of the east–west leg that followed. As so often happened, however, the Russians put an end to our plans in that regard.

The Narwa–Waiwara–Wesenberg railway line ran parallel to this east–west axis of the Narwa, about eight kilometers to the north. Another 800 meters to the north was the Rollbahn. From there it was another five to six kilometers to the Baltic coast. The area between the river and the Rollbahn was completely marshy; the railway went over a reinforced embankment. The infantry units, which were supposed to occupy the east–west axis in order to form the planned bridgehead to the south, arrived too late.

One had assumed that the Russians had not yet advanced as far as the Narwa in that area. Because of the marshy terrain, one also considered it unlikely that the Russians would establish themselves north of the

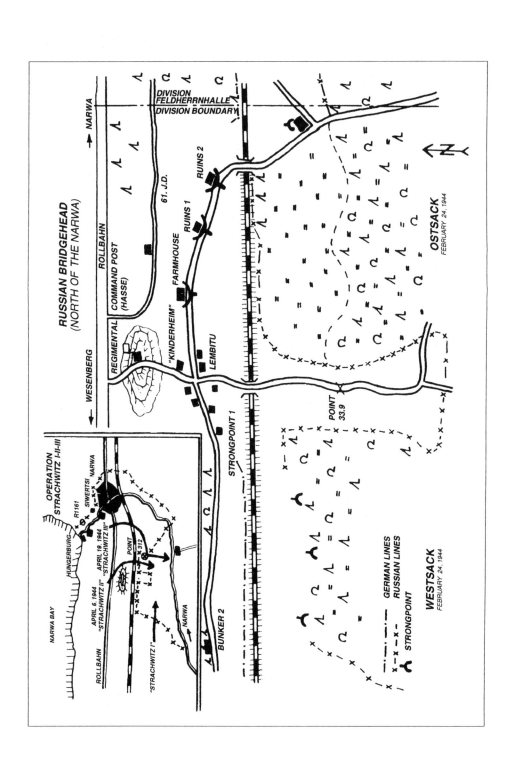

RUSSIAN BRIDGEHEAD
(NORTH OF THE NARWA)

← NARWA →

DIVISION
FELDHERRNHALLE
DIVISION BOUNDARY

61. J.D.

ROLLBAHN

RUINS 2

RUINS 1

COMMAND POST
(HASSE)

REGIMENTAL

WESENBERG

"KINDERHEIM"

FARMHOUSE

LEMBITU

OSTSACK
FEBRUARY 24, 1944

STRONGPOINT 1

POINT
33.9

N

NARWA BAY

OPERATION
STRACHWITZ I-II-III

HUNGERBURG

R1161

SIWERTSI

NARWA

APRIL 6, 1944
"STRACHWITZ II"

APRIL 19, 1944
"STRACHWITZ III"

POINT
312

ROLLBAHN

"STRACHWITZ I"

NARWA

BUNKER 2

WESTSACK
FEBRUARY 24, 1944

— · — GERMAN LINES
— x — RUSSIAN LINES
STRONGPOINT

river. According to the High Command, the marshy area was completely ill suited for establishing a position.

When our guys wanted to occupy their positions, however, they made the embarrassing discovery that Ivan had already pushed forward with strong forces between the northern bank of the Narwa and the Rollbahn. He had established a bridgehead there from which he threatened our troops in Narwa. Our units were too weak to force him back to the south over the river.

As a result of all these difficulties, our front line took on a highly original character. It ran north of the railway embankment and consisted of strongpoints. At about the middle of this leg, however, it pushed into the enemy bridgehead on both sides of a trail. There it had the shape of a boot. The northern portion of the Russian-occupied terrain was thus split into two parts, the "east sack" and the "west sack." Both of these "sacks" became standard terms in the Wehrmacht reports.

The trail, which led out of the boot to the north, went through the village of Limbitu after crossing the railway. After about another 800 meters, it reached some high ground that jutted out of the somewhat flat terrain like a large molehill. Just behind it, the trail emptied into the main Rollbahn. This trail was crossed by a second one in Limbitu.

It ran from the west, parallel to the railroad, and brushed past a farmhouse behind the edge of the village. From the farmhouse, it led diagonally to the railway embankment and reached a second railway crossing after about 130 meters. Along the leg from the farmhouse to the rail crossing, there were two additional houses located at approximately equidistant intervals.

I wanted to preface my upcoming narration with this detailed description of the terrain, so that the reader could form a mental picture of our operations in this area. The map provided in this chapter also gives additional information about the area where we fought it out with the Russians.

✠

When we returned from Riigi to the company trains, located about twenty-five kilometers west of Narwa in an area between the coast and the Rollbahn, I immediately drove on to the battalion command post to report to the commander. He asked me to relieve our company commander at Limbitu that same day. He was not in the best of health.

Our company was distributed among the individual infantry regiments. The company commander was at Limbitu with two "Tigers"; there were an additional four at the "west sack." Using a Kübel, I immediately drove to Limbitu in order to relieve the commander. As I drove down the road from the "Kinderheim"—that was the name given to the high ground north of Limbitu—I noticed where the front line ran from the amount of combat activity. The commander was happy that I had come so quickly and immediately disappeared with my Kübel.

Feldwebel Kerscher was sitting in the second vehicle and served as its commander. We always got along well. Whenever both of us were together, I always felt better in an operation. My comrades explained the situation to me. According to them, the Russians were sitting behind the railway embankment and making themselves at home there. The embankment was so high that one could easily dig tunnels into it. These served as bunkers.

Our men were in the farmhouse and in both of the houses between it and the "Russian" rail crossing. Our tanks were behind the farmhouse. At night, pairs of sentries had to maintain contact between the strong points. It had been decided against a trench system, as the regimental commander was of the opinion that the current lines were only temporary ones. His command post was located on the back slope of the "Kinderheim." It fell off so sharply on the eastern side that they had dug tunnels into the mountain. They were thus safe from any type of fire.

After the first night, I reached an agreement with the infantry commander that *we* should pull security during the day and his people at night. My men also needed to have a few hours of rest as long as it was possible.

We laid a wire from the farmhouse to a house west of the road crossing in the village. I was thus always able to be in position whenever something was happening. On the first evening, of course, we did not drive back to our "rest position." I wanted to take a look at the positions first. This was only possible during darkness.

The infantrymen were quite surprised when I expressed my desire to get acquainted with the positions. Apparently, they had never experienced that before. But I had my own ideas on that subject. How were we supposed to support people effectively when we really didn't know their positions inside and out?

How was teamwork supposed to function, if we didn't know one another better? For us tankers, positional warfare and any type of operation within the front lines was certainly nothing to shout about. We weren't born to hang around the countryside as large targets. Our missions were attack and counterattack, that is, operations on the move. But what were the poor guys there supposed to do without us? They were in a position that could not be held without tanks.

I therefore went to the nearest house with the first pair of sentries. It was about seventy meters away. The route could not be seen by the Russians at night, as there were small trees and marsh vegetation between us and the railway embankment.

The strongpoint had been occupied by a company, just like the farmhouse. One shouldn't be deceived by the word "company," however. That meant twenty-five to thirty men. This "imposing" number had only been achieved because replacements from home had arrived shortly before. Raw recruits who still needed to learn about the front were sitting there. They were astonishingly willing and eager to see action. I went with the roving sentries from this strongpoint to the third one, only thirty to forty meters from the railway embankment.

There was no cover to the right, but the Russians behind the railway embankment appeared to be concerned with themselves. Only occasionally did a shot ring through the night and force us facedown in the mud. Ivan probably only wanted to prove that he was still there. We were only a few meters away from the enemy in the most forward strongpoint. In general, the front was quiet. Only occasionally did a round from our artillery rustle close overhead through the air and explode on the other side of the railway embankment.

Once in awhile we heard the Russians call to one another and perceived sounds that made us assume that the construction of positions was in progress. The Russians had to fortify their dugouts—just like we did—and improve their roads to bring up heavy materiel.

The next company was located another 150 to 200 meters farther on in the woodline, which extended between the railway embankment and the Rollbahn. This guard therefore had to cover the longest stretch. We then went to the man at the right contact point of the next battalion, which belonged to the "Feldherrnhalle" Division. There, in the woods, a proper front line started. It ran along to the railway embankment heading east. The Russians had established their lines in another woodline 200 meters to the south.

No foot soldier enjoyed having completely open terrain to his back. It doesn't offer any cover and makes it practically impossible in a difficult situation to bring up reserves without the enemy being able to observe and disturb every movement. Our infantry found itself in just such a complicated situation in these positions. That made the necessity of our presence all the more obvious. If the Russians were to get the dumb idea to attack farther to the north, then our comrades could not have prevented a penetration without armor support.

Our infantry was busily engaged in building up the strongpoints into bunkers. The basements were reinforced with beams, firing ports were added, and the "duty stoker" ensured that the guards could always warm up. Compared to them, those of us in the tanks were quite bad off in the winter whenever we had to pull security for days and weeks on end, as we did there. We would have been happy to have a little bit of the heat that prevailed in the tanks in the summer. In the winter, it was like sitting in an icebox.

To warm us up a little bit once in a while, we had come up with the idea of burning a large petroleum lamp. While we were in training, it had been strictly forbidden to smoke in the tank. And there we were, allowing a petroleum lamp to burn at full throttle in front of the enemy! Thank God that an accident never occurred in any of the tanks of the company because of this carelessness. But there were other effects. For example, whenever all of us had dozed off and the pressure on the wick let up some, it began to smoke like there was no tomorrow.

We all looked like chimney sweeps. Because of the soot, the inside of all of our tanks could scarcely be called white anymore. The air wasn't the best either. I am amazed today that none of us was poisoned from smoke inhalation. A standard phrase applied back then: "Nobody has ever died from the stink, but a lot have from freezing."

Even the rations in the tank tasted of gas or oil. With time and in a pinch, however, people get used to everything. This smell of gas and old oil, this "tank smell," even became quite agreeable to us over the years.

In the gray of morning, a young soldier came running to my vehicle. He reported that his people in the nearest strongpoint had observed the Russians emplacing the first AT gun in the railway embankment.

Of course, I promised immediate countermeasures. An old truth: We had to show something to our infantry comrades to win their trust. If that was done, we could talk to them in a reasonable manner and not have to worry about dumb things happening.

Then both of us boldly drove out to the second strongpoint and lined up against the railway embankment. The Russian antitank gun was difficult to identify because it had been camouflaged magnificently. Only the muzzle brake peeked out. Because Ivan still hadn't fired up to then, he missed his chance. After a few rounds, the barrel of the gun pointed skyward, looking like it could have been that of an antiaircraft weapon.

Even though we were scarcely fifty meters in front of the thing, it could not be finished off with a single round. Ivan had emplaced it very skillfully in the railway embankment. We first had to soften up the exterior. During this minor operation, I could finally take a look at the terrain during the day. Without a doubt, the Russians had the advantage over us.

Behind the railway embankment were a few rows of high fir trees. The Russians were later able to dominate the entire terrain using sharpshooters from the peaks. Behind that, visible through the fir trees, was an open plain, which extended to the edge of a fairly tall set of woods in a marsh. The row of trees stopped at the railway crossing. The Russians had therefore let their front line move back at that point, because the embankment became lower to the east and didn't offer enough cover.

After our little "morning excursion," we drove back to the farmhouse. At that time, we had no idea that we would have to continue this monotonous existence of pulling security for weeks on end. We had scarcely arrived into position behind the farmhouse when a VW-Kübel came racing down the road from the "Kinderheim." Ivan could see this route without any problems and immediately began to "pepper" us with mortar rounds.

Fortunately, he didn't hit the Kübel. "Old Man Biermann," a career noncommissioned officer, climbed out of it. He ran the forward supply point and wouldn't hear of not bringing us rations, even in the most impossible of situations. He drove right up to us, and we were able to take our meal. I greeted him with a few choice words:

"You put your life on the line for this lumpy chow! Have you gone crazy?" Biermann gave a short reply: "Don't forget, I also want my warm food and my coffee. But if you didn't have anything here up front, then how are *we* supposed to enjoy our meal!"

That wasn't just dumb talk or idle bragging. His words came from the heart. Whenever there are shots fired in anger, all the idle bragging stops. It was that selfless comradeship and altruistic commitment that will never let us forget the difficult times at the front. It holds us together even today. Only when everyone has to show his true colors and substance counts—not a uniform or an external mask—does one really get to know a person. One can be sure that these comrades won't let one down in peacetime either.

Granted: A war isn't exactly necessary in order to get to really know a person. But the experience of comradeship, this bonding to the others

without regard for oneself, has convinced me that our time in the war
had not been lost. Instead, it has given all of us something to take with us
on the path of life. In my experience, the people who curse a blue streak
about their army time and talk about "stolen" years were usually poor
comrades and boundless egoists.

Of course, "Old Man Biermann" was only old for us young bucks. He
was probably in his midthirties. He had a family and had been a member
of the Social Democrats, a party that he still admitted belonging to. He
never attempted to conceal his opinions, but that didn't stop his becoming a noncommissioned officer. He was a tremendous soldier. None of us
ever asked to see someone's party membership book! No one, except for
the first sergeant who kept the company rolls, knew who belonged to
what religion.

Who cared whether someone was from Saxony or from the Pfalz,
from Berlin or from Austria! What counted was that he did his duty in
the group and that we could depend on him. To the enemy, everyone
was the same; the Russians didn't differentiate. On the other hand, whoever let us down at the front and couldn't get his act together was written
off by his fellow soldiers. He had a hard time being accepted back into
the community.

It was with Biermann that I liked to talk to about our options after
the war. We occasionally had the thought that we could lose it. We all
had our fantasies. Life after the war would be so nice if everyone
respected everyone else as we did in the company, without regard to
party, religion, and occupation. The main thing was that everyone did
his job the best way he could.

We believed back then that such ideals could be realized in a democ-
racy. But doubts also surfaced as to whether such ideal relationships
allowed themselves to be created in the world at all. We later had to
experience just how justified these doubts were. "Old Man Biermann"
liked to say: "The guy who sits at the feed trough gets to pig out. And if
he is the only one who is pigging out, then everybody else can still be satisfied." He may well have hit the nail on the head with that.

Following my little digression, let's return to the front at the Narwa.
Ivan continued to remain suspiciously quiet. Only when we allowed our
engines to warm up for a quarter of an hour did he start to "pepper" us.
He was probably assuming that we wanted to take off and stir up some

trouble where he was. As soon as we heard the "bam . . . bam . . . bam" of the firing, we quickly buttoned our hatches. A few seconds later, the mortar rounds were hitting in our vicinity. Because the fuses were very sensitive, they made any type of penetration into the frozen earth impossible. The rounds only left black marks in the snow after impacting. Later on, with the 15-cm mortars, things became a whole lot more uncomfortable.

The days passed by with dozing and freezing. In a comfortable civilian life, people have a hard time imagining how we could get used to the continuous cold. Despite it, we stripped off our old clothes twice a day to delouse ourselves. How thankful we would have been for a can of DDT powder! We hardly changed our underwear. Experience had taught us that our friendly "rear end roomers" felt better in clean laundry.

Therefore the underwear had to be so dirty that even the lice were disgusted. Only then was their urge to reproduce somewhat dampened.

Back then I possessed three utensils that reminded me of my distant civilian life. First there was a nail cleaner, highly valued by all of us. Then there was a comb, which also performed yeoman service. Finally, there was an old hairpin, which I used to clean my ears. It also circulated among the other comrades, and I was able to hold on to it throughout the war and prison camp.

The subject of water was a sore one. Washing and even shaving were not high on the list of priorities. Naturally, the few wells had become frozen. The infantrymen didn't have it any better than we did, either. But foot soldiers know how to take care of themselves, even in the craziest of situations. Whenever meatballs arrived with the rations at night, we ate them with our hands. Our skin became visible under the soot and the dirt again.

These things were of secondary importance to us anyway. We were all happy whenever we could sleep in a stretched-out position for at least a few hours during the night.

We drove back to the western outskirts of the village on the second night. In one house, we found a bunker constructed under the floor. Even if we didn't have a stove in there, we could at least sleep in a stretched-out position in our winter clothing. Due to our exhaustion, we didn't notice the cold at all. The truck with the fuel, ammunition, and rations came at midnight. For the first time, we ate with a real appetite.

During the day, we only forced something down reluctantly. Often, I wouldn't have eaten at all if my crew hadn't forced me to. The men simply did not let me light up a cigarette until I had finished my bread. My gunner, Unteroffizier Heinz Kramer, was extremely hard and unrelenting in this regard. It should be noted that we were extremely well fed, given the circumstances.

Our mess sergeant, Unteroffizier Pseidl, a barber by trade and from Vienna, spared no effort, even though he would have preferred to be in a tank again. He often provided us with dumplings and vegetables and avoided stews as much as possible.

The men who brought rations, fuel, and munitions up front deserve special praise. They had a difficult and responsible mission. These resourceful men had to find us right behind the front and arrive in one piece.

They always traveled at night, without lights and usually on unfamiliar routes, which were disrupted daily by new craters. Their mission was often more difficult than ours at the front. At least we were familiar with the local situation. They almost always had to count upon surprises. They were then expected to do the right thing based on their own initiative. Despite all that, we were never left without resupply.

We were quite happy with our new "night camp." The men in the lines could also be reassured; we had laid a field phone line from them to us. Shortly before daybreak, we would drive back to the farmhouse. There, someone usually came running to us to report what new things Ivan had done the previous night at the railway embankment.

Occasionally, there were also some humorous episodes. Once in a while, we shot off the crowns of the trees on the other side of the railway embankment because they appeared "suspicious." Ivan had sharpshooters in them. They breathed down our necks and prevented any type of free movement. During one such incident, a young infantryman, who clearly hadn't been at the front very long, came running out of breath to my tank.

He excitedly explained that the Russians had posted armored sharpshooters in the trees. He had observed exactly how our machine-gun ammo had bounced off them. He thought I really ought to be shooting in the trees with main gun rounds.

And what had the well-meaning youth actually seen? The tracers of our rounds flew in all directions after contact with a branch; at the same time, however, the trajectory of the machine-gun rounds was naturally quite different. Our comrade departed reassured. It should be noted, however, that he had only been a bit premature with the facts.

Later, after penetrating the "east sack," we were actually able to find body armor. It was worn primarily by the commissars and offered very nice protection against shrapnel and pistol rounds. In my opinion, though, this armor must have seriously impeded movement.

My men had to get used to a lot of things and did it without complaining. There was one requirement, however, that they only begrudgingly got used to and complained about a lot: no one was allowed to relieve themselves during an operation or while pulling security.

Personal relief had been "ordered" for the mornings and the evenings. If necessary, there was no other choice but to take care of business in the tank. With the passage of time, everyone got used to this rule and there weren't any more problems. There was a reason for this harsh action: the majority of the men were lost when they were outside the tank.

The Russians, who could observe their dismounting, immediately fired with rifles or mortars. Besides the senseless wounding of the men, there was the additional problem of getting equally good replacements from the home front. Because of my strict orders, we actually only had two more casualties outside of a tank, and these were with another Einsatzgruppe. Of course as tank commanders, we had to get out once in a while to go to the infantry. The men didn't like that either. Whenever I wanted to climb out of the turret, Kramer often held me by the legs. He was afraid I might catch a round.

On February 27, bomber units paid their respects for the first time. From then on, these nuisances came every night, sometimes even twice in a night. They apparently wanted to prepare our positions for an assault.

Shortly before the onset of darkness, the "pathfinder" flew in from the south and dropped the familiar "Christmas trees" behind our lines. Immediately after that, two-engined bombers appeared. They dropped their loads behind us on both sides of the Rollbahn. For the duration of the attack, Ivan fired red and pink flares toward us. They helped to orient the pilots so that they didn't drop bombs on their own lines. In addition, the Russians had stacked piles of wood behind the front line. These had the shape of a Soviet star and were ignited at the onset of darkness. Despite all of this, they sometimes dropped too short. In general, we didn't have anything to worry about right behind the front. In the following weeks, the Russians transformed the entire area on both sides of the Rollbahn from Narwa to us into a moonscape.

Because of the marshy land, the bombs burrowed deep into the earth before they blew up. They then scooped out high walls of earth. There were craters the size of single-family houses. They immediately filled up with water. We were well advised to take a close look at the terrain in the morning so we didn't drive into them in case of action. What could happen will be reported in another section.

Our Flak only took the "pathfinder" under fire, because then the ammunition was gone. Unfortunately, they didn't always succeed in hitting it. Even though we felt safe to a certain extent, this whole business still didn't give us a warm and cozy feeling. Whenever those guys dropped their bombs, we had the feeling that they were rushing straight at us. This feeling lasted until they finally landed at a safe distance and made the soft earth tremble. In the tank, we thought we were standing on a spring mattress.

Of course, we quickly set up our countermeasures. Whenever we saw the "pathfinder" approach over the bridgehead in the evening—it was dubbed the "duty NCO" because of its punctuality—we quickly moved back to our house in Lembitu. We did that so we weren't moving whenever the "Christmas tree" appeared in the heavens. This short move out of the danger zone wasn't a "retreat." We drove toward the west and parallel to the front.

We were then located in front of the so-called "boot shaft"; that is, we had Ivan right beside us. It was impossible for the bombers to hit us in the narrow "boot."

On the same evening, after our guests from the air had left us again, the division surgeon came to us riding in the resupply vehicle. He wanted to check out the health and welfare of the troops. No one was sick, but all of us had such swollen feet and legs that a few men had already cut open their boots somewhat to get relief.

We couldn't take the things off, since no one would have got them on again. It was at that point that the honorable division surgeon appeared and examined our legs. He caused a laugh riot when he, in all seriousness, proposed that we should take "foot baths" in the evenings.

We didn't even have water to wash our faces or a place to light a fire! It only would have betrayed us to the Russians. Two of my people absolutely had to be sent to the rear, he said, because their feet were especially bad. But nothing could convince them to ride to the rear and be relieved.

That was the spirit of our frontline comrades. Only the defective fantasy of a third-rate hack could dream up the fairy tale that a pistol had sometimes been necessary to force our subordinates into combat.

Calm Before the Storm

The signs of a imminent attack by the Russians increased. On the morning of February 28, we executed another maneuver against the Russian antitank position. Ivan had given it another try with an anti-tank gun. According to the infantry, he had also built a bunker in the embankment at the railway crossing.

He didn't let himself be distracted by our direct hits. Every evening he built something new, just like a mole. Without a doubt, the Russians were superior to us in the building of field fortifications. Equal parts natural talent and hard drill were responsible for that. They always dug in before we identified them. It should also be noted that the Russian anti-tank guns didn't let themselves get into a duel with us. The crew usually scrammed before we got into a good position.

A few days later, a report reached us from corps that a Russian radio transmission had been intercepted. It forbade antitank and tank fire by the frontline units in the bridgehead. That made it clear that they did not want to reveal their positions. Only in case of a German attack on the bridgehead were they allowed to open fire.

This order revealed two things. On the one hand, they certainly had respect for our tanks. On the other hand, it was clear that Ivan had already positioned tanks in the bridgehead. That clearly indicated an intention to attack. Tanks could only be envisioned for an attack. They were completely unsuitable for defending in the marshy woods, which allowed no repositioning. It also didn't require any tremendous strategic talent to realize that the Russians would risk everything to roll up the bothersome German bridgehead at Narwa from the south.

We had a lot of bad luck that evening. The rations had already been distributed, and we were chatting away with our comrades from the company trains, when Russian bomber formations approached. Generally, we didn't need to be especially worried right there behind the front lines. But this time, when Ivan dropped his bombs noticeably short, a few of us crawled under the tanks. The rest disappeared as soon as possible.

A lot of bombs even fell among the Russians. One fell directly behind one of my tanks. Both of the crew members underneath it were immediately killed by the concussion. The men sitting on the tanks were flung off them and escaped with the shock of their lives. This unfortunate incident was another lesson for us to remain alert, even in relatively quiet periods. As we lay down in our bunker, we were still shaken by the event. The old saying about bad luck seldom traveling alone was confirmed shortly thereafter.

We had laid down for scarcely an hour, when a guard woke us. We heard a suspicious crackling and rustling. A few idiots from another unit who didn't know anything about Russian heating had fired up the stove in the house above us.

The sparks were already flying, and the thatched roof immediately caught fire. Only with difficulty did we get out of the burning house, which then collapsed behind us. Ivan naturally fired at the good target. Once again, there was no such thing as a halfway peaceful night.

The next day brought new surprises. We dispatched an enemy anti-tank gun the first thing in the morning, whereupon the Russians didn't bring any more into position. Observation revealed that they had also brought artillery and heavy mortars close to the front. They occasionally showered us with their attentiveness. In the evening, after our airborne "duty NCO" had once again given the march order to his bomber formations, we moved back.

We found a small abandoned bunker in a patch of woods the size of a postage stamp. It was north of the trail and 1,000 meters to the west of the burned-down house. It became our nightly resting place from then on.

The tanks were parked well camouflaged between the trees, and we were more or less satisfied. That same night, however, the sentry reported to us that the glow of a large fire could be seen in the direction of our infantry strongpoints and that there was a lot of firing in progress. We immediately moved out and saw from afar that the farmhouse and both of the other strongpoints were burning brightly. The Russians had fired at them with incendiary munitions to remove our last cover. I had been afraid of that for a long time.

It had always upset me that no trenches had been built, if nothing else at least between the three strongpoints. Naturally, our soldiers had to get out of their bunkers during the fire. They were laying about in the terrain without cover. The losses would have been even greater during the day. The anticipated attack of the Russians did not happen.

They probably only wanted to create a better line of sight. Fortunately for us, the houses in the Narwa sector had stone foundations. They did not burn and continued to offer protection. During the following night, they had to be covered with new beams. This situation meant that we were completely naked for the world to see. We had to constantly observe the railway embankment so that the Russians didn't surprise us. For the time being, they didn't appear to have any desire to engage us in heavy firefights. That, too, was an indicator of an intention to carry out an attack of great magnitude.

By early morning, we had already moved the severely wounded back to the "Kinderheim." From then on we were the "jack of all trades" for the infantry—so that they didn't suffer even more casualties. Company strength had already shrunk to ten to twelve men anyway. Almost every night, I went to the regimental command post behind the "Kinderheim" and asked the commander to have the lines in our sector built up by digging trenches during the night.

Unfortunately, my proposals met with no success. In my opinion, everyone simply had to see that the weakest point of our front was there. But Major Haase was always only worried about his two battalions in the boot. Yet it had to be clear to him that further to the east we had to cover the sector boundary between two divisions. The enemy always liked to select such sectors for an attack.

Once the houses had also been burned to the ground, the situation was practically hopeless for the infantry in case of a Russian attack toward the Rollbahn from the "east sack." From now on, these three houses will be referred to as the three ruins.

I was finally able to arrange for a platoon of four well-camouflaged assault guns to be positioned even with and east of the "Kinderheim." Three 2-cm quad Flak guns also went into position 100 meters behind our farmhouse.

Whenever an infantry radio broke down, we drove to the "Kinderheim" and picked up a replacement. We also risked picking up rations on moonlit nights. I really could have stepped into it doing that. It would have been all over if a vehicle had been lost during such an action. But what was I supposed to do?

After all, I had to help the men as much as was possible. They were also thankful for it and sent us their regards long after we were employed in a completely different sector.

We also had our worries about our loyal Biermann. He appeared punctually every morning with his hot coffee, even though he risked his neck with every trip. We simply didn't have the heart to tell him that we would have preferred our rest to drinking coffee. That was because the Russians accompanied every trip by Biermann with sortie wild fireworks. One morning, he only got out by the skin of his teeth. In the process he got two blowouts. He finally listened to my advice and dispensed with the "dangerous" coffee. The infantry and the Flak crews were also happy. It always took a good half hour after Biermann's Kübel had shown up until Ivan had quieted down again and stopped his dumb shooting.

During one of those nights, we had an interesting experience in our bunker. I myself was the center of attraction. I must preface that by saying that we received an unwanted visit every night by a so-called "lame duck" or "sewing machine." Those were the names we gave to the Russian biplanes. These planes flew up and down behind the front, quite low, almost to the point we could grab them. Besides hand grenades and mines, they also dropped small bombs.

One could also call these machines the "hot-rod bombers," because the engine was always throttled before the pilot threw something out. He held the stick firmly between his knees when doing this. We were therefore always ready for the drop, that is, if we were awake.

One night, however, we were sound asleep when one of these strange birds showed up. By chance, one of his bombs fell directly on the corner of the bunker. It raised a great cloud of dirt, and two guys were slightly wounded by shrapnel. Everybody ran out of the bunker. They missed me outside and went back in.

They found me lying there as if dead and began to undress me to see where I had been hit. Not until they were in the process of undressing me did I wake up. I noticed that I was covered in dirt and snow, completely unscratched. I had slept as soundly and as deeply as only a completely exhausted man can.

The whole affair may sound improbable nowadays, but a doubting Thomas could easily be set straight by my Feldwebel Kerscher. Even today, he still likes to talk about this basically humorous incident. Front-line soldiers don't need a bed or pills to sleep like the dead.

Living in a tank for weeks at a time wasn't something to shout about. One needs a little bit of fantasy to be able to imagine it in real terms. The confinement and the grim cold took its toll after a while. Our health was under considerable attack, even though we didn't want to admit it to ourselves. The results showed up later, however.

Moisture from our breath and the petroleum lamp settled onto the inner walls of the tank. It soon froze and formed a thick, white coat of frost. If one of the crew nodded off and wound up with his hair on the wall of the tank, then it was actually frozen to it when he woke up. To a certain extent, we could only hunch down and shiver ourselves warm.

The infantrymen in their positions hardly envied us at all. We could not move about in the tank and never had the opportunity to warm ourselves by a stove. I therefore wasn't surprised when one day I started carrying a pleurisy around with me, as the doctor was later able to diagnose. My left knee, which often lay against the wall of the tank, also had frostbitten spots.

The deceptive calm before the storm continued until March 15. We were hit by a mortar round on that day. We had always been able to avoid one up to that point by means of skillful evasive driving. I radioed to the company that the radiator was leaking. Fortunately, two vehicles had just come back from the repair shop and were ready to roll. They could relieve us the next morning. In the previous few days, the Russians had appeared with more and more heavy equipment from out of the depths of the bridgehead. They didn't fire much, however, so we assumed that they only wanted to zero in their guns. Up front, the infantry frequently made out the sounds of tracked vehicles. One assumed that it was tractors that were bringing the artillery pieces forward. At any rate, the striking quiet of the previous few days told us that nothing good was happening.

Toward evening, Feldwebel Kerscher towed me back to our bunker. On the next morning, the 16th, Oberfeldwebel Zwetti arrived with two vehicles to relieve us. Before the break of day, I went with him to the farmhouse and oriented him on the terrain. We then went in Kerscher's tow in the direction of "home."

We were extremely happy to be able to have at least a few days of rest, to bathe and, finally, to sleep to our heart's content. On our move parallel to the front line along the "west sack," we passed the place where the three vehicles commanded by Oberfeldwebel Göring were. It was where the trail turned north toward the Rollbahn.

His position was better than ours in the "east sack." The crews had picked a cemetery as overnight accommodations. The tanks were parked right against the cemetery wall, and the men slept in a grave vault, which had been lined with bricks and reinforced above with beams. Looked at from a peacetime perspective, one would consider that to be blasphemous. But the law of war overrides the law of peace everywhere. The men were happy to be able to get into the frozen ground any way possible. Whoever had the misfortune to become a prisoner of the Russians later on had the opportunity to see even more blasphemous things happen at cemeteries.

Our forward support base, company commander, and first sergeant were located in Sillamä at that time. The town is directly on the Baltic coast, about twenty-five kilometers west of Narwa and north of the Rollbahn. We first greeted all our comrades in the company. We hadn't seen them for a long time, and they scarcely recognized us with our beards.

They had already heated the sauna for us, which was right on the beach. We really looked forward to the bath we hadn't had in such a long time. I then reported to the commander in his area. His tank was parked next to the house in front of the window as protection against artillery shrapnel. His greeting was not overwhelming.

"Once again, you're not wearing a tie. It's no wonder that I continually have to dress down one of the men when you set such a poor example. Where is our respect supposed to come from, if *we* let ourselves go like that!"

It should be noted that I always only wore a black scarf. I knew that von Schiller didn't like that. His words weren't spoken in an unfriendly manner, but they were completely serious. I only said:

"If the respect of my men depends completely on my tie, then there must be something wrong with me."

I had known von Schiller from my time as a recruit. He had immediately offered to use the familiar "du" with me after we had arrived in Russia with the 502nd. He was my only superior in the battalion and never gave me an actual order. He knew that I always acted according to my own discretion when I was on my own anyway.

And when I was at the front, that was all the time. He never had a bad experience because of it. Our "du" relationship was also the reason that I constantly had to sit on the fence post. Whenever members of the company were present, I observed military decorum and the "du" didn't exist anymore. I was always the man in the middle between the company and its commander and had to mediate, sometimes for one side, sometimes for the other.

Whoever claims he has never perceived an oppressive feeling of fear has certainly never been to the front. The prerequisite for bravery is fear, just as the fear of dying and the uncertainty of what follows this earthly existence are the prerequisites for the origin and existence of every religion. *Real* bravery is overcoming the fear of one's own death through the greater determination to be an example to one's soldiers and to support them.

Probably none of us were free from fear. Before some operations, I did not feel the best. But as soon as the tank was rolling, I was distracted by so many things that I scarcely thought about the danger. After the first shot had been fired, our nerves quieted down on their own. Nothing went quite right when we were agitated. During the fighting, I could often transfer my outer calm to others through a short, humorous radio transmission.

Von Schiller shouldn't have been surprised if his people didn't like him, since he didn't impress them in combat. As a consequence, no one could stand his arrogance. It probably functioned as some sort of self-defense for him. We knew each other too well to put something over on one another. I forgave him things that hardly any other friend would have been able to forgive. One couldn't demand the same tolerance from the men. After all, their employment at the front—to include the ultimate sacrifice—was demanded as a matter of course.

Occasionally, his criticism was also completely justified. There was the embarrassing story concerning using code names on the radio. Von Schiller was briefing me on the situation in the bridgehead. He looked at me in an accusatory manner: "These radio games in the clear have to come to a complete stop! You're not only endangering your own people with it."

Wisely, I kept my silence; he really wasn't incorrect. I couldn't or simply didn't want to get used to the silly code names. During an operation, was I always supposed to radio, "Nightcap, this is Wood Grouse" and similar messages? Our men felt a whole lot better when they were addressed with their real names. I naturally made use of the code names when radioing the battalion and the supply point. With the men up front, however, I had addressed and continued to address them with their real names. Even more scorned was the unofficial radio traffic.

We often heard a voice on the radio: "What's the word in smoking circles?" That meant that cigarettes had once again become scarce and Otto Carius had to prove himself as a friend in need. It should be noted that I was well supplied from home.

Ten to fifteen small packages of cigarettes arrived with every mail call. My mother organized things on a grand scale for me. I immediately distributed the packages among the individual tanks. There was a short greeting on every one of the packages. These greetings were carefully packed away by the soldiers.

Naturally, the Russians listened in. Because of the transmissions in the clear, they knew right away that wherever the "Tigers" showed up,

there were always also the same men. The code names were changed
every few days at the latest, whereas our names of course always remained
the same. But Ivan would have noticed something anyway if we disappeared at Newel, for example, and reappeared at Narwa. For all appearances, we were a thorn in their side.

One time, for instance, they announced via a loudspeaker unit in the
"east sack" at Lembitu that our infantry should hand me over to them.
They would receive their choice of thirty soldiers in return. They
demanded that our men finally defang the "bloodhound" who was continually forcing them to hold out! My comrades in the infantry only let the
guy talk for a little while. They then shot the loudspeaker to pieces when
it got to be too much for them. They seemed to have an unfortunate liking for this "bloodhound." Ivan continued his loudspeaker activities without flinching, which proved the great respect he had for our battalion.

After I was wounded at Dünaburg, the Russians announced over the
radio that I had been killed. The Soviet officer who delivered the lost
map board with my name on it to prove his success was decorated. My
first sergeant wrote me this news to cheer me up while I was in the hospital. It's well known, after all, that those given up for dead often manage
to live the longest.

✠

Naturally, we enjoyed our involuntary impromptu vacation in the
support base. The sauna had let us become human again, and we felt
like newborn babes. As a result of this opportunity, I also sweated out my
pleurisy and was again healthy to the core. We didn't have any idea, however, how short our rest would be.

At the front, you were wont to make use of the good times and not
think about "later" and "for how long." We had scarcely got used to the
nice warm room, when the report came in from Oberfeldwebel Zwetti
that the radiator of his "Tiger" was also leaking. He also said the second
vehicle had been damaged in the running gear. Ivan was probably quite
satisfied in having damaged three of our vehicles. He was known to have
something against "Tigers."

For the time being, Feldwebel Zwetti remained in the village. In the
event of action, he could at least support the infantry with fire. I went to
my maintenance people to see how far the work on my radiator had pro-
gressed. There was no doubt in my mind that we had goofed off long
enough.

The work performed by the men in the maintenance section cannot be described using standard terms.

Nowadays, one would characterize their physical performance as humanly impossible. This self-sacrificing activity behind the front could not be brought about by orders. Instead, it presupposed an inner conviction and the will to help the combat troops by all means available. They wanted to have the damaged vehicles rolling to the front again as soon as possible.

Oberfeldwebel Delzeit, the leader of the maintenance section, was anything but easy to get along with. His good side was covered by a very rough exterior. He often chewed butt so thoroughly, that his men barely fit in their uniforms afterwards.

By the same token, he also treated his superiors with so little respect that we didn't have to have a picture painted for us to imagine what would happen to his people if they had done the same thing to him. But since everyone knew him, neither the gentlemen from above nor the men from below thought the worse of him.

Delzeit was a first-class professional, and he used all his abilities to get a defective vehicle in shape again. He was also a good comrade who *never* left his people in the lurch. The well being of his platoon took precedence over everything else.

They often worked day and night during operations. The men of the maintenance section certainly didn't lag behind the soldiers at the front in toughness. If Delzeit promised a vehicle at a certain time, one could depend on him. Those are the type of men that one needs at the front. What did it really matter that someone had a somewhat rough nature? Smooth-talking and constantly obliging types are out of place wherever men have to prove themselves. Their time to shine has always come *after* the catastrophes.

On March 16, 1944, our friend Delzeit had once again worked in an exacting and dependable manner. I discovered during my visit to the maintenance section's bunker that my tank would be finished at midnight.

Nothing therefore stood in the way of relieving the others. Our "pass" had lasted exactly twenty-four hours, but we had used it well. I also brought the news to Kerscher's crew that they didn't need to unpack their stuff completely. Instead, they were to get everything ready and lay down in order to be able to sleep comfortably for a few hours.

In the meantime, the remaining two companies and the battalion staff had been directed to the area around Pleskau. We remained by ourselves in the Narwa position. It thus came to pass that I never saw Major Jähde again.

He had been awarded the Knight's Cross on March 15 and was then transferred to the noncommissioned officer academy at Eisenach as its commander. That meant an award and the climbing of a few more steps up the career ladder, but his departure certainly wasn't easy for him.

We also didn't like to see him depart, because we had got along with him so magnificently. The comrades who were there when both the Knight's Cross and the departure were celebrated at the same time later told me *how* difficult the separation from the 502nd had been for Jähde.

He could not hide his tears when each of the men shook his hand. After the war, I discovered in a roundabout fashion, that the Russians had saddled him with a so-called "war crimes trial" in Eisenach. I have never been able to discover the verdict. Unfortunately, every trace of him is also missing. Perhaps we will get the happy news some day—possibly caused by this book—that Jähde is still living and we will be able to see him again.

In the evening, I sat together with von Schiller for a long time with a good bottle of whisky. He couldn't understand why I wanted to lay down a bit before my departure. He wasn't exactly wrong when he said that I would have ample opportunity to rest up at the front, despite the uncomfortable position.

Of course, Ivan also had something to contribute concerning that. We knew only too well that the deceptive calm would soon come to an end. I thus took leave of my company commander and lay down. We wanted to get started at four in the morning. That way, our comrades could be relieved before the break of day and get their defective vehicle out of sight of the Russians. I instructed the sentry to wake me in time.

Unfortunately, I hadn't counted on his "consideration." When Kerscher himself finally came for me around five o'clock, I was still lying in a deep sleep. The sentry resolutely claimed that he had awakened me according to orders.

I had even given a response, but I didn't want to know about any of that. I also had a hangover that didn't let me look forward to duty. To add insult to injury, I yelled at the innocent guard and ran to my vehicle. Everyone was already waiting for me there. It was high time.

We arrived at Zwetti's location shortly after seven. He was able to disappear just before daybreak. The contact with the infantry was completely in order and the battalion commander told me that the front was quiet. I therefore went back to sleep right away. If we were needed, we were always immediately available. It was also clear to the men up front that it was quieter in their positions whenever we weren't with them.

That only gave Ivan occasion to start his usual wild shooting, and another tank might have been lost.

Ivan Attacks

Shortly after daybreak, I was awakened more abruptly than I would have liked. The alarm clock this time was the Russians. Their methods were extremely disagreeable. Out of the blue, they laid down a barrage that left nothing to the imagination. It covered the entire front of our bridgehead. Only Ivan could lay down a barrage like that.

Even the Americans, whom I got to know later on in the west, couldn't compete with them. The Russians shot with every available weapon, from light mortars all the way on up to heavy artillery. They showed us that they had been doing everything but sleeping in the previous few weeks.

The entire 61st Infantry Division sector was covered with such a barrage that we thought all hell had broken loose. We were right in the middle of it, and it was completely impossible for us to get to our tanks from the bunker.

Whenever we got ready to dash after one salvo hit, the whistling sound of the next one forced us back to the bunker entrance. Due to the intensity of the fire, it was not possible to tell where the main point of the attack was. After all, the fact that the Russians were attacking was no longer a secret. Naturally, the line to the infantry was broken after the fire had been initiated. Everything was up in the air. We assumed that the Russians were attacking in our sector at Lembitu. But we also had to count on the possibility of the enemy infantry rounding us up before we even got to our tanks.

The Russians shifted their fire farther north after a good half hour—an eternity for us. It was then high time that we jumped into our tanks. The Russian attack was obviously in full swing. The skies above us also became alive.

Close air support, which hadn't appeared at all in the previous weeks, raced over us. They raced so close past us that we got the impression they wanted to take our hats with them. They thundered about wildly in the area and dropped smoke bombs north of our position so that the artillery observers were blinded.

From all appearances, Ivan had something quite big planned. He apparently wanted to reach the coast that day to cut off our bridgehead in front of Narwa from the rear. This would have encircled elements of the SS Panzer Corps, the Feldherrnhalle Division, and Wengler's infantry. The important question for us was whether we were inside or outside the pocket.

In the meantime, the situation had become extremely critical. Shortly before ten o'clock, a few ground troops came running past me heading west. Then came a 37-mm Flak gun with a twelve-ton prime mover. After that came another twenty to thirty men, all without weapons.

All this occurred during the barrage, which continued unabated. Although we were only about thirty meters in the woods, they didn't pay any attention to us at all. I had to run to them to find out that all three strongpoints had been evacuated. One of the assault guns east of the "Kinderheim" was burning, and the other had driven off.

The Russians were already heading toward the Rollbahn with tanks and infantry. There was no more time to be lost. It was clear that they were pushing north with strong forces in order to roll up our bridgehead at Narwa.

I immediately moved quickly to the vicinity of the farmhouse. Kerscher was right behind me, and I had him fan out to the left. He was supposed to concentrate on what was happening on the open plain. The Russians were moving on it in regimental strength north of our strongpoints. Five T34s were already closing at full speed on the Rollbahn. A sixth Russian tank had almost reached the "Kinderheim" before we caught sight of it. But first, I directed my attention to the five AT guns on the railway embankment that were threatening our flank. They were the most dangerous opponents at that moment. I was soon finished with them, but not before I had taken a few hits in the running gear. Fortunately, none of them caused serious damage.

While my gunner, Unteroffizier Kramer, was shooting it out with the Russian antitank guns, I looked to the left at just the right time. I discovered the T34 that had turned around when we showed up and was heading almost dead on toward Kerscher.

The situation had reached critical mass. It was literally a question of seconds. We were lucky that the Russians had buttoned up like they always did and could not size up the terrain fast enough. Kerscher hadn't

noticed the tank either because it was practically coming from the rear. It
was racing past him, barely thirty meters away.

I was able to notify Kerscher just in time: "Hey, Kerscher, a T34 right
behind you, watch out!" Everything happened in the blink of an eye.
Kerscher took care of the Russians with a direct hit. They careened into
a bomb crater and didn't come out.

We had a good reason to catch our breath. If Ivan had kept his
nerves and fired, both of us probably would have been finished. The
remaining five T34s didn't even get to fire. They probably also didn't
have a clue as to who knocked them out and from where.

All of the Soviet tanks had to cross the railroad crossing in a row
before they could deploy properly. Naturally, this maneuver delayed their
attack considerably. We had arrived a few minutes too early for them. We
were therefore unable to catch the rest of the tanks that were driving on
the far side of the railway embankment.

Ivan immediately pulled back into the protectiveness of the marshy
woods when we began to mop up among them. For the most part, his
infantry was also able to withdraw while we were occupied with the antitank guns and the tanks.

Naturally, our strongpoints had been completely abandoned. There
weren't any German infantrymen to be seen in the entire sector between
Lembitu and the point where the railway embankment disappeared in
the woods.

Only the machine gun on the right flank of the Feldherrnhalle Division started firing again in the late afternoon. We soon reached our old
front lines at the ruins, where we found ourselves all alone on the plain.
My report that the strongpoints had been evacuated by our infantry was
somehow denied by division. Later in the afternoon, I finally decided to
drive to the "Kinderheim" myself. I wanted to have at least a few people
rounded up in order to occupy the strongpoints that we had kept clear
of the enemy. By the time these men finally arrived, however, the Russians had already taken both forward ruins under the cover of darkness.
All in all, we had all sorts of frustration that day with the rearward command posts.

In the meantime, after a half-hour barrage in the early afternoon,
the Russians once again attacked our sector using armor support. We also
repulsed this attack and were able to knock out another five T34s and a
KVI. Knocked-out tanks are occasionally odious and malicious things. We
had to duck our heads at one point when a few of the tanks exploded
and all sorts of metal parts flew through the air. What made me mad was
the fact that our artillery could not be convinced to fire protective bar-

rages. It should be noted that the observers had been lost and division had the erroneous impression that the ruins were occupied.

As a result, our own people would have been in the area of the barrage. An hour and a half later, the Russians were once again staging for an attack with strong forces at the railway embankment. I wasn't able to guarantee that I could repulse a third attack with my remaining ammunition.

In the meantime, I had received a third tank and requested my company commander to also appear with his vehicle. He radioed a number of times that he was directly behind me in the woodline. I never did catch a glimpse of him, however, and I later discovered that his tank had never headed toward us at all.

Once again I had all sorts of reasons to be angry at my commander. But I didn't say anything because I was happy that von Schiller was at least able to get the artillery to finally initiate our protective fire. It was laid so well that the Russian attack position was completely destroyed.

Exactly one hour later, Ivan assembled in battalion strength and with armor support for another attack. He wanted to take our strongpoints at all costs. He didn't obtain his objective and lost another three T34s.

It was after this last unsuccessful attack of the Russians that I left two "Tigers" at the ruins and personally drove to the regimental command post at the "Kinderheim" to report on the actual situation. It should be noted that they were still maintaining the hypothesis that the ruins were occupied by our infantry.

It was through me that the regimental commander first discovered the real situation. He then gathered up a few people from his staff. Because that took a while, I had to displace about 200 meters from the ruins during darkness in order to have a field of fire and be safe against tank-killer teams. Only one "Tiger" stayed back at the farmhouse.

The farmhouse was also kept clear of the enemy until the ten men who had been picked arrived and occupied it. Another twenty-five men formed a line along a trail behind us.

The Russians didn't attempt any new attacks during the night but were able to occupy the ruins without resistance.

Two hours before midnight, we drove back to fetch supplies. Less than ten minutes after we had arrived at the bunker, both trucks of the company trains showed up. They had been on call at the supply point in Sillamä since the early afternoon.

I had arranged a point on the Rollbahn where they were supposed to meet me in case it had been necessary to resupply us with ammunition during the day. But because Feldwebel Gruber had made it through to us with a third tank, our supplies held out and we were able to wait out the darkness.

Hauptfeldwebel Sepp Rieger, the first sergeant, had also come up front with the resupply group to help celebrate the day. He wouldn't think of not congratulating us personally on our defensive success. Rieger was a splendid fellow, the likes of which one seldom sees. I believe it would have been hard to find a dozen first sergeants of his caliber in the entire Wehrmacht, which doesn't mean to say that the bulk of the first sergeants were bad.

Men like Rieger were an exception, however. He was an example to everyone, both as a soldier and as a person. He had a well-rounded personality: knowledgeable, without being pedantic, thrifty, without the slightest tendency toward stinginess. He had earned an Iron Cross First Class as a tank commander and platoon leader in the line.

He also knew that despite all sense of justice, it was impossible to do right by everyone. Occasionally, there were soldiers who complained, because Rieger was very strict in watching out for the equipment. But he was also responsible for it and knew how scarce everything was. I also never heard of him taking one more cigarette or bottle of schnapps from the canteen than was coming to him. For him, the combat troops came first. Then came the maintenance staff, followed by resupply and, finally, the trains. He was dear to the heart of everyone in the company, the superiors as well as the subordinates. Rieger was an exemplary comrade.

As a superior, he knew how to bring about respect without yelling. Everyone revered him and recognized his sense of fairness. That was our Sepp Rieger. Certainly no one who ever had the good fortune to be allowed to serve under him has ever forgotten him.

We then hauled gasoline and munitions to the tanks to stow it away. One hundred rounds and 200 liters of gasoline were needed for each "Tiger."

One can well imagine how we first had our work cut out for us before we could think about the warm meal. But then we switched over to feeding and war stories. Rieger told us how they had experienced "our" day in Sillamä. The company commander had ordered a line run from the receiver on his "Tiger," outside the window, to the loudspeaker on the field radio. They were thus able to listen in on our radio traffic. For every kill that was announced, Rieger treated his men to a schnapps.

There was one thing that the men could not understand, however, and that was why the commander hadn't taken off for us, even though I had urgently requested him to do so many times. They also thought badly of him for not initially being able to get the artillery support for us. That was because he didn't talk to the responsible party in person but on the telephone.

Not until toward evening, when I reported that the position could not be held anymore, did he finally drive to corps in his Kübel to insist on the final protective barrage. It was also initiated a half hour later. The behavior of the commander had the men in an uproar.

I had to make all sorts of effort to calm them down. Of course, I was also disappointed by von Schiller. I told the men, however, that we didn't need to get excited after the fact. After all, we had taken care of the matter all by ourselves, and the final protective barrage had arrived in the nick of time.

Toward midnight, we drove back to the ruins to give our infantry some moral support. I went to the "Kinderheim," where I spoke to the regimental commander about the plans for the next day. We agreed to retake the ruins at the morning twilight.

The attempt had to be made in any case, so that the Russians couldn't threaten us on our side of the railway embankment from the two sets of ruins. That could make the entire situation even more precarious. For our planned counterattack, we pulled out an additional sixteen men from our already meager strength.

Around five o'clock, we assembled for the attack in Tirtsu, a small spot on the map between the "Kinderheim" and Lembitu. Feldwebel Kerscher and I each had eight men assigned to us.

The attack began punctually at five o'clock in the morning. It was still completely dark, of course. Feldwebel Gruber had the mission of pinning down the Russians during our assault. First we fired at the western ruin from point-blank range using all three tanks. We then drove right up to it, and my eight men occupied it. The operation was completely successful, and we only had one wounded man to complain about. In contrast, the attack against the eastern ruin near the railway crossing was more difficult. It appeared to be of great importance to Ivan. In fact, he had set up five antitank guns, two artillery pieces, and a 47-mm antiaircraft gun during the night. We had to duke it out with them for a while.

It should be noted that that was typical for the Russians. If they sat anywhere for just a few hours—especially at night—they hauled up materiel like ants and dug into the ground like gophers. Even though we had constantly experienced that, we never could figure out how they actually did it. Despite all our efforts, we were not successful in regaining the second strongpoint. During our firefight, Ivan started a counterattack with two T34s and a small infantry unit.

We were able to beat them back, and their tanks were knocked out in the process. Shortly thereafter, heavy mortar and artillery fire of extremely heavy caliber began to arrive. We had two killed and two wounded. It was not possible for the remaining four to take the strong point, let alone hold it. Unfortunately, the leader of the infantry, a lieutenant from the staff, was killed when he assaulted the ruins shouting "Hurrah!"

The Russians continued to fire with an MG that we weren't able to silence. They couldn't afford to give up their position on our side of the railway embankment under any conditions. Running back would have been even more hopeless than holding out, since they then would have been without cover in our fields of fire.

For the time being, we had to recover our wounded. Using both "Tigers," we approached as close as possible so that we could load the wounded under the cover of the vehicles without falling victim to the machine-gun fire. The Russians had probably had thirty to forty men killed, yet the contested ruins continued to remain in enemy hands for the next few days.

Shortly after noon, following a fifteen-minute barrage, the Russians tried to win back the strongpoint and the farmhouse. They attacked in company strength using armor support. They were beaten back with heavy casualties and lost a T34 and a T60.

They finally appeared to have had enough for that day. We remained undisturbed until the next morning. When we returned to our bunker in the evening, the supply vehicles had already arrived.

Once again there were problems with our commander. Our people were already extremely upset with him. I had radioed a request for a Kübel so I could drive to the 61st Infantry Division command post during the night.

I also wanted to spare myself having to go to the regimental command post on foot. Each time that meant a distance of eight kilometers back and forth across country. To avoid the attention of the Russians, I didn't want to go with the tank. Besides, my crew deserved some rest whenever possible. The Kübel I requested did not show up, however. Biermann reported that the company commander apparently didn't have one available.

Not until a get-together after the war did I discover from one of the soldiers assigned to the orderly room that he and von Schiller had visited a female acquaintance on several evenings. She had come back from Narwa with them.

So that was the reason he needed the Kübel! Had I known that back then, I too would have finally blown my top. This knowledge was kept from me during the entire war, however, so as not to get me too worked up.

It also caused consternation among my men when the 2nd Company of the 502nd, "under the leadership of Oberleutnant von Schiller," was mentioned in the Wehrmacht daily bulletin. After all, our commander had contributed nothing to our success. This time it was difficult to calm the men down. I made it clear to them that the entire company had been honored in this fashion. Otherwise, only one platoon could have been mentioned. In the final analysis, the entire company had participated in our success.

It was good I didn't yet know anything about the unbelievable use of the Kübel for "joy rides." Otherwise, I certainly wouldn't have made any effort to calm down my men. It should be noted that we were rewarded in another manner: by a special mention in the corps order of the day, which was distributed to all the units of the corps and read aloud.

Only *our* tanks were mentioned in this order. It was stressed that through action on our own initiative we had stopped the Russian penetration to the coast and prevented the subsequent cutting off of all the units east of the "Kinderheim." In addition, we had held the recaptured front line for the entire day without infantry support.

Ivan didn't grant us any rest. He wanted to roll up or encircle the bridgehead at Narwa at all costs. Around noon on March 19, the enemy attacked west from the "east sack" after artillery and mortar preparation. He wanted to cut off the southern portion of the "boot," which had been held by us up to then. He then wanted to link the "east sack" with the "west sack" and create better jumping-off positions for further attacks.

We knocked out six T34s and a T60 and destroyed a 76.2-mm AT gun. Despite all that, the Russians were successful in penetrating our front lines.

Even before our own infantry could start the counterattack, we had to intervene in an emergency at another place. From the strongpoint north of the railway embankment came the report that four Russian assault guns had set up on the far side of the railway crossing in a small patch of woods. In addition, two Russian tanks had driven up to the right of the railway crossing. Feldwebel Kerscher and I had arrived just in the nick of time, because a mood of panic had already overcome our infantry. There were no antitank weapons available besides our "Tigers."

We were able to knock out the enemy tanks before they started to attack and also come back in time to effectively support the counterattack of our infantry to the south. We did this from Point 39.9 (along the route from the "Kinderheim" to the "boot sole").

The marshy terrain there gave us a lot of problems. It simply wasn't possible to drive off the road. It was only through our fire that we could help our infantry friends in holding down the enemy. Operations in marshes are unpleasant and, at the same time, unsatisfying for any tanker.

After three hours, the enemy was dislodged and our infantry had reached their old positions again. One officer deserves special mention here. Major Haase stormed the Russian positions with unforgettable dash and courage, at the head of his battalion.

This type of action reminded me of the stories my father told of how in World War I officers with drawn swords stormed ahead of their men. During the attack, we were able to destroy an additional two T34s. But the Russians didn't want to call it quits. By the next morning, at the break of dawn, they were again attacking at Lembitu in company-sized strength. They were thrown back after a one-hour struggle. An attack around noon suffered the same fate. Once again, they lost two tanks and a 45-mm antitank gun. But they still didn't give up. They selected an unusual hour to attack the next night: They charged our lines at three in the morning. We could only fire blindly in the darkness, and so Ivan finally succeeded in taking the ruins in the middle.

We had learned from the rebuff we had suffered at the strongpoint at the railway embankment and didn't wait too long this time. I executed a counterattack with ten infantrymen, and, two hours later, the ruins in the middle were again firmly in our hands. Despite the short time we had given the Russians, they had already hauled up two 76.2-mm AT guns. At first, these gave us a lot of trouble.

The reconquered set of ruins in the middle was of decisive importance to us. If it had been lost, the farmhouse would also have fallen soon after. The entire defensive front in our sector would have collapsed. Of course, it also had the same importance to the enemy.

They renewed their attack two hours later. The ruins finally had to be evacuated again after four infantrymen, among them the leader of the strongpoint, had been killed. The remaining six men couldn't hold out against the Russian infantry and sought shelter in the farmhouse.

We then arranged ourselves with all three tanks around the farmhouse. It had to be held at all costs. Because the infantry's radio had been knocked out by fire, I sent Feldwebel Gruber with his tank to the regimental command post to fetch replacements.

It was impossible for the infantrymen to go back on foot. The Russians were really playing "cat and mouse" with us. They always attacked at the point where we weren't. Because of that, they ran us all over the place. In the afternoon, Feldwebel Kerscher was able to knock out another two Russian tanks at Point 33.7.

Before the onset of darkness, we started a new counterattack against the middle ruins. A half hour later they were firmly in our hands. That was to be our final attack before we attacked the "east sack" later on and established a better front line further south as part of "Operation Strachwitz."

The great numbers of casualties in men and materiel forced the Russians to take a breather. Our magnificent infantry were primarily responsible for that. They had performed in a superhuman manner during those days. In terms of numbers, they should have been too weak to hold their positions against the superior forces.

Despite this, they had constantly attacked and displaced the enemy. This accomplishment can only be gauged by someone who has been in a similar situation. Words alone cannot describe such aggressiveness.

After the situation had been restored, I set up my "Tigers" on the plain to cover the railway crossing. That wasn't a lot of fun for us. Due to their artillery and mortar fire, the Russians forced us to constantly change positions.

We were completely without cover. The enemy could observe our every movement, especially since they had occupied the eastern ruins on our side of the railway embankment. They didn't give us any rest.

As was always the case in such situations, I had ordered that no tanks were allowed to back up without having a neighboring vehicle give directions by radio. The commander of a moving "Tiger" could not see directly behind his tank. He was always in danger of getting stuck when moving backward, especially since the driver was completely "blind."

The track of the neighboring tank also had to be observed. When moving backward, it could ride up on the teeth of the drive sprocket even during small turning movements—especially in mud and snow. If that happened, there was unbelievable tension and the tank was immobilized. There was nothing left to do but cut apart the tracks.

Despite all experience and reminders, there was a serious mishap. While under fire, Feldwebel Gruber suddenly put his tank in reverse and drove straight into a bomb crater in the excitement. Apparently, he hadn't set his radio properly and also didn't see my signaling. I was therefore unable to prevent his disappearing into the bomb crater.

Only the muzzle brake of his cannon peeked over the edge of the crater. All of a sudden, he once again had radio contact with me and was cursing like a sailor about his bad luck. None of the crew could get out because the Russians had observed everything and fired like madmen at Gruber's tank.

It was a sticky situation. Of course, I immediately thought about the "pleasant" prospects of recovering the tank the next night. On top of everything else, my "Tiger" had clutch damage and was not available for towing.

It was therefore our good fortune that Zwetti came up front that night in his freshly repaired tank. Together with Kerscher, he retrieved "little Max" and his crew out of the unpleasant situation. Unfortunately, not everything went smoothly.

The Russians began to shoot like crazy again at the appearance of the two tanks. They knew of course that we intended to recover our scuttled "Tiger." During the day, they had adjusted their sights on that stupid bomb crater.

One of those delayed-fuse 15-cm mortar rounds, especially designed for fighting tanks, penetrated the radio operator's hatch on one of our tanks. The round impacted almost vertically and the entire charge, together with parts of the hatch, smashed into the legs of the unfortunate radio operator. The last few days had gone by without casualties, and then, while recovering a vehicle, they had to get this guy. He had just arrived in the company.

He had probably just turned eighteen, and it was his first operation. In our bunker, we applied dressing to the poor guy. He must have had unbearable pain. He was complaining about the pain in his left foot. He hadn't noticed yet that it wasn't there anymore.

It was a terrible sight and one that moved me more deeply than all the operations of the last few days.

I saw a mixture of hope and fear in his eyes. After all, he was still just half a child who found himself lying there in the tank with shattered feet and horrific pains. He was only babbling incoherent sentences:

"Herr Lieutenant, she'll probably never see me again! Oh, it hurts so much in my left foot! Does it have to be amputated? I wonder whether she can still make it? She's already lost two sons, and now me. Herr Lieutenant, will you write to her?"

The babbling of the severely wounded youth, who continuously talked about his mother, shook me to the core. I comforted him as well as I could and made sure that he was immediately brought to the field hospital in a Kübel ambulance.

I was happy when I discovered that he had survived. They were forced to amputate his left lower leg, but he could see his mother again and that was the main thing. I later saw him in the replacement battalion, and both of us were very happy to see each other. Perhaps the leg that he lost also saved his life. Who can know for sure?

✠

On March 22, the Russians attacked Point 33.9 in the "boot" for the last time. They were beaten back with the loss of two additional tanks.

From then on, there was finally quiet in the "east sack." In the period from March 17 to 22, we had knocked out thirty-eight Russian tanks, four assault guns, and seventeen artillery pieces in the heavy defensive fighting.

We could therefore be quite satisfied with our success.

The only casualty was the severely wounded eighteen-year-old tanker. This also wouldn't have happened if we hadn't been forced to recover Gruber's tank.

Ivan made one more try to reach his objective. Because he realized he couldn't get anywhere attacking from the "east sack," he came up with the idea of landing from the sea. We already knew about this intention from prisoner statements. Even the trains near Sillamä were prepared for "Operation Sea Lion." The defensive countermeasures took place under this code name.

The Russians attempted their landings north of the "Kinderheim" at Mereküla. We immediately moved to the coast with a few tanks.

Most of the landing craft had already been destroyed at sea by the Pak guns of the Feldherrnhalle Division.

When we arrived, we only saw burning boats milling about on the water. A few Russians were able to reach the coast, but they were soon taken prisoner behind our front. As we determined later, they were magnificently well-equipped elite troops. According to their statements, the operation had been precisely practised.

It wasn't supposed to take place until the breakthrough in the "east sack" had succeeded. But even though Ivan had not been able to succeed there, the Russians attempted the landing anyway. As a result, there was only the senseless sacrifice of good soldiers.

Despite the Russian fiasco, the specter of "Operation Sea Lion" haunted us for a long time, especially at night. For the remainder of our stay in the Narwa sector, however, there wasn't a repeat performance of the operation.

At the end of March, our tanks were withdrawn from the 61st Infantry Division sector. We prepared for a new operation. It was called "The Elimination of the East Sack and the West Sack." Its execution was in the hands of Oberst Graf Strachwitz.

When we assembled in Sillamä, we were all in need of an overhaul—our "Tigers" needing one just as much as we did.

Mutiny in the Bunker

At our support base on the Baltic coast, we finally had a few days' time to recover. That was simply a must for the crews of our three tanks. During the previous few operations, they hadn't received any rest either by day or night. Despite all toughness and willingness to go to battle, an individual's ability to perform has its limits. In many respects, our rest period was interesting and relaxing for me. I especially enjoyed being able to hear good music on the radio again. In that regard, there was always a small fight going on with the commander. I was a lover of more serious music. He, on the other hand, liked modern and easy listening music.

In our rest area, I won the affection of a four-legged friend—Hasso, a German Shepherd. Von Schiller had picked him up from the military police for a bottle of schnapps. He was of no value to the police, after he had knocked out his teeth on a brick. Hasso was exceptionally well trained and brought me a lot of happiness. He climbed ladders effortlessly, jumped amazingly high, and even fetched things out of the strong current of the Baltic. He would guard a piece of wood until he was relieved of his duties by a command.

Hasso was the only dog I ever saw that let a piece of meat drop on command, even after he had already had it in his mouth. He accompanied me everywhere and placed his head on my feet at night on the sofa. Whenever it was time for him to relieve himself in the mornings, he licked my hand until I was awake and went out with him. Although he was a "company dog" and had a lot of masters, he was especially attached to me and also never forgot his good training. I was thus able to have all sorts of enjoyable diversion during my rest period. But my happiness didn't remain undisturbed.

The commander was always somewhat jealous of me, because I got along so well with everyone. He wasn't quite so jealous of all the hardships that went together with these successes. He was always surprised at our "hunter's luck," whereas he still hadn't been able to knock out a single tank. The fact that we were always in action—as opposed to him—must have escaped him. Whenever two "Tigers" in our company were mission capable, I was always sitting in one of them. After all, how long had we been forced to endure at Lembitu without accomplishing anything until we finally earned our keep? Von Schiller reminded me of the fair-weather hunter. He believed he could simply go into the woods to shoot the deer that was waiting for him.

I got along with him when both of us were alone, because I was mindful of his faults. Things also went well whenever I was on an operation and he held the company together at the support base. In Sillamä, however, the mood was often somewhat tense. I made it a habit to be with the men a lot. That didn't suit the commander at all. He had the opinion that one always had to maintain a distance. Thank God, I didn't find that necessary. I never experienced anyone "acting improperly" toward me. I was therefore always between a rock and a hard place.

I had to calm down the NCOs whenever they complained about the commander, and I also had to convince the CO constantly that our men where great guys whom you could depend on. Perhaps my men were also especially excitable because of the heavy action. In any case, a bomb exploded one day, and it exploded far worse than I had feared.

It was Ivan, moreover, who gave rise to the occasion. Even in our "reserve position," he didn't always allow us our well-earned rest. He fired over us and into the sea with long-range artillery, which was south of Narwa. Actually, he wanted to hit the Rollbahn, but his rounds flew too far. Whenever they raced over our heads, we had the feeling that they were taking the roof with them. We had an unpleasant barrage like that every couple of hours. We would hear the muffled report in the distance and could count off to the second to the point they raced past us. The sentry had to report the start of an artillery barrage immediately. It was a standing order that everyone then had to race into the cellar of the house. This order was completely justified, as was proven when the Russians shot short once. A sergeant from maintenance and a company clerk were killed by shrapnel when they were enroute to their bunkers but could not reach them in time. Therefore caution was completely in order; that much was certain.

It upset the NCOs who slept in the other room next to both of us, however, that the commander was always the first one jumping through the hole in the floor going to the cellar. He did this even though such haste wasn't called for. Besides, according to military tradition, the leader was supposed to be the last one to think about his personal safety. The company commo sergeant, Funkmeister Schotroff, an otherwise quiet, dependable man and an exemplary soldier, lost his nerves, insulted von

Schiller, and almost became physical. He thus had to be taken into custody for mutiny.

Von Schiller insisted that I immediately go with him to the court-martial authority. We had to go to a meeting anyway with the commander of the Großdeutschland Panzer Regiment, Oberst Graf Strachwitz. During the ride, I urged von Schiller not to destroy the entire life of a proven soldier such as Schotroff.

I finally got to the point that he became indecisive. Perhaps he also thought to himself that things could be said in front of a court-martial that would be unpleasant for him. In any case, and to my great relief, he didn't get out at the seat of the court-martial. Instead, he turned to me and said, "OK, Otto, I've thought it all over. Because of you, I want to personally punish Schotroff's unbelievable behavior. I will arrest him and then take him into combat with me."

I kept quiet; a great burden was lifted from my shoulders. Funkmeister Schotroff was thus given the most severe punishment a company commander could mandate; he received confinement to quarters. He then had to serve as the radio operator in the commander's tank during the next few operations. The latter "punishment" was doubly false psychologically.

First, assignment to the line elements could not be a punishment. It was required as a matter of course from all of us. It should be noted that Schotroff had frequently requested permission to participate in at least a few operations. He had always been turned down because his position could not be easily replaced. Finally, von Schiller would never have been allowed to take him along in his tank, as was soon determined.

"Operation Strachwitz"

Oberst der Reserve Hyazinth Graf Strachwitz was the type of man who, once encountered, was never forgotten. The Graf was a master of organization. On the other hand, he delegated the improvising to his subordinates as a matter of course. We had the good fortune to participate in a few operations under his command. They were perfect examples of the fact that everything that is planned well is already halfway on the road to success. Graf Strachwitz had received the Knight's Cross as a Major der Reserve and commander of the 1st Battalion of Panzer Regiment 2 on August 25, 1941. On November 17, 1942, he received the Oak Leaves. As an Oberst and the commander of the Panzer regiment of the Großdeutschland Division, he received the Swords on March 28, 1943. We would contribute some to the success of the upcoming operation. For its successful execution, he was recognized with the Diamonds on March 15, 1944.

Gossip mongers maintained that the Großdeutschland Panzer Regiment was taken away from Strachwitz because he had too many losses. I had justifiable doubts concerning this claim. Graf Strachwitz and his staff were always employed at hot spots on the front, where they had to carry out extremely pressing operations, for which every form of support was provided to them. Painful losses couldn't always be avoided during those types of operations. But it was through these losses that the lives of many soldiers from other units were saved.

Graf Strachwitz had brought along his staff from Großdeutschland, as well as a few tanks and armored personnel carriers. Our company played only a subordinate role in the first operation, designed to cut off the "west sack" and eliminate it. The attack was conducted from the west to the east near the "sole" of the "boot." Contact was then reestablished with the infantrymen in the "boot."

A line was established, and the pocket was finally eliminated. The trail that had to be used for that was not sufficiently wide and firm for our "Tigers." They therefore had to be satisfied with the Panzer IVs, about thirty tons lighter.

They had been brought along by the Graf. He personally rode in the point tank and thus won our confidence from the very beginning. For this operation, we were only responsible for holding back the pressure, which, quite naturally, came about in other areas of the "west sack" because of the attack.

The entire operation was supported by Stukas or, better said, was supposed to be supported by Stukas. They proved to be ineffective in the densely forested terrain, however, and were even dangerous to our own troops! The pilots couldn't identify their targets. The Ju87s had arrived on time and brazenly dived onto their assigned targets.

One of their bombs landed right in the middle of the only trail the attacking tanks could drive on. A minute later, and Graf Strachwitz himself would have been a victim of this bomb. He cursed a blue streak, and the attack had to be carried on by the infantry without armor support.

It should be noted that the line was supposed to be established regardless of the costs before the onset of darkness. Otherwise, there was the danger that the Russians would have escaped out of the pocket to the south or rolled up our own line, which was hanging in the air. Strachwitz did, in fact, reach his objective without tanks or Stukas.

On the next day, the pocket was reduced and eliminated. The majority of the Russians and all of their materiel fell into our hands. Only a few Russians had escaped to the south during the night, when Ivan initiated relief attacks there. This severe setback caused our enemy to pump up the "east sack" with more soldiers and materiel than ever. He didn't reckon that we would proceed there in quite a different fashion.

The Graf had his peculiarities. But no one thought the worse of him for them because he had won our respect and recognition. For example, he didn't allow himself to be addressed as "Herr Oberst." The men who had known him as a major said that he also didn't shy away from making high-ranking superiors aware that he was a Graf. He said that the title of Graf (count) meant more than the military rank.

During the first briefing, he left no doubts about how he envisioned the operation. The bold planning surprised us, but it also soon made a lot of sense.

"Well, gentlemen, this is how I see things," he said in his somewhat haughty manner. "Our Kampfgruppe will conduct a frontal attack against the so-called 'east sack.' Starting at the 'Kinderheim,' it will move across the plain to the rail crossing. Four 'Tigers' will drive point. After crossing the railway embankment, they will swing to the right and roll it up.

"The following four 'Tigers,' which will each have a squad of infantry mounted on them, will drive like the devil to the fork in the road, which is 100 meters southeast of the rail crossing. This fork must be reached as quickly as possible and kept open. That way, the four Panzer IVs and the APCs can advance and occupy the plain, which runs even with the bottom of the pocket." He pointed to the map. "So, that takes care of that.

"At night, a perimeter will be set up and held until another infantry regiment can follow and establish the front line. Contact will then be made to the west and east.

"The main thing I want to emphasize is that the entire operation has to run according to schedule. That means that no tank may remain on the road and block me. The success of the entire action may be jeopardized through delay. And I won't allow any of that.

"I hereby expressly order that every immobile tank be shoved into the marsh by any means possible so it doesn't hold up the other vehicles.

"The responsibility for the success of the operation lies squarely on the tank commander, regardless of his rank. Is everything clear?"

"Jawohl, Herr Graf!"

The Oberst twisted his mouth into a slightly sarcastic smile. It wasn't unbeknownst to him, that we had allowed ourselves a few remarks about his desired form of address. None of them were to be found in a handbook for good manners.

"Very well. So far it's also been quite simple. But now a different question for the 'Tiger' people. What battalion do you want to fight with?"

We looked at each other, astonished by the generosity of this offer. We immediately agreed upon a light infantry battalion we had already worked with.

"Very well, that's what you'll have." The Oberst turned to his adjutant. "Make sure that these people are extracted from the front at Narwa, where they currently are, and are brought here. We'll talk about the employment of flamethrowers, engineers, artillery observers, and all the other odds and ends later.

"The air superiority in the sector will be guaranteed by fighters. That has already been arranged with the air wing. You will have the necessary radio contact with the Stukas by a liaison APC available to you.

"Anything else? Oh, yes, of course! You will receive your own maps and aerial photos for the operation. They have been made especially for this operation. All areas important to you have been marked by numbers. In this way, there will be no misunderstandings and no unnecessary questions. Moreover, you'll be able to give your location quickly and accurately.

"That's all for today. Any other questions? No? Good, then. Thank you, gentlemen!"

A new type of mine-clearing device for tanks was ordered by air a few days before the beginning of the attack, which was supposed to be launched on April 6. It was a heavy roller that was pushed ahead of the tank. It caused the mines to explode before the tank could ride over them. The new device didn't pan out, however, because it slowed down the advance of the tanks too much. We refused to use it, despite the danger of mines.

"Operation Strachwitz" was then practised twice far behind the front in an area that resembled the "east sack." This was done without the Luftwaffe and artillery, of course, but live ammunition was used. The Supreme Commander of the Northern Front at the time was personally present and talked briefly to us after the exercise. He indicated the importance of the operation. The bridgehead in Narwa had to be held at all costs because of the presence of oil shale deposits in Estonia. The oil was needed urgently for our U-Boat support points.

Back then, we didn't think too much about why Estonian oil, of all things, was of such great importance to the German war effort. We were completely absorbed in the mission that lay ahead of us.

Shortly before the beginning of the attack, we rolled into our assembly areas behind the high ground of the "Kinderheim." We had to be excruciatingly careful to avoid any type of noise so as not to draw the attention of the Russians. As usual, the artillery fired an occasional round to serve as background noise. The Graf had thought of everything!

The infantry was already there, and every squad quickly found its tank since we already knew each other well from the training. Everything went like clockwork. Our four "Tigers" drove in the following order: Kerscher, me, Zwetti, and Gruber.

Graf Strachwitz had expressly forbidden the unit leader being first in line. That way, the attack wasn't stalled when the first tank ran onto a mine. Therefore, contrary to my usual custom, I had to ride second this time, even though in this closed-in terrain one could only properly size up the situation from the lead vehicle.

It was only natural that the "Tigers" drove point. Because of our previous employment there for a number of weeks, we knew the area around

Lembitu like the back of our hands. Every bomb crater was familiar to us, and we had even already had a glimpse behind the rail embankment.

The three tank commanders I had assembled around me represented the ideal type of tank commander. Such perfection is only rarely encountered. During the previous difficult months, I had experienced practically every operation with one of these comrades. Therefore, I hope I am permitted to single them out at this point, without appearing to value the other commanders such as Link, Wesely, Carpaneto, Göring, Riehl, Mayer, and Hermann any less.

The latter group just had less luck with their tanks. They had to "borrow" another vehicle occasionally and therefore didn't stand out as much. Basically, they were all equal, and I hope every future tank company commander has men of their caliber.

✠

Our lead group didn't have any mounted infantry. Gruber and Zwetti each had three combat engineers as "guests." They were supposed to help us if mines showed up. It should be noted that nothing happened to these engineers during the operation. Whenever we stopped, they immediately made themselves scarce in the surrounding terrain. Because of that, they had it better than we did in our tanks.

Graf Strachwitz had two bunkers constructed at the "Kinderheim," one for him and the other for his adjutant.

This amazing Graf had really thought of everything. During the attack, the infantrymen could move about better without winter clothing. For that reason, the winter clothing was collected and bundled by squad. Every bundle was marked with a sign and was supposed to be delivered by an APC after the objective had been reached. That way, the men wouldn't have to freeze after the attack.

In the days preceding the attack, the commander's aide had to find out at what minute in the morning it became light enough to properly see and shoot. The exact time of the attack was based on this determination.

The preparatory fire was supposed to start five minutes before the attack, and it was supposed to be shifted after another five minutes. By the end of the first five minutes, we were supposed to have already crossed the rail embankment.

✠

Shortly before the attack began, the Graf came to us with his traditional thin walking stick to observe the breakthrough from our position. We then experienced a barrage of fire such as we never again saw during the remainder of the war. Thirty-seven-millimeter rapid-fire Flak guns, 20-mm quads, and 88-mm Flak guns were set up in a half circle around the "east sack."

They fired with tracers, which formed an actual dome of fire we could drive under to reach the southern edge of the dome. A rocket regiment fired from farther to the rear, first with napalm rockets and then with high explosive munitions. The effect was devastating, as we were able to determine later. It should be noted that the low-hanging woods in the marshes didn't allow any pressure to escape upward. The flames thus scorched the trees for a height of several meters. All Russians who weren't in their bunkers were immediately killed by the concussion. At the same time, howitzer and artillery units, including 280-mm howitzers, fired everything they had.

During the barrage, we rolled toward the rail crossing at high speed. From the left set of ruins they had occupied, we saw the Russians running back to the railroad crossing in the trenches they had built. Our machine-gun fire was totally ineffective while moving at speed. In a flash, we were over the rail crossing. It was not mined, as expected, since Ivan needed that road to the south for his own supplies.

Our attack must have come as a complete surprise to the Russians. After our tanks had driven past the rail crossing to turn to the right, we saw a Russian standing like stone in his shirt and pants in front of us. He couldn't believe that we were already there. Kerscher finished off an antitank gun, which was apparently supposed to block the path. It still had the muzzle cap on the barrel, and the crew wasn't in position.

We then drove parallel to and not far from the rail embankment, heading west. The plain between the railroad and the woodline was mined, so we drove in one another's tracks and had to guide each other. Fortunately, the mines were laid in the open. The Russians had not been able to dig into the earth due to the frost. Besides, dug-in box mines became too wet in this marshy terrain. We were thus able to take our intermediate objective without any type of losses. We then turned to the right and saw the Russian positions from the rear for a change. Ivan had built bunkers into the rail embankment every couple of meters. Of course from their side, they didn't offer much protection anymore. Seven antitank guns that the surprised enemy hadn't been able to turn around were immediately rendered harmless.

We were in the best of moods because our breakthrough, upon which everything else depended right now, had succeeded beyond expectation. The terrific planning bore its first fruits. Our good mood was disturbed rather abruptly, however, by a very unpleasant interruption.

It was at this point that we suddenly started to receive heavy fire from our own 150-mm infantry howitzers, which were being directed from the "Kinderheim." The observer thought we were enemy tanks. Our silhouette barely peeked over the railway embankment, and we were shooting in the direction of our own lines.

We received a demonstration of how unpleasant the fire of these guns was. We heard every report quite distinctly and also saw the heavy rounds, which had a very flat trajectory, come straight at us. That certainly wasn't anything for weak nerves.

We were forced to drive back and forth across the mine-infested terrain to avoid the unfriendly "messengers." One might call something like that "a continual change of position." But who would want a 150-mm round landing on his head?

On top of everything else, our folks were shooting very well. Of course, I immediately radioed the observer at the "Kinderheim" to explain the mistake. It became more and more uncomfortable, because our people were continuing to fire all four guns unabated. Nothing else was left for me to do but fire a few rounds in front of the observer. That forced him to change positions, and we cleared out before he could again begin to become uncomfortable for us.

I later took the guy to task. He really hadn't recognized us and simply did not want to believe that we had driven behind the embankment so quickly. Not until our unexpected fire did he become nonplussed. He then straightened out the matter.

The "friendly fire" had additional unpleasant consequences. We had got through it all unscathed, to be sure, but the tense concentration and the continual driving back and forth had diverted our attention. So much so, that we didn't notice an antitank gun, which had gone into position in the woods behind us. We were then startled in a most disagreeable fashion. I was hit in the rear. Zwetti found the guy and covered the woodline to avoid further surprises. Almost at the same time, they hit Gruber from the right. Ivan had quickly turned around an antitank gun, which was in a small copse of trees near the rail crossing. It had not been spotted by us, and it knocked out Gruber. The first shot severely damaged the running gear. The second round penetrated. In the process, Gruber and the loader were wounded.

First, we silenced the antitank gun. Then Zwetti shepherded the tank out of the minefield in the direction of the rail crossing. It could drive under its own power only with great difficulty. Zwetti covered him and brought him back to the "Kinderheim." The good fortune in our misfortune was that Gruber's tank did not need to be towed, because all hell was breaking loose in our area. Even the Russian heavy artillery south of Narwa had joined the battle. Ivan wanted to turn the tide around at all costs.

We couldn't be concerned with the rest of the Russian infantry, because we had to follow the advance guard. It had long since passed the fork in the road at the rail crossing. Von Schiller held open the entrance to the marshy woods with his four vehicles and the accompanying infantry. Unfortunately, the light infantry battalion had heavy casualties due to Russian artillery.

The infantry had jumped into the ditch after reaching the fork in the road in order to look for cover. After the Russians had realized that we had broken through to the south, they had fired at precisely this spot with artillery and mortars. One round landed right in the middle of our infantry. Because the men were lying quite close together, the losses were very heavy. They should have dispersed themselves immediately. As we drove south through the woods, Ivan was on guard everywhere. We had to pay excruciating attention to avoid new unpleasant surprises. We saw mortars in position to the left and right in the woods. Next to them were infantry howitzers and antitank guns. We had only one goal and that was "forward, at all costs."

We were thus only able to deal with those Russian guns aimed directly at us while driving by. In front of the woods, we came across a cemetery that the Russians had set up for their dead. They always buried their dead right behind the front. When the pocket was mopped up later, we found out that the wooden crosses didn't even have names on them.

An incident proved how much our operation was also dependent upon chance. In addition to carefulness and bravery, a soldier needs a bit of luck—more so than someone in civilian life. A T34 suddenly surfaced out of a cut in the woods to the side. It was driving south along our trail. Of course, it had no intention of attacking. It just wanted to escape to the south. We, on the other hand, weren't going to knock it out, because it then would have blocked the all-important, and only, way for us. So for once, our intentions were the same.

Too much time would have been lost by the time the engineers had blown the tank out of the way, and I don't believe that our operation would have ended successfully. Plainly, the Russians in the tank were more interested in just getting through to the south than in spoiling our attack. A few Russian tanks in the portion of the pocket to the left and right of us were still firing arbitrarily. They were captured later because even Ivan could only drive along the trails and the corduroy roads. A breakthrough to the south was thus denied to him. When we reached the place where the forward elements had turned off to the east, I left two vehicles to pull security. I personally drove back to the plain to reinforce the defensive perimeter.

The forward elements had reached their objective without large losses. The situation made us realize how fortunate we were to have such good cartographic materials. Because of this, we were easily able to find every trail and clearing. That never would have been possible on a normal map.

The Night Was Hell

Up until that point, everything had gone reasonably well. We would have been happy, however, if we would have already made it through the night. It was clear to everyone that the Russians would try to counterattack us.

At the onset of darkness, two of our patrols left to establish contact to the east and west. The night from April 6 to 7, 1944, was probably one of the worst ones of the entire war for all of us. We were right in the middle of the Russians and didn't know whether they would cut off our way back.

Our APCs had driven back during the day to fetch the winter clothing. During the night, they had to bring ammunition and rations up front. That was a more than difficult mission, which demanded courage, stamina, and an extraordinary sense of duty. The men had to box their way through again and again, first to the north and then to the south. The Russians did everything to block their path. Many APCs fell victim to the exposed mines. The route could only be kept open thanks to the courage of Graf Strachwitz' aide, Lieutenant Günther Famula, who had been assigned this difficult mission. On April 22, Famula was killed by a bomb dropped from a Russian airplane during our next operation at Kriwasoo. He was never able to wear the Knight's Cross, which was awarded to him on May 15.

The Russians attacked our defensive perimeter with strong forces from all sides. The forces cut off by us in the north attempted to break out to the south. From the south, Ivan conducted vigorous relief attacks to destroy us and maintain his forward positions. It was a bitter night for the battalion. It was under heavy fire from the enemy the entire night and suffered heavy losses. The seriously wounded were transported to the rear in APCs; the slightly wounded preferred to stay with us.

Our Stuka squadrons brought us hardly any relief, because they couldn't drop their bombs right next to us. Besides, the heavy things would sink so far into the marshy ground that they made large craters but caused little damage. The Russians had also concentrated so many antiaircraft guns, primarily rapid-fire weapons, that it was impossible for our Stukas to dive low enough. The times where our Stukas were able to demoralize the enemy were long gone. The forward observers of the artillery units helped us the most. They were able to give us some breathing space occasionally due to their superbly directed fire.

We hardly believed it when morning finally came and we were still alive. Ivan still hadn't given up his efforts to dislodge us, but everything looked different with the onset of daylight. The oppressive darkness, in which you could identify neither friend nor foe, was gone. We could see who was in front of us again. During the morning, the ground began to soften up under the influence of the April sun. Soon our tanks had sunk so deeply into the marshy ground that they were practically sitting on their hulls. We just managed to get to the trail and set up security there.

The first elements of the infantry regiment then came forward and occupied the new front lines. The rest combed the pocket from north to south. One of our tanks, Wesely's, had been hit the previous evening right at the fork in the road. A heavy artillery round had crippled him, and he sat helpless in the open, exposed to possible attacks by Russian patrols. Our commander had driven back to the "Kinderheim" during the evening. I called Schotroff several times and told him that he needed to tow Wesely. Von Schiller was once again not in his tank and also didn't return after some time. I finally went myself and freed Wesely from his miserable situation.

We could scarcely recognize the commander and the men of the fusilier battalion who had survived the hell of the past few days. They appeared to have been aged by years.

We were withdrawn at the conclusion of the operation. We then drove back along the Rollbahn toward Sillamä. Well beyond the front a Russian observation balloon observed the ridgeline that the road crossed.

It was well known that the Russians immediately opened fire at any movement along the roads. I gave the express order that hatches were to be closed in this sector or, at the very least, that heads had to be kept in the tank.

Feldwebel Link didn't bother with that and was exposed down to the belt buckle in his cupola. Three tanks had already gone by the high ground when the first salvo landed to the right and left of the Rollbahn. At the same moment, I saw Link collapse into the turret looking like he had been struck by lightning. Because the tank didn't stop, I brought it to a halt by radio. The crew hadn't noticed that its commander had been seriously wounded.

He hadn't made a sound. We attempted to pull him out of the turret, but he cried out in pain as if we wanted to tear him in pieces. A large piece of shrapnel had penetrated through the hip and ripped open all of one side. He looked terrible, and we were afraid that we would not be able to bring him to the field hospital alive.

To our relief, the doctor determined that no vital organs had been hit. After a few weeks, we received the news that Link had gone on convalescent leave. Once again we had got off easy, but these unnecessary casualties always upset me more than any heavy combat.

Fact or Fiction?

We finally had a few days of rest and were able to get our damaged vehicles back in shape. One morning, we received a surprise visit from a vehicle from the public radio section of a propaganda company.

These folks had the mission of recording our defensive fighting of March 17. This was to occur in an "authentic manner" on wax records.

At first, all sorts of stories were told, until the electrician had laid a wire from the commander's tank into our room. It connected the radio in the tank with the recording device next to us. When everything finally worked, I had to get into the tank, while the propaganda man took the place of the radio operator. The drama was ready to begin.

I had to give a semblance of the radio traffic and orders that I had given out on the day of the battle. Of course, fire commands and similar things were also given. Von Schiller sat in the room and played my partner as the company commander.

After all, he had been named in the Wehrmacht daily report. The "Front Line Report" needed to refer to that.

When I had enough of this gruesome game, we called it quits. The record was played back right away, but it did not find approval under the demanding eyes of the experts. We had to repeat everything once again.

At certain intervals, the propaganda man gave his fantasy-filled description of the events. In a realistic fashion, he portrayed how the tanks were burning, how they fired, how they were hit, and how all hell was breaking loose everywhere.

The second recording finally met with approval. Then a few comrades who had record players at home were allowed to make a recording as a sort of letter. It was sent to the folks back home. No one recognized his own voice anymore when the record was played back. Only the text revealed who had actually spoken.

In general, these propaganda guys weren't to our liking. By that, it shouldn't be inferred there weren't terrific guys among them who took their job seriously and were also good soldiers to boot. But exceptions prove the rule. Usually, they were strange types who showed up dressed as soldiers in their pseudo officer uniforms.

This hybrid between not quite soldier and not quite civilian was very unfortunate. Besides, we saw most of the propaganda men as the darlings of the propaganda ministry. They only viewed the war as a pleasant change of pace.

They were also allowed all sorts of preferential treatment compared to the foot soldier at the front. That was why we enjoyed the exceptions, as I already noted, even more so. Unfortunately, there were some among them who gave their life for their country.

We heard our propaganda report a few days later during the normal radio program.

We were amazed at how well the sounds of battle had been added in Berlin. We could barely understand our own voices for all the shooting going on. For that reason, the report unleashed all sorts of laughter among us. After that experience, we never again took a report from the front seriously.

When our guests departed, I was supposed to sign a paper certifying that the propaganda man who filed the report had sat in my tank. I left this to the company commander, who could do that with a clear conscience. It was, after all, his tank in which the story had taken place.

It didn't become clear to us what great good fortune we had that the operation was a success until the prisoners had been interrogated. Among other officers, our advance guard had taken prisoner the operations officer of the division in the "east sack."

The rapidly advancing tanks of the Großdeutschland Division had reached the division command post located at the base of the pocket so quickly that the Russian divisional commander still hadn't received any word of our breakthrough. All the lines had been broken during the preparatory fire.

The surprised operations officer was still only in his shirt upon our arrival and had to dress quickly in order to be taken captive. The Russian general, it should be noted, had already taken off for the south.

We discovered through our prisoners that an entire Russian division had been assembled in the pocket. It had been equipped with a lot of heavy weapons. The Russian hadn't considered such a catastrophe possible.

The remainder of their tank brigade, which had already suffered considerably in the previous defensive fighting, was likewise still in the marshy woods where it had no maneuver room at all. It fell into our hands without a scratch.

The interrogation of the Russian captain was very informative. It should be noted that he made a superior impression, even in his clothing.

I saw that the Russians had returned to the wide shoulder boards that had been forbidden for a while. Medals were also awarded and worn again. The other side had also come to the conclusion that soldiers place value on being able to show their combat skills to the outside world by the wearing of awards.

Based on the statements of the Russian captain, our attack had come as a complete surprise to them. They had never expected a frontal assault from the north. They thought that the northern front at Lembitu had been fortified so well that nothing could happen to it by any stretch of the imagination.

I also wouldn't have wanted to experience what would have happened had we got stuck at the railway embankment and the ten Russian antitank positions had been occupied. The Russians had expected our attack along the bottom of the "sack" from the east and west.

That was the shortest route, and the "west sack" had also been liquidated in this fashion. To avoid the repetition of just such a disaster, the Russian lines on both sides of the bottom of the "sack" had been mined in all sorts of tricky ways.

Even the trees had been connected with trip wires. No infantryman would have been able to get through there in one piece, regardless of whether he walked, stooped, or crawled on the ground. But this mining proved fateful to the Russians themselves. After our breakthrough, they were no longer able to break out to the side and withdraw.

The Russians cursed their commissars as much as we did our own Nazi political officers. They were also becoming an increasing nuisance to us at the front. They usually hung around division headquarters, however. We only noticed their presence through the circulars that were occasionally sent to the frontline units. Politics didn't play any role at all for those of us at the front.

It would have appeared idiotic to me, if I had said "Heil Hitler" to my men during morning formation. After all, the most varied types of people were thrown together in the same struggle and subject to the same harsh laws. There were Nazis and opponents of the regime, as well as completely disinterested parties. They were united in comradeship. It was completely unimportant whether one did his job for the Fuhrer or for his country or out of a sense of duty.

The political or nonpolitical opinions of the others didn't interest anyone. The main thing was that he was a good comrade and a halfway decent soldier. If that was true, then everything worked out.

After all the difficulties that lay behind us, we enjoyed our breather in Sillamä to its fullest. But something pulled me back to the site of the carnage. I wanted to see it one more time in a more "peaceful" atmosphere. So I left on the spur of the moment in my Kübel and paid a visit to the "former east sack."

Since I didn't have to concentrate on the enemy anymore, I realized how ghastly the terrain appeared that had been so bitterly and continuously contested for the previous few weeks. As I drove back in the darkness, my flesh crawled. The air was still full of the stink that burned-out tanks always left behind. The materiel of the Russians lay scattered all over the place. On the plain, I found a Russian tank turret all by itself. It had survived all the artillery fire. At the beginning of the fighting, we had knocked out this Russian tank.

The turret had been ripped off the hull by the explosion and flew through the air. We ducked our heads, and, in fact, the turret didn't land too far from us. The cannon bored into the marshy ground almost up to the gun mantlet, while the turret jutted upright as if on a stick. Almost all the trees in the woods south of the railway embankment were charred black and shot to pieces. It created a ghostly impression, as if all life had completely died out.

Not a single living creature was to be seen in these dead woods. The birds had withdrawn after all of nature had been trampled on by the humans.

It was always interesting for us to see how well the Russians were capable of constructing positions even under the most difficult circumstances. The artillery pieces and the mortars had been built up on corduroy stands and completely protected by beams against shrapnel. No human could dig in deeply in that marshy terrain.

The shallow Russian "bunkers" (if that's what one wants to call their dugouts) actually protected against the fire of heavy weapons; unless they received a direct hit. We were able to determine that all the Russians who had been in their provisional bunkers had gotten off with a good scare.

Even the connecting trenches between the rail crossing and our former eastward strongpoint had been constructed in an exemplary fashion.

This showed me that it was possible to dig in quickly despite frost and marshy terrain. Our regimental commander had considered this impossible.

Strongpoints without heavy weapons and without contact with one another will always be lost whenever a massed attack starts. The man dug into the ground has already been psychologically prevented from giving his best. He finds himself in constant fear that he may not be able to get out of his foxhole during an enemy breakthrough because he is a goner in the open.

Therefore, he will logically do that which our guys did when the Russians penetrated. That is to say, he will attempt to get to safety during the artillery barrage.

In Praise of the "Tiger"

In my book so far, there has been much talk about knocking out tanks and the destruction of Russian antitank guns. This portrayal could create the impression that to a certain extent these successes were child's play. If that is the case, then this book has been misunderstood.

The paramount mission of an armor unit is the engagement and destruction of enemy tanks and antitank weapons. The psychological support of the infantry during covering missions is only of secondary importance.

There was no such thing as a life insurance policy in a tank and there can't be any. Our "Tiger" was the most ideal tank, however, that I was acquainted with. It probably hasn't been surpassed, even by the current state of weaponry. In any case, that certainly applies to the west; the Russians could possibly surprise us with new designs.

The strength of a tank lies in its armor, its mobility and, finally, in its armament. These three factors have to be weighed against each other so a maximum in performance is achieved. This ideal appeared to be realized in our "Tiger." The 88-mm cannon was good enough to defeat every tank, assuming that you hit it in the right place. Our "Tigers" were strong enough up front to defeat a few rounds. We couldn't afford to let ourselves be hit on the side or in the rear or, especially, on top. Just that alone required a lot of prudence and experience.

Our guidelines were: "Shoot *first*, but if you can't do that, at least hit first." The prerequisite for that, of course, is fully functioning communications from tank to tank and also among the crew. Furthermore, quick and accurate gun-laying systems need to be present. In most instances, the Russians lacked both of these prerequisites. Because of that, they often came out on the short end of the stick, even though they frequently didn't lag behind us in armor, weapons, and maneuverability. With the Stalin tanks, they were even superior to us.

The most important consideration came after all the material conditions were filled. The personal aggressiveness of the commander while observing was decisive for success against numerically vastly superior enemy formations. The lack of good observation by the Russians often resulted in the defeat of large units. Tank commanders who slam their hatches shut at the beginning of an attack and don't open them again until the objective has been reached are useless, or at least second rate. There are, of course, six to eight vision blocks mounted in a circle in every cupola that allow observation. But they are only good for a certain sector of the terrain, limited by the size of the individual vision block. If the commander is looking through the left vision block when an anti-tank gun opens fire from the right, then he will need a long time before he identifies it from inside the buttoned-up tank.

Unfortunately, impacting rounds are felt before the sound of the enemy gun's report, because the speed of the round is greater than the speed of sound. Therefore, a tank commander's eyes are more important than his ears. As a result of rounds exploding in the vicinity, one doesn't hear the gun's report at all in the tank. It is quite different whenever the tank commander raises his head occasionally in an open hatch to survey the terrain. If he happens to look halfway to the left while an enemy antitank gun opens fire halfway to the right, his eye will subconsciously catch the shimmer of the yellow muzzle flash. His attention will immediately be directed toward the new direction and the target will usually be identified in time. Everything depends on the prompt identification of a dangerous target. Usually, seconds decide. What I said above also applies to tanks that have been equipped with a periscope.

The destruction of an antitank gun was often accepted as nothing special by lay people and soldiers from other branches. Only the destruction of other tanks counted as a success. On the other hand, antitank guns counted twice as much to the experienced tanker. They were much more dangerous to us. The antitank cannon waited in ambush, well camouflaged, and magnificently set up in the terrain. Because of that, it was very difficult to identify. It was also very difficult to hit because of its low height. Usually, we didn't make out the antitank guns until they had fired the first shot. We were often hit right away, if the antitank crew was on top of things, because we had run into a wall of antitank guns. It was then advisable to keep as cool as possible and take care of the enemy, before the second aimed shot was fired.

No one can deny that the many casualties among the officers and other tank commanders were due to exposing their heads. But these men didn't die in vain. If they had moved with closed hatches, then many more men would have found their death or been severely wounded inside the tanks. The large Russian tank losses is proof of the correctness of this assertion. Fortunately, for us, they almost always drove cross-country buttoned up. Of course, every tank commander had to be careful while peering out during positional warfare. Especially since the turret hatches of tanks in the front lines were continuously watched by enemy sharpshooters. Even a short exposure could be fatal for the tank commander. I had commandeered a folding artillery scope for just such cases. Actually, such a scope shouldn't be missing in any fighting vehicle.

For a long time, the Russians had only four-man crews. The commander had to observe, aim, and fire all at the same time. Because of that, they were always inferior to an enemy who divided these important functions between two men. Shortly after the beginning of the war, the Russians had recognized the advantages that were to be found in the five-man crew. They eventually redesigned their tanks. They put a cupola on the turret and added a commander's station. I have never quite understood why, for example, the English developed a new heavy tank after the war that was only crewed by four men.

We were completely satisfied with our "Tigers" and our infantry no less so. After all, we had stood our ground with them during all the difficult defensive fighting in the east and west. Many a tanker owes a debt of gratitude to this first-rate tank; he survived to enjoy a peaceful existence nowadays.

Failure and Farewell

The objective of a new operation that was planned was to eliminate the remaining Russian bridgehead. Its depth from north to south was almost twice that of both portions of the bridgehead already wiped out.

On April 15, 1944, we were once again ordered to a meeting with the Graf. The subject matter was preparations for the third "Operation Strachwitz." Although we were already familiar with his leadership methods to a certain extent, his careful, methodical planning amazed us once again.

When he entered his command post, where we had all assembled, he sized us up once again with that somewhat caustic glance of his. After he had put aside his cap and walking stick, he stepped up to the map table.

"Very well, gentlemen, this time we want to eliminate the remainder of the Russian bridgehead, which sits like a thorn in our sides. Its depth, as you know, is almost twice that of both portions of the bridgehead we wiped out. But that shouldn't bother us.

"The Kampfgruppe that will be assembled for this operation has the same strength and organization as the one for our affair in the 'east sack.' You gentlemen know one another already. That will make some things easier." While saying this, the Oberst pointed to the map. "We will assemble in this piece of woods. To get to it, you'll have to turn south from the Rollbahn east of the 'Kinderheim.'

"Our own front lines, about two kilometers from the assembly area, will be crossed during the preparatory fire. They will be crossed at the point where they run from north to south along the side of the bridgehead. The Russian front lines will be broken violently in one continuous advance.

"I will now ask you to follow all additional information on the maps, which were handed out to you at the beginning of the conference. These maps are photocopies of the aerial photography taken of the area of operations. They turned out first-rate and put our other map material to shame.

"The first battle objective is Point 312. You can see how the road turns at a 90-degree angle to the south at that point. From then on, it runs in a practically straight line until it reaches the Narwa at a larger village. The trail from the north that joins into our avenue of approach at this bend will be secured by the lead element until the rest of the Kampfgruppe has passed Point 312 heading south. The Kampfgruppe will thrust to the Narwa; it will occupy and hold the aforementioned village until the bridgehead has been split by other units into individual sectors and eliminated.

"At the same time, a second Kampfgruppe will advance south along the axis 'Kinderheim-boot sole.' It will then follow this trail east and reach the axis of advance using that. A third Kampfgruppe has the mission to penetrate the enemy lines 1,500 meters south of and parallel to that trail. As you see, there is a low-lying wooded ridgeline running east to west between this Kampfgruppe and you. That's the plan of attack so far."

The Graf stopped for a moment and looked at us in succession. Since we didn't have any questions at that point, he continued.

"Looked at superficially, this operation is very similar to both of our previous ones. Only this time, there are probably going to be considerably more difficulties.

"Mark my words! The basic object has not changed. You still have to advance without stopping. You must reach the Narwa without the Russians being able to gather their wits. It is undoubtedly clear to all of you that you cannot reach your objective if, for some reason, the lead elements should come to a standstill. That's the entire problem for the 'Tigers.' There is marsh to the right and left of your avenue of approach. Therefore, you can't deviate from the trail. Moreover, the trail is also only wide enough for one of your 'Tigers' to be able to drive on it without problems. The only advantage that you have compared to the previous operations is that the road is somewhat elevated and has a good foundation. From Point 312 onward, it proceeds through a reasonably tall set of marshy woods, which extends to the Narwa. For us tankers, it is something completely and singularly undesired. But we can't change that at all.

"How far we will be able to get with keeping everything a secret this time is another question. We have already surprised the Russians twice in their bridgehead. They know that this bridgehead is a pain for us. A third surprise will therefore probably not be possible. Especially since they know that a new attack can only be carried out on this road. This naturally diminishes our chances of success compared to the previous operations where we were successful in using the element of surprise.

"Fortunately, we also know a few things. According to prisoner statements, the trail from the Russian front lines to Point 312 has been mined.

Ivan has packed the culverts in the road embankment full of explosives. These are located about every thirty meters. He can ignite these demo chambers all at once from a bunker, which is—as you can see—in the woods somewhat east of Point 312. We want to try to counteract the danger of everything being blown. During the preparatory fire, we will fire an entire battalion of 280-mm artillery just at this bunker. This will undoubtedly cut the demo lines, and the route will remain negotiable.

"To provide cover for the lead elements, a platoon of combat engineers will follow the 'Tigers.' After the breakthrough, it will advance in the ditches to the right and left of the trail. It will cut the lines that lead to the demo chambers. It's better to be safe than sorry. Besides, it must be assumed that the Russians probably won't ignite the charges until the tanks are on the mined sections. Otherwise, their preparations don't make any sense. If, contrary to our expectations, the lines are still intact despite the artillery fire, then the engineers can still prevent their demolition in a timely fashion.

"What's going on?" Reluctantly, the Graf turned to his adjutant. He had just entered the room, flushed with excitement.

The officer straightened up. "Herr Graf, I would like to report that the announcement has been made in the news that the Fuhrer had awarded you the Diamonds to the Knight's Cross! If I may take the liberty, I would like to be the first one to congratulate you!"

We were also extremely happy about the award and wanted to congratulate him ourselves. Likewise, we wanted to celebrate this honor in a suitable manner. After all, we had also contributed quite a bit to it. Before we were able to say a word, however, the Graf made an abrupt sign of disapproval.

"First, the news is not an official source of information. Second, I don't have any time for that now and don't wish to be disturbed again!" That was meant for the adjutant, who turned beet red. He raised his hand to his cap and disappeared rapidly. The Oberst then turned back to us as if nothing had happened.

"Behind the Russian lines, there is still a knocked-out T34 along the route of advance. It can be clearly identified in the aerial photo. In my opinion, it blocks the road and must be removed. To accomplish this, an APC with engineers will follow behind the second 'Tiger.' They will blow the wreck out of the way with prepared charges. Did you want to say something, Carius?"

"Yes, Herr Graf. There is a ditch in front of the T34 behind the Russian lines. It, too, can be clearly identified in the aerial photo. A wooden bridge used to cross this ditch. It has since been removed. Only a small footbridge can be seen in its place. Naturally, our 'Tigers' can't go over it. The wooden bridge with its small span would have held a Tiger, but the footbridge . . ."

The Graf interrupted me. "You'll also get over this ridiculous ditch without a bridge!"

"With all due respect, no, Herr Graf. I still know this area from the time when the Russians hadn't yet advanced so far, and they were just getting ready to infiltrate across the Narwa. Back then, of course, I studied the terrain intensely. Because even if the ditch isn't an obstacle for infantry, for tanks it is . . ."

The Graf had placed his hands in his pants pockets and looked at me with interest. Because of his gaze, I hesitated for a moment in my explanation. He drew up the corner of his mouth and then repeated in his haughty manner, " . . . for tanks it is?"

The question mark was not to be ignored.

I pulled myself together. "This is what I mean, Herr Graf. The area surrounding the ditch is completely marshy. Getting over it without a bridge is something completely impossible. Besides that, you can see quite clearly from the aerial photo that the ditch has been cut to have steep sides. That tells us that the Russians have quite intentionally created an obstacle.

"They have made this ditch in the marshy terrain into an antitank ditch. Quite simply, it is an obstacle, and it is also intended to be one."

I hadn't held back with my opinion. I considered it to be my duty to my comrades to surface my doubts here. After all, if anyone were to get stuck in this damned ditch, it would be us and not the Graf. I looked him straight in the eyes, "unflinchingly, but not insolently," as the regulation puts it so nicely.

The Oberst took his right hand out of his pocket and moved it along the ditch on the map. "Take note of this, Carius," he said in a friendly manner. "If I say that this ditch doesn't exist as an antitank ditch to me, then it doesn't exist. Do we understand each other?"

In my entire military career, I had never experienced such an elegant and, at the same time, unmistakable rebuff. Graf Strachwitz didn't want to see an antitank ditch. So, there was none there. Period—end of discussion. I was so nonplussed by that, that I could only choke out a short "Yes, sir!"

Still smiling in his slightly caustic manner, the Oberst nodded and continued his briefing. The other officers had also piped up and asked their questions, none of which remained unanswered. After the meeting, when no one said anything following the usual "any more questions?," the Graf turned to me one more time.

"I've thought about the matter one more time, Carius. Do you still foresee difficulties with the ditch?"

"Yes, Herr Graf!"

"Well, I don't want to spoil your fun. Especially not when there really could be something to the matter. Do you have a suggestion?"

"I believe that wooden beams should be set aside and brought forward in APCs at the right moment. We can then lay these beams over the ditch, which would only cause a minor delay."

Graf Strachwitz nodded. "Approved!" he said. "I will cause the necessary things to happen." He then reached for his walking stick and cap and turned to go. Somehow I got the impression deep inside that even the Oberst didn't quite believe in the success of the plan just discussed. He himself would have preferred to call off the entire affair.

The preparatory measures corresponded in scope to those that had been taken for the previous operations under the Graf. Our fighters from Reval ensured absolute air superiority. Our Stuka comrades had the difficult mission of destroying the main bridge and both of the pontoon bridges that had been built by the Russians over the Narwa. This was intended to cut off supplies in the bridgehead and to prevent the enemy from falling back over the river.

Without a doubt, the entire concept was tremendous, the preparations magnificent, and the organization excellent. Despite that, we thought our chances were quite slim. That may not sound logical. One must not forget, however, that we had enjoyed amazing luck and the advantage of surprise during the first two Strachwitz operations. But no one dared to hope for the luck we needed for the new operation. We knew that if we actually made it to the Narwa in accordance with the plan, we would then be sitting in a trap in the midst of the Russians. They would have the understandable desire to hold the bridgehead at all costs. Ivan would only have to close the door behind us, and no one would get out again. An assault gun or a tank, set up behind us on the road, would make every forward or rearward movement impossible.

We thus drove back to Sillamä with mixed feelings. We briefed the tank commanders on the new plan. Von Schiller insisted that he lead the forward elements. I tried in vain to dissuade him. He probably wanted to prove to all of us that the bad opinion of him was wrong. But somehow he had picked out the one operation that was almost hopeless. No one else could have been successful either. It was to be his last operation with the company.

According to plan, we reached our assembly area in the early morning hours of April 19. The Russians kept both exceptionally and suspiciously still. We expected an artillery attack at any moment on our piece of woods. Ivan could easily see into them. He also must have heard us, since the area was quite level. Strange: nothing happened, nothing at all! Those guys had most likely been armed to the teeth and just wanted to take a look at us from close-up. That was my firm belief.

Graf Strachwitz had ordered his command post built in this piece of woods. The drivers of the APCs with our breaching beams were also in the bunkers. They would wait there until they were called forward to supply us if needed.

The other APCs were in line on the road with the Panzer IVs of their regiment. They were participating in the breakthrough and transporting the infantry. They were mixed in behind our eight "Tigers."

An APC was located behind the second "Tiger" of the lead group. It was bringing our engineers forward and also had to take along the forward observer of the artillery. A squad of infantry was attached to each of my four "Tigers." They were already standing on the tanks and checking out how they could best make themselves small behind the turret and hold on.

It was probably still about ten minutes before the beginning of the attack. I was walking down the column to see whether everything was all right. It was then, at the last minute, that we had an unfortunate incident, which served as an ominous omen. I had barely gone fifty meters to the rear when, with a start, I heard a machine-gun salvo behind me.

I knew right away that someone overly anxious had already loaded. A few rounds had gone off on the unlucky guy. I almost had a heart attack when I realized that this had happened to *my* loader, of all people. Bad luck seldom travels alone.

He had also depressed the weapon so that two infantrymen on the "Tiger" in front of me were severely wounded. Naturally, our comrades in the fusilier battalion were besides themselves, and their confidence in us was shaken to the core.

The wounded were quickly evacuated in an APC, because the attack was supposed to begin. If Ivan really hadn't noticed anything up until that point, then everything must have been clear to him after that incident.

The matter continued to bother me throughout the operation, but there wasn't anything else that could be done about it then. I just couldn't understand how such a thing had happened to such an old hand. It should be noted that it was strictly forbidden to load or even depress weapons before the attack was rolling and a clear field of fire was present.

In the assembly area shortly before H-hour, only the radio operators were allowed to tune in their equipment. Everything else had to wait. And it was on that morning, of all mornings, that we would have had many hours of time to load our weapons. We would soon find that out.

Naturally, my loader was virtually useless that day. I also had it up to the chin line. Later on, we were only able to avoid a court-martial with great difficulty. Who would have benefited from a conviction of the unfortunate fellow?

Although the cause of the accident had been wear on the breach of the machine gun, the loader's guilt was indisputable, if for no other reason than that the weapons should have been elevated. The gunner would also have been charged because he had not exercised his supervisory duty. I was extremely happy that I avoided punishment for both of them.

Despite everything, the attack rolled on time. Our point had just crossed the front line when the column unexpectedly came to a halt.

After some time had elapsed, information was passed on the radio that the lead tank had run onto a mine and was immobile. The attack thus came to a standstill, and it was clear to me that we would never reach the Narwa.

We then waited in completely open terrain, a good target. Ivan had already started to show signs of life. He was firing with artillery and mortars of every caliber and, in addition, had also alarmed his close air support. Fortunately, our fighters were at least able to keep the skies clear. They shot down two Russian ground-attack planes. The others didn't come too close after that.

Three Russian observation balloons floated over the bridgehead. They directed the heavy artillery. We didn't receive a single direct hit even though we were there for hours on end. We also only had limited capability to move forward and backward because we could not leave the road. That just proves how difficult it is to render a tank harmless at great distances—even with directed fire.

In some respects, the Russians are magicians. For example, it was amazing how quickly the balloons disappeared onto the ground whenever a German fighter approached. Those guys were up in the air again just as quickly.

Our fighters couldn't approach at low level, because the Russians had employed countless antiaircraft weapons. These weapons, especially the twin and quad light cannons, laid down a terrific wall of fire whenever the fighters appeared.

The Stukas, which attacked the Narwa bridgehead in the course of the day, suffered the same fate as the fighters. It's hard enough to hit a bridge in a steep dive. It was impossible there because the bombs had to be dropped at high altitudes.

Two of our machines were even shot down by the Russian antiaircraft weapons. It should be noted that we later found out that the bridges constructed by the engineers were scarcely detectable from the air. They ran just under the water surface.

One could only identify them by the slight agitation of the water. Such "underwater bridges" could not be approached from the air, let alone be hit. In any case, Ivan hadn't been sleeping, and his defensive measures presented us with an unsolvable problem.

The other two attack groups had also become as hung up as we were. The group that had attacked out of the former "boot" wasn't able to use a single reinforced road. The Panzer IVs soon became stuck in the mud.

During our orders conference, we had joked that the Graf wanted to report the elimination of the Narwa bridgehead to the "Führer" as a birthday present on April 20. After just a few hours, the entire affair already bore very little resemblance to a birthday present.

Our Stukas dropped bombs several times on the ridge farther to the south and around Point 312. Perhaps these attacks had a psychological effect, but no serious damage was inflicted upon the enemy. The smoke had scarcely dissipated when the Russians came back to life.

The company commander, von Schiller, remained quiet in his tank, without trying to do anything. At regular intervals, Graf Strachwitz inquired about the situation. He received the same answer each time: "Location unchanged. Forward advance impossible!"

We held out until about noon in this fashion. But then the Graf lost his patience. Von Schiller and I were ordered back to the command post. Of course, I couldn't imagine anything good happening and made my way on foot with the commander. We finally reached the command post, more crawling than walking.

Graf Strachwitz was already awaiting us in front of his bunker. He nervously swung his customary walking stick back and forth. And then he let loose: "Von Schiller, I am shocked! You didn't give a single order the entire time! I think you would still be at the same spot tomorrow, without having done anything! I have to demand somewhat more personal initiative from the commander of a 'Tiger' company! This is really incredible! Simply close your hatches and wait until the situation clears up by itself! I will investigate the matter and then take appropriate action."

The Graf finished off von Schiller in this manner. Strachwitz was beside himself with rage and was scarcely able to stop. He then gave *me* the order to assume the "welcome" mission and put the completely derailed operation back on track. He announced he would soon visit the lead elements. "You haven't seen anything yet," he said, "if I personally have to get the entire affair rolling again."

With mixed feelings, I made my way back to the front. I told the men by radio that command had been transferred to me. Unteroffizier Carpaneto, who, as the lead tank, had suffered the misfortune with the mine, then immediately attempted to move his vehicle to the right and into the marsh using his one track.

I helped push him a little bit from behind and then got past him without problems. Of course, we could have executed the same maneuver during the morning. Carpaneto had not moved, however, because von Schiller had not made an effort to get past him.

Carpaneto couldn't stand the commander at all and had probably waited for a long time to do him in. The incident with the mine helped him do that. One could have possibly characterized his obstinate waiting for an order as unsoldierly or not in the spirit of comradeship, but, in the long run, he saved all of us with his stubbornness and his dislike of von Schiller.

Even with a speedy advance, there was no doubt that Ivan would have finished us off that time. Unteroffizier Alfredo Carpaneto was an academy-trained painter from Vienna. He was a daredevil and a fabulous tank commander and comrade. One could do anything with him, provided one had his trust and confidence.

As one could imagine, he wasn't born for parade ground drill and ceremony. He cut a less than imposing figure on the drill field. One never could have made a "Prussian" out of him, but his soldierly attitude and his unconditional comradeship weren't too far removed from the real Prussian spirit of old. Of course, that type of man always tried to get the goat of people like von Schiller. I therefore couldn't understand why

Otto Carius in dress uniform, wearing Knight's Cross with Oak Leaves. Probably a studio portrait on the award of the Oak Leaves.

Receipt of, training on, and initial firing of the "Tigers." Ploermel in the Bretagne in Southern France in 1943. (Translator's note: Notice the new state and factory finish of the tanks.)

The author's first "Tiger."

Oberfeldwebel Rudolf Zwetti's "Tiger." From the left, facing the camera: Gefreiter Lippmann (radio operator), Unteroffizier Spallek (gunner), Gefreiter Schochart (loader), the author, and Oberfeldwebel Zwetti. In the driver's hatch is Gefreiter Monses.

Shallow-fording operations. Another early production "Tiger" with the high-silhouette commander's cupola. Factory finish without anti-magnetic mine paste.

Major Willey Jähde, our battalion commander. Unfortunately, he left much too early to take on even greater responsibilities. He is shown here with his crew.

This was the way an attack was led from the front. "Diving" at the right moment was essential. (Readily apparent are the disadvantages of the commander's cupolas of the first "Tigers": the welding and the prominent hatch.)

Knocked-out T34 at Narwa.

"Tiger" 233 with the old cupola.

My two officers in the company in a VW-Kübel. In the front is Lieutenant Nienst-edt, in the rear Lieutenant Eichhorn.

Visiting a mine layer in Reval Bay. Just one day after my arrival, I received a telegram: "Return imediately to your unit!"

Discussing the operation on my tank south of Dünaburg. It can be easily seen how much more practical the new commander's cupola was! (Translator's note: This picture stems from a Wochenschau and is mistakenly identified as being on the Western Front. Of interest is the fact that several soldiers are wearing the two-piece mouse grey Panzer overalls.)

The heavy companies of the battalions had Panzer IIIs and IVs.

The first prisoners are collected in the vicinity of Wilna. This shot is taken from the viewpoint of a Panzer II, a vehicle present in the battalion combat reconnaissance platoon.

The advance continues. A typical "Rollbahn" can be seen here. When the term "Rollbahn" is encountered in the text, this is the image that should come to mind.

A maintenance halt is conducted with all of the vehicles nose-to-tail. Since the 1st Battalion was following the lead battalion, there was little to no danger to these vehicles. Note that all the armored vehicle crewmen wore one-piece overalls over their black Panzer uniforms.

The 1st Battalion moves off the "Rollbahn" and to the flanks to cover the advance. Panzerschülte Otto Carius is seen on top of his Panzer 38(t). Unteroffizier August Dehler, the tank commander, stands to the side of his vehicle. Unteroffizier Dehler was later killed by accident when his tank ran over him while it was being positioned in icy terrain.

A 37-mm Pak gun from the antitank platoon of the 1st Battalion headquarters. This platoon usually worked closely with the trains and provided them protection.

The effect of a round on the author's tank can be seen here. The radio operator lost an arm due to the penetration, while the author came away with the loss of some teeth and flesh wounds.

Panzer IIIs from the 4th Company.

A Panzer III from the 4th Company.

The awesome power of the "Stuka zu Fuß" can be seen to good advantage. Although not as accurate as precision weapons, they could be employed as an area weapon in places such as woods with good results. In addition, their psychological effect was enormous.

Other means of crossing a river. . . . One had to be very careful, since the riverbed quickly eroded under the weight of the tracked vehicles and the ford could then become impassable. One crew member of the follow-on vehicle stands by on the riverbank to observe the results of this crossing.

A Panzer II from the combat reconnaissance platoon.

A knocked-out Russian BA32 armoured car.

A Russian T34 with a 76-mm main gun. These proved to be worrisome for the Germans.

An early version of the T34 here with a BT7.

German soldiers inspect one of the first knocked-out T34s.

A view of a knocked-out KVI (also 76-mm main gun), another Russian vehicle that commanded a great deal of respect.

The Panzer 38(t), which formed the bulk of the 21st Panzer Regiment, was virtually helpless against the T34 and the KVI. The only weapons that could often help were the long-barreled 75-mm Pak guns and the 88-mm Flak gun (pictured), pressed into ground service.

An abandoned Russian antiaircraft gun.

In Orscha on the Dnieper, July 1941.

The capture of Smolensk, late July 1941.

The capture of Smolensk, late July 1941.

Attempts were made to camouflage vehicles during rest halts. In the wide open spaces of Russia, this could be a difficult undertaking.

The man shaking hands with the soldier in overalls is Unteroffizier Meier, a tank commander in the 21st Panzer Regiment. Meier was later promoted to lieutenant and served as the commander of the 3rd Company of Heavy Panzer Battalion 502. He was killed in action north of Gatschina in 1944.

The author, now a Feldwebel and officer candidate, is seen here in the spring of 1942 supervising the recovery operation of a supply column moving up to the front.

Feldwebel Carius is seen here sitting on his tank during a visit by Hauptmann Jung, the adjutant of the 92nd Artillery Regiment of the 20th Panzer Division. Carius and Jung were friends from school. Jung was killed in action approximately four weeks after this picture was taken in the spring of 1942.

Obergefreiter Schimmel posing with the company dinner in the spring of 1942. Obergefreiter Schimmel was the only enlisted man in the author's company who had been awarded the Iron Cross 1st Class. He was later killed during an artillery barrage by a shrapnel wound through his heart.

Panzerjäger Is (probably from the 92nd Armoured Antitank Battalion)

Promoted to lieutenant in the autumn of 1942, Otto Carius was permitted to go on his first leave home from the Eastern Front.

This photo shows von Schiller's "Tiger" with other vehicles of the company in a road march.

The author's original tank. The old tank commander's cupola can be clearly seen. It was welded on, had a hatch that stood straight up, and could be seen from afar! The later version was flat, with a hatch that swung out sideways.

Another view of the author's original tank.

Lieutenant Bölter, Major Schwaner, the author, Lieutenant Eichhorn, Oberleutnant Schütze.

Lieutenant Hans Bölter is seen in his "Tiger" in the summer of 1943. Lieutenant Bölter was one of the company officers of the 2nd Company. He was later transferred to the 1st Company, where he was its commander.

Portrait shot of our "Tiger" in Tschernowo. (Translator's note: The tank is still in the factory finish and is missing the first outer road wheel.)

Feldwebel Hermann was not exactly known for his luck with his "Tiger." He got to know the recovery section of the maintenance platoon so well that his fellow tank commanders jokingly referred to him as a "Hero of the Soviet Union."

Feldwebel Hermann bogged down with his tank.

The newly awarded Knight's Cross winner was granted three weeks of home leave in May 1944. Although two weeks of that leave were taken up by travel, the author was able to enjoy a week with his parents and younger brother at this home in Zweibrücken. His father, a major in the engineers, ended the war as a battalion commander. His younger brother, shown here as an officer candidate, later ended the war as a lieutenant and platoon leader in a Panzer regiment in Italy.

Author in black Panzer uniform. Knight's Cross, Iron Cross First Class, Wound Badge in Silver, *Panzerkampfabzeichen* (Tank Battle Badge) in Silver.

von Schiller had ordered this sergeant, of all sergeants, to drive point in front of him.

This demonstrated von Schiller's psychological inexperience and lack of perceptiveness once again. It finally became his undoing.

We then broke through the Russian lines at a fast clip and reached the ominous antitank ditch, which forced us to halt again. I immediately reported our new location. Graf Strachwitz thereupon ordered that our attack would not continue until the following morning. The engineers were supposed to make the ditch passable during the night and blow up the T34 on the right side of the road.

God knows, our position was not to be envied! All around us were the Russians, and we were practically condemned to almost complete immobility.

When I portray everything here in a dispassionate manner, one cannot easily envision how difficult everything was, even though we had become used to all sorts of things. Every tank down the line provided cover, alternating to the right and left. Only the lead tank covered to the front, as the others didn't have any fields of fire in that direction.

Each of us had to keep up a constant, vigilant lookout so the Russians couldn't spring a nasty surprise on us. When we waited in such situations, it naturally gnawed at our nerves. We yearned for the night to pass by.

The tank ditch was covered by a Russian antitank gun, which had been set up in a piece of woods off to the right. A tank obstacle is worthless unless covered. We exchanged fire with these guys until we finally had some quiet.

We knew that if the Russians were true to form, they would have new pieces ready in the same position by morning. It should be noted that the firefight wasn't too spirited. I suspected that the Russians wanted to let us advance some more because they were so sure of themselves. They could survey the entire Kampfgruppe on the open road and assign their targets.

Our left flank posed a special problem for the continued advance to Point 312. The high ground paralleled it. With its wooded crown, the high ground seemed as if it were created for the emplacement of defensive weapons. Because of that, the trailing tanks had to constantly fire at the assault guns that had driven up onto the high ground from the south to threaten us. If Ivan got a bit too impertinent, then our artillery observers put a little damper on things. We were soon able to see Russian infantry march up to the high ground.

They walked around the area unconcerned, as if our tanks were only there for their enjoyment. This too indicated that Ivan had gotten a grip on things for some time and wasn't thinking at all about turning tail. He undoubtedly knew that we couldn't become a serious threat to him there.

The Russian artillery fired exceptionally well. For the time being, however, it only appeared to be sizing us up. At that point, there still weren't any massive artillery barrages. The prisoners we had taken in the "east sack" said during their interrogation that the heavy Russian artillery was crewed by women. Perhaps that was the actual reason for the greater precision in aiming.

Experience had shown that a female Russian in uniform was even more fanatical than her male counterpart. For Ivan, there were never any resupply problems along short stretches in difficult terrain. If, for example, the vehicles could not drive all the way to the front, then the surrounding population, without regard to age or gender, was used to transport things. Everyone gave his best effort to fill his "obligation."

✠

We were extremely happy when it became dark. As usual, the Russian bomber formations flew past us and bombarded the city of Narwa and our bridgehead. The city had probably already been leveled to the ground. Whenever the fires lit up the evening sky to our rear, we could hardly believe that there was still anything flammable left.

The night was so dark, that we couldn't see our hands in front of our eyes. I had a portion of the crews dismount with their machine pistols so that they could provide cover to the left and right of the road a short distance away. Ivan would have been able to easily surprise us in the tanks since we couldn't see his approach.

With Kerscher and Zwetti, I went back to the assembly area where our supply staff brought up munitions, fuel, and food. From that point on, the troops were supplied by APCs. The "can do" attitude of these men from Großdeutschland and their leader, Lieutenant Famula, was magnificent. No matter how often I went to their bunker with a request during those nights, I never heard anyone curse when he was torn away from his sleep and once again had to drive to us up front.

Kerscher brought the munitions and fuel up front, based on the reported needs of the individual tanks. I followed with the engineer squad, which had loaded the beams for the antitank ditch. The Russians were scarcely firing their heavy weapons anymore. An occasional machine gun to the right and left of the road could be heard.

Wild confusion reigned behind the Russian lines as far forward as the antitank ditch. Ivan was exploring the area with numerous reconnaissance patrols. Often we yelled at someone who was standing in our way and didn't realize it was a Russian until he took off. Of course, none of us let himself get involved in a firefight. But despite that, or perhaps because of it, the night was especially unnerving. The Russians must have been interested in snatching one of us, and this certainty sufficed for us to practise the greatest of caution.

In the afternoon, we had wanted the nightfall; during the night, we waited impatiently for the morning. At least then we could see what was going on in our immediate proximity. Whereas in the darkness, however, the men were running back and forth, the APCs were moving about, and the Russians were interspersed among them.

For that reason, we could not begin any firefights; we were afraid of hitting one of our comrades. We had already had enough bad experience with that.

During the early morning hours of April 20—the Führer's birthday—the antitank ditch had been "leveled," and the T34 prepared for demolition. Our engineers had packed everything imaginable into it, so that it actually would disappear from the road after the demolition. We therefore preferred to get back into our tanks for a short time. The engineers had called out to us while moving by that the demolition fuze was already burning.

The thing flew apart with a murderous explosion. We assumed that Ivan would come to life after that, but nothing appeared to stir him. He had time and knew how strong he was. I made my way to the command post once again to discuss the operation with the commander of the fusilier battalion.

Graf Strachwitz allowed himself to be disturbed during the night only by exceptional circumstances. Lieutenant Famula reported that the Graf was sound asleep—and in pajamas, as usual. Famula added that he only rarely allowed himself to be talked out of doing that. It couldn't really be that bad, Famula said, if the Graf was showing such calmness.

Because the Graf wasn't there, we discussed matters with the battalion commander. At H-hour, a Nebelwerfer regiment was supposed to fire a five-minute barrage on Point 312. The observer could employ the artillery according to our wishes.

In the meantime, the infantry battalion had already arrived at our positions. It was in the ditches along the road left and right of the tanks and waited for the attack order. I looked at my watch somewhat nervously.

That was probably about five minutes before the initiation of the preparatory fire. We were already warming up the engines. None of us felt quite right. Everyone had thought to themselves that the Graf would call off the operation during the night. That would have saved us a lot of men and materiel, but it turned out that we would have to wait on an hour-by-hour basis for two complete days for the order to withdraw.

At H-hour, we heard the howling caused by the punctual firing of the Nebelwerfer batteries behind us. I was just about to observe where the fire fell, when terrible detonations made the earth shake all around us. It appeared that all hell had broken loose. All of the hatches flew open because of the air pressure. We had the feeling that our lungs would burst. My first thought was that Ivan had monitored our radio traffic and had started their attack at the same time we did. Unfortunately, that was a false conclusion.

But how could I have known that our own "wonder boys" were shooting too short! Those unwelcome rockets with their deafening noise came at us from the rear! I had experienced the fire of a Stalin organ often enough, but compared to what happened there at the time, the Russians were rank amateurs. I immediately radioed the command post but without success. Once the command to fire was given, then the planned salvo was fired off.

Only rarely did we succeed in stopping it. We thus had to endure those terrible five minutes, and anyone who experienced them will never forget it. We were helpless in the barrage of our own Nebelwerfer. Even Ivan, if he had wanted to decimate our attack position, could not have shot better.

I was never able to find out then or later how this miserable situation came about and who was responsible for it. The Nebelwerfer units had the same maps we did. It was a mystery how something like that could happen. When we were operating in the "east sack," I had requested rocket fire and it had been denied because I had requested that it be fired eighty meters in front of us. The distance was considered too short. The same people now fired on their own accord right on top of us!

Unfortunately, we couldn't talk to them to hold them accountable because the Nebelwerfer units quickly displaced and disappeared after every fire mission. That way, Ivan couldn't return the favor. After this incident, I could very well understand his feelings in that regard.

As a result of the screwup, the infantry battalion was smashed to pieces. Most of the men were wounded or dead. It was a gruesome sight. The neatly arranged beams in the antitank ditch had also been decimated.

Despite all that, I got over to the other side of the ditch without problems. I set up with three tanks, so the Russians couldn't seriously interfere with the evacuation of the wounded and dead infantrymen. Lieutenant Famula immediately sent a few APCs forward to load the wounded. We thought the time had finally come to give up our intentions. Instead of that, an order was sent: "Determine whether you can advance. A new battalion is being sent to you." Some may consider that insanity or—depending on the times—a crime. But one can't judge the requirements of such a critical defensive battle from a civilian or peacetime perspective.

As a minimum, I wanted to reach Point 312 to have a better jumping-off point for an attack south next morning. At the same time, it was also completely clear to me that we could never reach the Narwa. Ivan had long since mined the road through the woods. We moved out but only a short distance.

A tank had already become disabled, and the road had to be cleared again. I wanted to light up a cigarette. Kramer gave me a light, and, at the same moment, a solid hit shook our tank. It must have been a colossal caliber, fired by an assault gun.

This time, however, it came from the Russian side. The guns were located on the high ground to the left of us. The men to my rear had already identified the target and took it under fire. The entire commander's cupola had flown off my "Tiger." I had shrapnel in my temple and face. The wounds bled profusely, of course, but nothing had happened otherwise. The entire affair could have turned out considerably worse. Kramer had always chastised my smoking. But he had been taught a lesson; if I hadn't bent over to light up my cigarette, then my head would have been in the cupola at the critical moment. It hardly needs to be mentioned that I would have "lost my head" in the truest sense of the word.

I wouldn't have been the first one that had happened to. The reason could be found in a design failure. On the initial "Tigers," the cupola was still welded. It rose up high and had direct vision slits. The cupola hatch stood up vertically when it was opened. Thus, from a distance, anyone could recognize that the tank was vulnerable from the top.

A high explosive round only had to hit the hatch, and the entire charge then came down on the commander's head. If a commander wanted to close the opened hatch, he had to lean over on the outside of the vehicle and expose himself to the hip to unhitch a safety latch that released it. This faulty design was soon changed. Thereafter, the cupola was rounded off. The commander looked indirectly through the vision slits with mirrors, and the hatch could be swung right horizontally and closed.

The round that hit had ripped off the cupola right at the weld line. I was very lucky because if the round had hit somewhat higher on the hatch I wouldn't have got off so easily, despite the saving grace of the cigarette.

To finally get out of the Russian line of sight, we moved rapidly to Point 312, which then meant that we were in the woods. I turned to the right to cover the path that ran into our road from the north. It was intended that the tank following me would provide security to the south. I immediately identified a Russian assault gun to the north and had my gunner take aim. Ivan bailed out, however, when he noticed that we were laying our sights on him.

Kramer fired and at the same time another Russian assault gun hit us between the turret and the hull. The following tank had not reached Point 312 yet. It remains a mystery to me how we got out of our "Tiger." In any case, it happened as fast as lightning—we gathered in the ditch. I still had my headphones on, the only thing we saved.

Naturally, we quickly disappeared into the next "Tiger." The column started to move back to the antitank ditch, covering to all sides. In the process, another tank was knocked out and had to be pushed into the marsh to the left of the road.

We intended to recover the damaged tank later. As one could imagine, we were fed up with everything. If the Russians had kept the overall situation in mind and waited a little bit longer to fire, we all would have certainly come back on foot. That marked the conclusion of our "birthday present to the Führer."

After moving back, we didn't suffer any more losses. In the meantime, the Graf had pulled a battalion out of our old frontline to cover us. The Kampfgruppe, which had advanced from the north, also got hung up.

According to reports from its command, the Kampfgruppe advancing to the south of us had reached the road between Point 312 and the town on the Narwa. That was probably also the reason why we had to continue to wait. Perhaps they could have opened up the road from that location. On the next day, we knocked out two enemy tanks during a Russian counterattack.

Our damaged "Tiger" had to be blown in place by the engineers because it could not be recovered. On April 22, we moved our positions a little bit forward to make possible the towing of the second tank. The "Tiger" was towed back during the night. The Russians didn't hold back on their ammunition anymore, once they knew that our operation had failed. We received a few hits from antitank guns, because both exhaust pipes of our tank were glowing red and offered a good target. We dropped the one "Tiger" in front of the ditch.

Further to the rear, we picked up Carpaneto's disabled tank. The Russian "lame duck" biplane considerably disrupted our movement to the rear. (The superb Lieutenant Famula also fell victim to one of these bombs. He was surprised by one and mortally wounded by shrapnel while standing on the road.) We finally reached our assembly area in good shape.

We set up there in case of a Russian counterattack. At the same time, the infantry went back to its old positions. Von Schiller, together with Oberfeldwebel Delzeit, moved forward to recover another disabled vehicle. While mounting up, a piece of antitank shrapnel sought out Delzeit's hindquarters. He vented his spleen by continuously cursing up a storm.

The "Tiger" we had left on the far side of the ditch also had to be blown in place because the infantry could not hold out under the Russian pressure. They had to withdraw that same night. That was the way the third "Operation Strachwitz" ended. We didn't gain one yard of ground but sacrificed many soldiers and tanks in the process.

Our operations in the northern sector of the Eastern Front, especially the last few ones along the Narwa, hadn't made us happy despite the successes we had gained. Everyone realized, however, that our presence had been desperately needed. The infantry by itself was simply too weak to fight against such a superior foe. We had to reinforce the front by becoming the "stays in the corset." Just the psychological support that only we could often provide sufficed to keep our "ground pounders" from giving up. Unfortunately, the losses sustained by indirect fire as a result of too much milling about were too high. The mechanical problems in the marshy terrain also occurred more frequently than usual.

Proper tank terrain, where an entire company could be employed as a unit, was a seldom sight in the pathless areas of the north. Because of that, we often had to fill the vacancy of the missing defensive weapons.

"The spirit of armor is the spirit of cavalry," a former company commander of mine used to say. He, like many tank officers, came from the cavalry. This comparison is very apt and demonstrates how the employment of tanks requires the room to maneuver, something which was never available in that sector. Only by attacking and counterattacking were we fully able to use our maneuverability and the long range of the 88-mm cannon. In the northern sector, where Ivan was always eluding us, we could only rarely inflict serious damage on him. Without our presence, however, the Narwa sector could not have been held at all. We made every effort possible to come to terms with the difficulties of the terrain and, in the process, approached the limits of what was humanly possible. Even if we often cursed about vegetating in the marshy terrain, we were proud that the infantry had confidence in us and was, by and large, satisfied with us.

The final "Operation Strachwitz" was our farewell performance in the Narwa sector. We assembled at our support base in Sillamä. Most of the tanks were being repaired and had to be overhauled from the ground up. Fortunately, Ivan also appeared to need some rest, and there was no major fighting in the following few weeks.

Knight's Cross at the Hospital

Our time in the Narwa area was thus brought to a close. At the end of April, the company received the order to follow our battalion to the area around Pleskau. Pleskau is the traffic junction on the Leningrad–Dünaburg road. It lies directly south of Lake Pleskau, which stretches north toward Lake Peipus. From Sillamä, we set out to the west to our railhead. Even without the direct intervention of the enemy, one can still have a lot of headaches with a tank. The infamous rain and mud period had arrived, and even the road was barely negotiable. The wheeled vehicles sank up to their axles, and we were afraid that our tanks would sink to their hulls. Every "Tiger" had one to two trucks in tow. The trucks couldn't move forward using their own power. The mud dammed up in front of the radiators. If the tow cable was strong enough, it ripped out the truck's front axle along with its wheels. When we finally arrived at the train station, most of the vehicles were ready for the repair shop. The bulk of them had to be towed onto the railcars.

We looked forward to the train trip. We could stretch out on the straw in the cars for the enlisted men and finally sleep undisturbed for the first time in a long time. We didn't anticipate any alerts at all during the trip. We therefore took good advantage of the time, since no one knew what awaited us in the area around Pleskau! Of course, I had also taken our company dog, Hasso, along with us. But when I woke up at a stop, he had disappeared. According to accounts from the men, he had jumped out of the moving train, probably to fetch something that somebody had thrown out. I thus lost a good friend whom I sorely missed, even if he was only the four-legged kind.

The battalion had reserved a village for us where we were supposed to draw quarters. It appeared we were supposed to enjoy a few weeks of quiet. This fact didn't sink in on me until the new commander, Major Schwaner, paid us a visit shortly after our arrival. At the time, we didn't know him. He asked me to draw up training schedules for the next four weeks. That didn't go down too well with me. I was of the opinion that the men should first recuperate from the long, difficult operations. Nat-

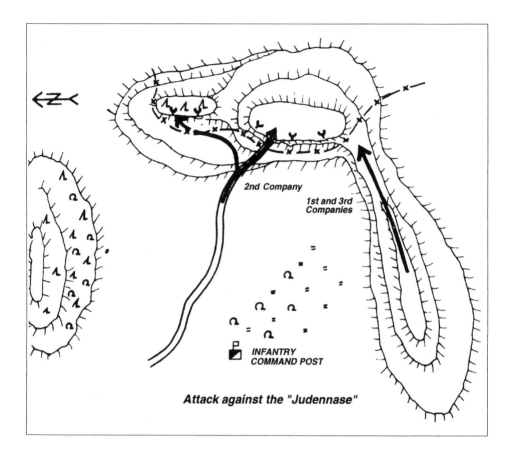

2nd Company

1st and 3rd Companies

INFANTRY COMMAND POST

Attack against the "Judennase"

urally, even in a rearward rest position, the necessary duties still had to be performed during the day. But I really had no patience at all for gunnery instruction and similar nonsense, especially since there were no green troops among us.

Amazingly enough, the rest didn't do me any good. I found out that even with the best intentions there are limits to physical stamina. I got asthma attacks, which soon became so severe that I had to stop after every step. I could only move about with a "Wolchow" walking stick. The battalion physician, Doctor Schönbeck, looked after me. I was ordered to bed and was allowed neither tobacco nor alcohol. The fact that I also didn't have any desire for them told me how really bad off I was. But after a week I had recovered enough so that I could again carry out route reconnaissance missions toward the front. We had to inspect the roads and bridges in our new area behind the front lines. We also had to establish contact with the troops in their positions so that we knew our way about in case we were employed there.

For our operations in the Narwa sector, I had been awarded the Knight's Cross on May 4. The company claimed that I had become sick only to be able to get out of the battalion formation, which had been scheduled for me. The award was therefore brought to me in my billets. The guys drank to my health, while the commander kept an eye on me so that I didn't partake of any alcohol. Everyone shared my happiness. They knew that I would be there when we went to our next operation.

Two new officers, Lieutenants Nienstedt and Eichhorn, arrived a few days later to relieve me. The state of my health had improved noticeably. Based on the peaceful situation in that sector of the front, I was granted a four-week convalescent leave. As is well known, however, one should never count his chickens before they are hatched. I was barely home for five days when a telegram summoned me back to the unit. The frontline soldier must always be prepared for such eventualities. In wartime, usually only the soldiers in the occupied territories were able to enjoy an uninterrupted leave, even though they were already quite well off while "in action" there. One gets the impression that these privileged men are the ones who complain the most now about the "miserable army" and the "horrible war." Among their ranks today one also finds those who discriminate against the decent German soldiers and spinelessly support the consciously directed hate from other countries.

In Riga, on the trip back to the front, I met Lieutenant Schürer from the 3rd Company. He had received the same telegram as I did. He cursed up a storm and probably didn't even notice how happy I was to have some company on the trip. That made the sudden departure from home easier. When we both arrived at our destination train station and asked about our units, we found out that they had already been moved somewhere else. We then looked up Hauptmann Schmidt, the commander of an assault gun battalion, whom we both knew. He promised to put a Kübel and a driver at our disposal, which would take us to our units.

At the time, however, he wanted to party with us. We were thus able to drown our sorrows about the leave being cut short. The carousing was so high-spirited that we weren't even aware of our departure. We didn't come back to our senses until we stopped in front of the battalion command post. Instead of an enemy attack awaiting us there, as we had assumed, there was another party. Schürer had been promoted to Oberleutnant. We thus had all sorts of reasons to wash down our anger. Our comrades had summoned us back from leave without any type of operation ahead of us that would have demanded it.

✠

The next day, I drove to the company. It was quartered a fair distance away in a village. At first, the first sergeant didn't recognize me at all. He was about to salute by the book because he thought I was a new officer who had been transferred to the company. The mistake was soon rectified. Happy to see each other, we shook hands. It should be noted that I had brought back a new and completely "regulation" overseas cap from leave. It greatly changed my customary appearance. Up to then, I had always worn a form of headgear that bore no resemblance to that in the regulations. It had been sent to me by my mother at the time I was promoted to lieutenant. Since then, the cap had become completely washed out, more gray than black. It sat quite well on my head and didn't have an eagle or a cockade any more; they had fallen off over time. It had always been a sore point with my battalion and company commanders. Despite numerous requests, however, I could not separate myself from my old cap. It had always served me well and sat so comfortably on my head, that the headphones didn't bother me. Even during a heavy storm, I didn't have to worry about losing it. But this was a new field cap. I only wore it in the rear area, however. As soon as I put on my old "assault cap," my men knew what was going on. The first sentry who saw me immediately woke up the crews. He knew for certain that things would be happening shortly.

I had the opportunity during my first night back to pack my "official cap" in my trunk. That was because the Russians had broken through at Ostrow, south of Pleskau. I could be grateful to them that they had waited for my return. We rolled out in the early morning hours. We reached the Rossitten–Pleskau Rollbahn and approached the area of our operations. Ivan had broken through from the east toward the Rollbahn and controlled it. We were supposed to immediately force him back with a counterattack.

We arrived at the infantry command post exactly fifteen minutes before the start of the attack. As always, I sat outside the turret with the gunner during our move. I was to the left of and next to the cannon. By doing that, we could see better in the darkness and help the driver. In the process, I had apparently nodded off and suddenly tumbled past the driver's hatch and onto the road. Once again, luck was on my side. My driver, Baresch, reacted as quickly as lightning and braked before the track could grab me. Without his presence of mind I would have died a less than glorious death. Unfortunately, a messenger had worse luck than I did. He passed a tank and cut in front of it to turn right. When he lost control because of a pothole, was run over and killed.

Major Schwaner, our new commander, was participating in his first operation with the entire battalion. He was very proud to have all of his companies together and went to the regimental command post to discuss the operation. It wasn't as easy to talk to Schwaner as it was with the unforgettable Jähde. I had already clearly stated it was impossible to begin the attack at 8 A.M. I urgently requested that the time be postponed until at least 9 A.M. Schwaner had a different opinion. He soon came back from the command post and, despite my misgivings, we had to move immediately. The entire operation was thus condemned to failure from the very beginning. The coordination among the commanders was of secondary importance. It was important, however, that the tankers be given the opportunity to establish contact with the leaders of the infantry units. They had to agree upon the measures needed to work together with us. There was no time left for that, and the results were soon apparent. After a short distance, the infantry went to ground and were not seen anymore. In their inexperience, the men had bunched together like grapes behind and next to the tanks. That drew the fire of the Russians' heavy weapons and resulted in the infantry suffering heavy casualties. Those who had not been wounded threw themselves to the ground to the left and right. Naturally, with the heavy fire, none of them dared to get up again. It was a complete mess. None of us knew a single one of the officers, and no one knew who actually belonged to whom. It was thus practically of no value that we reached the objective with our tanks. At the onset of darkness, we had to evacuate the position because we had no opportunity to mop up the Russian trenches and occupy them ourselves. Ivan was quite aware of that and didn't make any efforts to withdraw. He remained in his bunkers in front of us, feeling quite safe.

The high ground from which our people had been tossed off was called, quite simply, the "Judennase" or "Jew's nose." Readers with some misgivings needn't take offense at this designation. It had nothing to do with anti-Semitism. It simply said something about the shape of the high ground in terms that everyone could understand.

The "Judennase" was fortified in such a manner that it continues to remain a mystery to me how it could have been lost. The Russians had taken it in a raid at night. This reverse can only be explained by the presumed carelessness of our men who felt too secure and hadn't been alert.

The ridgeline rose steeply. The most direct way to it led through a narrow defile, perhaps fifty meters long. Only one "Tiger" could fit in it. To the left and the right of the defile were trench systems, which were arranged in a terraced format along the slope up to the crest. The trenches, which connected the bunkers with one another, were dug into the hill and must have been completely safe against direct fire. The Russians had a reversed front in this defensive system. We had a detailed "fortifications map" at our disposal and thus knew the location of every bunker and trench. I was supposed to conduct a frontal attack with the company. At the same time, the rest of the battalion, almost at full strength after its rest and refitting, was to advance to the right of us on a ridgeline that ran into the "Judennase." That would have meant that the entire battalion would have assembled there, one tank after another, to become an easy target for the Russian artillery. That, of course, provided another opportunity for a falling out with the commander. He was already ill-disposed to me because of my objections to the start time of the attack. I said that I considered it nonsense to attack such a small objective with the entire battalion. For this operation, one company would have sufficed completely. If it had been up to me, I would have taken four tanks with me and another four tanks would have advanced along the ridgeline so that no more than eight tanks could have been lost. If those eight tanks couldn't do it, then neither could the entire battalion because the vehicles would have interfered with each other's fields of fire. My arguments were not accepted, and I was dressed down. According to the lessons taught by the "sand table," the entire battalion just had to be employed. Unfortunately, I couldn't change any of that. One always had a good feeling, however, when there were still a few vehicles held in reserve that could recover the others. . . .

I drove off quickly and reached the defile ahead of the others. We weren't in the best of moods while moving through there. Ivan could toss shaped charges down upon us with very little effort from the trenches and the upper edge of the defile. Each of us had to watch out for the others in order to avoid a gigantic mess. We arrived at the military crest without problems, however. Two tanks had turned off to the left at the foot of the "Judennase." They followed a trail that ran diagonally along the slope to the crest and reached the edge of a patch of woods, at the other end of which we were located. I had scarcely stuck my nose over the crest, however, when I heard a decent-sized round rush past me. That made it appear advisable to remain on the back side of the crest. I later discovered that Ivan had set up assault guns and artillery not far in front of the far side of the slope. They completely dominated the crest. Any advance would have been suicide. Besides, we had reached our former positions. They only needed to be occupied. Our infantry was kilometers to the rear, however, and appeared to be sleeping. In any case, I didn't see a single infantryman for the rest of the day.

In the meantime, the rest of the battalion approached us from the right. Although I was in radio contact with the battalion commander, my own boss, he hit me from the right with an antitank round between the glacis plate and the turret. He had gone with the other group. The round knocked the wind out of our sails. If he had aimed a little bit more to the left, none of us would probably have had enough time to get out a single curse. Fortunately, he finally recognized us, and the matter stopped with just the one hit. He simply couldn't understand how I had already reached my objective.

Lieutenant Naumann, a new man in the battalion and in combat for the first time, drove at high speed at the front of the Kampfgruppe to the right. He stood exposed in the turret and could be seen down to his belt buckle. That sort of thing had nothing to do with boldness. It was suicidal madness. The life of the crew was also irresponsibly placed on the line. I immediately switched over to his company's frequency and continuously transmitted that he should drive more slowly and be more careful. When none of that helped, I gave him the exact distance he still had to drive before Ivan saw him and knocked him out. I could observe everything, after all, and knew how far forward we dared to go.

But Naumann didn't hear, or he simply didn't want to hear. He got up to the place I had specified and promptly received a devastating direct hit. His tank disappeared from view for a short time. His crew became the only one listed as missing in our battalion; no one in the tank came back. None of us approached the "Tiger" because it was in the middle of extremely heavy enemy fire. How could a tank commander sacrifice his crew so senselessly! I could not comprehend it then. Even today I still cannot understand the actions of that young comrade.

The 3rd Company had recently received a new company commander, Hauptmann Leonhard. We were lucky and won the grand prize with him. Leonhard was the kind of man whom everyone wants to have as a company commander. I owe him a lot of thanks. He always helped me, the "little lieutenant," whenever I wanted to convince the commander of something for the company.

There we were, on the crest of the hill, waiting for our infantry. Actually, only the optimists among us waited because the infantry usually didn't follow. If we wanted them to come along, we had to take them with us during the advance. At any rate, these men had taken such heavy losses in wounded that they would not have been strong enough to hold the position through the night. The Russians fired with increasing frequency and accuracy. Their observers probably sat in the trenches behind us to the left. They had simply stayed in their positions, because they had no reason to give up ground to us. What could we have done to them?

We thus lost one tank after another, especially in the right-hand battle group, which was in an even more disadvantageous position than we were. Von Wesely, who was all the way on the left on the far side of the little patch of woods, soon reported that he had received a hit in the turret from an assault gun that rendered him combat ineffective.

Von Wesely had moved up to engage the enemy and give us a little breathing space. The Russians were sharp, however, and didn't even let him get off a shot. He had barely stuck his nose over the crest when a muzzle report was heard. After four tanks in the right-hand group, one of mine, and then that of Wesely had become disabled, the commander pulled back with the rest of his "Tigers" to fetch the infantry. I was supposed to hold the crest for as long as was needed.

During the day, we could still do that even though we saw Ivan being continuously reinforced and, above all, becoming quite lively to our rear. We wouldn't have had any chance at all at night. At the onset of darkness and without waiting for orders, I decided to drive back through the defile. No human in his right mind could have demanded that I remain there overnight with the three remaining combat-ready tanks or that I try to get back through the defile in complete darkness. We made it through that dangerous area without incident and also picked up the crew of Lieutenant Eichhorn enroute. His vehicle wouldn't start anymore, and no one had looked out for him. That meant that yet another "Tiger" was left in the open, a really depressing conclusion to our efforts.

When I finally arrived at the jumping-off position, I discovered that none of the infantry entertained thoughts about coming forward that night. I was thus thoroughly pleased with my decision not to remain there. Major Schwaner didn't raise any objections and probably realized that I had been right with my moaning and groaning in the morning. Everyone has to pay dearly for experience.

✠

In the early morning hours of the next day we brought our infantry halfway up to the "Judennase," so it would have a shorter distance to our objective. The men formed a skirmish line there and were able to occupy the old positions with the remaining forces without any problems. The terrain was somewhat flat, but wooded in places, and good camouflage was possible.

To the left of the trail that led to the "Judennase," we could see a ridgeline about 800 meters away, which ran parallel to us. A Russian attack was in progress there. I could observe the close quarters combat with my binoculars and immediately fired into Ivan's flank. That helped our guys somewhat.

The Russian lines ran into a depression halfway to the left in front of us. They were about a kilometer away and could be easily seen from above. The Russians moved about in such a happy-go-lucky manner that we had to fire off a few rounds to make them be more careful. Their brazenness was often amazing. Around noon they drove with their prime movers, artillery pieces, and ammunition trailers onto the open area of the forward slope as if we didn't exist at all! We let them advance far enough down so that they couldn't quickly disappear over the crest and then lobbed a few rounds in front of them. The distance was too great to hit with any accuracy, and the drivers were able to save themselves before we hit their transportation and their tractors burned.

The Russians realized that we had redeployed, and they abstained from attacking that day. It was clear that they were going to reinforce their positions on the "Judennase." They could certainly count on us attacking a second time. In the final analysis, the retaking of these "fortifications" was absolutely essential to us. The front to the left and right of us could not be held otherwise. The high ground we had lost dominated the terrain completely. It absolutely had to be retaken.

The German Fighters Didn't Show

The infantry reinforcements arrived the following night. Using the exact drawings of our "fortress," I discussed the attack to be conducted in the morning in great detail with the battalion commander in his bunker. Every squad could thus be given a precise mission. Artillery support was also assured for the upcoming operation. Since all four of my tanks had been disabled during the day, four vehicles were attached to me from the third company. That meant I had to work with unfamiliar people. Despite that, everything went well because they already knew me.

We moved out quickly at the onset of the preparatory fire. We reached the foot of the hill in front of the defile before the batteries shifted fire onto the high ground. The Russians hadn't even stuck their noses out of the trenches, and we were already covering them with fire. According to our agreement, the infantry had advanced almost as far as us by then.

We covered the trenches with heavy fire while our men charged and occupied the first trench along the lower edge of the precipice. The rear two tanks shot it out with the two Russian antitank guns that had set up in the little patch of woods. They kept our flanks clear by doing that. These two tanks also had the mission to move up the path heading diagonally to the left along the slope. At the same time, I had to move through the defile with my two tanks. I waited until our artillery had shifted and then moved in quickly in order to get that defile behind me.

Fortunately, I saw in time that the path had been blocked by exposed German mines. It was a critical situation, because time was pressing. After all, the entire operation could not be allowed to fail because of two German mines. Therefore there was nothing left for me to do but climb out and toss both of them to the side.

I dismounted somewhat apprehensively while my comrades gave me cover and forced Ivan to keep his head in the trench. Miraculously, I actually got back into the tank in one piece, and we then slinked through our "alleyway." Nowadays we can smile about it, but a tremendous load

146

was lifted off our shoulders when we arrived unscathed at the top. Without a little bit of luck, even the best soldier can't do a whole lot. . . .

Our infantry cleared the trench system while we were covered with unbelievable artillery fire. We were lucky that the Russians didn't get a single direct hit. But what did our good old "Tigers" look like after this barrage?

The dirt was so deep on them that we could have planted a small vegetable garden. It really was a miracle that we got out of that affair unscathed. On top of everything else and to our astonishment, a few waves of close support aircraft also attacked us. They swept so closely over the crest that we thought we would be rammed. But even their numerous bombs and rockets didn't hit us. Unfortunately, as usual, there wasn't anything to be seen of our flyboys.

Our infantry comrades sang the Czarist "Volga Boatman" whenever Russian fighter bombers or Ratas preyed and swooped above them in such a carefree and unimpeded manner. It was supplied with a different and more appropriate text, however. Its ending went like this:

"You have a lot of fighter planes back home!

So send me just one, yes one of them on loan!"

We spent a lot of time on the crest and were continuously targeted by the Russian artillery. We were not destined to get out of that jam unscathed. While changing positions and backing up, the other tank threw a track due to a sloppy turning maneuver.

The "Tiger" stood there, immobilized. The two other tanks, which had moved up on the reverse slope farther to the left, didn't let Wesely's disabled tank dissuade them. They also tried their luck. Of course, both of them were promptly hit. I immediately had to come to their aid. It was impossible for the crews to bail out in the heavy fire.

The Russians observed every movement, and none of the men would have got out alive. I positioned myself next to both of the tanks in such a way that the men of one tank could climb out of a hatch and into my vehicle without being caught by enemy fire. All of them had been slightly wounded. I then recovered the crew of the second tank. The tank commander had a severe head wound. I immediately had to drive him back to the battalion command post, because his life would have been in danger otherwise.

The good major must have been all eyes when I returned alone with my "Tiger." Before I could even make my report, he was already yelling at me. How was it possible to drive back alone and leave my comrades up front. My answer was very short.

"Sir, every tank is immobilized! The rest of the men will come back on foot any minute now." I then left abruptly, so he couldn't see how the tears welled up in my eyes because I had lost another three of my faithful "Tigers." My nerves were shot after all the tremendous demands placed on them. Despite everything, we had reason to be satisfied. The infantry was back in its old positions, and the stated objective had been reached.

The nighttime was used to recover the shot-up tanks. Right at the onset of darkness, I moved out with two tanks to tow back the vehicles that were right behind our lines. We then brought along personnel from the maintenance squad. They had to weld together the track of the one "Tiger" on the "Judennase." The tank was just in front of our lines in no-man's-land. The light, which is unavoidable when welding, was screened by shelter halves. I placed my tank in front of the other vehicle to protect the men who were working.

Once again, we had our problems with the infantry. One could only drum it into their heads so often not to fire illumination rounds while men were occupied with recovering a tank. There were always people who had to have their own way and shot those things sky-high. In the process, Ivan couldn't help but figure out what we were doing there since we stood out like a sore thumb in the glow of the flares. Fortunately, everything went well and without casualties during that operation. It is difficult for the uninitiated to conceptualize such work.

One really has to have experienced just how a "Tiger" with only one track lets itself be towed cross-country. In our case, this also meant downhill and through a defile. Once past the defile, we started receiving machine-gun fire from Wesely's destroyed tank. Ivan had already "settled in" underneath the "Tiger" on the hilltop. On top of everything else, the towed tank also slid sideways and into a small bomb crater. We were ecstatic when we finally got it out of the danger zone.

Lieutenant Eichhorn's driver, Obergefreiter Lustig, whose name means "funny" in German, lived up to his name on that day. Without saying a word at the trains, he simply took off to check up on his disabled tank. He found it right in front of our front lines in no-man's-land. It was in a condition that readily indicated that Ivan had already rummaged through everything. To the joy of our friend Lustig, however, he found a bottle of liqueur that the Russians had probably overlooked. He drank himself a little courage from the bottle and then actually got his tank running again. When we were ready to tow the next "Tiger" and were moving up the defile, "brother Lustig" approached us. We immediately latched on to him so we could simultaneously recover both of the tanks that were still on the high ground. Lustig was so tipsy that he couldn't drive a straight line. We were often close to bogging down with yet another tank. The recovery took its toll of nerves and patience by the time we had finally done it.

By morning, we had brought back all the "Tigers," except for Wesely's tank, where the Russians had settled in. Supported by a patrol of infantry, we also tried to get to this vehicle the following night. Our intentions came to naught, and we gave up on the recovery effort to spare the infantry even more casualties.

We shot Wesely's "Tiger" into flames in the morning. Despite the debilitating losses, we only had one complete loss to complain about. It had been proven once again: The recovery of a tank after an operation usually cost more in nerves than the operation itself. Because of that, I tended to go into action with as few "Tigers" as possible whenever we found ourselves on the defense.

Our success had proven me right. We had reached the old front lines on the "Judennase" *by ourselves,* that is, the same objective which the entire battalion had failed to reach before. Making our second effort even more difficult was the fact that the Russians had been able to reinforce and build up their positions in the meantime.

They were also prepared for a new attack during the second operation. By contrast, surprise certainly would have contributed to the success of the operation during the first attempt, had it succeeded. When we were successful on the second attempt despite those disadvantages, it was really no miracle. On the contrary, it showed the benefits of a thorough discussion of every phase of the operation with the infantry and the artillery. If our commander had allowed the first operation to be delayed in order to prepare the attack in detail, then the entire matter would have become a Sunday drive in the country, especially since the entire battalion was attacking and the Russians hadn't properly set up yet. Decisive in every operation is the degree to which units don't work beside one another but with one another!

I always found that a proper infantryman, who had already been at the front for a while, couldn't be talked into a tank, even by threat of force. He certainly appreciated the advantage that our armor offered us, but he also knew the disadvantages of our "tin crates." We presented the enemy with a much larger target and had to put up with the barrages that seemed to concentrate on us. The infantryman, on the other hand, could keep his distance. He skillfully exploited every depression in the ground to bury his nose in the protective earth.

The armor leader was always responsible for the success of an attack. It was thus in his own best interest to ensure that the infantry followed along. But that could not be done if one closed his hatches and blindly headed off for the objective. The foot soldiers never followed once contact with them was lost. The fighting on the first day of the attack, which had ended without any success, had proven that one more time. There is now talk about constructing helmets with built-in receivers. Even if radio contact from the tank to every infantryman should come to pass in a modern war, the need for personal contact will never go away. This is especially true when the troops are an unknown quantity to the armor leader. One could transmit for a long time before the infantry went to the "receive" mode! Every good tank commander has to leave the comfort of his vehicle, even if it is often very difficult to do. He has to show the infantry there is life in those "tin cans," and that we tankers are also willing to hold our own in the open without our usual protection.

I was consistently successful in getting a completely bogged-down attack rolling again. I never had the experience where our troops remained in place whenever a tanker preceded them, setting a good example. There was something else that helped: none of us tankers had a helmet. That created the completely undesired impression of being especially gutsy soldiers. A helmet was certainly part of our basic issue, but those things hung outside the turret of every tank. They took up too much space in the vehicle. Consequently, they quickly got lost. No one could wear a helmet in the tank because there was then no room for the headphones. Besides, the thing was uncomfortable. A helmet was sometimes offered to me by considerate infantrymen whenever I went on reconnaissance with them. But the right size was never found, not unusual for people with big heads like me who wear a size $7\frac{3}{8}$.

The tankers who were new at the front also had something to learn in this respect. For example, they concluded that they were near the front because the infantry had their helmets on their heads or slung back around their necks. They had drawn a false conclusion, however. The soldiers simply didn't know any more comfortable way of carrying their helmets around with them. It was more of a hindrance on the belt or anywhere else than where it actually belonged. When we were outside of the tank, we tried to justify our situation with the words of Lieutenant Rieger: "What do I need a helmet for, if I get shot in the belly!" There was a bloody irony to these words. During the retreat to the Narwa position, Rieger actually died from a stomach wound.

"Report immediately to the unit"

After its successful operation at the "Judennase," the battalion returned to its assembly area in the rear. Lieutenant Karl Ruppel from the 3rd Company and I were sent to the forward area rest center at Ravel to be able to recuperate a bit. That was probably intended to make amends for the home leave that had been so abruptly interrupted.

Besides, we were always immediately available in Reval in case we were needed. We were to find out how much we were needed sooner than we would have liked. More about that later.

My referral to the rest center at Reval was based on a statement written by the battalion doctor. A physical had been conducted after my premature return from convalescent leave. The document stated that no more indications of a weakness in the functioning of the heart had been determined. This condition had first been detected in the fall of 1943. That meant that I had recovered surprisingly quickly! But then the findings went on:

"A four-week stay at a rest center would be appropriate due to the instability of his circulation and his reduced general state of well-being, *despite* the leave. Strict abstinence from nicotine and alcohol is another prerequisite for attaining complete readiness for duty. New heart asthma attacks can be counted on in case of future physical stress of long duration."

Karl Ruppel and I pulled out with the "express" to Reval. It is difficult nowadays to believe that we were en route for eight days. That wasn't too much fun for us "vacationers."

The train would hardly move any distance at all before the locomotive started to switch railcars once again. For a change of pace there was another stop: partisans. This unpleasant pace continued all the way to Reval.

To my surprise, the manager of the home, who already knew me from 1943, sent a vehicle to the train station. We received magnificent rooms with running water, flushing toilets, and a bath. All the men were accommodated that way. One could get back in superb shape with the excellent food and the complete quiet there.

On the first morning, we had breakfast with the proprietors of the home. We were in the process of telling them what had happened to us in the recent past, when an aide appeared. He handed each of us a telegram.

We each made a nasty face, because I had already made a wager with Ruppel during our trip that we would never have three weeks of rest in Reval. I already knew my bet was as good as won. On the evening of our arrival, we had heard about the breakthrough of the Russians along the front at Witebsk on the Wehrmacht news report.

I naturally had an idea what was in the telegram: "Report immediately to the unit!" We cursed up a storm, and my good upbringing prevents me from repeating it. We were less upset about being needed than having made the boring trip completely in vain. We had the same trip ahead of us one more time. We thus returned to the troops even more on edge than when we left.

We discovered at the front control point at Pleskau that our unit had already been yanked into the area south of Dünaburg. It had been thrown at the open flank of the Russians who were already making a rapid advance toward Wilna.

The enemy had learned a lot from us and was now marching along the same route that we had taken in 1941 unfortunately, in the opposite direction. Originally, it was Wilna–Minsk–Witebsk–Smolensk. This time, Ivan marched Smolensk–Witebsk–Minsk–Wilna! The gods of war had ruled against us, a process in which the incredibly superior strength of our many enemies also contributed a lot.

Refusal to Obey Orders

Our "vacation train" had to be divided into ready reaction forces along the Rossitten–Dünaburg stretch of the route because the area was already threatened by partisans. We arrived in Dünaburg without incident, however, where we were immediately transported to our units. It was incredible; everything looked like peacetime! The tanks were scattered about in a state of recovery, so to speak. The men who belonged to them had also pitched tents. They were sunning themselves and writing letters. Naturally, everyone knew that this nice state of affairs couldn't last very long.

Because the trains were still located with the combat elements, we had quite extraordinary rations compared to what we normally received. Whatever had been too monotonous during operations was overcompensated here to the point of luxury. Not one person ate the soup, because it was too fatty. Who even wanted the official meal, when anyone could scavenge for himself to his heart's content. It should be mentioned that the unit raised a large herd of livestock in the form of cows, pigs, geese, ducks, and chickens. A special section was set up for "maintaining" the livestock. Soldiers in Russian captivity later received sentences of twenty-five years for such "crimes." In any case, we lived luxuriously during that period. So much so, that the people back home could have envied us for a change. We ate all the delicacies on hand. No one knows as well as a soldier how fleeting earthly goods are.

Ivan frequently led us about by the nose. He pursued the objective of tying up our forces. He never conducted a massed attack to the north from his flanks. We were occasionally alerted by a regiment, but it never amounted to anything.

On July 11, near Karasino, we had our first real contact with the enemy. The Russians weren't quite in agreement with the way our positions ran there and the fact that we were slowly starting to rebuild them. We therefore had to help our friends in the infantry in occupying the dominating high ground. That was not a big problem for us, because the Russians themselves were not strong and hardly had any tank forces available. They were concentrating exclusively on the advance to the west.

During the operation, we had the opportunity to knock out a single T34, which had shown up along a wood line. Compared to what we were used to, it was a harmless incident.

It was harmless, that is, except for our valiant Oberfeldwebel Zwetti, a rascally fellow from the Styria area of Austria. After everything had already been taken care of and we were resupplying behind high ground far away from the line of sight of the Russians, a ricochet hit him like a bolt from the blue. He was standing up on his tank and was helping to load ammunition when it hit him, of all places, on that part of the body so often covered in literature. In the Middle Ages, in Germany at least, you could still say in polite society that it hit him "ärschlings" or "ass first." Besides everything else, we also laughed, which made him intensely furious. Zwetti, who had never had anything happen to him in combat, had to leave the company due to this unfortunate incident. The flesh wound would not heal without a stay in a hospital. I later saw him again at the 502nd Replacement Battalion in Paderborn, where he was his old self.

Two days later, the Russians came to life again at Karasino. We were employed in Grenadier Regiment 380's sector when I met Lieutenant der Reserve Bernd Schäzle. He had received the Knight's Cross as a platoon leader during the winter and was serving as a liaison officer to us. As a real Swabian, he also had a real Swabian name that meant something akin to "little treasure" in English. After I was severely wounded, I met him again on the ship that was supposed to take us home. Schäzle was only wounded in the arm that time, and could still walk. I therefore didn't lay about so helpless and abandoned. He made sure that I could rest on the deck and took care of me during the entire long journey.

During the orders conference in front of the command post of the 380th Light Infantry Regiment, we received an unexpected visit. A film reporter made an unannounced visit, and his film was actually used in a newsreel. To make his clip even more realistic, he asked permission to ride with me during the next operation. I was not inclined to do it, because it was already cramped in our vehicles. But since the operation probably wouldn't be all that bad, I let myself to be talked into it. For the first and last time!

The gentleman from the newsreels got in the loader's position, so that he could film out of the turret hatch. Our operation revolved around straightening out the front somewhat. Feldwebel Kerscher advanced to the east, a little bit too far, with the result that he almost became stuck in a swamp with his three tanks. I took up a position on the high ground and had great observation of the Russian positions. The enemy demonstrated little understanding for the intentions of the film man and was presumptuous enough to fire a few rounds at us. In short, the man never once got his camera out of the hatch. He always screamed "target," whenever we fired a shot. He made me so furious by doing that, that I remained on the hill until Feldwebel Kerscher had returned. If I had been by myself, I would have long since disappeared behind the hill, but common courtesy to my guest demanded that he also experience something.

Shortly before our return, the Russians came driving up with two tanks along the wood line about 1,200 meters in front of us. They didn't want to have anything to do with us, however. Instead, they drove across our front. I intentionally held back long enough so our man had his camera "ready to fire." He could thus film the actual destruction of a Russian tank. But that didn't happen. My first round missed, at which point the Russians hurriedly disappeared into the protection of the woods. The effects of our round were even greater on the cameraman. He let himself sink into the turret, as if hit, when the round went off. Our loader, impeded by that, couldn't load of course. Both of the Russians owe their good fortune to this reporter. I don't believe that our cameraman friend ever again uttered the wish during the war to be permitted to ride along in a tank. Ambition and readiness to do combat are two different things, especially in front of the enemy.

I was ordered to division on July 15. I was attached to a Kampfgruppe, which had constructed a defensive line with weak forces at Maruga, farther to the west. The leader of the Kampfgruppe had been the commander of a large city in the occupied eastern territories before his employment at the front. He wasn't quite in charge of the situation. In my presence, the divisional commander calmed him down on the telephone and assured him that I would show up by morning with my "Tigers."

Right at six o'clock in the morning, Lieutenant Eichhorn and I arrived in a Kübel at the command post of the Kampfgruppe. To be mobile, it had been set up in a bus. I reported to the general, who was visibly surprised that he hadn't heard the approaching "Tigers." He was even more astonished when I reported to him in a succinct manner that my vehicles were probably en route but would not arrive until around eight o'clock at the earliest. The high-ranking gentleman said in an affable manner: "Well, my friend, you certainly are lucky! Our attack, for your information, begins at eight o'clock!" Sometimes it isn't easy to talk to a general, especially at such critical moments. I tried to explain to him there was no way I could be combat ready at eight o'clock, because I had to conduct a reconnaissance of the routes up to the front. Besides, a meeting with the commander of the infantry battalion was absolutely necessary. The high-ranking gentleman was of a different opinion and quickly became impatient.

"The roads and the bridges have already been checked out by the assault gun people. Wherever they can drive, you too can also get through with your vehicles!"

Many a person would have simply clicked their heels and left by then. There was too much at stake, however. I explained that an assault gun had barely half of our weight and that, as a matter of principle, I never relied on reconnaissance conducted by others. I had already had a lot of bad experiences as a result of faulty reconnaissance. By then, however, my general had lost his patience. He thundered, "You! I will not tolerate 'prima donna' behavior by young officers. You will attack at 0800!"

Nothing was left for me to do but roll over and play dead. "I respectfully request the general's forgiveness," I said and turned around. Lieutenant Eichhorn had already disappeared. He didn't have a good feeling. There was absolutely no doubt in my mind that I would *not* attack at 0800. I didn't want to put the old man's nerves even more on edge, however, and I drove off. The commander of the infantry battalion was very happy when he saw my black uniform. He immediately told me, however, that he couldn't possibly be ready for the attack at eight o'clock. We were in immediate agreement with one another and set H-hour for ten. Kerscher's repaired tank had been promised by that time by the maintenance squad. As always, I could depend—down to the minute—on the tank being ready. Besides, the infantry didn't have its wire in place yet, and the commander had no communications with his companies. We went up to the front line together, and the major briefed me on the terrain. The objective of the attack was high ground, which we could see off to the right of us about three to four kilometers in the distance. It dominated the terrain in all directions. Once this high ground was in our hands, the position could be held with significantly weaker forces. By contrast, the present one was very weak. It should be mentioned that Ivan was sitting in front of us along a wood line. In comparison, our lines practically ran across open terrain. They were completely dominated by the Russians.

In the meantime, my "Tigers" had arrived at the command post. The general himself arrived around half past nine in order to view the attack. We could see that he had come to terms with the new H-hour. The day was to be more exciting for him than for us. We certainly had more experience than he did, and it wasn't so easy to get us stirred up. We were just about to move out slowly to reach the most forward lines on time, when a wild firefight started up front. It was reported that the Russians had broken through. The general was completely beside himself, but I was able to calm him down quickly. Only infantry had attacked, after all, and this type of thing was really no problem for us.

We moved out. As I was making my way over the first rise in the ground, Kerscher checked in with me on the radio. I saw him moving behind me. Such was the reliability of Delzeit and his men! We reached the old lines without difficulty. A few Russians were still slinking about in the terrain, because they had not been able to get out in time. Our men were able to reoccupy their old positions. I initiated the attack right at ten o'clock. The general directed his praise to me via the battalion signals section, which maintained contact with the Kampfgruppe. He was obviously delighted, even though there was no reason for it up to then.

The terrain was crisscrossed by many small rises in the ground, and the depressions were somewhat marshy. We could only work our way forward along the edges of the rises. It was fortunate that our objective, clearly elevated, continuously rose in front of us. Otherwise, we would have certainly lost our orientation as a result of the constant changes of direction.

When we finally had the objective directly in front of our eyes, Feldwebel Kerscher noticed that the Russians were putting two antitank guns into position on top. We were driving broadside to the high ground and toward the right in order to go around a marshy area that separated us from the objective. From that point on, two of us constantly covered the movement of the other tanks. God knows, there are a lot of things a tanker can imagine that are nicer than being forced to show his broadside to the enemy. But what could we have done differently in that situation? We had to approach the high ground regardless, and Kerscher soon finished off the antitank guns.

It was thus even more incomprehensible to me that the tank behind me did not follow. A Feldwebel, who had recently arrived from the replacement battalion, was its commander. Up to then, it had always been a matter of course for every tank commander to at least move even with me. I even had to hold back the men most of the time, so they didn't range too far ahead of me. Feldwebel Kerscher had taken care of the Russian antitank guns. He could not follow me, however, because the other vehicle impeded him. I had reached my limit, and I ordered the gunner to relieve the commander. The radio operator had to replace the gunner, and the "new" Feldwebel had to cool his heels in the radio operator's seat. How many of the men in the company were just waiting to be made tank commanders! And this one didn't even appear to have a whole lot of desire for the job! When we got back in the evening, I transferred him to the trains where he could make himself useful. In any case, he couldn't be used up front with us.

We then reached the high ground and remained there until the onset of darkness. The terrain we had driven through was completely clear of the enemy, except for this high ground. Naturally, Ivan also considered it important. Only the line across from our main line was thinly held. But for reasons unknown to me, our infantry didn't move at all. That was a decisive factor for me. While we were still able to see our tracks somewhat, I reported to the Kampfgruppe that we would be coming back. I wasn't about to remain alone in the midst of the Russians and have myself blown sky-high during the night. Nothing could be seen of the group with assault guns that was supposed to make its way to us from the enemy's rear, off to the right. During the afternoon, we had heard a short firefight from that direction but nothing else. Our mission was therefore completed, and we returned to the command post of the Kampfgruppe without incident. The question remains unanswered as to whether we should have stayed there from the very beginning. After all, the loss of the two antitank guns hadn't weakened the Russians, and we had used more fuel and ammunition than the entire thing was worth.

Nonetheless, our general was mightily proud of our accomplishment. In an affable manner, he said to me, "Of course, prima donna behavior is forgiven, if the performance on stage is worthy of a prima donna." Basically, the high-ranking gentleman was extremely happy that it hadn't become as critical in his sector as he had feared. In his eyes, we were the main reason for that.

We received another small mission farther to the west. I was once again able to get out of it before it came to its execution. Ivan had positioned artillery to cover his flank. Any movement to either the west or the east right behind the front caused the Russians to cry out or scream: "Tiiigriii! Tiiigriii!" Immediately afterward, the artillery guys fired a protective barrage along the entire front. It was thus best for us to keep quiet until something really did happen.

It should be noted that the Russians weren't about to display their tanks to us at all. They constantly appeared behind some high ground with their vehicles and got the infantry in an uproar. But before we arrived, the apparition had disappeared. The most that we then heard was the sound of diesel motors moving away. Ivan just didn't want to let us get any rest. Massed attacks never took place. Our enemy also didn't have the strength for them. His main columns drove steadily to the west, and, unfortunately, we were much too weak to be able to cut off his advance. For that reason it remained relatively calm on the flank where we were.

As our general put it, the new line in the sector of the Kampfgruppe made an "unsightly" bend to the north. He therefore wanted to have that section straightened out. To do that, we were supposed to take a village. The front line was then supposed to run in a straight line through it. I drove there with my Kübel to take a look at the matter for myself. The regimental commander briefed me. When I told him the general's intent, he indicated he thought the general was crazy. The entire village was located in a valley, in no-man's-land. Our lines ran along the high ground along a wood line to the north of it. The Russians were also on a slope to the south of the village. It would have been sheer insanity to occupy the village. During the day, one wouldn't have made it there at all—perhaps those of us in the tanks, but certainly no infantryman. By comparison, our current lines could be held by our weak forces without a problem, because they dominated the approaches. Even if this line didn't look very "pretty" on the map, it was the only possible one in this terrain.

The general soon called the regimental commander and ordered the attack on the village. The colonel was beside himself. To his relief, I declared I was prepared to drive immediately to General Berlin, to whom the Kampfgruppe was attached, to prevent the ordered operation. General Berlin recognized the correctness of my ideas and smiled about the minor "mutiny." He called up his Kampfgruppe commander, and our front lines remained as they were. Our infantry and our "Tigers" were too good for such nonsense.

This example shows, as do many others in my book, that it was completely possible, even in the Third Reich, to refuse to obey an order, if done in a suitable manner, or at least not follow it to the letter. It goes without saying that the responsibility for such action has to be borne alone by the officer or the man in question. That is also certainly demanded of the modern German soldier. In any event, I would like to see how many officers, especially young officers, will refuse to carry out an order, if it should ever come to that again—which no normal human can hope for. Most of the time, they will not be familiar enough with the situation to be able to decide to take this step. We were directly attached to the army corps back then and, therefore, in the lucky position of having an overview of the fighting in the entire sector. We could thus form an objective opinion. But each of us always had to carry complete responsibility for any operations on our own initiative, especially for the changing of an order or the refusal to carry it out. Enthusiastic acceptance of responsibility is the most prominent characteristic which must be demanded of an officer. That is nothing new, and everyone who was in the war will be able to cite examples of that. If a "small fry" undertook a tiny advance at his own initiative and the thing succeeded, then he was praised. Under some conditions, he was rewarded. If the operation failed, on the other hand, then he stood in front of a court-martial.

Given those conditions, we too were able to make decisions on our own back then. Those were decisions whose necessity later became self-evident. It's clear that such opportunities were offered much less frequently to the platoon leader or company commander of an infantry unit than to a subordinate leader of an army-level battalion, such as we were. But that won't be any different in the new armed forces. The requirement to obey *only* "sensible orders" stems from false assumptions. It will also be very rare in the future to have people who refuse to obey orders and are then not punished. It has to be that way. Military success is impossible whenever everyone carries out only the order which appears to be sensible and necessary to him (as observed from his perspective).

By this time, we were only providing security at the command post of the battalion with which we had conducted the attack at Maruga. When I woke up one morning, Feldwebel Kerscher had disappeared. I asked around and heard to my surprise that I had summoned him while I was sleeping. I had ordered him to move to the front lines and pull security there. I couldn't remember that. I also never would have sent a tank to pull security by itself, especially at night. Feldwebel Kerscher was a good man, however, and drove out there in accordance with my order. I called him back via the radio. A similar occurrence happened to me with a wheeled vehicle driver. He reported to me because I had requested him from the support base to go on reconnaissance. Half asleep, I sent the good man away again and stood there without any means of transportation after I had finally woken up.

To avoid further misunderstandings of this type, I dictated that I wasn't to be considered of sound mind until I had stood upright! All of us were so tired back then that we only regained our senses with difficulty after we had fallen asleep wherever we were at the time. Oberfeldwebel Delzeit found the best solution. If I slept somewhere whenever there were a few minutes of time and he wanted something from me, he grabbed me by the collar and sat me upright. Everything was OK then; it really woke me up! Looked at from a present-day perspective, of course, that was a very bizarre method.

Our former company commander, von Schiller, whom I had to relieve from command, was transferred back home to a service school as a tactics instructor during this time. He was fortunate that Graf Strachwitz went back to Germany then for the award of the Diamonds to the Knight's Cross and that we had been pulled out of the Narwa sector. I never found out anything about proceedings against him because no one wanted to bring up the unpleasant topic. Only Oberfeldwebel Zwetti had been questioned, as far as I knew. But otherwise, the entire affair appeared to have blown over. As far as I was concerned, it was for the best that way. Von Schiller remained as a "special purpose officer" in the battalion until his transfer in July 1944. I had been given temporary command of the company. Actually, both of us were probably fortunate that fate had brought us together. Had I had a different company commander, I never would have had such a satisfactory assignment or any of my success. In addition, von Schiller never would have been a company commander for so long, if he had received a less circumspect and understanding officer in the company. Anyone else would have probably reported him long before the matter took its own course. He even became a Hauptmann ahead of others and thus escaped with only a black eye. I believe that both of us are aware of this if we are honest with ourselves.

Defensive Fighting at Dünaburg

In the night before July 20, 1944, that is, not too many hours before Oberst Graf Stauffenberg undertook the assassination attempt against Hitler, a report reached us from battalion. It stated that the Russians had broken through northeast of Dünaburg in the sector of the 190th Infantry Division and were advancing in the direction of the Dünaburg–Rossitten Rollbahn. From ninety to a hundred Russian tanks were mentioned in the report.

I was somewhat skeptical, because I knew from experience that not only drunkards but infantrymen managed to see double especially when they are surprised at night by tanks. I thus counted on fifty tanks at the most, something one didn't like to hear either. Besides everything else, we were still about fifty kilometers away from Dünaburg.

The order to move the company immediately toward Dünaburg also arrived simultaneously with the battalion report.

Our briefing was planned to take place at the entrance to the railroad bridge, which was the only one over the Düna that was negotiable by "Tigers." Our company was ready to move in the early morning hours of July 20.

We reached the bridge over the Düna around eleven o'clock. There were two additional vehicles from the company on the far side of the river. They had arrived from the workshop freshly repaired. I thus had the handsome sum of eight "Tigers" at my disposal. It was a battle strength that we almost never reached otherwise. Five to six tanks were usually out of action due to the enemy or mechanical damage.

The cemetery west of the Dünaburg–Rossitten Rollbahn had been selected as the resupply point for the battalion. It was about five kilometers northeast of the city.

We arrived as the last of the three companies. We had made the longest march by far. Oberleutnant Bölter and his 3rd Company were already finished with refueling and resupplying. He had just enough time to call out to me while driving by. He said I could take my time.

"By the time you guys arrive, we'll have already taken care of everything ourselves!" he said in departing. I wished him good luck and then went to the battalion command post to inform myself about the situation.

What I discovered there certainly didn't look too rosy. Using massed armored forces, the Russians had launched an attack in the area of the 190th Infantry Division. They obviously had the objective of reaching the Dünaburg–Rossitten Rollbahn, cutting it, and then advancing on the city from the north. They had succeeded in making a deep penetration.

Our command still didn't have a clear picture of whether it was a breakthrough. Most of the infantry units were moving, and they had already moved the division command post back considerably.

Ivan had quite correctly recognized that the German command had tossed all available defensive weapons into the area around Dünaburg to protect the open flank, which soon reached all the way to Vilna. He also cleverly understood how to tie up these forces.

Sometimes he attacked here, sometimes there, using a few armor and infantry units, but never with a lot of pressure. The German front lines were practically stripped of all heavy defensive weapons, so the opportunity for a Russian attack appeared to be more than likely. Success couldn't remain far behind. The Russian objective was to cross the Rollbahn, advance to the west, swing to the south, and take Dünaburg. In the process, they would encircle the 190th Infantry Division and eliminate it.

The German command had assembled all the defensive weapons south of Dünaburg. It then shifted back to the other extreme. It concentrated all of the Pak, assault gun, Flak, and "Tiger" units in Dünaburg. From there, it moved them in the direction of Polozk with the mission to straighten out the Russian penetration and restore the old front lines.

When my company reached the resupply point, we were the last unit. The way things appeared, it promised to be a nice day. It was barely conceivable that the firepower that was already rolling to the east would leave any tanks left for us to knock out.

It was noon, and we had just finished topping off and resupplying. The engines were already running when a divisional vehicle suddenly came racing up from the front. A major with red general staff stripes on his pants jumped out of the vehicle, which was still rolling. He talked excitedly to the first soldier he nabbed. He wanted to talk to the leader of the unit.

I stepped in right there. It turned out that the Russians had renewed their attack first thing in the morning. The division command post could not be found anymore at the designated point. The entire situation appeared to be up in the air and critical.

Besides everything else, the entire divisional staff had been moved farther to the west a few days before. Only the operations officer had remained behind, and he wasn't able to influence the new commander, an Oberst.

We moved out on the Rollbahn toward Rossitten and then, after about three kilometers on the Rollbahn heading east, toward Polozk. We continued obstinately eastward. After all, we had to run into resistance somewhere.

The midsummer sun burned down relentlessly. We had to grant our vehicles a maintenance halt every forty-five minutes. During such halts, the crews sat on the tanks.

The drivers busied themselves with the engines and checked the oil and water. Only one question concerned all of us: "What was it like at the front?"

I suddenly heard noises in the distance. I called up Kerscher and indicated toward the north, where weapons firing was clearly heard—the unmistakable, hard barking of tank cannons. Had the Russians already advanced to the west farther north and parallel to us?

Acting quickly, I got into the VW-Kübel with Kerscher. Using field paths, we took off toward the northwest to the Dünaburg–Rossitten Rollbahn.

What transpired in front of our eyes is barely capable of description. It wasn't a withdrawal anymore, but a panic-stricken, headlong flight.

Everything and everybody was heading toward Dünaburg—trucks, wheeled vehicles, motorcycles. Everything was completely loaded down. No one could be persuaded to stop. It was like a river that swells whenever its tributaries flow into it after a rainstorm.

The road could scarcely contain the turbulent traffic. This spectacle said it all to us. It proved that the Russians must have actually penetrated deeper and had scared off all the train's elements.

The panicky race to the south slowly subsided. Only occasional vehicles still passed by us. Finally, we were able to move toward the north to find out whether the Rollbahn there was still free of the enemy.

We had scarcely driven a few kilometers, when we saw an Unteroffizier running in the ditch, as if he were running for his life. Agitated, he stopped us and cried out: "There are already Russian tanks in the next village."

We were happy to finally discover something definite and took him along in our Kübel, where he started to breathe more easily. But he was visibly nonplussed that we continued to travel north.

"I really did see two T34s," he said, out of breath. He probably had the impression that we didn't believe him.

The Rollbahn soon climbed slightly. Our guest made it clear to all of us that behind the rise, somewhere in the valley, was the village he had mentioned in which there were already Russian tanks. The village was called Malinava.

We left our Kübel on the reverse slope. We crossed the terrain and sought a place where we could see the village without difficulty with the binoculars.

It was about a kilometer in front of us and was over a kilometer long—a typical linear village in Russia. We could clearly make out two Russian tanks at the entrance to the village.

They couldn't have been there very long, because movement in the village could still be recognized. More tanks were moving over the Rollbahn.

We clearly saw that Ivan was setting his vehicles up to "circle the wagons" and await the main body.

We soon received a new visitor. A motorcycle raced up to us from the south. An Oberleutnant climbed out of it. We then received the information we desired about the firefight that had caused our reconnaissance trip.

The Oberleutnant reported that there was an assault gun battalion north of Malinava that had tried to break through to the south.

The commander had ordered the village attacked, but the only result had been the total loss of seven assault guns.

Using the motorcycle, the adjutant was supposed to try to get through to Dünaburg at all costs and request a unit from the south that would hack his battalion out. Full of despair, he was now returning from Dünaburg.

He had found out that there were no more armor-defeating weapons in Dünaburg. I was able to raise the crestfallen man's spirits when I suggested to him that he should link up with us and wait to see what happened.

It would not have made any sense for him to detour around the village, sweeping farther out to the west and looking for his guys.

I promised him that he could drive on the Rollbahn to his commander in two hours, at the latest.

We then raced back to the company as quickly as possible and let our "reconnaissance NCO" off at the Rollbahn. We didn't have any more time to lose.

The Ambush

I led my company up to the village along the route we had just reconnoitered. We then stopped, and I discussed the operation with the platoon leaders and the tank commanders. What I said back then remains in my memory to this day:

"We are completely on our own. Besides that, the situation is completely unclear. It would be too dangerous for us to attack the village on line. We have to get through this without losses, if at all possible. Behind the village, an assault gun battalion has already suffered heavy casualties. But that's not going to happen to us! We're going to orchestrate everything as follows:

"Two tanks will drive into the village at full speed and surprise Ivan. He must not be allowed to fire a shot. Lieutenant Nienstedt will bring up the remaining six tanks. Herr Nienstedt! You will remain on the reverse slope until I give you further orders. Let's just hope that the patron saint of radios isn't sleeping! Herr Nienstedt, this is your first operation with us. Remember one thing more than anything else: as long as you are patient, everything will work. The first two are Kerscher and me. Everything else should be obvious. What will happen later will be determined by the situation as it develops."

That was our short orders conference and that was all that was needed. I then took my "trackmate" aside and discussed everything with him that was important. Complete success was dependent upon our penetration into the village, better said, upon our surprise.

"I'll lead and both of us will advance to the center of the village as quickly as possible where we will quickly get our bearings. You will orient to the rear and I'll orient to the front. We will then take care of anything that stands in our way. I estimate that at least one company is in the village, unless the rest of the Russian battalion has closed in the meantime."

I patted Kerscher on the shoulder. After a short "Let's go!" we were sitting in our tanks. We quickly checked our radios, and the engines were started up. In a flash, we were over the slight rise and in the Russians'

166

line of sight. My driver, the outstanding Baresch, got everything out of our "crate" that he could. Each of us knew at that point that only speed was decisive. Both of the Russian tanks covering toward our side didn't initially react at all. Not a shot was fired. I immediately drove just past the center of the village. It is difficult to recount what took place after that due to the abrupt and lightning-fast chain of events. Kerscher, who had approached the village about 150 meters behind me, noticed that the turrets of both Russian tanks were moving. He immediately stopped and knocked out both of them. At the same instant, I also began to mop up on the other end of the village.

After Kerscher had closed on me, he radioed and pointed to the right. A "Stalin" tank was broadside to us next to a barn. It was a vehicle that we hadn't yet seen in the Northern Sector of the front. We were startled for a moment, because the tank was outfitted with an extremely long 122-mm cannon.

This was the first Russian tank cannon with a muzzle brake. Moreover, the "Stalin" tank looked somewhat similar in its shape to our "King Tiger." After I initially hesitated, just as Kerscher did, it occurred to me immediately that only the running gear was typically Russian. I fired and the tank burst into flames. After this short digression, we finished off all of Ivan's vehicles in the village, just as we had arranged earlier.

Kerscher and I later had to laugh because we had thought for a moment that we had had a "King Tiger" in front of us that had been captured by the Russians. In the heat of battle, however, such things could sometimes come to pass.

At the same time I started firing in the village, I gave Lieutenant Nienstedt the order to move slowly over the high ground. He was to ensure that no Russians could flee from the village. They could have then warned the main body of the enemy, which was closing. This measure proved to be of great importance for the later conduct of our operation.

The entire affair in the village hadn't lasted a quarter of an hour. Only two Russian tanks tried to flee to the east. None of the others found any opportunity to move. After my entire company had reached the village and three tanks had been positioned to provide cover on the eastern side of it, we dismounted to briefly discuss the new situation.

We had reason to be satisfied. The surprise attack had succeeded without a hitch because we had arrived at precisely the right time. As it turned out, the Russians had reported to their unit that everything was in order on the road. The main body could proceed without alarm. Based on that information, we could formulate our new plan.

The Russians had dragged their wounded to the road. I had them, together with the those capable of walking, brought by the assault gun battalion to Dünaburg. We couldn't do anything at all with those people with our assets. Shortly thereafter, a motorcycle with a sidecar came racing into the village from the north.

The commander of the assault gun battalion climbed out of it. He was so happy, he practically hugged me. He had already given up on his encircled unit. In addition to everything else, we then delivered his adjutant to him.

There had been no Russian infantry in the village. Anyone who was still crawling around alive was from the tank crews. They had felt completely safe. To judge by the lack of movement by most of the enemy tanks, the drivers and the radio operators had probably gone out to plunder in the houses when we appeared out of the clear blue. The village was cleared of the enemy. At that point, it was important to advance east to build up a front line as far in that direction as possible. That would make the Rollbahn negotiable again.

I quickly took stock of the situation and sent a standard report to the battalion. One of the battalion's signals sections (mounted in an armored personnel carrier) had been attached to me. Using medium-wave radio, I gave the commander my location and the results of the engagement (seventeen "Stalins" and five T34s). I also gave him the objective of my new attack, which I had determined myself. It was a village that was located about ten kilometers east of our present location. I then additionally requested that the scattered elements of the infantry division be gathered together. They were to wait until I arrived at the battalion command post with the trucks.

In the short time that all of this happened, my covering tanks had noticed that two Russians were attempting to get away from one of the two "Stalin" tanks that had fled a few hundred meters farther to the east. They moved extraordinarily well in the terrain, and one of them had something that looked like a map board under his arm.

One of my "Tigers" drove after them, but it only brought back the map board. The Russian officer, a major, had shot himself at the last minute. He was the commander of the 1st Tank Brigade "Josef Stalin," as we determined later. His comrade had been mortally wounded.

The major was a "hero of the Soviet Union" and wore the Order of Lenin on his breast. I had never seen that award up close before. Both of the Soviet officers were buried in the village during the afternoon by their comrades. I discovered that the next day when I came back and pulled security near the grave. The major's maps were very informative to me because the intended advance of the Russians was shown in grease pencil. According to them, this Russian battalion was supposed to advance toward Dünaburg on the Rollbahn after the arrival of the remaining companies. At the same time, another battle group was supposed to advance past Dünaburg to the north to reach this city from the northwest. It will be shown later how little this important map was used by our higher headquarters.

After we had passed on the necessary report, we moved east along a small field path, which led to the Rollbahn from the southern end of the village. We stopped ahead of each village that we had to drive through and quickly checked things out so as not to be surprised. But nothing could be seen of Ivan anywhere.

We thus reached our objective at 5 P.M. without any delays. The village I selected on the map was about ten kilometers east on the Rollbahn from the "tank graveyard" that we had just established. A small, brackish creek flowed north past the edge of the village. A decaying wooden bridge, which could not possibly hold a "Tiger," crossed it.

I set up my tank on the edge of the village. I had the men camouflage it well. I took Feldwebel Kerscher and Lieutenant Nienstedt in my VW-Kübel, which I brought along to every operation, whenever possible.

The VW always had to drive behind the tanks, except, of course, during battle. It always had to be handy, however, and the driver of the VW had earned his Iron Cross honestly. Because a few VWs were damaged during my beloved reconnaissance missions, they had given me the name "VW-death" in the battalion. That was a gross exaggeration, however, because I cannot remember one case where we had the total loss of a VW.

In any case, even though it was ordered by the battalion to ride in an armored personnel carrier—we called the things "coffins"—it was too slow and unreliable for me. That was because the tracks of these half-tracked vehicles frequently jumped off. One then became immobile and wasted a lot of time. The armor plating also wasn't much better than the sheet metal of the Volkswagen.

While the battalion radio operator was passing the new location report to the battalion, we were already moving out. We wanted to get to the wider road that the Russians had probably used. According to the map, it ran into the Rollbahn about ten kilometers north of our village of Malinava.

We reached this road after about four kilometers and found our suspicions confirmed: fresh tank tracks! If our luck held, then we could wait there and surprise the remainder of the Russian brigade. That is, of course, assuming that no report about the new situation had reached it yet.

One difficulty still had to be cleared out of the way. The road could not be seen from the company's location. On our way back we looked for, and found downstream, a usable fording site. We carefully moved the tanks across the creek so none of them became stuck.

Everything went well for the first six "Tigers," but the seventh sank to its hull and could only be freed up with difficulty and by moving it backward. It therefore seemed advisable not to have the remaining two tanks drive through the creek.

Our six cannons would have to suffice to take care of the affair that we had taken upon ourselves. Later on I would be happy that I had left these two "Tigers" on the near side of the bank. We needed them to help the six vehicles involved in the operation cross the creek again. Time was pressing, and I had the six "Tigers" go into position as quickly as possible behind a small rise in the ground. They were set up in such a manner that they had a field of fire onto the road where we expected Ivan. The position was magnificently camouflaged by my men.

I then had the commanders come to the high ground. I described the course of the road to them. We controlled from there for a length of about two to three kilometers. It disappeared behind a rise to the left of us.

If the Russians really were to come, just as we wanted them to, then we had to let them move their first tank to just before this high ground before opening fire. By doing that, we could nab the most enemy vehicles. It was only a question of nerves and discipline in ensuring that no one opened fire too soon. But, thank God, we had practised that so often already, that it had to work. The fields of fire were assigned in detail. In doing so, however, it was only important that the left tank fired at the first tank and the right "Tiger" fired at the last Russian tank. All "Tigers" were supposed to open fire at my command simultaneously.

I sat in with Kerscher as his radio operator, since my vehicle was one of the two that we had not taken along over the creek. Kerscher was the farthest left. If we were lucky, then everything would work out just like on the range. I was happy for Lieutenant Nienstedt, who was chomping at the bit to finally get a few enemy tanks in his sights.

We were in the greatest of suspense for about the next half hour. In such situations, minutes became eternities. We finally recognized some dust clouds to the east. If they weren't from our comrades in the other companies, then they had to be Russians. Using my scope, I was soon able to identify the tanks that were slowly approaching.

Our hopes had panned out. Ivan didn't know anything about the bad luck of his advance guard because infantry was sitting on the tanks, the cannons were in the travel position, and the Russians were moving as if on a road march behind the front. We could also make out trucks between the tanks. These were most likely transporting fuel and munitions.

Those guys were moving past us, directly in front of our eyes, as if on parade. At most, they were a kilometer away. Ten to fifteen men were standing or sitting on every tank. They had no idea that we were lying in wait for them there.

Just as the first Russian tank wanted to disappear behind the protective high ground, I gave the order to fire. What then took place would make the heart of every tanker beat faster. I was so beside myself, that I jumped out of the tank to better view the spectacle.

The panic was unimaginable. Not a single shot was fired from a Russian tank. Naturally, we didn't have any time to spend with the fleeing Russian infantry.

After we had finished off all the vehicles, there wasn't a Russian to be seen. They had slunk away into the fields, if they hadn't been surprised on their tanks. The entire column of vehicles was burning. Some of the trucks were overturned.

One truck drove into another. And not a single one could escape. By the time the Russians knew where the shooting was coming from, everything had already been knocked out—a really horribly beautiful sight! Twenty-eight tanks were in front of us, burning and smoldering. With each passing moment, a fuel tank exploded; the ammunition rattled and ripped the turrets apart. We had done a great job. I was firmly convinced that we had given Ivan something to think about. It would certainly suffice to guarantee us a few peaceful nights.

We then withdrew our tanks back to the village, and I was happy when I got all of them across the creek. This brackish ditch was welcome protection for the coming night.

The communications vehicle passed on the report of our success. My men were then ordered to rest, so that they could be alert during the night. I took a radio operator along with me in the Kübel. He would be used to guide in the supply vehicles. I scurried back in the direction of the Rollbahn to the forward supply point.

The first sergeant had set it up in the meantime in the vicinity of where the easterly Rollbahn branched off from the main Rollbahn. That was the point where we had turned off at noon. He probably still didn't know that he had to look for us in a completely different place from where he assumed we were. I still didn't have any radio contact with him.

When we arrived at the support point, there was a big, friendly reception for us, because the assault gun personnel had already reported our ambush. When we reported the additional kills, however, there was no end to the celebration.

The Hauptfeldwebel immediately dispensed a bottle of cognac for every crew. Food, fuel, and ammo were soon ready to roll. Lünneker, my "master of the airwaves," assumed the leadership of the column so that the crews were quickly resupplied. I rapidly moved on to the battalion, whose command post was located with the divisional one.

I wanted to get informed about the situation and see to it that at least a company of infantry was attached before the onset of darkness. A nighttime without our infantry friends was not something for us, because we didn't feel comfortable without them. The Hauptfeldwebel was instructed to keep trucks ready for transporting the infantry.

My commander approached me halfway to the command post. It was as if he had been transformed. He congratulated me on our success. He told me about the elation that predominated at division headquarters because the situation had been saved in such an elegant fashion at a critical moment. By the same token, it was also the first big success of the battalion since Major Schwaner had become its commander. He was thus completely satisfied, and the old quarrel between us was buried and forgotten. Men at the front don't hold grudges.

On the way to the scene of our operation, I discussed the measures that had to be taken. I also had to describe exactly how we had executed our operation. I mentioned that Ivan would not have had to suffer this setback, if he had left six to eight tanks as a reserve outside the village. Schwaner looked pleased at the remark.

"But then, Herr Carius, you would have certainly taken a beating in the village!"

I was able to counter by saying that my six "Tigers" had been ready to spring to free me in that eventuality, something which had been planned for. But, I admitted, everything certainly would not have gone so smoothly.

While riding to the front, we encountered the operations officer of the infantry division, who had the great misfortune of having to work with the new divisional commander. He had taken a look at the knocked-out Russian tanks on the Rollbahn, and we discussed the rebuilding of the front line, as had been worked out by division. The new front line was intended to be in place by the following morning, and contact to the north and south was also intended to have been made by then. Major Schwaner placed all of our trucks at the disposal of the infantry for transporting their men. We thus entertained hopes that the front would again be in order by the gray of morning.

We then drove on to the first objective of our attack, Malinava, where some of the tanks were still smoldering. We inspected a "Stalin" that was, to a certain extent, still in one piece. The 122-mm long-barreled cannon was already capable of instilling some respect in us. Disadvantageous was the fact that one-piece rounds were not used in the "Stalin."

Instead, the shell and the powder had to be loaded separately. The armor and the shape were better than our "Tiger," but we liked our weapons a lot more. A "Stalin" that had not burned out was supposed to have been brought to Dünaburg for transporting to Berlin, but the Russians didn't allow us any time for that.

A Fateful Difference of Opinion

When we got back to division headquarters, I was introduced to the new division commander. It was an Oberst who up to then had been the commandant of one city or another in East Prussia or in Lithuania. He then thought he had discovered the "strategist" in himself. He was a man who never allowed a word in edgewise from his operations officer, who had been in a combat division on the Eastern Front from the beginning. I've always regretted having to work with two divisional commanders of this caliber, especially in the last weeks and days before my forced departure home. This was especially true after having experienced only terrific men up to then. I still think back to the men in those positions with eternal gratitude and the greatest of respect. They were tactically proficient and good human beings. Initially, of course, the Oberst was very nice and asked me to turn in the awards recommendations. He had cigarettes brought to my men. When we started to talk about the evaluation of the captured maps and the statements of the prisoners, however, our opinions were already clashing. After a short time, Major Schwaner and I "accepted our place," said a short "Jawohl!," and left.

It should be noted that the Oberst was of the opinion that the Russians had only made the markings on the map *to lead us astray!* In his, the colonel's, opinion the Russian main thrust would undoubtedly be made east of the Dünaburg–Rossitten Rollbahn, heading south in the direction of Dünaburg. An envelopment around Dünaburg was entirely out of the question! Unfortunately, a few days later, I would find out with my own body how correct we had been in our opinion.

I had procured a few additional men from a road construction unit for night security. I was able to bring them along in a truck. Such protection, of course, was mostly for psychological support. It would be enough, however, if these men paid attention and kept their ears open. That was already help enough for us, because I wanted my crews to rest up somewhat whenever possible.

At the forward supply point, I met Lieutenant Eichhorn. His tank had just come out of the workshop. Along with him and the truck, I drove forward to the company. We arrived there shortly before midnight. Lieutenant Nienstedt made his report. Up to then, everything had been quiet, and nothing had been seen or heard of the enemy. Nienstedt had set up our tanks to pull security at the edge of the village. They were facing the creek and, following my suggestion, in such a manner that the vehicles were backed up to the creek. The cannons were turned to the rear, so that we could quickly "back up" by driving forward if necessary. This method had always proven itself whenever we were all by ourselves in no-man's-land. At nighttime, we tankers were somewhat helpless because we were not able to fire an aimed shot with our weapons. Because of that, every infantryman was in an unquestionably superior position to us, if he had guts and did his work in a halfway clever manner. We went into an abandoned Russian house. The peasants had already left the village in the evening, not perceiving anything good. There, using the map, I discussed with both of my platoon leaders what was supposed to happen during the night on the part of the infantry. The infantry had the mission of digging in about three kilometers west of us by the early morning hours. It also had to establish contact with our northern neighbors and then pass us through the new front lines. We therefore had to hold out the few hours until then in no-man's-land.

We sat for about an hour in the abandoned farmhouse. We were talking good-naturedly, when a guard suddenly came in. He was excited and reported he had distinctly heard Russians calling out to one another in the part of the village on the far side of the creek. That didn't seem possible to us. We still went to our tanks, however, and lo and behold, the young soldier had heard right. We now had to keep absolutely quiet so as not to draw the Russians' attention to us. All the tank commanders were then informed. That wasn't so easy, because our crews were so sound asleep after the many long nights, that it was only possible to wake them by shaking them vigorously. Yelling was impossible and whispering made little sense with frontline soldiers. I will not repeat what slipped out of the men's mouths in their half sleep when we tore them from their dreams. I breathed a lot easier when I finally had all of them halfway together. It would have been so easy for Ivan to capture us, if he had thought we were still there and had kept quiet!

The enemy on the far side of the creek became increasingly lively. We soon heard a tank moving on the other side; it was guided with a lot of yelling and flashlights. It was now time to withdraw behind the village in order to have open fields of fire and be able to survey the situation. After all, it wouldn't take much longer before the first Russians crossed the little bridge toward us.

We let loose with a suitable barrage of fire from all vehicles simultaneously. I would have been only too glad to have seen what a dumb look Ivan had on his face. We then drove out of the village. After about 600 to 800 meters, we set up a new position to wait there until morning so that the infantry behind us could dig in undisturbed. Using tracers, we shot a few houses in the village into flames. That way, we wouldn't be surprised and could also see something. Except for a few mortar barrages, we generally had quiet. Only a single Russian tank fired wildly in our direction, without precision and much too wide. It was apparently the tank that they had guided in earlier. Lieutenant Eichhorn aimed at the muzzle fire, and, after the third shot, the Russians literally flew in the air. Pure luck! When the morning dawned, we heard heavy armor noises to the east and northeast, but no Russians let themselves be seen.

At daybreak, we drove back the same way we had come and found our new front lines already occupied. I established contact with the commander of the infantry battalion. I had two vehicles remain with him. Two other vehicles were placed with the neighboring battalion. I took the remaining vehicles with me to the Rollbahn. We set up to screen in Malinava, where the Russians had been twenty hours before with their screen. The day was completely quiet, but we knew that Ivan was getting ready again and it was the calm before the storm.

The continuous sound of heavy armor was to be heard in the wooded terrain that began one to two kilometers northeast of us. We waited for the Russians to start the attack. We were mistaken, however. We were not subjected to any more attacks there. We only saw occasional figures, who took a look at us using binoculars from the edge of the woods. Whenever they became too bold, we sent a few steel greetings on over to them and the rascals then disappeared into the woods.

The wildest rumors were spread the following night: Russian cavalry had broken through, and enemy tanks were attacking, among other things. But the Russians weren't even considering running up against our defensive front. Unfortunately, we made it much easier for them later, when the front at Dünaburg was shifted and the Rollbahn evacuated.

The situation was as follows: The division had set up all armor-defeating weapons (assault guns, "Tigers," antitank guns, and antiaircraft guns) along the road that went from my supply point toward Polozk. These were to turn back the anticipated Russian attack to the south. Someone was located every fifty to eighty meters and waited for Russian tanks. But Ivan didn't come. . . .

The next day also went by quietly. The Russians brought more and more tanks into their assembly areas, however. A "Stalin" played a dirty trick on me when it shot off my right drive sprocket. I didn't find that out until I wanted to back up after the unexpected concussion and explosion. Feldwebel Kerscher identified the guy right away. He also hit him in the front, but our 88-mm cannon couldn't penetrate the heavy armor of a "Stalin" from that angle at that distance. Despite that, the Russians still preferred to withdraw.

July 23 didn't bring the expected attack either. Unusual quiet reigned on both sides. The only surprise attack against us came from two propaganda men who came racing up in a divisional Kübel. They inquired their way through to my tank and asked about my particulars. They wanted to gain insight into the situation. As the first mortar barrage arrived, however, they had heard enough. They disappeared as fast as they had arrived. I could barely recognize the situation anymore in the report about our operation that circulated through the press: There was so much shooting going on, and we tankers were so brave. If my name hadn't been mentioned in the report, I really wouldn't have recognized our operation.

Unfortunately, this type of reporting is still par for the course even today. Apparently, a reporter is seldom found who understands how to portray a situation factually and soberly and in a manner that corresponds to reality.

A report reached me the following night that our immediate "high command" had decided to pull back our main line to a position north of the Dünaburg–Polozk Rollbahn by dawn. The line that we had previously held with great effort and difficulty was shifted. It had run from north to south. It was subsequently intended to run from east to west. As I discovered the next day, the line ended at the last houses northwest of Dünaburg. An 88-mm antitank gun was posted there which had no contact to the east or west. The latter instance could not have pleased the crew, because absolutely no one else was to the left of them. I immediately drove to the division command post after receiving the report. It was at the fork in the road north of Dünaburg at which met the Rollbahn to Polozk and the one to Rossitten. It was thus at the point where we had departed east a few days before.

I also met my commander at the command post. We briefly discussed the new decision of the division commander and then immediately called on him. We wanted to be sure that at least the bridges over the culverts under the road wouldn't be demolished. It should be noted that all of them had already been prepared for demolition. During my nighttime trip, I had seen that an engineer was next to every bridge. He was just waiting there until he could blow the thing sky-high. That would mean, however, that my "Tigers" couldn't return. After this conversation, there was nothing left for me to do but drive immediately to our forward supply point in my Kübel. There I picked out a number of my men and posted one at every demo site. He had to delay the premature demolition of the bridges by our engineer friends.

I was completely against the demolition of the bridges if we had to shift the front lines back, because we weren't able to control the Rollbahn anymore. Ivan could move west over the road without danger to his flanks, something that we had always been able to prevent until then.

Despite support from the operations officer, our arguments to the divisional commander were not successful. The high-ranking "Herr" desired that we, together with countless other weapons, should await the Russian attack that he anticipated would come from the north, east of the Dünaburg–Rossitten Rollbahn. One didn't need to be a fortune-teller to see that this attack would never come. It was as clear as daylight to me, and to every soldier who used some reason, that Ivan would cross the road as soon as we had pulled our tanks back. He would do this without being noticed by us, let alone being hindered. He would then detour around the city of Dünaburg from the north and take it from the northwest. There wasn't a single German soldier there, much less armor-defeating weapons. The Russians could thus advance into the city without any enemy contact and take the bridges. They would then have us in a pocket one more time.

I got my tanks back into the new line just in the nick of time at dawn, before the demolitions began. The explosions clearly showed the Russians, in case they hadn't noticed it already, that we weren't there anymore. They could move out at their leisure. Meanwhile I still didn't want to come to terms with this type of "suicide." In the early morning of July 24, I once again spoke to division. I requested they allow me to pull my company back in order to block the Dünaburg–Riga Rollbahn. Even this request was not granted. At that point, I lost my patience. I asked Major Schwaner to release at least four of my tanks and order them to that position. As logic dictated, he agreed and had me move with these four tanks. After all, there wasn't anything to be gained there at division. I also knew, however, that my "Tigers" would be sorely missed elsewhere. I pulled Feldwebel Kerscher, Oberfeldwebel Göring, and Lieutenant Eichhorn out of the line. I had them wait at the cemetery at the Rollbahn, where we had refueled a few days before. The headquarters company was still at the same spot and could resupply us right away.

I intended to hold up the Russian tanks for at least twenty-four hours on the Rollbahn to Riga, which was completely unguarded. Then, when the pressure became too strong, I would pull back to the city and build bridgeheads. We would thus cover the rearward passage of lines by the troops, ensuring that unnecessary casualties didn't arise. As our last action, we would have then driven over the railroad bridge and conducted a passage of lines through the newly established front line west of the Düna. Unfortunately, I was not able to execute this plan to its end. Fate had something else in mind for me.

Many will ask themselves with astonishment why we continued to fight on so doggedly after everything already appeared to have been lost. One doesn't have to search very far to find a reason for our behavior. Everyone in the east, from the high command down to the lowliest platoon leader, was convinced that the enemy had to be kept from the German border for as long as possible to save as many women and children from the Russians as possible. Besides that, it was not permissible to allow the retreat to degenerate into headlong flight in order to prevent even more comrades from being encircled and falling into captivity. If events had taken the course the way that those who nowadays curse at the evil "warmongers" had wanted, then many of our women and children, and also many a true comrade, would not be alive now. I believe that every German, if not the entire "free" world, has come to the conclusion it would have been better for everyone if the Russians had not occupied half of Germany.

After all, we didn't fight for a man or a system. On the contrary, we gave our best and our all for Germany and, in the process, for ourselves. One has to consider our decision to do something on our own initiative from this perspective. We simply didn't want to remain sitting in a trap. The army had to get back over the Düna and, because of that, the crossing points had to be kept open.

Knocking on Death's Door!

On the morning of July 24—a day I'll never forget as long as I'm alive—I was with the four tanks resupplying at the headquarters company. Major Schwaner had also showed up. Once again, we briefly discussed the operation as I conceived it. In accordance with the plan, the "Tigers" under the command of Lieutenant Eichhorn were supposed to move through Dünaburg and wait for me at the edge of town on the Rollbahn to Riga. I wanted to drive ahead to reconnoiter the terrain and then meet my people at the agreed-upon place.

I still remember exactly how the battalion cook prepared a favorite of mine, cucumber salad, which I hadn't had for a long time. Major Schwaner jokingly said to me, "Carius, don't eat so much. That's not good for a stomach wound!" As he had done so often before, the commander also threatened that he would punish me if something should happen to me during my cruising with the VW and motorcycle. Fortunately, neither of us knew how right he was that time. This day would mean "contact with the enemy" in the truest sense of the word! Unfortunately, the last running Volkswagen in my company was disabled. I therefore moved out with the medic's motorcycle and sidecar. The medic himself steered. This vehicle didn't bother me; I had never believed in superstition. I also wouldn't have been any better off with another vehicle.

There was also an incident that wasn't without its comic side. In the early morning hours, the driver of my Volkswagen Kübel had came running up to me out of breath. He excitedly told me that he had been knocked out by a Russian antitank gun. The motor was destroyed, and he had left the vehicle standing on the Rollbahn. It would have been very unpleasant for me if he had really been right. I then carefully drove back the two kilometers, dutifully staying on the alert, and waited for the first hit that the antitank gun would deliver. Nothing stirred, however, and we were finally in front of our Volkswagen. I carefully got out to see from which side it had been hit. I couldn't find any penetration, however. A puddle of oil on the ground led us to solving the puzzle.

A piston had penetrated the oil pan. The bang in the middle of the night had shocked the poor guy so much that he only thought he was hit. He disappeared in a flash. That could even happen to an old vet. Nobody needs to be embarrassed if sometime something similar should happen to him. The worst thing about the entire matter was that my last Kübel was out of commission.

Riding the motorcycle, I drove through Dünaburg and then northwest on the Rollbahn to Riga. After a journey of about eight kilometers, we turned off the road to the northeast and went through a few small villages. We crossed a railroad track and then had the wooded terrain in front of us. It extended north of Dünaburg from west to east as far as the Dünaburg–Rossitten Rollbahn. There was nothing to be seen of the Russians far and wide. En route I met Oberleutnant Wolff, who led the battalion's reconnaissance platoon. He had just come back from the woods and had covered the same route that we intended to do, but in the opposite direction. I asked him to wait with my tanks, which had probably already arrived at the northwest outskirts of Dünaburg. For the evening, I invited him for some sauerkraut and dumplings, his favorite meal, which my mess personnel had promised me. This invitation possibly saved my life, a fact which I wasn't to discover until later. If his Kübel had not been available, I wouldn't have reached the hospital in time.

Riding in the motorcycle, we then drove east into the woods until the Dünaburg city line. We turned south and reached the antitank gun that formed our boundary on the extreme left of the front, but which didn't have contact to the right. At first, however, the men who were covering to the north assumed we were Russians. They recognized us, thank God, just in time. I briefly explained to the commander of the piece what we intended and that we would soon assume positions to the left of him. If we intended to pull back to Dünaburg, I would inform him.

In the meantime, it had become afternoon, and I had returned to my tanks on the Rollbahn. I took along both of the "Tigers," which had set up for security about two kilometers north of the road. The tank commanders were Eichhorn and Göring. The other two tanks followed, and we then drove the same way that I had previously reconnoitered with the motorcycle. We had to cross over a few small bridges after we had turned off the Rollbahn to the northeast. These planked bridges were so short that they held even our tanks. Only one of them was too long. Fortunately, however, we found a ford and finally got to the railroad line without incident. The trains were backed up there, some of them with wounded, and every one wanted to go to Riga. The line was completely blocked, however. The railroad men were already preparing to leave the trains, because they thought the Russians were approaching. They already imagined that they had heard a few shots. When they saw our "Tigers," they calmed down again somewhat, especially when I assured them that they could wait with confidence, at least until the evening and our return. Perhaps they could continue then with their trains. They did in fact actually succeed in getting away by train later.

I had a man from the reconnaissance platoon placed at each of the bridges we passed because all of them were already prepared for demolition. The engineers weren't there anymore, by the way, but it would have been easy for anyone to light the fuses before we had returned. I wanted to avoid that at all costs. The engineers had been very active everywhere. They had even turned around the signs in the hope that Ivan would perhaps drive the wrong way! That would succeed with the Americans in certain situations on the Western Front later on but certainly not with the Russians.

We crossed the railroad tracks and approached the village where I wanted to set up my tanks. From the northern edge of the village, we had woods in front of us about a kilometer away. We could cover everything superbly until the night fell. I wanted to drive back to the Rollbahn at night after a decent-sized salvo of fire. That was so the Russians would think that we were still there! I stopped as I approached the entrance to the village. It was a small village, whose street in the center made a right-angled turn toward the northwest and continued as a field path. Something or other didn't appear to be right to me. People sometimes get a sort of sixth sense in extraordinary situations in their lives. I looked over the houses with my binoculars and found it strange that there wasn't one person to be seen on the street. The women were gaping behind the windows, however. A boy came running up to me from the village, and I stopped him. I asked the boy in my "terrific" Russian: "Ruski soldat suda?" Amazingly, he immediately answered: "Tri kilometro!" How could he know that so well? I had just come through there a few hours before, after all, without noticing one Russian soldier.

Lieutenant Eichhorn pleaded insistently with me to drive *behind* both of the tanks with my motorcycle, because everything also seemed strange to him. Despite that, I drove into the village in front of both of the tanks and directed them into position at the northern edge. I had left Feldwebel Kerscher and Unteroffizier Kramer, the latter in my "Tiger," to pull security at the turnoff at the Rollbahn to Riga. They were supposed to wait there until we came back at the onset of darkness.

Nothing stirred far and wide. I drove along the field path in my motorcycle toward the northwest. I wanted to observe the terrain better from some high ground and survey the woods some more. I saw the roof of a farmhouse peek out from behind the high ground. It was to the left of the road. We had passed it a few hours before during our reconnaissance run.

We drove just up to the high ground, where I ordered a halt. I then engrossed myself in my map board to orient myself on the ground. Suddenly, my driver shouted: "Russians in the farmhouse!" They were already firing. I glanced to the left and shouted out: "Turn around!" Lokey, the driver, killed the machine—a 700cc Zündapp. Everything else happened as fast as lightning. We jumped from the motorcycle. Lokey reached the ditch intact, but a shot shattered my left thigh. Crawling, we attempted to get back to the village, but my strength soon left me. I ordered Lokey to scram and alert Lieutenant Eichhorn, but the loyal man didn't want to leave me in the lurch. He drove me even crazier with his remarks that Ivan was coming closer and closer. Every time we raised our heads over the edge of the road, the Russians fired like crazy. I shouted out Eichhorn's name again and again, as if he could have heard me! But people do many senseless things at such moments.

Despite my wound, I slowly crawled on as best I could. The Russians, however, came closer and closer. They certainly hadn't noticed our tanks, because they couldn't see into the village from the farmhouse due to the high ground in between.

I had also lost my map board in the meantime. My ever-present field cap had already fallen off during the jump into the ditch, a bad sign. Marwitz, who found it later, saved it as a talisman through the long period of his Russian captivity.

In the meantime, the Russians had crossed over the road and into our ditch. Every time we moved, they fired. The bullets whizzing past me didn't hit Lokey either, because he was covered by me. In the end, he got away with a flesh wound. I intercepted the other rounds. I received a shot that penetrated through my upper left arm and another four hits in the back. Because the many wounds, especially those in the back, were bleeding heavily, I was soon completely exhausted and didn't get any farther. When we didn't move anymore, the shooting stopped. Suddenly, my rapidly dwindling will to live was revived. The engine noise of my tanks could be heard clearly—the sound of salvation to my ears! Eichhorn and Göring had heard the shooting and moved out to see what was going on. In addition to my elation, my hopes were revived that I would get out of that fix alive.

But then death suddenly stood in front of me! Three Russians had approached our rear and suddenly surfaced three meters behind me. I will never forget that sight for the rest of my life. I was bleeding from my many wounds, had no more strength, and heard the engines of my "Tigers," which were probably coming too late after all.

Like an animal shot in the belly who sees the hunter coming and can no longer escape, I looked around me. A Soviet officer stood in the middle. He called out, "Ruki werch!"—"Hands up!" The soldiers to his right and left held machine pistols aimed at us.

It was fortunate that the Russians were still afraid that I could get the dumb idea to shoot. The same thing would have probably happened to me in his place. He had no idea at all what state of mind I was in. Nothing was further from my mind than shooting.

I couldn't think at all at that moment. It would have been impossible for me to draw my weapon since I was lying on my healthy right arm. My tanks came racing up then. With machine guns firing wildly into the area while on the move, they didn't hit anything. The sudden appearance of the "Tigers" naturally gave the Russians a shock. Both soldiers ran away immediately, but the Soviet officer raised his pistol to finish me off. In my condition I didn't desire to look death in the eye. I turned toward my approaching tanks. That was my good fortune and my salvation!

The Russian pulled the trigger three times, but he was so excited that two shots went wide and only one hit. The round went extremely close to the spinal cord in my neck, but miraculously not one tendon or artery was hit. So it didn't turn out to be a bullet in the head after all. I was amazed that I was still alive. In any case, if I hadn't turned toward my "Tigers," the shot would have gone through the larynx and these lines here would never have been written! Quite literally, my comrades had arrived at the very last second!

Lieutenant Eichhorn rolled on past me, while Oberfeldwebel Göring immediately stopped next to me. I am not capable of expressing the wonderful feeling of security that filled me then. The thought didn't even enter my mind that something could possibly happen to me during the continued shooting. Stabsgefreiter Marwitz, Göring's gunner, swung out of his hatch in the turret and landed with a leap in the ditch next to me.

He hardly knew where he should start to dress me or apply tourniquets. After all, I was bleeding everywhere. The overalls that I was wearing were just rags. Marwitz unfastened his suspenders and firmly tied off my thigh above the wound. Fortunately for me, these suspenders were of top quality and elastic; otherwise I would have lost my leg due to the tourniquet!

Afterward, I was often asked whether I had felt pain. No one could imagine how I really didn't feel anything at all as a result of the excitement and the exhaustion through the large loss of blood. I was just pleasantly tired and also afraid of losing consciousness. I perceived the bullets only as blows against me and not at all as pain.

When the leg was tied off, Marwitz propped me up from behind onto the rear deck of the tank. Even today it remains a mystery to me how I got up there at all. I then actually stood behind the turret, one leg hanging loose in the air. I hung on tightly to the edge of the turret. Suddenly, on top of everything else, there was more shooting from behind. It was then clear to me why no Russians had been seen before in the village: a few Ivans had already ventured up to the houses and were surprised by us. When faced with the tanks, they preferred to remain completely under cover. But then they came to life. I called out to Göring to traverse the turret to the rear.

He reacted so quickly that he jammed my unscathed foot between the turret and the hull. Because of that, I came within an inch of having permanent injury inflicted on my unscathed leg. Even today, I can't understand why not even one shot hit me while I was standing exposed on the rear of the tank. And shortly before, while dismounting the motorcycle, I had to receive an immediate hit!

We fought our way back through the village and reached Oberleutnant Wolff on the outskirts. With clever foresight, he had waited with his Kübel outside the village. By doing so, nothing had happened to him.

They then put me, as best they could, in the rear seat of the vehicle. I once again ordered Leutnant Eichhorn to immediately drive back to the road, just as we had already discussed. He was to blow the bridges, where our people stood as guards and awaited our return. Unfortunately, Eichhorn didn't follow my order.

When the Kübel finally moved and I knew I was finally saved, I collapsed completely. I was completely bled out and could only talk softly. Wolff came from Pirmasens, which was only twenty-four kilometers from my hometown. He held my head in his lap and boosted my spirits. I could only whisper: "Tell my parents how everything was and that I couldn't do anything to prevent it. I feel like it's just about all over for me!" Wolff also didn't believe that I would survive the trip, as he later wrote me. But I came home healthy, however, while my comrade died a soldier's death in East Prussia shortly before the end of the war.

I didn't come back to my senses until they wanted to transfer me to a medical vehicle. By then we had long crossed the Düna. I deeply regretted that I had not been able to say good-bye to Kerscher and Kramer. The people attending to me had also dispensed with driving me by the battalion as I had desired to do prior to my evacuation. Of course, it didn't occur to me why they took everything so seriously as they hurried along. In my misery, I also didn't receive anything to drink, although I had a terrible thirst after my large loss of blood. The conscientious medics were afraid, however, that I could have a stomach wound. Today, I have to agree with them, but back then I cursed up a storm. I had been wounded around 8 P.M. and regained my senses at the main dressing station around 1 A.M. Even today, I see Hermann Wolff dashing about like a madman looking for a doctor. After Wolff had finally found one, the doctor determined that my leg probably couldn't be saved, because it had been tied off for so long. Fortunately, however, blood began to circulate again after half an hour and no artery had been damaged. I was thus able to keep it. The doctor gave me a shot of morphine. When I woke up again, I was the "prisoner" of a cast. With the exception of my right arm, my right leg, and my head, nothing could be seen of me. I felt more than uncomfortable. I then received another blood transfusion, after which I noticeably revived. It should be noted that the donor was also someone from Pirmasens: He also wrote me later in the hospital.

Like a package, they placed me in the barracks. All the beds around me had been filled with the severely wounded. When I saw the suffering of these comrades, who continuously moaned in agony, I felt, besides compassion, deep gratitude that I had got off relatively well. I didn't feel any pain at all. I had enjoyed unbelievably good luck in that the many shots had not penetrated any nerve endings. I was able to talk in a coherent fashion with the minister who made his rounds in the morning.

The first one to visit me the next day was my commander, Major Schwaner. Tears welled up in both our eyes when we saw each other again. I then made my report: "Contact made with the enemy." When he saw me, he even forgot to chew me out because of the motorcycle, which was now in the junk pile. It had been the last one in the company.

Oberfeldwebel Delzeit appeared after Major Schwaner. I felt how difficult it was for him to keep the truth from me. I then knew for certain that I had to say farewell, the most difficult farewell of my life up to then. Of course, I talked some rubbish about how I would soon be back in the company again. Delzeit believed even less than I did that I really could keep that promise.

As a consolation, the battalion adjutant brought some news along for me. After our big success, the corps headquarters had turned in my name for the Oak Leaves. I wouldn't discover until back home that this report wasn't just a consolation.

My condition improved noticeably during the day. I noticed this change because I got an urge for a cigarette. The doctor, who wanted to deny me the cigarette, remarked that I had been shot in the lungs, something which strictly ruled out smoking. I continued to plead, however. It was precisely through smoking that I could prove that my lungs were in order: In case my lungs had been penetrated, the smoke would have to escape out of the wounds in my back. The medical man couldn't deny my logic. My persistency in begging had probably convinced him that things were looking up for me again.

I continued to grumble about my fate, however. I simply couldn't understand why I had to get shot right then, when my fellow soldiers needed me so much. On the day I was wounded, of all days, I had officially been named company commander by battalion order. Unfortunately, the pleasure of receiving that post had been of short duration.

At first, I was supposed to be flown back to Germany in a Storch, but there were so many soldiers who needed the transport more urgently and sooner than I did. I was thus in the main dressing station for another two days. During their daily visits, my comrades reported all the news that had happened to our unit. They told me that Lieutenant Eichhorn had not moved back on that night and that on the next day he had let himself be misled into frontally attacking a village, which was occupied by strong Russian tank forces. Of course, he had been repulsed. Eichhorn was a superb officer, but he still lacked the necessary experience. He had only been in the company for a short time, after he, a former paymaster, had voluntarily attended the school for armor forces.

The men also related how he had only reached the Rollbahn, which Ivan already controlled with his tanks, to Riga with great difficulty. The unit had run the gauntlet between "Stalins" and T85s. Only one "Tiger" had reached the bridge over the Düna, which was already under enemy fire. Our company had more casualties dead and wounded on this one unlucky day than in all previous operations. The men who could get out of their burning tanks had to swim across the Düna to get to safety. Our company never recovered from this severe blood-letting. Nienstedt and Eichhorn were soon wounded, and new officers arrived who weren't so close to the troops. Major Schwaner was also later replaced by a commander who was a complete failure. The rest of our tanks were farmed out individually and were lost one after another.

With a heavy heart, I went back to the homeland. I was loaded on a ship in Reval. The Russians had already broken all rail connections. After fourteen days, I arrived in Germany. In Swinemünde, we were put on wonderfully clean hospital trains. For the first time in a long time, I lay in fresh, white sheets, almost too good for a common soldier such as myself.

When I arrived in Lingen on the Ems, I weighed all of eighty-seven pounds. At that time, I didn't believe I would be making my first attempts at walking by the end of September.

It was in the hospital that I first read in an old newspaper that a fellow soldier had brought with him that I had been awarded the Oak Leaves on July 27, 1944. I was the 535th soldier of the Wehrmacht to receive that award.

Rapid Recovery in the Hospital

Of all the untold good wishes from the front and from home, I enjoyed the letters that my company sent me in the hospital the most of all. Of those, I especially enjoyed the writings of my fatherly friend, the term that I really must apply to our Stabsfeldwebel. I was always up-to-date on the company through his letters. Rieger had written quite guardedly to my mother when he couldn't find out anything definite about me. He wanted to determine whether I had made it home alive.

We were corresponding with one another shortly thereafter. It still makes me happy today that my mother put away and saved all correspondence from that time.

In the first lines I sent to the company from the hospital, I asked whether Kerscher, Kramer, Göring, and Lönneker had received the awards I had requested for them while still at the main dressing station. In response to that, I received the following reply from Rieger on September 5: "Göring, Kerscher, and Kramer haven't been submitted yet. There is no longer an officer in the company who will pursue the matter!"

I wrote to the battalion by return post and received the following good news on November 17: "Feldwebel Kerscher and Unteroffizier Kramer have been awarded the Knight's Cross; Oberfeldwebel Göring the German Cross in Gold. The concerns that burden you have been eliminated by the presentation of these awards. I am especially proud that they are the first sergeants of the battalion to whom this high decoration has been awarded."

My recovery actually proceeded too quickly. The doctor determined that my upper thigh bones had already become so set during the fourteen days my medical evacuation lasted, that an adjustment of their length appeared impossible. Despite that, I was still put in a Thomas stretch splint. That was a fine affair! Despite all efforts, however, my leg remained shorter. I was just happy that it had set so quickly.

One morning I received a letter with the return address of Department P5 of the OKH, also known as the medal department. In it, I was asked to report my ability to walk so I could be ordered to Hitler's head-quarters for the official award of my Oak Leaves.

I replied, asking whether they couldn't also send me this award. The answer: "Because the Führer has reserved to himself the right to hand out the Oak Leaves, a transmittal of the award through the home-front High Command of the VI Army Corps is not possible. As soon as you are able to personally report to the Führer, you need to report that to OKH/PA/P 5 1 in a timely fashion, so that an appropriate report can be initiated here."

The only aspect about these laconic lines that made me happy was the short, handwritten greeting at the bottom: "With best wishes for a speedy recovery! Johannmeyer, Major." I thus discovered that this superb man was still alive. We had given up hope on him at Newel.

In the middle of September, I made the first attempts at walking after the weights had been removed from my leg. Walking on crutches has to be learned, however. I made this unfortunate discovery during my first excursion.

It was, of course, a forbidden flight to a certain locale. Everyone looks forward to this place after they have been chained to a bed for a long time. Of course, I wanted to go down the first step leg-first instead of with the crutches. I promptly fell, naturally on the injured leg. My first thought was that my thigh bone, which hurt like hell, had been broken again. Besides everything else, the doctor would make short work of me. But I was lucky. The medic brought me back to bed. Walking went better the next day. Through hard training, I got to the point after fourteen days that I could walk with two canes. After an additional fourteen days, things were working with only one cane. I then sent off my report that I was "ready to roll." I was eager to learn when I would be ordered to the Führer's Headquarters. I wanted to see, once and for all, what the mood was there, because I had already had my doubts about the successful con-clusion of the war for some time.

At the end of October, I was ready. I was ordered to Salzburg, where I was supposed to report to the local commander for additional instruc-tions.

Traveling by train back then was no longer a simple procedure. The Lingen–Salzburg route wasn't exactly short either. Our train didn't even enter Salzburg. The final stop was a small station in the suburbs, where I shaved to get myself "inspection ready." Suddenly, there was an air raid alarm. Everybody ran into the air raid shelter, except for two other soldiers and me. We looked at the bomber formations out in the open.

They were flying a straight course in neat formations toward Munich. They didn't even let themselves be bothered by the antiaircraft guns, which were well represented. Their fire no longer even had a psychological effect.

Those guys came back on the same route a short time later. Only one straggler flew somewhat low. He appeared to be hit. We wanted to view its demise, of course, when the plane suddenly dropped its bombs scarcely 100 meters in front of us. Apparently, he had been saving them for Salzburg. We soon lay with our noses pressed in the dirt, but we got off with a scare.

The bomber got the worst end of the deal. It was hit by flak and slammed into the mountains. But then my fine "inspection uniform" looked like I had just come directly from the front!

My suspicions were confirmed at the city commander's office. The Führer's Headquarters wasn't in this area at all. It was intended that Himmler give out the decoration. His staff was located in a suburb of Salzburg. Himmler wasn't just the leader of the SS. He was also simultaneously the head of all police, the minister of the interior, and the commander of the replacement army, that is, of the replacement units of the army itself.

All the offices were housed in a special train located directly in front of a tunnel. During air raid alerts, it was shunted into it. I had envisioned the guards being more exacting. Two sentries made their rounds on each side of the train. They didn't even ask us for our identification papers when we climbed onto the train steps.

The army liaison officer, a Major, attended to me and directed me to a compartment in the guest car. He said I didn't need to hurry since my meeting with Himmler wouldn't occur for another two days, at a minimum.

He also said that the commander of the 1st Company of the 502nd, Oberleutnant Bölter, had departed a day before. He had received the Oak Leaves three months after I did and had also come to that location for the award. It was very upsetting that I had missed him. Up to this day, I have never seen him again.

I was then a guest of the staff. All the officers were happy whenever they had a visit because they were then allowed to attack the bottle of schnapps reserved for honoring the guests. Himmler was very strict. He didn't drink alcohol himself. And everyone, from the general down to the lieutenant, had to peel their own boiled potatoes during the meal.

The major guided me through the individual sections of the train. I was amazed that so many offices were housed in the cars. Of course, one question interested me the most: "What course will the war take, and what do they think about it here?"

Many new weapons were being shown in the movies: jets and manned antiaircraft rockets. There were already so many reports of volunteers to crew the rockets that only a small portion of them could be used.

I saw these reports on the volunteers with my own eyes! It was intended to bring down several bombers at one time with these rockets. Other items had been shown: remote-controlled antiaircraft bombs, new types of poisonous gases (Tabun), and new submarines that couldn't be detected by sonar. There were also night vision devices for tanks and long-range bombers, which could reach America.

The "smashing of the atom" was also portrayed by means of a model. That was a process I couldn't follow with my knowledge back then. It didn't become clear to me until after the war in the course of my studies. I also discovered that "heavy water" was required for this process.

Through treachery, our factory in Norway had fallen victim to an attack. Even the two railcars that were able to be saved were blown sky-high on the ferry that was intended to bring them to Germany. It was claimed that this loss had set us back a minimum of two years. Because of that, the Eastern and Western Fronts had to be kept clear of the German borders for at least a year. Of course, the details of the assassination attempt of July 20, 1944, were also discussed. For me, the only "resistance fighter" in the true sense of the word was Graf Stauffenberg. Initially an enthusiastic frontline officer, he became acquainted with the actual situation of the war after his wounding and subsequent assignment to the Führer's Headquarters. He decided to act, and he followed his convictions. It is perhaps noteworthy that it was a proven frontline officer, of all people, who took action and sacrificed himself for his convictions.

He was among the most capable General Staff officers in the army. On top of that, he was a man who had lost all of his right hand, part of his left, and also an eye through wounds. The fact that Graf Stauffenberg didn't join the resistance group until late is proof positive of the indecisiveness of all the others who had planned an assassination since 1938 but who had never found an executioner. In all those years, no one was found who could simply draw his pistol and fire the decisive shot.

Almost all of us front soldiers believed that we were putting our lives on the line for something good and that we would win the war, but no one knew for certain. The leaders of the resistance groups were not only convinced that their sacrifice would be beneficial to the fatherland, but they also *knew* that only the *timely* liquidation of Hitler could save Germany.

This is according to statements of the survivors and the judgment of the biographers. From every soldier in the world, it is demanded that he put his life on the line for his country during war. He must do this without asking whether he will sacrifice himself for a good and just cause, or even for one that promises success.

Why then are we supposed to relieve the men of the resistance groups of their obligation to go into action in a timely and ruthless fashion? They knew, after all, that their deeds and their sacrifices could only save Germany when they acted in a timely fashion. The failure to act on that last factor remains incomprehensible to us combat soldiers.

What would have happened if Hitler really would have been killed on July 20, 1944? What hopes could Germany have placed in these men who, after so many years, didn't understand how to plan an attack on Hitler that simply *had* to be successful? The conspirators never would have been in control. In any case, as can be proven, the laughing third party was the Allies, who never were ready to offer guarantees to the resistance group.

The hate of the western world, and the even more justifiable hate of the Russians, didn't just apply to Hitler. It applied to the entire German population as well. Just look at the treaty in Yalta and the negotiations that led to it.

Whoever wants to start a revolution has to place his bet on one card. Either that or he has to give up the rebelling and submerge among the army of gripers and saboteurs who were, are, and always will be in every state and every regime. Every decent combat soldier will resist, and rightly so, the fact that secret grumbling and treacherous sabotage are valued higher than the risk of one's life at the front, especially when the survivors and those in on the secret of the resistance groups often allowed modesty, which characterizes true idealists, to disappear after 1945.

Unfortunately, the men who were executed after July 20, 1944, didn't obtain anything for their people. Many of them acted out of conviction. In no way, however, have they earned more recognition and respect than any soldier who died faithfully and silently at the front for his homeland. The dead of the resistance groups did not risk or lose any less, but also not any more, than those who fell in battle: their lives.

A Visit with Heinrich Himmler

The time finally arrived that I was supposed to report to Heinrich Himmler. The major reemphasized to me that I shouldn't mince words. Himmler liked it when someone openly expressed his opinion. I was supposed to do just that during our conversation.

The staff headquarters was in a villa, where Himmler lived as long as the train wasn't going somewhere. I had to check my briefcase at the entrance cottage. Nobody asked me for my pistol! Before I was admitted, an SS-officer briefed me one more time. Himmler was addressed, as I already knew, simply as "Reichsführer" and not as "Herr Reichsführer." Furthermore, my hat had to be tucked under my arm before I entered. That was in contrast to the Wehrmacht, where we reported to our superiors under cover. Everything was understood, and we could start. I had no illusions after everything I had heard about Himmler. It didn't help that we didn't have any great love of the SS either.

I reported succinctly: "Oberleutnant Carius, commander of the 2nd Company of the 502nd Heavy Panzer Battalion, reports as ordered, following convalescence." It did cost me some effort, however, to leave out the customary "respectfully reports . . ." I also had to make an effort not to address him in the third person but rather just use the word "you." Once in a while the "power of convention" scored a victory, especially during the conversation after the meal. But I didn't lose my head because of it or because I asked everything that was on my mind.

Himmler had stood up. "In the name of the Führer, I am presenting you the Oak Leaves to the Knight's Cross, which were awarded on July 27, 1944. The Führer extends an apology, because up to now he has always personally presented the award. The Führer is overburdened. He has empowered me as the Chief of Staff of the Replacement Army to present the Oak Leaves to you and to extend his best wishes for a speedy and complete recovery of your health. I personally congratulate you from the bottom of my heart. You can certainly be proud, because you are the youngest bearer of this award in the entire army!" Himmler approached me, shook my hand, and gave me the Oak Leaves in a case. He then said in a friendly manner:

"We'll now want to go over to dinner. The guests are probably already waiting. We will be able to converse in private after dinner."

After a short, military thank-you, I put the little box into my breast pocket and went into the anteroom. Himmler was already next to me, however, and said: "My dear Carius, that simply won't be allowed. I'm going to introduce you shortly as 'freshly decorated,' after all. You are going to have to have that thing around your neck, for better or for worse!"

He removed the "paper clip," which held the Knight's Cross securely on the ribbon, and added the Oak Leaves. He then tapped me on the chest and said: "That's probably your own invention? I will recommend it to my men. Some of them are also wearers of that kind of necktie." He was talking about the elastic band from the driving glasses. It could be placed comfortably around the neck regardless of neck size. This manner of wearing it was especially practical with shirts.

My first impressions of this man, whom his opponents called a "bloodhound," had really pleasantly surprised me. I wasn't apprehensive about the upcoming "cozy" conversation anymore.

Himmler and I went to the dining room, where approximately fifteen to twenty men rose from their places. I was introduced to the entire group and was given the seat to the right of Himmler. I was soon able to determine that the majority present were generals, together with a few men in civilian clothing. The conversations were extremely interesting for me. Two SS-generals had been ordered back from Yugoslavia to discuss the additional measures that were intended to be undertaken there. It should be noted that the partisans were at odds with one another. The old animosity between the Serbians and the Croatians continued to exist and had been exploited by our leadership for a long time. We thus supplied the Croatians with weapons. We now wanted to recruit them and use them for ourselves.

A few of the civilians were from the armaments industry. According to them, the main problem that had to be solved soon and under all circumstances was air defense. Of course, that was also clear to any layman who had viewed and been horrified at the devastation of our cities. I would have been only too happy to discuss that topic even longer with those men, especially since this was the only place where I could have discovered whether there still could have been the chance of a successful conclusion to the war.

The meal was appropriately simple, given the times. There was soup, followed by meatballs, vegetables, and potatoes. It should be noted that in honor of the guest the potatoes were peeled and not in their jackets! Finishing up were preserved pears. At any rate, it was certainly no luxurious meal. When I was finished with the first serving, I naturally wanted to stop.

Himmler gestured to the orderlies, who were all SS-Scharführer, and personally put some more on my plate. He was in a good mood and said: "Eat up, Carius. You don't look as though you need to hold back. On the contrary, you ought to gain some weight. Otherwise, a quick release from the hospital is not at all conceivable." To the laughter of all assembled, he pointed to a general who had already put on a little fat. "Carius, you have to put on at least half of that weight!"

Himmler had on a simple field grey uniform. He didn't wear any type of piping or decorations. It amazed me that this man was supposed to be so dangerous. I thought that probably anyone who has to ensure order behind the front in a country at war is unpopular, because he is forced to be uncompromising.

Coffee was then poured. Himmler had it brought into his work area, where he renewed his official discussions. It should be noted that he neither smoked nor drank any alcohol. As the "guest of honor," I was given time to drink my coffee in a leisurely manner and smoke a cigarette. Then came the big moment, when I started my long conversation with Heinrich Himmler. Based on memory, I will attempt to render our conversation as accurately as possible.

Himmler's work area was decidedly modest. The room was very large, but nothing more remains in my memory than a large desk. It was off to the right rear and against the corner. A comfortable grouping of armchairs was in the opposite corner.

We sat down in a relaxed manner in the chairs next to a small, round table. Later on, I've often had to think about this conversation whenever it was said that one could never get close to the "big men" of the Third Reich. For half an hour, I sat alone with Himmler at the table, at ease and with a pistol.

At that point, our informal conversation began. It is still vivid in my mind even today. After a few friendly introductory words, Himmler asked: "Oberleutnant Carius, do you believe that armor will soon be outmoded and eliminated by the development of handheld weapons?"

I answered very frankly: "Reichsführer, I do not share this opinion. You know that the Russians have used hunter/killer troops for a long time. They have almost never achieved anything, however, whenever our tanks were employed together and they covered each other. If infantry was also there, then it was difficult for anything to happen. The probability of a hit with bazookas and similar weapons at greater distances is very small. If the tank crews are alert, then soldiers with those weapons can definitely only shoot one time. Hunter/killer teams have had an easy time of it with the English and the Russians, whenever they drove with closed hatches. Our battalion, however, has only lost a single tank to this method. That was on the Newa. It was due to the stupid employment of a single 'Tiger,' and it was our own fault. Besides, for our antipersonnel security, we also have six close-in mines on the turret. When needed, they can be set off from inside. But I've never needed to make use of them."

Himmler had listened attentively and then suddenly changed the topic: "What do you think about the attitude of the people back home? You've certainly had the opportunity forced upon you to gain an impression here as well."

I didn't feel one bit shy about this very direct question, and I said quite openly what I thought about it.

"Reichsführer, there is no doubt at all that the people have become rather unnerved by the terror attacks. Everyone is waiting for a weapon that can knock this horrible enemy out of the air." I hesitated for a moment and then continued without concern:

"Many people, myself included, are disgusted by the boastful speeches of certain party people who always act as if the war were already won and our final victory a given." Himmler now looked at me with great attentiveness.

"In my opinion," I continued without hesitation, "our people have already shown that they are strong enough to discover the truth. They also know that we will have to continue to work hard to change the fortunes of war. Could it be arranged that experienced and decorated frontline generals occasionally come to Germany and talk to the people? These people enjoy more respect than the party people, who actually know nothing at all about the front themselves. Because of that, they only speak empty words, probably directed from higher up."

Would Himmler blow up now, I thought to myself, after I had described certain party people in such a derogatory manner? Nothing of the sort. The Reichsführer-SS answered quite calmly:

"I am aware of the suffering of our people. I also know that the fundamental condition for our continued holding out has to be our new aerial defenses. In a relatively short time, we will be able to prevent the Americans from flying in 'parade formation' above us. Our new jet aircraft will soon be put into operation. New flak rockets, some manned and some radio controlled, have already been tested. A little while ago, you sat at the table with the responsible gentlemen. You are correct, my dear Carius. Without wide-reaching prevention of the bombing, we will not be able to hold out much longer, but all that will look completely different shortly."

At that point, Himmler hesitated for a moment. "The prerequisite, to be sure, is that our fronts can be held at all costs for another year. We need this one, uninterrupted year to finish the weapons that we're building to surprise the enemy!" With these words, I thought about the old saying: "I hear the message fine; it's just believing it that's hard!" But at the same time I glimpsed a ray of new hope. Himmler continued:

"Concerning your criticism of the party leadership, I also have to admit you're right, Carius. You yourself know that the best people are at the front. I simply could no longer disapprove their requests to volunteer. When we win the war, and we have to win it, then we will soon remedy the abuses that prevail here right now. We will replace the incapable men with proven ones!"

He suddenly changed the topic again:

"Wouldn't you like to switch to the SS? We are looking for young and proven people. In a few weeks, you could be a Hauptsturmführer!" Nothing was further from my mind than leaving my tankers. I answered promptly:

"No, Reichsführer. My conservative background forbids me from 'abandoning the flag.' I only want to return to my old company. I also don't intend to go active. I think that the rivalry between the Wehrmacht and the SS up to now has only had a negative effect for everyone. Without any reservations, we in the army recognize the great achievements of the SS at the front. But you also can't forget that the SS-units have the best people and the best material; that is, they have continuously received preferential treatment. That's already frequently caused bad blood with the other units."

Even these remarks didn't produce a rise from Himmler.

"In regard to your worries about the rivalry between the Wehrmacht and the SS, I can tell you today that efforts have been under way for some time now to combine both forces. It should be noted that these efforts have continuously failed due to the stubbornness of the Wehrmacht generals."

This remark by Himmler made me happy, because it proved to me that our generals really did have more backbone than one usually assumed. The introduction of the "German greeting," or Nazi salute, after July 20 had already made me extremely upset.

I hoped the generals would remain resolute. The SS could join us after all, since we were certainly there first, but many things indicated that the SS wanted to swallow the Wehrmacht. Himmler was already the chief of staff of the entire Replacement Army, which included all elements of the Wehrmacht. In that capacity, he had just given me the Oak Leaves. Himmler then began to talk about personal matters.

"Do you have any personal wish that I can fulfill? Perhaps special leave, or something similar?"

I immediately requested a certificate from him that my duty status would be changed to "return to duty" after my return. I also requested that I should be sent immediately to my unit by the replacement battalion.

Himmler smiled in disapproval.

"That's really not going to happen, my dear Carius. I can't let you go back to the front for another two months. You can't finish yourself off before the end of the war. You have to recover for another couple of weeks or months in the replacement battalion. There is still enough time in the spring to return to your unit. You people at the front always want superbly trained replacements, but you never feel like training a few men yourselves."

After a little give and take, I finally succeeded in receiving something in writing. In it, I was to be considered as capable of returning to duty effective January 1, if I so desired, and I was to be transferred immediately to my old company, if I didn't want something else. I was later able to use this piece of writing quite effectively.

Our conversation drew to a close. Himmler asked me whether I was acquainted with Salzburg and its vicinity. When I answered negatively, he kindly placed a car and driver at my disposal. In departure, he reached out his hand to me and said: "If you should ever have difficulties anytime or anywhere, please don't hesitate to write to me. You can turn to me at anytime! With that, I was dismissed in "good graces."

I described my visit with Heinrich Himmler in such detail, because he really surprised me. After the conversation in his staff headquarters, I gathered some hope for a successful conclusion to the war. That was after I had already considered a defeat almost certain.

It doesn't matter what view one has of the Third Reich; the truth requires one to describe those men as they really were. I received a vehicle from Himmler for a short joyride. The driver introduced me to the wonderful region. He drove me to Berchtesgaden to the "Tea House," which was commonly called the "Eagles' Nest."

Besides that, he also showed me the Obersalzberg Mountain. I would have also enjoyed visiting my father, who was employed on the Yugoslavian border. Unfortunately, I couldn't find out his location and didn't discover until after the war that I could have easily made that detour in three days. That would have brought me the greatest happiness back then.

During the time I lived in the special train following my award ceremony, reports that came in from the front were constantly being discussed. The commander of the IVth SS Panzer Corps, General Gille, telephoned quite frequently. His corps had been brought back up to strength and was in reserve in the Northern Sector of the Eastern Front, right behind the front lines. Of course, that was extremely interesting for me.

We discovered that the Russians had assembled massive forces in this area with which they wanted to start their big offensive. This later ended with the capture of Berlin, thanks to the western powers who politely waited in place to give the Russians the honors.

Hitler, however, did little justice to his title as "the greatest commander-in-chief." In any case, his directives back then were more than unfortunate. For instance, he pulled Panzer divisions out of the Northern Sector shortly before the Russian attack and moved them to the south, where we intended to initiate an offensive. According to Hitler's plan, this advance was supposed to cause the Russians to withdraw a portion of their forces to the south and thus spread themselves out. But they didn't do us the favor. The times had long since past where Ivan was taken in by such maneuvers. Unfortunately, the Russians knew what condition we were in. In any event, the divisions were shipped to the south and ordered to attack immediately.

The result was that the Russians had an easy time of it. In some cases, the infantry attacked first without the tanks; in others, just the opposite occurred. Our attack in the south was repulsed and the divisions were, for the most part, wiped out.

Contrary to all strategic and operational dictates, General Gille had to remain right behind the front. His corps was thus unable to deploy to the front after the Russian breakthrough. His units were immediately overrun during the initial Russian advance and drawn into the general confusion of the withdrawal.

They were thus unable to bring their influence to bear. If the requests of Gille and other commanders had been granted (to move the corps farther to the rear in reserve), then these well-equipped men could have certainly stopped the Russians. Later, their advance couldn't be stopped anymore. The advance guard of the Russian tanks had already showed up at the gates of Küstrin in January.

By then, I had become acquainted with the region around Salzburg and waited for my return to the hospital. After three days, two SS-officers who wanted to drive to Berlin gave me a ride. I was happy to be spared the long train trip.

It was also nice that I had the opportunity to drop in on the Army Personnel Office in Berlin. I had to make do with the train afterward. On the trip from Salzburg to Berlin via Munich, I learned to appreciate the car radio, which I normally didn't care for much at all. That was because we could hear where low-flying planes were reported. Only because of that did some people escape being engaged. Whenever low-flying planes were reported, we drove under a highway bridge and waited until they had disappeared.

TREASON ON THE PRODUCTION LINE
We left our route from Munich to Berlin at the Autobahn exit in Halle and made a small detour to the Leuna synthetic oil facility. The SS-officers had a meeting there with the top engineers of the plant. As far as I can remember, it concerned the moving of individual elements of the operation underground for which technical difficulties still stood in the way.

This visit to the Leuna facility was very interesting for me. As is well known, and very understandable, the fuel production sites were always targets of the enemy's bombing raids. That shouldn't excuse the fact, however, that bombs were dropped arbitrarily and senselessly into the middle of the residential areas of the cities during the terror raids. While talking to Leuna's directors, I discovered that the attacks were only expected whenever partial production resumed. If the factory was put out of commission, then the enemy bided his time. They waited until a portion of the facility had been restored enough by the tireless women and men who worked day and night until production was again possible. They could then count on the facilities being bombed to pieces right on the evening of the first workday. Because the enemy couldn't just produce the exact times of the reconstruction work out of thin air, it was crystal clear to everyone that the traitors had to be sitting in their own factory. Despite all precautionary measures and surveillance, however, they could not be discovered.

Barrage balloons floated in the air all around the factory, which stretched on and on. But the Americans usually flew so high that the balloons didn't help at all. The Flak also had little effect. The great height of the approaching enemy formations also had its good side, because the chance of a hit was much less. Unfortunately, the Americans were even informed about the *effect* of their raids. They continued to fly to their targets until they were successful with their bombs.

Production had just started up again on the day of our visit. Because of this, the director recommended to us that we try to leave the area before the onset of darkness. Despite that, we stayed longer on our visit than we had planned. We had just reached the Autobahn when the enemy formations approached. We wanted to observe if what was said had been true. We stopped at the next overpass to see whether the Americans were once again in the know that day. It was a horrifying sight. Unfortunately, our workers were completely right. The bombers dropped their entire load on the factory, and we had the impression that this time they didn't need to fly any more missions. They had certainly done a great job. Our workers, as busy as bees, continued to partially rebuild the facilities despite everything. But that good will and industry couldn't help by themselves. The traitors were in the midst of them, as in other places, and the enemy could wipe out the entire tiresome labor in a few minutes.

The Catastrophe Looms

The trip to Berlin went without incident. I stayed at the apartment of the SS-officer who had given me a ride in his vehicle. The first thing next morning, I headed for the Army Personnel Office. I wanted to extract marching orders to my old company from them. Even though I left my old man's walking stick outside the door, just like I had when visiting Himmler, I didn't succeed in realizing an immediate transfer to my old unit at the front. I wanted to circumvent the replacement battalion, but the staff officers were inflexible. They dismissed me politely but firmly.

I took the train back to my hospital in Westphalia. The hospital was no longer in Lingen. That was because I had arranged to have myself transferred to a hospital in the area where my uncle was the chief surgeon. I was hoping to be able to achieve more there. At the same time, I was practically among family. I had been told to send a telegram before my arrival, but they didn't know me very well if they really hoped I would do that. The sister in charge of the kitchen had baked me a three-layered cake, and we celebrated together in an intimate atmosphere. During my stay in both of the hospitals, I had become acquainted with the food provided by the nuns. I must say that all the wounded were enthusiastic about the rations. For example, even for Christmas in 1944, every hospital patient received half a chicken. Mark my words! *Every* wounded man and not just the officers, as spiteful people like to claim. The wonderful sisters performed superhuman feats. The hospital, as can be imagined, was overfilled. My uncle operated practically around the clock.

The party functionaries in the area insisted on sponsoring an official celebration for me in the movie theater. They intended to invite the public to it. I told them right away that such events didn't interest me at all, especially since everyone really had other worries at that point in the war. No one should count on my appearing. The "hero's ceremony" was thus held on a small scale in an adjoining room of an inn. Only my fellow soldiers from the hospital and the friends of my uncle were present. The district leader also appeared with his following, but he left the gathering in a conspicuous manner after I had finished making my thank-you speech. I shouldn't fail to mention that I had given an overview of the situation from my perspective in my speech.

In the meantime, the enemy had come closer and closer to the western borders of the Reich. By December, we could see fully packed cars in Westphalia that had supposedly pulled back from the front. The men were usually so excited when reporting that one would think that the Americans were already just a few kilometers away. Of course, we had our own thoughts on the matter. Where was all of that supposed to lead? If all of the stragglers on the Western Front had moved back this far, then the Allies would soon be reaching the Rhine. In the meantime, the western districts had already been evacuated. I took advantage of the opportunity to visit my mother one more time for a little while after Christmas and helped her save a few things from home.

On the return trip, I made another detour to Berlin. I checked to see whether there was any opportunity to get to East Prussia. My old company had landed there in the meantime. I had written to my comrades that I could walk quite well again and had been feeling strong enough to go to the front for some time, but that I had been hindered in doing so by the replacement battalion. On December 2, I received the following reply: "Herr Lieutenant, with your wound, you can really consider yourself lucky that you are still among the living and don't have to be left out at the next census. When can we count on seeing you again in the company? It goes without saying that that would be the greatest Christmas present for the company." Of course, I thought the same thing as my terrific comrades.

It upset me when the Army Personnel Office informed me that no more opportunities existed to get to East Prussia. The troops there were being brought back. It would thus be completely senseless to send me there. Instead, I was supposed to report to Paderborn. In the units that were being drawn up, they were missing officers with frontline experience. I would find a satisfying assignment there.

I was very disappointed of course and quickly visited my brother who was taking an officer candidate course in Krampnitz. When I arrived there, excitement was in the air. All the men in the course were getting ready to move to occupy the positions around Berlin. I was lucky, because on the next day I wouldn't have seen my brother anymore. It should be mentioned that the Russians had already surfaced a few days before at Küstrin. Hauptmann Fromme had quickly assembled a battalion out of all the available training tanks. If I had just shown up a day earlier, I would have been able to take over a company immediately, because no suitable officer had been available. Hauptmann Fromme was a tough old soldier, whom I already knew from earlier times. It was said that he had been demoted in peacetime because he had struck a commander due to a difference of opinion while under the influence of alcohol. This old go-getter had become an officer again during the war, starting at the bottom. By 1941, he had already received the Knight's Cross. Fromme showed the Russians at Küstrin that the way to Berlin wasn't yet quite all the way open. He shot up the Russian armored advance guard and he thus prevented the Russians from obtaining the Oder crossings by surprise.

At the hospital, I packed my suitcase quickly and left, as ordered, for Paderborn.

The commander of the replacement battalion at Paderborn wanted to palm off a training company on me right away. I told him that I didn't feel confident with the training of a 300-man company. I wanted to be transferred to a combat unit that was being drawn up. He then became unpleasant. I remembered the correspondence that Himmler had given me. When I presented it to him, he abandoned his intentions. But then I had to wait around without doing anything until something suitable was found.

The 3rd Company of the 502nd under Hauptmann Leonhard had been pulled out of Russia and was in Sennelager. The company had received the new "King Tigers" and was getting ready for combat. I saw my maintenance team there, along with Oberfeldwebel Delzeit, who continued to lead it with his old vigor. I also saw old, familiar faces in the combat elements. Oberfeldwebel Zwetti was there as a tank commander and Lieutenant Ruwiedel as a platoon leader. How happy it would have made me to have been transferred to my old gang, because there was still hope that this company would be shipped back to the battalion on the Eastern Front. The commander of the replacement battalion ruined those plans, however. He was just about through with me.

By then everything had already gone completely crazy. Everyone in the replacement battalion lived according to the questionable motto: "Enjoy the war! The peace will be terrible!"

This dissoluteness and all the senseless partying according to the principle of *"Après nous le déluge!"* was deeply repugnant to me. I wasn't the only one who thought that about the way they carried on, but our circle was relatively small. In any case, it was clear to me that I wouldn't stay long in Paderborn. The catastrophe was already casting its bitter shadows.

The Ruhr Pocket

Hauptmann Scherr was the commander of the 512th "Hunting Tiger" Battalion. I was grateful to him for accepting me as a company commander. I had to disappoint the wounded from my old company. Although these men were lying around doing nothing, their transfer to the front was strictly forbidden by the commander of the replacement battalion. I regretted not being able to keep those men whom I knew and who were so tried and true. After a great deal of effort, I at least got Lustig as my personal driver.

Our equipment situation was quite complicated. The "Hunting Tigers" came from the Hindenburg Facilities in St. Valentin near Linz; the cannons, on the other hand, came from Breslau. The Russians had already advanced beyond that, however, so we were only able to equip thirty "Hunting Tigers" with cannons. Each company received only ten vehicles. In the final analysis, that was sufficient, since we couldn't man any more. The ammunition was drawn from Magdeburg. The ammunition details that picked it up had radios with them to report every stop. Our employment was that important to the high command! The tanks were transported by rail to Paderborn. The companies were assembled there in Sennelager. We had the impression that we were considered the secret weapon that could still save Germany.

Because the vehicle parts were stockpiled in Döllersheim near Vienna, I had to commute the 1,000 kilometers between Paderborn and Vienna on a continuous basis. That wasn't a lot of fun in the dark and with the constant air raids. Although I drove with blackout lights, we had a lot of problems with the civilian population, which felt threatened. But how could I have covered that stretch if I had stopped for every air raid and waited for the all-clear signal?

In Kassel, I once again had a lot of luck while making such a trip. We were in the middle of the city when the sirens suddenly started wailing. Everybody ran into the air raid shelter. My first sergeant, who unfortunately bore no resemblance to Hauptfeldwebel Rieger, wanted to get out of the vehicle at all costs and disappear into a bunker. I didn't allow him to dissuade me and stepped on the gas to get to the edge of the city. We scarcely had the railroad crossing behind us, when the bombs of "our liberators" were rushing through the air. Fortunately, the carpet bombing began farther to our right. The entire portion of the city where the first sergeant wanted to get out lay in ruins. Once again, I had had a sixth sense and was greatly relieved not to have paid attention to the requests of my Hauptfeldwebel.

When the assault guns were calibrated in Sennelager, we experienced our first failure. Despite its eighty-two tons, our "Hunting Tiger" didn't want to act like we wanted it to. Only its armor was satisfactory; its maneuverability left a lot to be desired. In addition, it was an assault gun. There was no traversing turret, just an enclosed, armored housing. Any large traversing of the cannon had to be effected by movement of the entire vehicle. Because of that, transmissions and steering differentials were soon out of order. That such a monstrosity had to be constructed in the final phase of the war—of all times! A better idea for the travel lock of the eight-meter-long cannon of our "Hunting Tiger" was also absolutely necessary. It had to be removed *from the outside* during contact with the enemy!

Locking down the barrel during a road march was necessary, of course. Otherwise the mounting brackets would have been worn out too quickly and exact aiming would have been impossible. All these problems were compounded by the fact that a tanker cannot feel comfortable in an assault gun. We want to be able to turn our weapons 360 degrees. If not, we have no feeling of security or superiority, but rather that someone is breathing down our necks.

During the calibration, Stabsgefreiter Sepp Moser set up the targets in the countryside. From Passau, he was a man with a powerful body and a heart of gold. He was with the maintenance squad that had been withdrawn from Russia with the 3rd Company of our battalion and reorganized in Paderborn. Whenever Sepp took matters in hand, things worked.

Moser drove a prime mover. In civilian life, on the other hand, he drove a beer truck. His wife took care of his correspondence with the laconic remark that otherwise the pen would break in his hands. I heard from another comrade, who saw Sepp again after the war in Passau, that he was content. He proudly noted that he got thirty liters of beer free every week. The comrade then asked him in amazement what he was able to do with all that beer. He received a classic reply to that question:

"Well, whatever I still need, I just have to buy for myself!" Sepp Moser gave it his all during calibration of the assault guns.

We missed everything in such a manner that we were soon fed up with it. Finally, the ordnance technician checked the matter out, and everything then worked better. We discovered that the cannon, because of its enormous length, was battered about so much as a result of even a short move off the road that its alignment no longer agreed with that of the optics. That promised to be a lot of fun—things didn't want to work, *before* we even met the enemy!

My company was the first to be loaded. On the last night, I gave my soldiers an evening pass and was both amazed and overjoyed that no one was missing in the morning. Our goal was the train station in Siegburg. The almost panicky haste was understandable. We knew that the Americans had already crossed the Rhine at Remagen, after the bridge had fallen into their hands intact. In spite of the total chaos that already prevailed then, we had all of our things complete and together. That was an accomplishment, all the same!

Three transport trains had been made available. The loading went according to plan because the enemy air force spared the train station in Sennelager for some unknown reason, although all our assault guns were assembled there. I preferred to drive in my vehicle to check out the new operational area before the arrival of my company. Due to the low-flying aircraft, of course, the transports only rolled at night. Using the Kübel, I had to drive up and down the rail line constantly, so that the trains didn't get held up too long. The tracks were frequently interdicted by the fighter-bombers which were a nuisance. There was hardly any air defense anymore. Besides, a strange attitude was prevalent. It could be summed up as follows: "Do anything but shoot! The pilots could discover our position!" The ease with which the enemy fighters circled over us in broad daylight made me furious. We had no way to defend ourselves against them, however. The air superiority of the enemy was simply devastating.

Because of that, during the day, our trains stayed in tunnels or along protective slopes where they weren't exactly safe. The field mess hadn't shown up yet, so I had to be a jack of all trades—driver, courier, transportation officer, and company commander, depending on the situation. Occasionally, I could even get warm food for my men. Fuel and rations were readily available in the depots. They either fell into the hands of the Americans or were senselessly destroyed.

When I finally knew for certain that the first transport would arrive in Siegburg in the morning, I drove ahead. I found out that the Yanks were already shooting as far as the loading ramp. That meant it could get lively!

In Siegburg, after a long search, I found a former commander of the 502nd, Major Schmidt. He led the "Armor Liaison Staff in the West" and was more than a little surprised to see me there. I actually had to sit down when Major Schmidt told me that he had no idea what was supposed to happen to us and where we were supposed to be employed. Then even crazier things happened. For instance, one of my motorcycle messengers appeared and proudly informed me that our first train was in the process of unloading in Duisburg. It was supposed to have gone to Siegburg, and it landed up in Duisburg! There had to be something fishy going on! I ordered the messenger to squeeze everything possible out of his machine so that he reached Duisburg before the empty train left again. Where was I supposed to get the special cars needed to load the vehicles again? The motorcycle messenger was able to get there, and the train in fact reached the area around Siegburg the next night.

In the meantime, Major Schmidt had called around to all possible units and staffs. Even the commander of Army Group B, Generalfeldmarschall Model, didn't know about our planned employment in his area. I was ordered to report to him after the arrival of my vehicles.

While waiting, I wanted to finally get some sleep. After all, who knew when I would get some peace and quiet again. I was just lying down on my wooden bed when a guard appeared and reported Oberleutnant Held to me. That was it for the sleep! Held was my platoon leader when I was a recruit. I hadn't seen him since 1941. I was very happy to be able to shoot the breeze with an old acquaintance. We talked the entire night.

We couldn't unload in Siegburg because of the very heavy fire. We therefore let the first train stay in a tunnel until the onset of darkness and brought the vehicles onto the road during the night. Not a single wheeled vehicle was ready for action. All the tires had been shot up, and it took days until we had the supply trucks halfway in order.

Intervention at Remagen was no longer a possibility because the Americans had already advanced across the Autobahn. The Yanks must have been really grateful to Hitler for creating these super highways. If only we had found such roads during our advance into Russia! We then would have reached Moscow and not have remained stuck in the mud.

At that point, I was attached to General Bayerlein. I had the first platoon occupy positions in a little patch of woods right behind the front lines. I myself scarcely sat in a combat vehicle anymore, because the individual assault guns were attached across the entire corps sector. I constantly drove from platoon to platoon, from "Hunting Tiger" to "Hunting

Tiger," and from regiment to regiment to direct the engagements. Soon the distances weren't very big anymore, because the Ruhr pocket collapsed more and more upon itself.

An incident occurred that proved to me how deeply the fighting morale among the men and the officers had sunk. My executive officer was pulling security in my "Hunting Tiger" in the piece of woods already mentioned. He had also taken my crew. Suddenly, my driver Lustig approached me on foot halfway from the front lines. I already had a bad feeling. The good man was completely out of breath and had to catch it first before he could report to me what had happened. His first remark said everything. "I almost slugged my tank commander just now! If we were still in Russia, he'd be dead now!" He then explained what had happened. His vehicle was located with another "Hunting Tiger," well camouflaged, at the wood line. A long column of enemy tanks had driven across their front at about one and a half kilometers distance. Lustig now considered it a given that the tank commander would give the order to fire. Why else were our assault guns there? The man refused to fire a shot, however. A heated argument started among the members of the crew. This strange officer justified his refusal to fire with the reason that he would expose himself if he opened fire and he would then draw the attention of the fighter-bombers!

To make a long story short, not a single shot was actually fired, although this distance was practically ideal for our cannons. The enemy would have had no opportunity to endanger our "Hunting Tigers."

It wasn't enough, however, that this strange officer didn't fire. He also ordered his vehicle to back up out of the woods shortly thereafter. It was then that he really did reveal his position. He was lucky that no planes were in the air at that time. He cleared out to the rear without notifying the vehicle commander of the second "Hunting Tiger" at all. That commander promptly followed, and both of them raced off as if the devil were behind them. Of course, no enemy was to be seen far and wide! Because of the careless driving of the completely inexperienced crew, the second vehicle was immediately disabled. The "fearless" Oberleutnant didn't worry about the vehicle at all. On the contrary, he obstinately drove on until his vehicle also became disabled. At least the Oberfeldwebel in the second assault gun blew up his own vehicle.

Lustig had then departed on foot and insisted that I forward his report to the battalion. In that phase of the war, however, it didn't make any sense anymore. Everyone had to decide for themselves whether they wanted to experience the end decently or as a louse. Troops from all dif-

ferent branches were lying about in the woods by the hundreds and waiting for the end. Their morale was completely gone.

In Siegen, I went to my battalion staff to report the situation to my
commander. As I entered the command post, I was congratulated from
all sides. The rumor had gone around, so it seems, that my guys had
knocked out about forty enemy tanks. I sobered them up when I made it
known that we hadn't knocked out a single Yank, and we had two complete losses to show for it. Had only two or three tank commanders and
crews from my company in Russia been there with me, then the rumor
could have easily been true. All of my old comrades would have enjoyed
firing up those Yanks "on parade." Five Russians were, after all, more
dangerous than thirty Americans. We had already noticed that in the few
days we had been employed in the west.

In the meantime, it had become clear to us that we were completely
encircled. The "Ruhr Pocket" had been formed.

Feldmarschall Model wanted to break through with all his forces at
Marburg and escape the encirclement while there was still time. That
would not have been difficult at all. The supreme command had a different opinion, however, and ordered us to hold out in the pocket for as
long as possible! Our withdrawal route followed the Sieg River through
Eitorf–Betzdorf–Kirchen. The first objective was Siegen, which was supposed to be held for a long time. A few assault guns had already become
disabled on the road march. Despite good intentions, the inexperienced
drivers were not able to master the situation in the mountainous terrain.
The men really had a good attitude, but they had neither experience
with heavy vehicles nor enough training.

The Chaos Grows

We encountered chaos everywhere. The roads were completely clogged, and the vehicles were easy prey for the enemy aircraft that completely dominated the skies. By means of handouts, the civilian population was requested by our leadership to abandon its domiciles and pull back with the troops. Only a small percentage followed this request.

We had a hunch that our army intended to employ Tabun, a new gas that promptly incapacitated the nervous system. The high command had probably distanced itself from using it because our own civilian population would have been wiped out and even this weapon would not have turned the tide of the war. The majority of the civilians remained home and awaited the Americans. Of course, only a few of them believed in the silly fairy tale about the "liberators," which had long since been refuted by the bombed-out ruins. But all desired the inevitable end to the dangers and the fears. After all, there were no Russians to be feared in the west, from whom the poor people in the eastern districts were fleeing in panicky fear in snow and ice.

On the go around the clock, continuously hounded by fighters and bombers, that's how we reached Siegen. Although we hid the assault guns in barns or under straw during the day, another two were rendered combat ineffective by fighters and had to be blown up. How I envied those comrades who didn't have to experience this hopeless struggle during the last few weeks on the Western Front!

In Siegen I found a magnificent position on the high ground where the military posts were. From there we had great fields of fire through a cut in the woods onto the road that led into the valley on the far side of the Sieg River. We waited for the Americans at this location, but we weren't granted any kills here either, even though I had remained in my assault gun to prevent a new failure. That was because the Yanks had confederates among us. The civilians who had nestled into the dugouts on the opposite slope stopped the American vehicles before they came into our line of sight. I still wonder even today whether such a thing could be possible in another nation.

I then withdrew my company toward Weidenau and covered the tank obstacle there. I set up my command post in the air raid bunker of a factory. I discovered from a civilian that a portion of the civilian population was cooperating *with the enemy,* the other portion with us. I didn't have any problem understanding that the people there were apathetic and tired of war, but that they would betray their own countrymen to the enemy I didn't want to believe at first. In the beginning, we had also let the people run to the Yanks, if they wanted to fetch some things. We didn't check anyone who came back. I soon noticed, however, that the Americans always fired wherever one of my assault guns was located, even though they couldn't see the targets at all. From that point on, we naturally sealed off the main battle line.

Practically all of our Kübels were disabled. We therefore decided one evening to fetch us replacements from the Americans. No one should think that that was a heroic deed! The Yanks slept in the houses at night, as was proper for "combat soldiers." Who was going to disturb them anyway! At the most, one sentry was located outside, but only if there was good weather. The war started in the evenings only whenever our troops pulled back and they followed. If, by chance, a German machine gun actually fired, then the air force was requested as backup, but not until the next day.

Around midnight, we departed with four men and returned after not too long of a time with two jeeps. It was convenient that we didn't need any keys for them. Only a small latch needed to be switched and the vehicles were ready to start. Long after we had reached our lines again, the Yanks began to fire wildly in the air, probably to settle their nerves. If a night had been long enough, we could have easily driven to Paris.

A small attack was planned for the next day just east of Weidenau. It had the objective of taking high ground from which the enemy had too good of a view into our positions. Infantry was not attached to me, although "foot soldiers" were lying about in great quantities. What could we have done with men whose fighting morale had been totally extinguished! The enemy propaganda had worked with great success. Besides, there was something else.

These units had been stationed in France for a long time and the fear of *this* enemy and of being taken prisoner was, compared to the east, very minimal. Everyone thought that it only mattered to just appear to "go the distance." Later, as we were pressed tighter and tighter into the "pocket," we encountered hordes of former German soldiers who, according to their papers, had been properly discharged from the Wehrmacht. A quite clever city commandant had thought that the Americans would fall for such a trick. For the time being, however, the enemy snapped up all civilians, all the way from the junior in high school to grandpa. They assumed that there was a criminal behind every German. In reality, the hate directed against Germany was much more virulent than anything that our propaganda had ever formulated. Even the current atrocity stories can't alter that fact.

We assembled for our "small" operation with four assault guns. Even though I could barely count on success, I intended to show the Yanks that, in any case, there was still a war on. The only evidence of that was in the ruins, of which they were perhaps still proud! We were used to an opponent the stature of the Russians; we were amazed at the contrast. During the entire war, I never saw soldiers disperse so head over heels even though virtually nothing was happening. After all, what could we achieve by ourselves? We advanced a few hundred meters to the south and reached our objective. I finally recognized one enemy tank, which drove wildly behind a house and disappeared. For once I wanted to try out our 128-mm cannon. I took a chance and fired at the house with a delayed fuze. The result showed us the monstrous penetrating capability of our cannon. After the second round, the American tank went up in flames. But what benefit were the best weapons in this phase of the war! The Yanks now came to life, of course, because someone was really shooting at them! We were soon in the middle of heavy artillery fire, and the bombers appeared to "punish" us. Fortunately, there were no casualties. At the onset of darkness, we withdrew back to our old lines because no infantry had showed up to occupy the new line. One of my assault guns became disabled when it landed in a bomb crater.

The next day, the order arrived to withdraw the assault guns somewhat to the north and establish them in a better position to cover the road. Toward midnight, I had my company move out and followed later in my Kübel. Just as I wanted to pass the column, a terrible blast shook the air. Everything came to a halt, and I saw that an assault gun was burning. The crews ran into the countryside, because they assumed that Americans could have infiltrated. I immediately had my doubts. Americans at night against tanks! And on foot! No, that was out of the question!

Everyone was under cover, weapons at the ready. Figures then surfaced, and I recognized German helmets, among them some from the First World War. These hearty souls made their way forward carefully, until I broke the spell and called out to them in German. It turned out that we had the "last reserves" in front of us, the Volkssturm! The men had never seen a German assault gun before, of course, and were firmly convinced that they had the "bad guys" in front of them. One of them finally got some nerve and fired a Panzerfaust. Both sides had gotten off easy.

Finally, Generalfeldmarschall Model made me happy with the order to transport my "Hunting Tigers" to Unna. I had been complaining about insufficient fields of fire; I hoped to find that in the open plain between Unna and Werl.

We were still in the process of loading in Gummersbach when the Americans broke through at Weidenau. It was very difficult for us to get away. The rail lines were interdicted by the fighter-bombers on an hourly basis, and the train personnel refused to take responsibility for the trip. Our men thus had to man the locomotives themselves. Using a small shunting engine, an advance force rode the rails to check them for their completeness. The condition of the rail bed could change hourly.

The Russians would never have given us so much time! But look at how long it took the Americans to liquidate a pocket where one can scarcely talk about any kind of serious resistance. A well-equipped force of German soldiers would have easily eliminated the entire "Ruhr Pocket" in a week at the outside.

I moved quickly with the reconnaissance platoon to Unna to check out the area and the operational possibilities. Unfortunately, there wasn't too much left of the good fields of fire that I had hoped to find there. Advancing from the east, the enemy had already taken Werl.

A Strange City Commandant

I was attached to the city commandant in Unna. Even the unit commanders were supposed to subordinate themselves to his directives. In reality, however, they scarcely took notice of this man who acted as if he were a great field commander. In any case, I had to report in to him. The command post was in the military reservation west of State Highway 233 and south of the Ruhr Highway. I finally found the entrance to the bunker. Thirty steps led down into a deep cellar, which had probably been set up as an air raid shelter earlier. Above ground was a wet-behind-the-ears sentry who took his duties very seriously. At first, he didn't want to give out any information. He finally confirmed, however, that the main headquarters was there. Downstairs I had to go through a dark passageway, where a sentry led me to the "boss." When the door was opened, I couldn't believe my eyes.

Sitting around a huge table covered with maps were numerous SS-officers in magnificent uniforms, stylish and clean. A liqueur glass was in front of each of the gentlemen. In short, a unique type of command post!

I reported and gave my combat strength. With the intonation of a practised master of ceremonies, the commandant explained the situation to me. He showed me on the map where his positions around Unna were supposedly occupied, how many men were under his command, how magnificently Unna was fortified, and how impregnable it was. Of course, my seven "Hunting Tigers" were also placed on the map immediately. I really didn't know whether to laugh or to cry. From the positions that were given to me, I could neither fire a shot nor see fifty meters, since they were located behind a railroad embankment. I had already driven around the area and sought out my position. With regard to my objections, the "man in charge" said jovially: "My dear friend! I think you'll find your way around soon enough. For the time being, the danger of an attack is most threatening from the east and the northeast. We'll show the Americans soon enough!"

216

I respectfully said "Jawohl!" and made my way to get to some fresh air. When I opened the door, the young sentry came running in all excited and made the following report:

"Impacting artillery in map sector XY."

Outside, I asked the guard about his duties. According to him, he had to report the position of every impacting enemy round or bomb immediately. "The Führer" never came upstairs, not even to go to the bathroom. Everything was conducted in a comfortable manner from the telephone. What a difference from the SS-units that we had seen in the east! At that point, at least, I knew that we could run the war there as we saw fit. I just had to make sure that our strange "bird" didn't fly out of his nest without me noticing it.

I set up two assault guns to cover the Ruhr Highway and put the remaining ones on the northern outskirts of Unna, facing Kamen. My command post was in the living room of a house near the second group. There were hardly any civilians to be seen in the city anymore. In the house that we had occupied, there was still a little old lady who took good care of us. I was almost always on the go to check out the situation so that we didn't unexpectedly fall into a trap.

The next day, enemy tanks were already firing into the town, although from a very great distance. I drove from my command post to the military post to check out the mood of "Fortress Headquarters Unna." The frustrated "Napoleon" immediately called out to me.

"Unheard of impudence by these Yanks! They are simply shooting into the city with their tanks. My observation post in the Flak tower reports to me that those guys have moved up onto open ground in rows with their tanks!" He also recommended that I climb up the Flak tower once and take a "peek at their cards." He himself was impeded from climbing stairs by bone fractures and moved about with a walking stick.

The Yank tanks actually did interest me, and I climbed up the Flak tower. From there, I immediately saw approximately twenty enemy tanks set up in a neat little row about two and a half kilometers away. Now and then, they fired a salvo into the city. I thought to myself that we really ought to show these guys for once that we too had a few rounds of ammunition left. If they had already come over the "big pond" and had to be subjected to so much unnecessary fear, then they ought to be able to at least talk about one live round after their return home. That's the type of mean people we Germans are!

I wanted our "Napoleon" to have a part in our operation, however. The bone fractures wouldn't bother him in my tank, after all. I thus went back to the command post and extended my invitation to him. Of course, he couldn't say no! Using two "Hunting Tigers," which I withdrew from the Ruhr Highway, we drove to a small rise east of the reservation. From there, we could enjoy magnificent observation of the enemy. Unfortunately, I noticed when opening fire that the Yanks were at least a good three kilometers from us after all. It thus took too long before our fire to sit well. In the meantime, the enemy tanks had crawled into a small patch of woods. Of course, they quickly asked for support against this "superior force." It didn't take too long before the enemy put fire of a very unfriendly caliber onto our high ground. Actually, I didn't have any other business there, but as the gracious host I wanted to allow the city commandant to experience at least a few impacting rounds up close. The danger of a direct hit was certainly slim, because the Yanks were shooting with long-range artillery. The psychological effect of their salvos was greater than expected, however. Our "Führer" and grand strategist ran back into his bunker, leaving behind his walking stick!

I kept both vehicles there and placed them in the cemetery south of the post to cover to the east. The crews diligently camouflaged their vehicles, and I exhorted them to hurry up even more, because a "lame duck" with an artillery observer in it was buzzing around in the air. In a real war, these things, which resembled our Fieseler Storch, would have been destroyed immediately. In a situation where we had neither aircraft nor Flak, they could fly around without risk and direct the fire of their batteries with precision. Whenever our troops fired into the air with a machine gun, the Yanks immediately disappeared.

I saw two or three planes shot down during the fighting in the Ruhr Pocket, but they were purely lucky hits. In reality, any flying on the part of the enemy during the final weeks of the war was completely safe. The "lame duck" had discovered us, and soon there was a shot from the Yanks, which landed about 150 meters behind us.

"Get in your vehicles as quick as possible!" I screamed out, but the young guys simply didn't listen. They just didn't have any experience and didn't believe there was any danger. The second round landed perhaps eighty meters in front of us. A fire for effect by the entire enemy battery followed immediately after that. A heavy round landed in the middle of our group. I was standing only a few meters from the impact but miraculously received only a small piece of shrapnel. By then, of course, everybody who could still run had suddenly disappeared into the assault guns. Three soldiers remained on the ground, however, and they cried out horribly. They had been severely hit. A piece of shrapnel had ripped open my loader's entire back and slightly damaged the vertebrae. I packed all three into my Kübel and sent the driver directly to the hospital in Iserlohn, where I was well acquainted with the doctors. Despite the efforts of these men, one of the three wounded died shortly after admission. All of that was the sole consequence of insufficient training.

When I got back to the "headquarters" and was about to descend the steps, I heard nearby machine-gun fire. My Feldwebel and I investigated the matter immediately. Just inside the reservation boundary, we saw a soldier from an unknown unit. He was amazed to find German soldiers still there. He belonged to a scattered unit, which had broken through on its own initiative. They had run into an enemy reconnaissance patrol, during which the shooting that we had noticed had started. It should be noted that he said that none of the men had seen anything resembling an occupied line.

That made me quite curious about the situation report of our "commander." I went back to the bunker. We didn't have to worry about the Yanks advancing farther during the night anyway.

I found the group in its customary composure and cheerful ambience. I asked about the latest reports from the front. Full of pride, the city commandant briefed me.

"Our fortress is holding like a ring of iron. Up to now, only the northern elements on the road to Kamen have had contact with the enemy."

I answered with a little less swagger, but just as precisely.

"If you don't immediately alert your reserve companies on the base, you will be captured before the Yanks even bother to call you on the phone!" His answer was classic: "Don't get nervous just yet, my young friend!" These were the types of men the Americans had to deal with! The man thought he needed to calm me down. I bid my "sincerest" farewells and intended to drive to my command post as fast as possible in my Kübel. I wanted to pull both of my assault guns back from the connecting road to Kamen and to give orders to those on the Ruhr Highway to immediately move out of Unna in case the Yanks intended to overrun them. I drove along Federal Highway 233 to the north. About fifty meters before the intersection of that road with the Ruhr Highway, I was taken aback. I stepped on the brakes. In front of us, vehicles were driving from east to west. We could only make out shadows and therefore sneaked closer on foot. Our suspicions were quickly confirmed.

American wheeled and rubber-padded tracked vehicles were rolling quietly past Unna toward Dortmund. They had absolutely no idea that there were still German soldiers around. Not a soul slowed them down in their enterprise. That's how "firm" the ring around Unna was! My "Hunting Tigers" hadn't fired yet. They probably didn't want to reveal themselves. I raced back and fetched the "Führer" out of his bunker to show him the strange spectacle.

We had just arrived back at the old position near the intersection, when I heard the cannons of my assault guns fire. The traffic immediately broke up, and a few jeeps drove wildly back and forth in front of our eyes. I continued into the city by myself, because my commandant preferred to walk back on foot. He was really afraid, because I drove in one of the jeeps captured at Siegen. It had the Yank star displayed on it! Although my Feldwebel comforted him with the remark that the Americans would certainly take more offense at the uniform than the jeep, he didn't let himself be persuaded to make the return trip with us. My jeep had already performed good service for me a few times when I wanted to occupy the command posts directed to me by corps and wasn't able to ascertain the presence of Americans until already at the location in question.

After the wild shooting, the Yank vehicles pulled back to the eastern edge of the city during the morning hours. The Americans' fear had delayed the fall of "Fortress Unna" once again. The "bravery" of the commandant and his garrison had little to do with it.

Today, I frequently wonder why we simply didn't allow ourselves to be snapped up. Everything had obviously been lost, and the soldiers scarcely offered resistance anymore. But we didn't want to, nor could we believe, that all our sacrifices had been in vain. If our opponents had at least shown a little pluck, we would have possibly capitulated more easily. At least then we would have been able to hope for fair treatment. No real combat soldier found it in his heart, however, to allow himself to be captured prematurely by these "half steppers," while at the same time our comrades on the Eastern Front were still bravely defending against the Russians.

From corps headquarters, I quickly drove back to Unna to reach the city before the break of day. Just before the Ruhr Highway, a red light was blinking. Could that be the Yanks? We still credited them with too much. We finally saw an SS-man who was waving energetically with the flashlight. He said:

"You can't drive into the city anymore. All the tank obstacles have been closed. Unna will be defended to the last man!"

Saying "Without me!," I drove past the surprised young man. We soon reached the first tank obstacle. Any car could have easily driven around it off the road to the left or the right. I reached the military post without enemy contact. A straggler told me the good news that the "commandant" had departed. Before doing that, he had sent a radio transmission to the Führer's headquarters: "Unna encircled. Holding out to the last man! Long live the Führer!" According to the latest order, the Unna garrison was supposed to assemble in Iserlohn.

I fetched my "Hunting Tigers" and led them south to the next village. We soon noticed that there was still a war on. An American tank became a nuisance. I quickly brought a "Hunting Tiger" into position on the eastern edge of the village and personally drove in the Kübel to a small patch of high ground to gain a vantage point. The enemy had already reached Federal Highway 233, and five tanks were right before our eyes under the trees. The distance was barely 600 meters. I quickly grabbed one of my assault guns to give the enemy something to think about.

The commander of the "Hunting Tiger," a Stabsfeldwebel without experience at the front, wanted to handle the matter himself. To be on the safe side, I first led him on foot to the high ground. I showed him the enemy and told him the distance, so nothing could really go wrong. It was like at the training area. The Stabsfeldwebel then went to his vehicle, and I remained to observe.

The unfortunate man then made a fatal mistake. He didn't crank the cannon down to its right position until he had almost arrived on the high ground. Of course, the Americans heard the sound of the motor and reacted accordingly. Two of the tanks scrammed, but the other three opened fire. The Stabsfeldwebel's vehicle was soon hit in the front and hadn't fired one shot itself. Instead of finally firing, the lunatic turned around on the high ground when he simply could have rolled backward. When the Yanks had the broad side of the "Hunting Tiger" in front of them, they let our vehicle have it. It immediately went up in flames. Other hits followed, and not one of the six-man crew could save himself, probably because everyone got in each other's way. This example serves to prove that the best weapon and the greatest of enthusiasm are useless when thorough basic training has not been conducted.

Approaching the End

From our positions, we could observe how the Volkssturm was leaving its lines and streaming back into the city. The war was over for these men. The Americans peacefully advanced in long columns along the Ruhr Highway toward Dortmund. Using my scope, I could observe how the women and girls were waving to the "liberators." White flags were suddenly waving everywhere. The city, as quiet as a grave just a little before, came back to life. A line from "Deutschland, Deutschland über alles" suddenly sprang to mind: "German women, German fidelity . . ."

What did we soldiers care if others raised the white flag! We "didn't want to break our oath, to be the same as rotten scoundrels."

I had to employ a trick to get more fuel. In a display of German thoroughness, the Feldwebel on duty in a supply depot referred to his "regulations." I bawled him out when he did that:

"Let me then see your pay book, please. That way, I can report to Feldmarschall Model who is responsible for me not being able to move my remaining vehicles."

I immediately received fuel in abundance. I had so much that I wasn't able to drive it all off before the "Ruhr Pocket" finally went up in smoke. Despite the aircraft, we were able to get back to our unit in one piece. We then continued to "advance to the rear."

By then, the pocket was so small that at least the communications functioned well. There had been scarcely any contact between Model and his divisions in the previous few weeks.

I set up my next to last command post in a house right next to a railroad line. We slept on the floor. I had scarcely nodded off, when a terrible blast ripped through the air. Of course, we immediately assumed it was enemy bombers, but it was a German railway gun that was sending its last greetings over our heads to the north. We made ourselves scarce before the fighter-bombers came, especially since the railway gun had disappeared in a tunnel.

During my last contact with the enemy, I also experienced surrendering a village for the first time, with a truce and everything else that goes with it. I had only known about this from hearsay. It was something that those who had only experienced the Eastern Front had never considered possible.

We were covering a larger village. I had the order to hold it at all costs for as long as possible, because the Ruhr Pocket would have collapsed after giving up this critical point.

The Americans didn't appear to be ready for any more resistance and came driving up the road with their tanks. After we had knocked out the first few, no more let themselves be seen. For doing that, the head doctor of the hospitals came racing out of the village. He vehemently reproached me because we had even bothered to shoot. The hospitals were full to the rafters. Even the private homes were occupied with wounded. The entire village, the head doctor said, was like a large field hospital. It was then completely clear to me that we had to evacuate without a fight even though I also knew that the pocket would collapse with the surrender of this position.

Despite that, I decided to deal with the Americans. When I took off toward the enemy with my Feldwebel, I had an uncomfortable feeling in the pit of my stomach. That was a leftover from my time in Russia. What had the Red Cross meant there? Here, however, the weapons were quiet, because both sides were attending to their wounded.

The matter didn't go down too well with my Feldwebel either. He was fearful for me and kept on talking to me about it. But everything went well. The Americans had dismounted from their tanks, probably so we didn't have any fears. I was received by the commander of the tank unit, who had a Jewish translator with him. Of course, the first question was, "You SS?" I was able to calm the good man down. He most likely believed that a bloodthirsty scoundrel was hiding behind the uniform of every member of the Waffen SS. I assured him, that we tankers had worn the death's head on our uniforms well before the SS-units.

I then expressed my desires, and the American lieutenant drove along to our corps as an intermediary. He didn't say a word during the ride. When I asked him whether he belonged to such and such an armor regiment, because this number was sewn to his sleeve, he answered succinctly that he hadn't asked me for the number of our regiment. His answer was probably quite proper. I was only surprised, however, that the Americans also wore their numbers in combat. By point of contrast, our insignia had disappeared during the war.

Everything was discussed at corps, and the evacuation was approved. Why should we have continued the senseless endangerment of the wounded? It should be noted that the American didn't take a cigarette from our general, let alone something to drink! Were they that afraid of us?

It was then laid out exactly how the Americans would occupy the city while we left it. The time of the truce was set precisely. I felt like I was on a football field at halftime!

I brought the lieutenant back and bid farewell to the commander of the American armored advance guard. He wanted to offer me a cup of coffee and was amazed when I declined. Then he asked me why we were continuing to fight at all. I gave him my answer: as a soldier and an officer, I probably really didn't need to give him an explanation for it. He advised me to protect my men, since we would soon require every soldier for the execution of joint missions. This remark gave me some hope again. It could only refer to a joint campaign against Russia, after all. Perhaps reason would triumph over hate among our western opponents. That was probably also the case among the enemy combat troops. Unfortunately, the politicians had the last word.

I had scarcely driven out of the village with my tanks when the Russians, who had been prisoners in the camps, began to plunder and descend like animals on the civilian population. I had to turn to the Americans again with a request to bring about order. They cleaned up like I never would have dreamed possible. The Russians were soon behind barbed wire again. This ruthless proceeding allowed me to believe even more that the western powers would march against the east after our capitulation.

After another two days, I ended up in the village where I had stayed in the hospital. Everything looked different from back then. The place looked like an army camp because everyone who hadn't been taken prisoner yet was heading there. Nobody thought about putting up a defense anymore. We were in a patch of woods; our maintenance squad was working on our last "Hunting Tigers." The news then came that the Americans were in the village. We blew up the barrels of our assault guns. I had the company assemble for the last time. I cannot express in words how I felt at this last formation and what the faces of the soldiers revealed to me when we said good-bye. A few still wanted to break through, but we all saw one another in the camps again.

Feldmarschall Model escaped being taken prisoner by committing suicide in some woods near Duisberg. How unfortunate for this wonderful troop commander! Even he hadn't been able to prevent the defeat. It was a comfort to me that this exemplary soldier escaped delivery to the

Russians through his suicide. That certainly would have taken place after his being taken prisoner. He didn't want to live through the collapse of his homeland.

The Heathens are Often the Better Christians

We followed the news from the Eastern Front up until the end. We continued to have the opportunity in our hospital, the "golden cage," to hear the last German radio stations. We were glad that our comrades in the east continued to fight on bitterly to hold up Ivan for as long as possible. Unfortunately, their sacrifices were in vain! The Americans stopped at the Elbe. Our hopes for a joint struggle against the Russians dwindled with that. How easy this advance would have been and how willingly our units would have marched to the east! All the units were still together. The Yanks would only have had to take over the supply! The last opportunity to lead a low-risk preventive war was thrown away, when, blinded by hate, they allied themselves with the devil against Germany. The only goal that held the Allies together had been reached: Germany ceased to exist. The Americans could not have won the war anyway; it had already been decided before their intervention. They had the option of losing the peace.

Großadmiral Dönitz spoke on the radio after the announcement of Hitler's death. The officers gathered with the doctors in the officers' club. We had all put on our uniforms one more time, and we knew that it was the last time.

A few days later, by order of the Americans, the first inmates of the hospital were evacuated to a prison camp. Together with a slightly wounded Oberstleutnant, I volunteered and left with another six officers. This was the first time we were to get acquainted with the American soldiers, whom we, more or less, had only heard rumors about in combat. Technological progress is to be welcomed. When it serves as a replacement for good upbringing, however, then the behavior looks like what we had to experience at the hands of the enemy officers and soldiers. Only men who had not participated in combat could act in *such* a manner. These were men who only judged us by the atrocity propaganda.

Not only the *losing*, but also the winning a war demands human greatness. This greatness was completely missing in our opponents. I had the impression that the occupying powers wanted to prove at all costs that they weren't better than we were, rather worse!

We were then rounded up by the thousands on a playing field. That meant that hardly anyone had the opportunity to stretch out. There were no rations, even though our units had brought fully loaded trucks along. These were pushed over and the food burned! Even worse, not a drop of water was brought. Not until a mutiny threatened to break out were a few soldiers allowed to fetch a small container of water. When the desired liquid came, a major attempted in vain to create order so everyone could get something. That worked for the old soldiers, but the Yanks had also snatched up civilians, who immediately rebelled and ran like cattle toward the container. They simply let the water run, and, in the end, nobody at all had a drop!

A few days later, the recently amputated were brought to us, because the entire hospital had been ordered to be evacuated. Dressings were not furnished. We cut up our blankets to help our comrades as best we could. They died truly wretched deaths, and we had to watch them die without being able to help!

At night, our lives were in danger, even if we were only moving around. They immediately opened fire if someone wanted to go to the bathroom. I personally saw how three soldiers lost their lives in this manner, *before* they had even crossed the marked line. Those were the "liberators" who wanted to teach us to be humane. The so-called interrogations were also something else.

The men were supposed to give statements on things about which they had absolutely no idea. They were put in holes in the ground that came to a point at the bottom. They had to endure that for as long as it took until they admitted their "crimes." They had others kneel on sharp iron surfaces to break their resistance! What actually happened in Remagen, Kreuznach, Landau, or even in the SS-camps or during the infamous Malmedy trails could give a few concentration camp guards some good tips.

Fate was merciful to me, by the way. I was soon released because of my miserable appearance. I borrowed a civilian coat, gave my occupation as a "farmer's apprentice" and my address as that of my uncle, the doctor. I thus showed up unexpectedly as a free man at my uncle's hospital. We were both happy to see one another, and the doctors envied me, because they were still prisoners.

But for me, the war was really over. A new life had begun.

In Closing

Meanwhile, many years have passed. The allies of today have evolved from the enemies of yesterday. From the hate that the western powers brought against the German combat soldier—a hate that they continued to let us feel for many years after the armistice—has come the recognition that this German soldier did nothing but his duty for four and a half years—properly, bravely, and loyally. That our own country repeatedly fails to recognize this is another story. It will remain a blemish on our people for all times.

The old spirit of combat comradeship could not be eliminated, despite all the humiliation that we were subjected to and all the injustice that we endured. Shared suffering binds you, shared experience obligates you. Whom should it have surprised then, that we tankers tried to get in contact with one another after our return from captivity?

I was very lucky to be one of the first to come home. I experienced great happiness there, because our entire family had survived the war in one piece. It was an unforgettable day! My father had arrived the evening before. He had found my brother and my mother there. On the following evening, we were all happily reunited. Although none of us had known anything of the others, we had all returned home within twenty-four hours of each other. Fate was thus merciful to us.

The first one from our old unit that I was able to establish contact with was Delzeit. Köstler, Rieger, Stadler, and many more followed. Today, we have contacted more than fifty men from our tank unit. We celebrated our first get-together as a small group in Holzkirchen, near Munich. Our comrades from Austria also came. In 1955, we met in See-walchen on the Attersee and brought our wives along to this gathering. We decided then to get together again every year at Pentecost and not to rest or slack off until one day *all* the members of the 2nd Company of the 502nd Heavy Tank Battalion have gathered together. This book is dedicated to those soldiers and especially to our dead comrades, who are always among us at our gatherings.

Afterword to the English-Language Edition

One writes the history of a war to keep remembrances alive. One reads these memoirs to discover what happened. Above all, hopefully, it is intended that the younger generation learns from these readings and draws lessons for leadership, training, and weaponry from them.

The second World War took place more than forty-five years ago. Many will ask themselves: Hasn't the face of war changed fundamentally? Can one still learn from the events back then? Have nuclear, biological, and chemical weapons created completely new conditions that invalidate the former principles?

The development of weapons in the last world war contributed increasingly to the destruction of large masses of people and the objects of civilization. Nuclear, biological, and chemical weapons have established a new set of priorities in the conduct of a war. Their employment carries the risk that the enemy will defend himself with the same weapons. Since no state desires to commit suicide, the balance of terror will hopefully function. Every thinking person certainly has to wonder why all the industrial states continue to develop new nuclear, biological, and chemical weapons, even though the deactivation of the nuclear, biological, and chemical weapons already on hand and more or less safely stored poses great problems and will probably last decades.

Three well-known examples from the past are cited as proof:

Nuclear weapons: In Hiroshima and Nagasaki, generations suffer from hereditary damage caused by the employment of nuclear weapons.

Biological weapons: The island off the coast of England where resistant anthrax pathogens were tested on sheep still cannot be entered by humans. (This was supposed to be dropped on Hamburg!) It is impossible to live on this island.

Chemical weapons: The future damage due to the employment of dioxin agents in Vietnam for defoliating the forests cannot be foreseen among either friend or foe. This is evident from the fact that a law was passed to care for the affected American Vietnam veterans.

The numbers of those injured during the course of atomic and other testing with special weapons is intentionally kept secret by all the atomic powers.

Dr. Jacob Segal, professor for general biology at the Humboldt University in Berlin, still adheres to his theory that the AIDS virus is a man-made product intended for biological warfare, created by a recombination of genes from the Visna virus and the human HTL V1 virus. Even if this remains a theory, just the fact alone that such a possibility has been considered by a prominent biologist gives us pause to think. As a rule, politicians and military leaders are not biologists or chemists or physicists. In this case, the scientists carry full responsibility. I hope that these people will finally put a stop to this madness and that the conscience of these men and women is stronger than their ambition and desire for material gain.

In my opinion, the leading soldiers in the East and West are well aware that military leadership ends wherever nuclear, biological, and chemical weapons are employed. There will only be the question of survival and picking up the pieces. Operational leadership on the nuclear battlefield is no longer possible. I hope that the politicians in the military are prepared to admit this. The lowest level of leadership is the one most adversely affected in the case of nuclear, biological, and chemical contamination. Many agents do not take effect for days. Subjectively, the soldier is still ready for combat, but he only has a minimal chance of survival even if he is treated immediately. Should the company commander continue to employ those soldiers since they are as good as lost? The psychological stress on the soldier as well as the superior can scarcely be imagined!

The war can continue to be waged at some distance away from the nuclear, biological, and chemical contamination, of course. The more often nuclear, biological, and chemical weapons are employed, the less opportunity there is to lead troops; the less frequently they are used, the more conventional the war. And, basically, that war will not be that much different from the one that took place from 1939–45 in Europe. The quality and effectiveness of modern conventional arms, the equipment, the organization, and the distribution of the troops on the battlefield continue their dynamic development. The "combined arms battle" runs its course more quickly, and the weapons become more deadly and technically complicated. Only man remains the same, perhaps becoming even more delicate. I am therefore of the opinion that, aside from or even without the effect of nuclear, biological, and chemical weapons, the fundamental principles of leadership, as well as the movement and employment of troops with their weapons in relation to time and space, in short, that which our forefathers called maneuvering, has changed very little.

Finally, the excessive use of computers on the equipment and by the leadership is frequently an additional psychological burden on the soldier at the front. A soldier, regardless of his rank, who doesn't remember he has a brain until the computer breaks down and doesn't begin to use it until then will always be in second place. In no case must leadership be dependant upon computers!

Looked at from the standpoint represented above, the lessons from the second World War appear to have kept their value. It is worthwhile to look at them, to take them to heart, and to develop them further.

Glossary

AG	Assault gun
Alter Fritz	Carius's nickname for SS-Brigadeführer Fritz von Scholz (comparison with Friedrich the Great who was also called "alter Fritz," which means "old Fritz")
APC	Armored personnel carrier
Armee	Army
Armee-Korps	Army corps
AT	Antitank (allied units)
Bataillon	Battalion
Brigadeführer	Waffen-SS rank equivalent to brigadier general
Bundeswehr	West German Armed Forces
Deutschland	Germany
Deutschlandlied	German national anthem. Sometimes called "Deutschland Über Alles."
Einsatzgruppe	Ad hoc group formed at or below company level for conducting an operation. (Not to be confused with the same word used by the SS to indicate liquidation squads.)
Feldherrnhalle	One of two German army divisions named after the monument in honor of German military leaders in Munich. After the attempted Putsch in 1923, this monument also became a Nazi shrine, and a special SA detachment was formed to guard it. Personnel from this detachment were later used to provide cadre for the first army division to bear this honorary accolade.
Feldmarschall	Field marshal (five-star general)
Feldwebel	Staff sergeant. Can also be used generically to refer to noncommissioned officers as a whole.

Flak	Antiaircraft cannon (German forces). Flak = Flugabwehrkanone. It can be used generically to mean any type of antiaircraft cannon-based unit.
Funkmeister	Master radio operator
Gefreiter	Corporal
Generalfeldmarshall	Field marshal (five-star general)
Generalleutnant	Lieutenant general
Generaloberst	Colonel general (roughly equivalent to a four-star general)
Graf	Count
Grenadier-Regiment	Grenadier regiment (light infantry)
Großadmiral	Grand admiral
Großdeutschland	Elite German Army Division. Großdeutschland means "Greater Germany."
Hauptfeldwebel	Master sergeant
Hauptmann	Captain
Hauptsturmführer	Waffen-SS captain
Herr __Leutnant__	Traditional form of address in the German army. Roughly equivalent to "sir." (Rank follows the word Herr.)
Infanterie-Division	Infantry division
Jagdtiger	"Hunting Tiger" (tank destroyer version of the "Tiger")
Ju87	German dive bomber, more familiarly known as the Stuka
Judennase	Name given to a terrain feature that figures prominently in a series of operations in the text. Judennase means "Jew's nose."
Kampfgruppe	Battle group. Somewhat similar to a combat command or, in modern terms, a task force. It was an ad hoc organization composed of several different branches, which was formed to perform a specific mission.
Kampftruppenschule II	Combat Arms School II (Bundeswehr combined arms mechanized school)
KIA	Killed in action
Kinderheim	Name of a terrain feature that figures prominently in many of the operations on the Newel front. Kinderheim means "children's home."

Kommandeur	Commander
Kompanie	Company
Kristallnacht	Crystal night (night of Nazi party-sponsored attacks against the Jews in 1934)
Kübel (Kübelwagen)	Wartime precursor to the Volkswagen "Beetle." German equivalent to the jeep. An amphibious version was also produced.
KV85	Heavily armored late-war Russian tank armed with a long-barreled 85-mm main gun.
KVI	Early-war Russian heavy tank. It was heavily armored and featured a 76.2-mm main gun.
Leutnant	Lieutenant
Leutnant der Reserve	Lieutenant in the reserves. The suffix ". . . der Reserve" can be added to any rank, although it was uncommon beyond field grade (Oberstz).
Luftwaffe	German Air Force
MG42	Model 42 machine gun
MIA	Missing in action
NBC	Nuclear, biological, and chemical
NCO	Noncommissioned officer
Nebelwerfer	Rocket launcher. The term Nebelwerfer literally means "smoke launcher."
Nordland	Waffen-SS division composed primarily of volunteers from the Scandinavian countries. Nordland literally means northern land.
Oberfeldarzt	Medical Corps lieutenant colonel
Oberfeldwebel	Sergeant first class
Obergefreiter	Senior corporal
Oberkommando des Heeres	High command of the German army
Oberleutnant	First lieutenant
Oberst	Colonel
Oberstleutnant	Lieutenant colonel
OKH	*See* Oberkommando des Heeres
Operation See Lion	Reference to the aborted amphibious invasion of England by the Germans
Pak	Antitank cannon (German forces). Pak = Panzer-Abwehr-Kanone or antitank cannon. It can be used generically to mean any type of antitank cannon-based unit.

Panzer	Tank when referring to vehicles. Armor when referring to the concept or an organization.
Panzer-Abteilung	Tank battalion
Panzer-Division	Armor division
Panzer-Kompanie	Tank company
Panzerfaust	Handheld antitank rocket launcher developed and used in the latter half of the war.
Panzergrenadier	Mechanized infantryman
Panzerjäger	Private in an antitank unit. Can also be used in titles to denote antitank units.
Panzerkampfabzeichen	Panzer Assault Badge (combat award based on number of days in combat, several levels)
Panzerschütze	Private in the armored corps
PD	*See* Panzer-Division
Pionier-Bataillon	Engineer battalion
Rata	Type of Russian biplane.
Reichsführer	Title given to Heinrich Himmler as the leader of the SS.
Reichsmark	German currency in the World War II era.
Rollbahn	Generally, an improved road. It can be used to denote an axis of advance or a combination of the two; therefore it is not usually translated.
Scharführer	SS staff sergeant
Schütze	Private
Schwerpunkt	Point of main effort. Usually not translated.
Sherman	Standard American medium tank (M4). Sent to the Russians as part of the lend-lease program.
Sicherungs-Division	Security division (responsible for rear area security)
Soldat	Soldier
SS	Schutzstaffeln. Literally, protective staff. The term was used for the elite security services of the Nazi party. The field force of the SS was known as the Waffen SS (SS Armed Forces)
SS-Panzer-Korps	SS armor corps
SS-Scharführer	SS staff sergeant
Ssyms	Name given to the special railroad car used for transporting "Tiger" tanks.

Stabsfeldwebel	Senior master sergeant
Stabsgefreiter	Senior corporal
Stuka	German dive bomber
Styria	Region of Austria
Swabian	Coming from Swabia, a region of southwestern Germany.
T34	Russian medium tank
T43	German designation given to the T34 tank armed with the 85-mm main gun
T60	Russian light tank armed with a 45-mm main gun
Tabun	Nerve gas
Unteroffizier	Sergeant
Untersturmführer	SS second lieutenant
V1	Unmanned rocket introduced in 1944 as one of Hitler's "wonder weapons."
Volkssturm	"People's Army." Hitler's last-ditch effort to raise personnel for combat units. Composed of those either too young or too old for normal military service. Despite this, they were employed in large numbers at the front at the end of the war.
Waffen-SS	Armed SS (military branch of the SS)
Wehrmacht	German Armed Forces (World War II era)

Documents

Notes to First Six Documents

DOCUMENT 1:

This after-action report details some of the problems encountered during the establishment of the first "Tiger" battalions. This report is written from the commander's point of view and details some of the first operations of the 502nd Heavy Panzer Battalion as well as listing some recommendations for organization and employment of these organizations. This report was written before Otto Carius joined the unit.

DOCUMENT 2:

This after-action report was written by the maintenance personnel of the 502nd Heavy Panzer Battalion. It lists some of the problems encountered with the initial production run of the "Tiger" tank.

DOCUMENT 3:

The operations at the "Judennase" are detailed in this after-action report by the battalion commander, Major Schwaner. (*See* chapter: "Knight's Cross at the Hospital")

DOCUMENT 4:

The operations in and around Dünaburg, which eventually led to the awarding of the Oak Leaves to the Knight's Cross for Otto Carius, are detailed in this battalion-level after-action report by Major Schwaner.

DOCUMENT 5:

This report from the engineer staff section of the L Army Corps discusses the measures needed to be taken to reinforce the road network for the employment of "Tigers." The report is based on input provided by the battalion commander at the time, Hauptmann Schmidt, and Lieutenant Carius.

DOCUMENT 6:

This after-action report, written by Lieutenant Carius himself, describes the operations in and around Lembitu in March 1944, which are covered in the main text beginning with the chapter "Ivan Attacks."

Document 1

Hauptmann Lange   In the field
2nd Company   January 29, 1943
502nd Heavy Panzer Battalion

AFTER-ACTION REPORT

I. Activation

The company was activated as part of the battalion in May 1942. The first two "Tigers" were allocated on September 25, 1942; they had to be transferred to the 1st Company of the 502nd (Wolchow) on October 13, 1942. During the time period mentioned, the drivers were tested by Technical Officer Hering and tank training was initiated; most of the time, both "Tigers" were in the workshop. Until outfitting was complete, training was limited to classroom instruction based on requisitioned training charts and general weapons and terrain training.

On December 21 and 22, 1942, one "Tiger" was received each day; on December 25 two "Tigers" were received; on December 26 three "Tigers"; and, on December 28 two "Tigers." Time for training was limited to a few hours on these days, because outfitting, modifications, and basic issue items took up the entire time. In addition, all of the work left undone by maintenance had to be performed. Elements of the maintenance squads and the Panzer VI drivers of the company, as well as the specialists, shop foreman, and supervisor of the maintenance platoon at battalion had been detached to the 503rd Panzer Battalion from the beginning of December until December 21. All of the "Tigers" were zeroed in Fallingbostel, even though the order was in effect for the last two to be left on the Ssyms railcars. Despite this, all three transport trains rolled at the ordered times. From Fallingbostel: the first train at 2000 on December 27; the second train at 0500 on December 28; the third train at 1100 on December 29, 1942.

Problems were intensified because the attachment of the company to Army Group Don was not ordered by teletype until the evening of

December 23; this was the first time it was certain that the company was being separated from the battalion. In the meantime, however, all of the replacement parts consolidated by the headquarters company were at the battalion on the Wolchow River. To ensure supply of the company, trucks were requested (immediately attached by the General Army Office) and picked up by the company by December 26. The drivers arrived from the replacement battalions late in the morning of December 27. All of the Panzer VIs continued to be delivered without bore brushes (for the Model 36 main gun), to cite one example. These were not procured until special couriers were dispatched to Krupp and Wegmann.

No time had been allocated for any training at organizational level. It is advisable that all "Tiger" units have at least three weeks' time for training after receiving their last tank. Moreover, it is necessary to loan them experienced officers as advisors on a temporary basis, who can train with the soldiers and start sharing their experience during activation. Doing things too quickly leads to a lack of success during an operation or to the premature breakdown of the Panzer VI as a result of inadequate technical knowledge. It is recommended that the tank battalions of the established regiments be equipped with "Tigers" because a firm foundation with regard to tactical and technical knowledge is already present there.

II. Employment

On January 5 and 6, 1943, the three trains were unloaded in Proletarskaja and, on January 7, the company was attached to the 17th Panzer-Division and directed to Ssungar (Kuberle sector). The 107 kilometers were covered without mechanical failure during a ten and a half hour road march. A short maintenance halt was made every twenty kilometers.

January 8, 1943

Mission: The company was attached to Panzer Battalion 39. Together with Panzer Company "Sander," it attacked six villages on the left flank forward of the left wing of the division (Schwerpunkt: Osserskij and Nish-Sserebjakowka) and eliminated the enemy wherever he appeared. After the first village was set on fire (twelve kilometers west of Ilowaskij), a radio message from the division was received: "Immediately turn around through the Kuberle sector in order to destroy the attack of two Russian regiments, supported by armor, coming from Osserskij."

In the course of this operation, two tanks, eight antitank guns, and approximately 1,000 Russians were destroyed by the company, for the most part by rolling over them. In addition, many antitank rifles and light infantry weapons were destroyed; by this action, the attack in front of friendly infantry was completely destroyed.

Distance covered:	65 kilometers on this day
Losses:	1 Panzer VI through transmission damage
	2 Panzer IIIs through enemy fire
Casualties:	1 dead
	5 missing in action
	3 wounded
Weather:	Heavy snowstorm with ice formation in the morning, later clear visibility

January 9, 1943

Mission: Mop up the southwestern portion of Ilowaskij in conjunction with Panzer Company "Sander"

The attack began in the morning twilight and ended with the destruction of five 7.62-mm antitank guns, two light field cannons, and one weak Russian battalion.

The unit assembled in the northern portion of Ilowaskij after performing the mission.

0900—New mission: Engage and destroy fifteen enemy tanks approaching Bratskij

Because the "Tiger" company could not cross the bridge over the Kuberle at Bratskij, the attack was conducted in the form of a pincer. The company crossed the Kuberle embankment on its own east of Ilowaskij and advanced north. A strong enemy antitank line approximately 1,000 meters in front of our own lines was destroyed by attacking it (partly by employing smoke).

In the process, eight antitank guns were destroyed.

Following that, the company pivoted toward Bratskij to link up with Panzer Company "Sander." In the meantime, the Russian tanks had turned off in the direction of Ssal. After linking up with Panzer Company "Sander," the attack on Osserskij was ordered. Portions of the village were shot into flames after knocking out four flanking antitank guns. Following this, the company marched back in convoy with the tanks that had fallen out.

Distance covered:	48 kilometers on this day	
Losses:	1 Panzer VI	Hit on commander's cupola (76.2 mm)—cupola lifted, welded seam cracked, cupola bolts broken. Temporary damage to the elevating mechanism, apparently due to the hit
	1 Panzer VI	Due to shifting difficulties
	1 Panzer VI	Due to motor fire, which was extinguished by the automatic fire extinguisher
	1 Panzer III	Right drive sprocket shot off
Casualties:	1 dead	(Lt. Dr. Taubert: killed by an antitank hit on the rear deck while checking the motor after the fire)
Weather:	Cloud cover, clear visibility	

January 10, 1943

Mission: In conjunction with Panzer Company "Sander," conduct attack against enemy armor northwest of Budjenny

In the process, eleven tanks, two antitank guns, and one Russian battalion were destroyed (3 T34s, 1 KV1, 7 T60s).

Vehicular losses and personnel casualties: None

By order of corps, all battle-ready tanks had to be attached immediately to the 16th Motorized Infantry Division. Three Panzer VIs and six Panzer IIIs were sent. The Panzer VIs remained at the 16th ID until January 15 and the Panzer IIIs until January 24, where they were involved in a number of battles, but generally just had to cover large distances. On

January 14, three Panzer VIs received a mission to cover the withdrawal of the 16th ID to Kamarow three kilometers to the west (north of Nowo-Ssadkowskij) and then to road march back to the company at Proletarskaja. The Panzer IIIs remained attached to the division. All three Panzer VIs broke down on the return march due to mechanical problems and had to wait up to thirty hours in the steppes until they could be recovered (due to a lack of prime movers).

On January 10, the remainder of the company and the broken-down tanks in Ssungar were ordered to withdraw to Proletarskaja. The march back ran into great difficulties because the recovery elements were not turned around in time, due to the Russians having captured a portion of the supply route. Despite this, everything was recovered, to a large extent with tanks that were moving back with the rear guard, which had been made driveable through improvised measures.

On January 16 and 17, the mission-capable elements were employed as cover at Stalinski Pud and were involved on January 17 in defending against a Russian infantry attack. At the onset of darkness, the withdrawal of the 2nd Company of the 502nd was ordered. It had been attached to the 503rd Panzer Battalion in the meantime. The march to Rostow was conducted in phases until January 22. Four "Tigers" and three Panzer IIIs were loaded in Ssalsk; the rest were towed to Rostow in a road march, primarily by two "Tigers," since the four prime movers were needed for loading or were, in part, themselves damaged. The march back and the towing operations were disrupted and made difficult by embankments, deep ravines, and heavy buildup of ice.

III. Evaluation:

Without exception, it must be ensured through the issuance of strict orders at all levels of command that "Tiger" units are never employed under company strength and that Panzer VIs and IIIs are never separated. The "Tigers" must be and remain the battering rams in an ongoing attack and the shielding buffers at the Schwerpunkt of the defense. The field elements are generally of the opinion that the "Tiger" can do everything. They do not understand that a new weapon has deficiencies and weaknesses, which can only be redressed through experience and further development. For this reason, the danger exists that "Tiger" units will be assigned missions that the normally equipped tank companies can solve without further ado. As a result of continuous movement, the subsequent heavy stress on running gear and motors, and the lack of time available for maintenance service, damage results, which cause "Tiger" units to break down when they are needed. The maintenance element must be able to work for as long as possible in one location (preferably a train station). When changing locations, it is especially important that it knows the "where to." For the time being, "Tiger" units must continue to remain the last reserve of the troop commander. They must be available and ready behind the Schwerpunkt of the sector in order to force the decision whenever all other means fail.

Road marches:

The winter grousers do not offer sufficient protection against sliding sideways, something which came to light in the many iced-over ravines and embankments. March speed satisfies all demands made.

Effect of enemy fire:

At no time did fire from 76.2-mm antitank guns result in a penetration or heavy damage among the "Tigers" of the company. In one case, the commander's cupola was lifted somewhat by a hit on the upper edge of its forward side as a result of the welding seam breaking open; in addition, the bolts inside snapped off.

The Russian Model 42 antitank rifle obtained penetrations of up to 17 mm, as measured on the front slope in front of the driver's position. This rifle was encountered quite frequently and can be recognized by its prominent muzzle flash. In one case, an oblique hit was made against the forward vision slit of the commander's cupola. Its corner broke off and ricocheted, rendering the Kinon vision block unusable. The result of a direct hit: probable penetration. The rounds of the antitank rifle usually impact in the vicinity of the vision slot. One hit on the jacket tube of the 88-mm main gun (probably a 45-mm antitank gun) resulted in a severe indentation in the jacket tube and a very slight dent in the gun liner. Because the crew did not think the gun tube had been damaged, they continued firing without interruption.

Firefight:

The best firing distance is up to 1,500 meters; perfect hits with well-zeroed weapons. Up to now, effectiveness and penetration ability of the 88-mm is more than satisfactory for all targets.

The ratio of the ammunition basic load must be 1:1—armor piercing to high explosive. As a minimum, it must be delivered in this ratio by supply elements in order to adjust daily for the requirements of the fighting. During the final battles, only armor-piercing rounds were available.

Some of the shell casings were too thick, so that stoppages occurred because the breach block was jammed by them.

The travel lock for the weapon must be capable of being operated with a handle. The ability to fire suffers due to the current travel lock and leads to delays of at least one minute. Under battle conditions, movement without locking down the weapon is not possible, as the weapons show severe elevation alignment problems after a short period of time.

Observation of fire is sufficient for the commander; for the gunner, there is heavy degradation through the cloud of smoke caused by the discharge. In any case, a wiper for the optics is necessary. At present, unit-level improvisation is being tested and has proven itself well.

Modification requests:

Commander: The commander's cupola must be lower. The vision slits must be adjustable. The turret hatch—as has already been requested—must be capable of being opened to the side. The cable for headphones and microphone is too short. The auxiliary handwheel for the traversing mechanism at the commander's location must get a neutral position; periscopes for the commander's cupola would be useful.

Gunner: Capability to sit normally without turning at the hip. Place the handwheel for the elevating mechanism higher and outfit it with a cover. The optics freeze up during severe temperatures, so that the indicator slips; setting the range is impossible. The locking mechanism for the turret must engage from above, since it disengages in its current configuration. An additional locking mechanism for six o'clock is necessary, because the turret drifts to the side during towing.

Loader: The machine gun is too close to the main gun; because of this, loading belts is made difficult. Many stoppages on the machine gun, because the sear linkage easily breaks or bends. Ammunition racks for the 88 mm are inconveniently located, especially the lower ones. The emergency escape hatch has to be able to be opened like a door. Hinges like those on the radio operator's hatch (mount inside). In its current configuration, the emergency escape hatch can be opened from the inside but not closed. The hatch is not only there for dismounting when in great danger, however, but also for evacuation of wounded, for establishing contact with the infantry, for tossing out spent casings, and for extinguishing engine compartment fires in battle (from the hatch by turning the turret to three o'clock). It is also used for dismounting to conduct the work necessary for towing disabled tanks in battle.

Driver: Vision slit jams easily. Install pivoting sideview optics (periscopes for the driver and the radio operator). Access hatch in the firewall between the fighting compartment and the engine compartment must be bigger for allowing easier work. Put the blackout driving light under armor protection, because otherwise it is constantly destroyed. Put the toolbox in the vehicle or in the storage box, otherwise it is constantly lost.

Radio operator: Tank poorly debugged for radio interference. For command vehicles, to include the company commander, medium-wave radio is appropriate to remain in direct and constant contact with division. Its nonavailability was considered very disruptive at the 17th PD.

IV. Organization

The heavy tank battalion with two heavy companies represents very heavy fighting power. Reinforcement by a third company ("Tiger"), as is being sought to some extent, is not considered appropriate. The massing of "Tigers" at one place and to this extent is not possible at this time. The result is a division of the battalion and correspondingly increased difficulties in supply. Furthermore, the danger exists that the battalion then becomes so unwieldy that it can no longer do justice to its actual missions. Due to the poor road situation in Russia, road march difficulties and traffic jams have already occurred during movements by the battalion and its wheeled vehicles.

As an organization scheme for the company, the following setup is considered to be appropriate (it has been followed by the 2nd Company since its activation):

Command section:

> 2 Panzer VIs (Both equipped as command tanks; the second one, to be used as a reserve vehicle for the company commander, is still not on hand)
> 2 platoons, each with 4 Panzer VIs
> 2 platoons, each with 5 Panzer IIIs (with short 75-mm guns)

Justification:

Both "Tiger" platoons combine heavy firepower and can be maneuvered quickly by the company commander. In case a vehicle is lost, each platoon remains sufficiently combat effective and fire control is always firmly in the hand of the platoon leader.

Both Panzer III platoons can be used at any time for reconnaissance to the front and flanks, the protection of the Panzer VIs against close attacks, and fighting infantry and massed targets. The provisioning of replacement parts and the exact wartime tables of organization and tables of distribution and allowances must be established in consultation with officers who have evaluated experience gained in combat.

<u>In summary, it can be said that the "Tiger" will do complete justice to the demands that are placed on a heavy tank in battle after its teething problems are eliminated.</u>

Of the nine "Tigers" in the company, most have reached a reading of approximately 800 kilometers.

Document 2

Maintenance Platoon
502nd Heavy Panzer Battalion
Inspector Cenker
Shop Foreman Neubert

In the field
January 29, 1943

TECHNICAL AFTER-ACTION REPORT

I. Damage to the running gear

Flange fasteners for the outer road wheels loosen themselves while moving. Result: loss of the outer road wheels. Severe wear on road wheels, their rubber surfaces, and road wheel rims.

Cause:

a) The flange for attaching the outer road wheels is much too small. The fastening screws are too weak and too short. The threads on the screws are much too coarse.

b) When the rubber outer layer of the road wheel is damaged, the road wheel rims jam on the track, bend the outer edge of the rim, and cannot be used anymore.

c) Too narrow mounting of the road wheels between the outer and inner ones; a space of 10 mm at the most.

d) Bending of the second lifting arm from the front.

e) Current lockdown devices insufficient. Great care must be taken in mounting the flanges.

Remedy:

for a) Make the fastening flange larger. Make the screws for them stronger and furnish them with fine threading; only employ screws where lock nuts can be used.

for b) When constructing the rubber outer layer on the road wheels, it should be ensured that the first layer of rubber (wire netting) is kept even with the rims. By doing this, it can be

ensured that the road wheels continue to roll on the first layer
of rubber or wire netting when the top layer of the rubber
layer becomes detached. Result: the heavy wear on the road
wheels and the rims can be avoided.

for c) The too-narrow mounting of the road wheels did not hold up
very well in the winter, with the result that heavy wear on the
rubber tires has occurred. If the vehicle moves in very poor
terrain with a lot of rocks and ice, the spaces between the
wheels jam up with sand and stones to such a degree that lifting arms are often bent and torsion bars broken. It is
requested (suggested) that the spaces between the road
wheels be kept somewhat greater.

for d) *See* c) above.

for e) As lockdowns for the screws, use the halfmoon-shaped piece
of sheet metal designed for two screws that was recently delivered from Henschel; however, both ends must be made
longer so that the lockdown clamps are higher. It must be
ensured during installation that the support ring is kept clean
(scratch away the paint).

II. Track pins sliding out

Reason:

Securing devices for the track pins are too weak (inside and outside).

Remedy:

Deeper indentation and stronger securing devices at the inside end
(track side); do not weld the fasteners on, but use screws for the track
pins.

III. Loosening of the fastening screws (cone-shaped screws) on the drive sprocket

Remedy:

Frequent tightening of the cone-shaped screws in the field or securing them by boring through the heads of the screws and locking them
down with wire.

Mounting of the running gear

Mounting and dismounting device for road wheels.

The following socket wrenches must be made stronger:

52 mm

27 mm

32 mm

Devices for fixing the lifting arms in place when changing torsion bars are needed.

IV. Damage to the cooling system

Reason:

Loss of coolant at the hose connectors. Poor hose connectors; connecting hoses and pipes too short.

Remedy:

SKF hose connector (like Maybach)

Presently fastened with wire by the troops. Longer connecting hoses. Lips at the end of the pipes.

Connecting pipe for the radiator water outlet from the motor to the right radiator

Reason:

When opening and closing the rear deck access hatch, one of the latches presses against the connecting pipe and pushes it down; because of this, the connecting pipe is twisted and the hose fastener loosened. Result: leakage and loss of radiator water.

Remedy:

Move the access hatch latch. At present, the troops are breaking off the far edge.

V. Damage to the fuel feed lines

Leaky fuel tanks; leaky connections from the upper tank to the lower tank.

Remedy:

Better installation; check the soldering during installation; pay special attention to the riveting of the reinforcement metal.

Loss of fuel

Reason:

Loosening of the membrane screws at the fuel pump. Bad seals on the sight indicators. Loosening of the lines to the fuel pump.

Remedy:

In general, better tightening of all screws and lines during installation at the plant. After longer road marches, retightening in the field as well. Lock down screws on the fuel lines.

Fuel feed line to the carburetor

Reason:

Material deforms.

Remedy:

Other material has already been planned by Maybach.

VI. Damage to the motor (carburetor fires)

Reason:

a)   When dismounting the air collection pipe, all seals are damaged (at present—cork seals).

b)   When the cork seals on the air collection pipe are damaged, a gap is created and, with it, the possibility of backfiring flames escaping.

c)   Leaky floats. Result: a change in fuel levels and overflowing of fuel.

Remedy:

for a) Use of special or not so easily damaged material or modification by the carburetor manufacturer.

for b) This malfunction can be eliminated by better seals.

for c) Thorough checking of the carburetor and floats by the manufacturer.

VII. Engine fires

Reason:

a)   Ignition of spilled oil (the result of poor outer crankshaft seals).

b)   Poor seating of the lines leading to the fuel pump. Result: leakage of fuel.

c)   Poor seating of the screw cap to the oil fill funnel. Result: leakage of oil.

This overflowing oil drops onto the muffler. Oil also leaks when the seal is missing.

Remedy:

for a) Use of better crankshaft seals.

for b) Tightening of all fuel feed lines and locking down the nuts.

for c) Tightening the fill cap screw with a wrench is not always possible during operations. For this reason, it is suggested that a larger-sized wing nut be used instead of a six-sided screw. That would guarantee good tightening, even by hand. The seal in the fill cap screw should be mounted in such a manner that its loss in the field is not possible.

It would be desirable if the driver had the opportunity while making a maintenance halt during an operation to check his oil level without opening the rear deck hatch.

VIII. Inadequate fire extinguishing system

Reason:

The crew has been given no chance to extinguish a fire in the engine compartment without leaving the fighting compartment whenever a fire starts.

1. For inexplicable reasons, the automatic fire extinguisher does not activate sometimes when there is a carburetor fire.

2. After two or three uses of the automatic fire extinguisher, it is empty and there is no opportunity for the troops in the field to refill or replace it.

Remedy:

It is suggested that an opening be installed in the firewall to the engine compartment so that the opportunity always exists of extinguishing the engine fire in the quickest manner possible without leaving the fighting compartment. It is absolutely necessary to mount a large five-liter Tetra carbon dioxide fire extinguisher in the fighting compartment so that any fire can be extinguished at any time.

IX. Transmission damage

Changing of the transfer devices; specifically, elongation of the wires (external). Result: changing of the shifting pattern.

Wearing out of the acceleration brake (first brake). Individual shifting cylinders displace on their own. Reinforcement and fastening of the individual actuation levers has been performed in such a faulty manner that, to a large extent, the Preson pins and cotter pins of the individual bolts are missing. Because these parts are located behind the transmission housing, checking them is impossible without dismantling the housing. Provide the line system in the transmission with better seals or tighten it down better during disassembly. Due to the poor mounting of the oil lines, pressure is lost in the transmission.

Remedy:

The much-too-large wear and tear on the acceleration brake is caused by shifting to the fourth or fifth gear. It is suggested that sturdier material be used by the production facility for this brake.

In manufacturing the transfer devices, great attention must be paid to the wire groups and assembly. In no case must easily malleable material be used. During the assembly and inspection of the transmissions by the manufacturer or the Army acceptance office, it must be ensured that all outside actuation levers and shafts are properly furnished with Preson pins and cotter pins. Because of these small deficiencies, vehicles have broken down. For the adjustment of the individual shafts, hours of work are often necessary by soldiers who have to perform this work without any type of aids. Likewise, it must be ensured by the manufacturer that the loosening of the oil pressure lines in the transmission as well as the displacement of shifting cylinders on their own is not possible.

For the most part, various deficiencies and disruptions in the shifting transmission could be avoided if the transmissions are not driven until they reach their proper operating temperature. This is frequently not possible. For this reason, measures must be taken so that the vehicles can be driven without damage even when they have not reached operating temperature.

AFTER-ACTION REPORT CONCERNING TOWING EQUIPMENT FOR THE PANZER VI

I. Towing operations with the Panzer VI have revealed that all of the towing equipment is inadequate and too weak. All of the tow bars bend and the bolts jam. Despite bracing of the equipment, the force exerted by the Panzer VI in steep terrain is so great that all of the towing equipment is bent.

II. The eighteen-ton prime movers are much too light; it is almost impossible to tow one Panzer VI in difficult terrain with three or four prime movers. In steep terrain, the tank pushes the prime movers out of the way. Greater braking power is absolutely necessary. In steep terrain, practice has shown that three prime movers have to be used in front with two in the rear acting as a brake in order to get the tank through it. It is suggested that every battalion be given two vehicles with a "Tiger" chassis for towing purposes (damaged vehicles).

III. Due to the length of the element, towing a "Tiger" along a route of advance with four or five prime movers impedes all of the traffic. Road marching within a column is very difficult. Approaching another column and sudden stops within one are practically impossible. Towing operations on longer road marches at night is impossible, because each bridge has to be checked for its load classification; narrow gullies or other obstacles can scarcely be negotiated at night.

IV. Towing a Panzer VI with four prime movers a distance of 150 kilometers has shown that clutch and transmission damage resulted in all four prime movers. Of those, one prime mover had such severe transmission damage that the entire transmission had to be overhauled.

V. The snow chains with the rubber padding for the prime movers are completely ill-suited in difficult terrain and for towing a Panzer VI. The chains are too weak and rip; the guide chains slip off and also rip off the rubber padding. The winch cables for winching a tank out are much too weak and rip. Five prime movers are necessary in order to winch out a Panzer VI on a 10 percent grade.

Besides the winching cables, the mounting screws to the drive on the winch rip out. These screws have only been rated for pulling seven and a third tons. Therefore, it is practically impossible to drag an immobile tank over an end ramp and onto a rail car despite two sets of block and tackle with two prime movers.

It is absolutely necessary to use stronger winch cables for the towing of Panzer VIs and to develop better towing systems. As practice has shown, recovery is most easily and quickly accomplished in difficult terrain by another Panzer VI.

VI. To recover a Panzer VI, a platoon must have at least six prime movers available (with one six-ton crane among them).

Because the 502nd Panzer Battalion was divided into two elements (each with a maintenance platoon), our 2nd Maintenance Platoon had only three prime movers at its disposal (of which one prime mover was lost due to transmission damage). Result: great difficulties in recovering Panzer VIs.

It is absolutely necessary that independent Tiger companies be equipped with six prime movers.

VII. Improvements in the towing equipment are being conducted in the field. Despite this, it is necessary to develop better towing equipment in Germany; it must be developed in such a form that it is delivered directly from the manufacturer with each tank.

It is suggested that the towing equipment be constructed in such a manner that it is mounted to the left and right of the exhaust mufflers. This will make it possible to tow a Panzer VI out of harm's way with another Panzer VI without special means of assistance (e.g. during battle because of breakdown, fire, or any other deficiency). Using tow cables to recover a Panzer VI in combat is very difficult.

1. This is due to the exhaustive work, the retrieval of the tow cables from the tank, and the connecting of the cables to the shackles.
2. The shackles delivered by the manufacturer have proven themselves to be completely inadequate.

Reason: a) The material is too brittle and it breaks.

b) The shackles warp and the bolts bend.

Result: More work in order to get the bent bolts and shackles out of the shackle mounting eyes on the tank.

VIII. Placing the track-mounting toolbox outside of the tank on the left side does not function well. The toolbox must be moved inside because it has been lost on almost all the tanks.

Document 3

Location classified
Carius, Lieutenant   March 24, 1944
2nd Company/
502nd Heavy Panzer Battalion

AFTER-ACTION REPORT FOR THE PERIOD FROM MARCH 17 TO 21, 1944

March 17, 1944

At 0900 on March 17, 1944, the artillery barrage in preparation of the large-scale Russian attack across the entire 61st Infantry Division sector was initiated. The Schwerpunkt could not be determined initially. My two "Tigers" were 1,000 meters west of Chundinurk, the reserve of the 162nd Grenadier Regiment. At 0930, during the artillery barrage, ten men passed me heading west from Chundinurk. These were then followed by a 3.7-cm Flak gun, a twelve-ton prime mover, and then twenty to thirty men without weapons. I asked one of the men whether he had come from the ruins. When I heard that both of the ruins and the farmstead had been evacuated and destroyed, I went into action. I didn't receive any more orders from above, because all the lines had been destroyed or cut by the artillery barrage. I immediately advanced rapidly to the farmstead and had the second vehicle sweep out somewhat to the left. I immediately saw that the enemy was already in battalion strength on the plain north of the rail embankment at Limbitu and that one tank was moving southeast of the Kinderheim. North of the railroad embankment, five additional T34s were moving rapidly north toward the Rollbahn. There were no defensive weapons on hand, because the assault guns had also moved north. Only the machine gun on the right flank of the Division Feldhermhalle had remained in place, and, late in the afternoon, it renewed fire. The T34 south of the Kinderheim turned around immediately when it saw us approach. It passed me heading toward Lembitu and was knocked out at point-blank range. The five T34s that were moving toward the Rollbahn were also knocked out within a few minutes. Five antitank guns were destroyed on the rail embankment. The majority of the Russian infantry on the plain were destroyed in a counterattack, and the old main battle line at the ruins was regained. The farmstead and the ruins were then held free of the enemy against all further attacks until the onset of darkness and would only have had to be reoccupied. By 1030 I had already informed Oberleutnant von Schiller that there were no more infantry there. This report was considered to be incorrect by the regiment, until I personally drove to their command post at the Kinderheim at 1700 and was responsible for a few people being assembled and ordered back to the old strongpoints. After a half hour preparation from heavy weapons, the Russians, using armor support, renewed the attack in battalion strength in the Lembitu sector at 1340. The main battle line was held by my tanks (at 1100 a third vehicle had been brought up), and the attack was repulsed with high casualties to the enemy. Five T34s and one KVI were destroyed. Our artillery did not support me, because the forward observers were no longer there. At 1515, the enemy assembled in regimental strength south of the rail embankment at Lembitu. Because my ammunition had run low and one had to reckon with additional attacks, I (through Oberleutnant von Schiller) had a barrage of army-level artillery initiated on preregistered targets around Lembitu. The fire came after about twenty minutes. It sat so well that the assembly area was completely destroyed. The Russians did not attack again until 1615. That time, it was in battalion strength. They wanted to take the strongpoints at all costs. At 1700 the attack was repulsed with heavy casualties to the enemy. The Russians had not accomplished anything. Three additional T34s were knocked out around Lembitu. After that fruitless attack by the Russians, I left two "Tigers" at the ruins and personally drove to the regimental command post. At 1600, it had been claimed by higher headquarters (relayed by Oberleutnant von Schiller) that the ruins had been occupied by us. Not until I told him did Major Haase hear about the mess-up in the morning. He then gathered a few people together. Because this lasted a long time, I had to drop back approximately 200 meters from the ruins when it became dark. I did this to be safe against hunter/killer teams and to have fields of fire. One "Tiger" remained at the farmstead. The farmstead was kept free of the enemy until the arrival of ten men at 2100. They simply reoccupied it. An additional twenty-five men formed a line in the vicinity of the Pirtsu–Auwere road. The Russians did not attempt any more attacks during the night; they occupied both ruins, however, without resistance. At 2130, I drove back to my base to resupply. At 2400, an additional two "Tigers" were sent to the Kinderheim as a reserve. I didn't need to employ them, however.

Destroyed: 14 T34s, 1 KVI, 5 7.62-mm antitank guns

March 18, 1944

Starting from Pirtsu at 0500, I initiated a counterattack against the ruins in conjunction with sixteen infantrymen. After a short destructive fire by all three vehicles on the western ruin, I rolled forward to it; eight men occupied the ruin. The attack on the eastern ruin was more difficult, because it had been occupied by forty men and was near the rail embankment. The Russians put up an extremely tough and bitter defense. During the night, they had emplaced five 76.2-mm antitank guns in the ruins. They were immediately destroyed; in addition, one 47-mm antiaircraft cannon and two short-barreled 76.2-mm infantry howitzers were destroyed. Two T34s, which counterattacked from the ruins of Lembitu, were destroyed. At 0545, heavy mortar and large-caliber artillery fire started. Four infantrymen became casualties, and the ruins could not be occupied, let alone held, by the remainder. I had the attack broken off to avoid further losses, including tanks. I brought the wounded back and drove to the support base. The eastern ruin was also left to the Russians in the following days. The Russians left thirty to forty dead in the ruins.

1445: Barrage-type preparation of heavy weapons on the ruins, farmstead, and the plain north of it. 1500: Counterattack of the Russians in company strength (with armor support) against the ruins and the farmstead. The attack was repulsed, and two T34s and one T60 were knocked out.

Destroyed: 4 T34s, 1 T60, 5 7.62-mm antitank guns, 2 7.62-mm
            short-barreled infantry howitzers, and 147-mm
            antiaircraft cannon

March 19, 1944

1200: After artillery and mortar preparation, attack against the north-south road at Point 38.9. Six T34s, one KVI, one T60, one 7.62-mm antitank gun destroyed. 1600: Counterattack south from Point 33.9. 1700: One T34 destroyed. 1800: One T34 destroyed. 1900: Old main battle line regained.

Destroyed: 8 T34s, 1 KVI, 1 T60, 17.62-mm antitank gun

March 20, 1944

0515: Russian attack in company strength around Lembitu. 0620: Repulsed. One T34 destroyed. 1145: Attack in company strength at Lembitu. 1230: Repulsed. One T34 and one 47-mm antitank gun knocked out.

Destroyed: 2 T34s, 147-mm antitank gun

March 21, 1944

0300: Middle ruins taken by the Russians. 0445: Counterattack with ten infantrymen against the middle ruins. 0620: Ruins firmly in our hands. Two 76.2-mm antitank guns destroyed.

0830: Ruins evacuated again. Four men dead; six men fled. 1205: Radio sets brought to the farmstead with a "Tiger" (the one there had broken down). Impossible by foot. Two T34s destroyed at Point 33.9.

1630: Counterattack against the middle ruins. 1700: Situation reestablished. One vehicle stuck. Damaged by direct mortar hit during recovery and one man wounded. Otherwise, the recovery went well.

Destroyed: 2 T34s, 2 76.2-mm antitank guns

March 22, 1944

1000: Attack at Point 33.9. Two T34s knocked out. Attack was repulsed.

Destroyed: 2 T34s

/signed/
Carius, Lieutenant
2nd Company/
502nd Heavy Panzer Battalion

Document 4

Corps command post
Corps Headquarters: L Army Corps   July 14, 1943
Ia./ K.Pi.F.—Stopi.
No. 93 / 43 g. Kdo.
Reference: A.O.K. 18. Ia No. 9945 / 43 geh. of June 12, 1943
SUBJECT: Employment of the Mark VI tank ("Tiger")

TO: A.O.K. 18
    A new route reconnaissance of the approach routes for areas of operation A-E in the corps sector was conducted by the commander of the 502nd Heavy Panzer Battalion, Hauptmann Schmidt, and platoon leader Lieutenant Carius. The following was determined:

Area of Operation A
    Debarking train station: Taizy
    Approach route: Taizy–Krasnoje Selo–Dreiecksdorf–river
                                 road
    The bridge over the Kikenka ditch between the Oranienbaum rail line and the river road can be circumvented for the time being by approaching on the rail embankment up to the high voltage line at the signalman's house, then moving 750 meters north, and then east to the road from Dreiecksdorf to the river road.

Work needed:
    Reinforcement of the railroad bridge over a ditch east of the signalman's house. Manufacture of a turn-off ramp from the rail embankment to the field path in the area of the signalman's house. The conduct of the work will encounter no serious problems and can be performed with expedient measures.
    The bridge over the Kikenka ditch on the road from Dreiecksdorf to the river road does not have to be reinforced initially.

A continuation of the Krasnoje Selo–Dreiecksdorf–river road approach route to Urizk is possible via the road through the collective farm at Proletarskij-trug up to the Oranienbaum rail line and from here on the road next to the railroad up to the outskirts of Urizk.

Work needed:

Reinforcement of both of the road bridges over the creek beds north of the fork in the tracks (at the western point of the fork in the tracks and in front of the middle of the fork in the tracks). This work can also be performed relatively quickly with expedient means.

Area of Operation B

Approach route: Taizy–Krasnoje Selo–Konstantinowka–
Dreiecksdorf–Puschkin Rollbahn

Where the route intersects the Dreiecksdorf–Puschkin Rollbahn, it can be negotiated further in the direction of Puschkin if the bridge over Duderhofer Creek, 600 meters east of the crossing, is upgraded to seventy tons. Rebuilding is necessary.

Crossing the Ligowski Canal is conditionally possible. The construction of a ford with surface reinforcement is desired.

Area of Operation C

Approach route: Taizy–Duderhof Ost–Groes Lager–
Finn.–Koirowo

The road bridge over a drainage ditch north of the reinforced bridge in Duderhof Ost must also be reinforced.

The remainder of the route from Groes Lager–Finn.–Koirowo is only negotiable when the ground is frozen.

Area of Operation D

Approach route: Taizy–Duderhof Ost–Groes Lager–
Niolajewka–Mal Kabosi–Rechkolowo

The larger bridges spanning ditches at Talikola, Ssolosi, Uskulja, and west of Nikolajewka which are on the east-west link from Mal Kabosi–Groes Lager must be reinforced.

Approach route: Gatschina–Kokkolowo–Mal Kabosi–
Rechkolowo

The crossing over the antitank ditch between Kowrowo–Pellelja must be made negotiable by filling it in.

Area of Operation E

Approach route: Gatschina–Pellelja–Ssobolewa–
                                         Sofija–Puschkin

The bridge over the creek bed south of Kirbusi must be upgraded to seventy tons.

Approach route: Gatschina–Romanowo–Innerer Ring–
                                         Antropschina–Sluzk–Puschkin

Reinforcement of the bridge over the drainage ditch 750 meters southwest of the Ishora is desired, but can be placed last in the construction sequence.

The crossing over Ligowka Creek at Romanowo cannot be forded. The bridge must be checked for a load capacity of seventy tons and, if necessary, reinforced.

Continued movement over the terrain starting from the northern outskirts of Antropschina appears questionable. An unimpeded advance is guaranteed by the reinforcement of the bridge over Slavianka Creek before it joins the Pokrowskaja–Sluzk road, the bridge on the northern outskirts of Pjaselewo, and the one prior to the hospital north of Sluzk.

All reinforced bridges and detours are to be marked with the tactical symbol used by the 502nd Heavy Panzer Battalion (an elephant).

For the corps headquarters,
The chief of staff

Document 5

502nd Heavy Panzer Battalion   In the East
S c h w a n e r, Hans-Joachim,   August 19, 1944
Major and Battalion Commander

**AFTER-ACTION REPORT ON THE EMPLOYMENT OF THE STAFF,
2ND COMPANY, AND 3RD COMPANY OF THE 502ND HEAVY
PANZER BATTALION IN THE AREA OF THE 18TH ARMY IN THE
PERIOD FROM JUNE 24 TO 30, 1944**

Attachment relationship

The staff, 2nd Company, and 3rd Company of the 502nd Heavy
Panzer Battalion were attached to the XXXVIII Army Corps; the 1st
Company was attached to L Army Corps (16th Army) on June 23, 1944.

Situation at XXXVIII Army Corps

On June 22 and 23, after heavy artillery preparation (heavy barrage
by sixty to eighty batteries), the enemy penetrated the main battle line
with strong infantry and armor forces. They penetrated in the 121st
Infantry Division sector (northeast of Ostroff) along an approximately
two-kilometer-long front. They took the high ground at Sujewo (Judennase)–Schapkowo–Bajewo–Wankowo. On the evening of 23 June, using
tanks and mounted infantry, they were advancing toward the Pleskau–
Ostroff road along the Sujewo–Judino ridgeline.

Alert and mission for the 502nd Heavy Panzer Battalion

At approximately 2000 on June 23, the 3rd Company of the 502nd
(billeted in Rubinjati, southwest of Ostroff) was alerted. The staff and
the 2nd Company were then alerted and directed by order of the
XXXVIII Army Corps to join the 121st ID in the area around Pyljai to
conduct a counterattack to regain the former main battle line. After a
thirty-kilometer road march with only minimal losses due to mechanical
problems, the companies assembled in the area ordered during the

night. The following tanks were combat ready: Staff—one command vehicle; 2nd Company—ten "Tigers" out of eleven; 3rd Company—eleven "Tigers" out of fourteen.

The orders conference at the 121st ID (Commander: Oberst Löhr) resulted in the following mission for the companies:

Starting from the tactical assembly areas (3rd Company in Pyljai; 2nd Company four kilometers to the north of it, just west of the village of Sseschtkino), the attack was to be initiated at X-hour on June 26 to regain the high ground at Sujewo. It was to be conducted along the path from the Kirowo state farm to Schapkowo in conjunction with the recently introduced 1st Battalion of the 94th Grenadier Regiment. The attack was to be started after heavy artillery preparation by reinforced divisional artillery. The 2nd Company was directed to work closely with the 1st Battalion of the 94th Grenadier Regiment. The staff and 3rd Company remained at the disposal of the division and were not to enter the attack until ordered to do so.

Simultaneously with the attack outlined above, a flanking attack was to be conducted by the 121st Engineer Battalion. It was to attack with assault guns and self-propelled guns along the Judino–Sujewo ridgeline toward the objectives of Sujewo and Woschtschinino.

June 24: Start of the attack—0730. By 0645, the 2nd Company had moved into its assembly area west of Sseschtkino and established contact with the 1st Battalion of the 94th. At 0720, the forward line of infantry was crossed with the intent to exploit our own artillery fire and attack simultaneously with the assaulting infantry. Our own infantry then went to ground at the woods east of the state farm in Kirowo due to the heavy enemy artillery fire. The "Tiger" Company, which had made good progress up to then, was forced by that to make an involuntary halt after 500 meters. It was identified by the Russians and immediately taken under concentrated artillery fire. The attack began to move again at 1030. Tanks and infantry fought their way forward, step-by-step, against hard-fighting enemy infantry, many medium and heavy antitank guns, and, occasionally, extremely heavy artillery fire of all calibers.

The attack of the right flank element, the 121st Engineer Battalion, proceeded much more easily. In acknowledgment of this situation (based on a suggestion to the division commander), the entire 3rd Company, originally given the mission to support the 2nd Company in its attack on Sujewo, was directed to support the 121st Engineer Battalion. It was to propel the energetic attack even further along, to provide relief for the attack of the heavily engaged 94th Grenadier Regiment and the 2nd Company, and to reach the objective without delay. This attack along the Judino–Sujewo ridgeline gained ground rapidly. At 1100, the 3rd Company was already at the southwestern edge of Woschtschinino. The Russian infantry, estimated at approximately three infantry regiments in the area of the breakthrough and supported by elements of a mixed armored brigade, was completely unnerved by the energetic pincers attack of the two assault groups supported by "Tigers." It evacuated the terrain in front of the objective (Judennase). About 1200, the 2nd and 3rd Companies reached the high ground around Sujewo without losses. They found themselves in the middle of the main Russian position, consisting of our own former bunkers and an expanded trench system, which was practically untraversable for tanks. Putting up a tough and bitter defense, the Russian infantry could only be partially expelled from their trenches. Many bunkers, machine gun, and mortar positions were blown apart. Several enemy tanks located in well-camouflaged positions in the ruins of the village of Sujewo were destroyed. The infantry, which followed both assault groups, had suffered high losses due to artillery fire and strong infantry resistance. They were completely worn out as a result of the summertime heat and the very difficult terrain—marshy conditions with shell craters. They could not establish contact with the tanks until the afternoon and then only with minimal forces. In this regard, both "Tiger" companies repeatedly dispatched one to two platoons to fetch infantry to clear out the enemy positions at the objective. As a result, a cut-off Russian infantry battalion was completely destroyed by the 2nd Company. By evening, three enemy counterattacks on the objective were repulsed by the "Tigers" of the two companies. Seven enemy tanks were destroyed, and infantry in at least battalion strength was eliminated in the process. Despite the fact that the positions on the high ground at Sujewo were still heavily occupied by Russian infantry, the enemy directed concentrated fire onto them to destroy the "Tigers." As a result, two "Tigers" were either immobilized or disabled by artillery fire. One of them was hit so hard that the crew had to dismount well in front of our own lines. In the evening, the second tank caught fire when trying to drive back under its own power. This was the result of damage to the fuel line. The fire was extinguished by the crew, however.

Because our infantry had not been able to clear and occupy the heights of Sujewo by 2100, both "Tiger" companies were withdrawn at 2200 (following a suggestion to division). The firepower of the "Tigers" alone did not lead to the desired success. They moved as far back as the battalion command posts to prepare themselves to beat back any new counterattacks. During the night, the entire 3rd Company was moved back to Pyljai where it resupplied and spent the night. Out of the 2nd Company, one platoon remained with the forward infantry elements at Schapkowo; the rest was also ordered to Pyljai.

Successes:	20 tanks (T34 and KVI) knocked out
	15 antitank guns destroyed
	At least two battalions of enemy infantry destroyed or wiped out
Friendly losses:	2 Panzer VIs:
	Of those, one in front of the enemy main battle line, the second vehicle in the middle of our own main battle line
KIA and WIA:	None

June 25, 1944: Situation

The enemy still possessed most of the Judennase. During June 25 and the night of 25 to 26 June, he reinforced his elements with infantry, antitank guns, and tanks.

The line, which had been taken on June 24 by the counterattack of the 94th Grenadier Regiment and the 121st Engineer Battalion (both closely supported by the "Tiger" companies), was held on June 25. It held out against a number of counterattacks by enemy infantry. It was intended to conduct our own counterattack in the evening to regain the old main battle line: specifically, by simultaneously attacking the Judennase and the area north of it to gain possession of the heights around Bajewo and Iwankowo. This attack was then slated for June 26 because the forces necessary for it (infantry battalion, artillery, and rocket launchers) did not arrive on time.

During the day, 2nd and 3rd Companies remained in their assembly area in Pyljai. In Schapkowo, one platoon from the 2nd Company was employed at the command post of the 1st Battalion of the 94th Grenadier Regiment. It beat back assorted small counterattacks of the enemy.

June 26, 1944: Mission

The mission was to continue the reduction of the enemy breakthrough at the Judennase and reestablish the old main battle line at

Sujewo. Using two Kampfgruppen, it was intended to conduct the attack in a manner similar to June 24. Employing six "Tigers" under the command of Hauptmann von Schiller, the 121st Engineer Battalion attacked to the right along the ridgeline from Woschtschinino to Sujewo. With six "Tigers" under the command of Lieutenant Carius, the 94th Grenadier Regiment attacked to the left. The start of the attack was initially set at 0900 but was moved up to 0600 during the night.

Conduct of the attack:

After heavy artillery preparation (a concentration of all available batteries) on the area of penetration and the heights of Sujewo, both assault groups assembled for the attack at 0615. The penetration into the enemy main battle line succeeded without great difficulty. Employing close and thorough teamwork between the tanks and the infantry, everything was rolled up on a trench-by-trench basis. The attack proceeded well as far as the heights of Sujewo and Woschtschinino. On the eastern edge of the high ground, the Panzer group of von Schiller destroyed two 12.2-cm antitank guns. As the attack continued, extremely difficult terrain conditions surfaced for the "Tigers." The enemy positions had been shot to pieces by the artillery fire from both sides. A lot of mud and muck had formed in the trenches and shell craters due to rain in the previous few days. The tanks could only work themselves forward on a step-by-step basis and had to direct each other by radio. As on June 24, heavy, concentric artillery fire of all calibers was employed against the tanks. At that point it became obvious that the commanding high ground of Bajewo (it was originally intended to attack it simultaneously) was not yet in our possession. Instead, a strong nest of enemy resistance had been formed from which the enemy could apply heavy flanking fire. With his observation posts, he could also overlook the entire terrain used by both assault groups. Attempting to block this dangerous northern flank through artillery fire was only partially successful and had little effect. The concentric artillery fire, antitank guns, and 15.2-cm assault guns caused losses within both groups of "Tigers." At Hauptmann von Schiller's location, two "Tigers" were damaged by artillery fire and made immobile; two "Tigers" were also damaged at Lieutenant Carius's location. Despite this, the attack to take possession of the Judennase was continued. The infantry of the right-hand assault group, the 121st Engineer Battalion, reached the objective. It worked closely with the tanks, advancing slowly and rolling up the heavily occupied enemy trenches in a series of rushes, sometimes using flamethrowers. The village of Woschtschinino and the trench system on the far side of the slope (which falls off to the east) were taken. The occupation and clearing of the high ground of Sujewo succeeded only partially for the left-hand assault group. The middle portion of the village was taken, while heavy, unresolved fighting took place for the northern portion of the village, dominated by the high ground of Bajewo from the flank. While bringing the infantry up to the old main battle line, the "Tigers" had to move up to the high ground of Sujewo. They were taken under fire there by concentrated antitank and assault gun fire from the east. One "Tiger" from Carius's group was knocked out by direct artillery and assault gun fire after two Russian assault guns had been knocked out at a distance of 1,500 meters. Two tanks from von Schiller's group were knocked out by the same fire. To avoid additional losses caused by moving up to or crossing over the high ground, all "Tigers" were ordered back to reverse slope positions where they could prepare to defend against tanks or conduct counterattacks in case of enemy penetrations. The positions on the eastern slope of the Judennase could only be taken by an infantry effort and with artillery support. Suffering heavy casualties, the infantry succeeded in occupying the old main battle line by 1300. It set up to defend against the expected enemy counterattack. The northern portion of the high ground of Sujewo continued to be in Russian hands. Under the command of Hauptmann Leonhardt, four additional combat-ready tanks arrived from Pyljai during the afternoon and were added to von Schiller's group in support of the defensive fighting of the engineers. Under the continuous employment of close air support and heavy artillery and mortars, an enemy counterattack with seven tanks (KVIs and Shermans) and approximately 400 infantry took place from the east around 1500. Two KVIs were destroyed by Hauptmann Leonhardt's tanks. The enemy infantry succeeded in dislodging the engineers on the forward slope of Sujewo. The battle for the Judennase continued to rage until the evening. Not until the onset of darkness did it quiet down enough to enable the tanks to withdraw somewhat from the line they had won. They set up near the battalion command post as ready reserves and an antitank defense. Together with the losses of June 24, nine "Tigers" in all had been knocked out on or right behind the newly won main battle line, having been immobilized by artillery or antitank hits. All fully capable "Tigers" were employed during the night to recover these tanks. By the morning of June 27, five damaged "Tigers" were successfully recovered from the front line.

Successes:	2 assault guns (15.2 cm) and 2 KVIs destroyed; 4 12.2-cm antitank guns and a number of anti- tank guns and self-propelled guns destroyed; Numerous enemy infantry weapons, mortars, and machine guns destroyed by fire or by being driven over; Approximately 500 enemy KIA
Friendly losses:	7 Panzer VI "Tigers" immobilized by fire; of those, five were recovered during the night
Personnel losses:	1 officer (Lieutenant Naumann), 1 noncommissioned officer, and 1 enlisted man MIA; 4 severely wounded and 2 slightly wounded.

June 27, 1944:

The situation remained unchanged at Sujewo (Judennase). To the north of it, a friendly attack to occupy the high ground of Iwankowo (Utkino–Gorodez) was conducted in the early morning hours using infantry and assault guns and employing the concentrated fire of the division artillery. Under the leadership of Lieutenant Carius, a platoon consisting of four "Tigers" supported the fighting by fire from the vicinity of Schapkowo. From there, the high ground of Utkino–Gorodez and Bajewo is thoroughly dominated. Carius's platoon had remained at the command post of the 1st Battalion of the 94th Grenadier Regiment during the night. The attack of the assault guns and the infantry did not succeed and was called off with considerable casualties after two hours. During the day, Lieutenant Carius remained at the command post of the 1st of the 94th as the reaction force. Hauptmann von Schiller—with four combat-ready "Tigers"—stood by at the command post of the 121st Engineer Battalion and later at the 1st Battalion of the 435th Grenadier Regiment to fight enemy counterattacks and armor penetrations. The situation remained unchanged during the day, except for various enemy artillery attacks and small-scale raids at the Judennase. Of the total of nine "Tigers" immobilized by fire, six had been recovered from the front by then. They had been towed to maintenance by the recovery platoon. Three shot-up "Tigers" remained along and in front of our own main battle line. They could only be reached by nighttime patrols with infantry and armor support. Because it was determined around 2200 that a Russian artillery observer was in the one "Tiger" located the farthest away from the main battle line, and it could also be gathered by motor noises (armor or tractors) that the Russians intended to tow that "Tiger" away, it was destroyed by our own guns on order of the division commander.

June 28–30, 1944

The situation remained unchanged. Except for a reaction force consisting of three "Tigers" (under the command of Lieutenant Eichhorn), which was held in readiness at the battalion command post one kilometer east of the state farm at Kirowo, no other "Tigers" were employed. The 2nd Company assembled near the division command post of the 121st ID at Telegina. The 3rd Company was in Pyljai. The vehicles were repaired by the maintenance squads, and a portion were sent to the maintenance section or the maintenance company (repairs of more than three days).

On the evening of June 28, the reaction force of Lieutenant Eichhorn knocked out two KVIs from a distance of 1,800 meters. On the morning of June 29, an American tank—a Sherman—was immobilized at a distance of 2,000 meters. A little while later a few artillery pieces of medium caliber were destroyed, which the enemy had emplaced between the high ground Utkino–Gorodez and Bajewo. The continual recovery attempts that Lieutenant Eichhorn tried at night failed. He attempted to recover the two "Tigers" in no-man's-land that had not been completely destroyed. It was impossible to approach these tanks without infantry support, because the Russians reacted with heavy artillery fire each time. Lieutenant Eichhorn and his tanks remained at his old location until July 4 in order to repeat the recovery attempts. Because the infantry situation remained unchanged, the enemy continued to remain strong defensively, and, finally, when Russian recovery efforts were identified trying to tow away both of the "Tigers," it was ordered on the evening of July 3 that both of these "Tigers" be destroyed by our own fire.

On July 1, 1944, the staff, the 2nd Company, and the 3rd Company (minus Eichhorn's reaction force) were withdrawn to the area northwest of Ostroff at Schabany–Wanino on the Wilikaja River. On July 2 at 2330, the battalion received the order from the army group to move to Dünaburg via rail. There it was to be at the disposal of the II Army Corps in the area of the 16th Army.

The 1st Company of the 502nd Heavy Panzer Battalion did not see action. On the evening of June 23, it was ordered by Army Group North to be the 16th Army reserve in the L Army Corps sector. It only conducted combat reconnaissance of a Russian penetration in the area of the 181st Infantry Division. On July 1, it received the order to move to Idriza in the X Army Corps sector. The company was employed there in two days of combat in the 281st Security Division sector.

Successes:	3 enemy tanks (2 KVIs, 1 Sherman) destroyed
	Several artillery pieces of medium caliber
	destroyed
	Numerous enemy KIA
Friendly losses:	2 Panzer VIs destroyed by our own gunfire because they could not be recovered from no-man's-land
Personnel losses:	None

SUMMARY AND LESSONS LEARNED CONCERNING EMPLOYMENT IN THE AREA NORTHEAST OF OSTROFF IN THE XXXVIII ARMY CORPS SECTOR

In close cooperation with an infantry regiment and an engineer battalion, as well as with heavy artillery support, the battalion with its staff and two companies conducted a successful counterattack as part of the 121st ID to clean up the penetration northeast of Ostroff and regain the old main battle line on the high ground of Sujewo (Judennase) and Woschtschinino. The fighting was conducted with heavy use of infantry, armor, and artillery forces on both sides. At times it assumed the aspect of a large battle of materiel for a dominating, fortress-like, built-up piece of high ground.

The attack was only possible using "Tiger" support and would not have been successful without them. Success had to be bought with the loss of a few "Tigers." These were caused by direct artillery hits and assault gunfire. During the attacks on June 24 and June 26, it became obvious in a very unpleasant way that the Russians were able to observe and flank all the terrain for the attack from the north. This would not have been the case if one had conducted a simultaneous attack further north to eliminate this flanking position. The infantry and artillery forces to do this, however, were missing. The teamwork with the light infantry went well on both days of the attack. On the first day of the attack, however, it did not lead to the desired success, because the assaulting infantry, the 94th Grenadier Regiment, was brought in just before the start of the attack. It had made a foot march of fifteen kilometers over softened terrain and only had a short time to be briefed. It should also be mentioned that our own infantry fought energetically and, at times, heroically on both days. On the second day of the attack, the fighting was made more difficult for the tanks. The enemy antitank defenses had been considerably reinforced by antitank guns, assault guns, and tanks firing from cleverly established positions. The artillery had apparently occupied even better observation posts than on the first day of the attack. From a leadership point of view, the fighting on June 26 was made more difficult by the Russians jamming the ultra shortwave radio frequencies. They spoke in German on those frequencies that were not jammed and issued misleading orders. A continuous effort was made to find frequencies not jammed on the radio and then to continue work on these. This meant, however, that the issuance of a battalion command by radio, for example, took more than an hour. Other means of transmitting commands or dismounting to deliver orders personally was not possible due to the heavy artillery fire. Looked at from equipment aspects, the outfitting of company vehicles with medium-wave radios would be necessary to send any orders when the frequencies are disrupted in such a manner.

The terrain offered tremendous difficulties in the attack sector. Aside from the frequent patches and strips of marshy land in the entire area between Pleskau and Ostroff, the terrain was heavily churned up by friendly and enemy artillery fire. Together with the old trench system and the bunker positions, it was practically impassable for tanks in some areas. The movement of the "Tigers" from their rear assembly area to the battle area was only made possible because route and bridge reconnaissance up to the main battle line was conducted by the battalion prior to the start of employment in the XXXVIII Army Corps sector. Reinforcement of the bridges and improvements to the routes (corduroy roads) were undertaken by division and corps engineers, based on recommendations from the battalion. Tactically and technically, the battalion had the best of relationships not only with the XXXVIII Army Corps, but also with the 121st ID. All suggestions and requests were considered. The battalion/companies remained attached to the division the entire time and were only directed to support the subordinate organizations. Thus it was possible for the battalion to work closely with the division commander, Oberst Löhr, or with the divisional operations officer. The division commander and the commanding general of the corps repeatedly praised the teamwork and the performance of the battalion.

For this attack, the 121st ID under the leadership of Oberst Löhr was mentioned in the Wehrmacht report. For "security reasons," the battalion was not named.

SUCCESSES IN THE PERIOD FROM JUNE 24 TO 30, 1944

Day	Battle	AG	Tank	A/T	Art.	Enemy KIA
June 24	Attack on Sujewo	-	20	15	-	600
June 26	Attack on Sujewo	2	2	4	-	500
June 28–June 30	Defense of Schapkowp	-	3	-	1	-
Totals:		2	25	19	1	1100

COMBAT-READY TANKS AND
PERFORMANCE OF THE MAINTENANCE SECTION

Day	Total in area of operations	Combat-ready	Number finished by maintenance section and repair shop
June 23	31	24	-
June 24	31	16	-
June 25	31	11	1
June 26	30	10	-
June 27	30	11	2
June 28	30	12	-
June 29	32	13	1
June 30	32	15	2

(The tanks repaired by the maintenance squads are not tallied.)

FRIENDLY LOSSES IN THE PERIOD FROM JUNE 24 TO 30, 1944

Personnel losses	Off.	NCO	Enlisted	Total
KIA	-	-	-	-
MIA	1	1	1	3
WIA (hospital)	-	1	12	13
WIA (with unit)	-	5	10	15
Total:	1	7	23	31

Material losses: 3 Panzer VIs totally lost with weapons and
                   equipment
                 6 Panzer VIs lost to enemy fire (recovered
                   from the battlefield and repaired in the
                   workshop)
                 2 half-tracks lost to fire (recovered and
                   repaired)

Ammunition consumption in the period from June 24 to 30, 1944

88-mm antitank round 39:	1,079 rounds
88-mm high explosive round:	1,132 rounds
Machine-gun ammunition:	64,000 rounds

Document 6

502nd Heavy Panzer Battalion,
S c h w a n e r, Hans-Joachim
Major and Battalion Commander

In the east
August 20, 1944

AFTER-ACTION REPORT ON THE EMPLOYMENT OF THE 502ND HEAVY PANZER BATTALION IN THE 16TH ARMY SECTOR FROM JULY 4 TO AUGUST 17 1944

Dünaburg area of operations from 4 to 27 July 1944

July 3, 1944

Command relationship:

The battalion (minus the 1st Company) was attached to the II Army Corps upon arrival of the staff, 2nd Company, and 3rd Company of the 502nd Heavy Panzer Battalion.

Situation at II Army Corps (right flank of the 16th Army and Army Group North):

Using strong infantry and armor forces, the enemy penetrated the main battle line at the juncture between Army Groups North and Center at Polotzk in the I Army Corps sector (and to the south of it) on June 22. The enemy forced the breakthrough to the west on both sides of the Düna on the southern wing of the I Army Corps. The II Army Corps, pulled out of the 16th Army sector, had the mission of establishing a new defensive front adjoining the right wing of the I Army Corps east and southeast of Dünaburg. It was ordered to build this front with newly arrived divisions (the bulk of these from the 18th Army sector; additional heavy weapons, the 502nd Heavy Panzer Battalion, several assault gun brigades and battalions, and Flak and heavy artillery battalions were also attached). The mission was accomplished by wrapping the main battle line around Dünaburg on the southern bank of the Düna. In the first few days of July, the infantry divisions occupied a security line that went roughly from Druja to Daugailiai via Braslow, Treswtaty, and Dokatas on the Dünaburg–Kauen road. One after another, the divisions were brought in by rail to Dünaburg and to Turmont, thirty kilometers south of Dünaburg. It was assumed that the enemy was trying to envelop the southern wing of the 16th Army in order to occupy Dünaburg, the important rail and road network. Originally, it was intended to close the gap in the front by linking up with the left wing of Army Group Center (IX Army Corps) and establish a firm defensive front with the forces recently attached to II Army Corps. The left wing of Army Group Center was continuously withdrawing west in the face of strong enemy pressure.

Along with the trains, the maintenance section, and a platoon from the repair company, the staff, the 2nd Company, and the 3rd Company of the 502nd were loaded for Dünaburg on July 3 and 4 in Briganowo and Ostroff. The trains arrived with the first elements in the evening of July 4. The remaining transports followed continuously until July 6. They were initially assembled in the woods north of Dünaburg. Then, after completion of bridge planking suitable for "Tigers" over the railroad bridge at Dünaburg, they were assembled in Peski and Laucesy, eight kilometers south of Dünaburg on the southern bank of the Düna.

The repair company and the trains remained on the northern bank of the Düna near Waldorf (Mezciema) and Stropi. A total of twenty-two "Tigers" were ready for action from the staff, the 2nd Company, and the 3rd Company.

July 4 to 8, 1944

After reporting to and holding discussions with the commander and the adjutant of II Army Corps and establishing contact with the 215th Infantry Division, continuous route and bridge reconnaissance east, southeast, and south of Dünaburg was conducted. Initially, this was done by five reconnaissance elements led by officers. By order of the 16th Army, the 680th Engineer Construction Battalion from the II Army Corps was directed to work with the battalion. Based on information provided by the battalion, it was used to construct bridges for "Tigers" and reinforce the bridges in that area, which usually only had the capacity to support ten tons (at the most twenty). Occasionally, the 3rd Engineer Construction Battalion and the engineer battalions of the 215th and 225th Infantry Divisions also helped with that work. Initially, the main march routes from Dünaburg to the new main battle line were built up. At the time, the railroad bridge in Dünaburg represented the only crossing possibility for "Tigers" over the Duna. Not only was a crossing not available for a distance of 100 kilometers east of Dünaburg, but there was also none for at least the same distance northwest of that town. Fording possibilities across the Düna were out of the question. Because of these reasons, the construction of a sixty-ton ferry over the Düna northwest of Dünaburg was planned. The construction was undertaken by the engineer platoon of the battalion, reinforced by a work force from the city commandant of Dünaburg. The 16th Army later installed a seventy-ton ferry (tank bridging equipment) at Livenhof, eighty kilometers northwest of Dünaburg. In the course of the reconnaissance operations, which took place in Volkswagens, motorcycles and—in areas not occupied by our own troops—in half-tracks, the route reconnaissance platoon leader of the battalion, Oberleutnant Wolf, became the first officer of Army Group North to establish contact with IX Army Corps of Army Group Center. Using three half-tracks, the scout platoon led by Lieutenant Ruwiedel conducted reconnaissance of the enemy forward of the main battle line to the south and southeast. He also conducted route reconnaissance for the employment of "Tigers." While doing this, he found out by July 8 that only weak groups of enemy infantry were forward of the main battle line. Continuous reports were made to the II Army Corps concerning the reinforcement of the road network and the continuous route and enemy reconnaissance. Because neither reconnaissance means nor sufficient reconnaissance aircraft were available to gather operational-level enemy intelligence, the picture of the enemy was extremely paltry and remained in part completely unclear.

July 9, 1944

Situation at II Army Corps:
    Advancing to the west, the enemy initially hit the defensive position around Dünaburg along the southern bank of the Düna (the 132nd Infantry Division sector). Coming from Dzina (sixty kilometers east of Dünaburg), he attacked Bruja. Further to the south, he also advanced west with strong forces. Using armor and infantry, he attacked combat reconnaissance elements of the 215th and 205th Infantry Divisions at Vidzy (twenty kilometers south of Dryswiaty) and Pilkoniai (fifteen kilometers southwest of Salakas). These reconnaissance elements had extended their feelers to the south from the divisional positions. The enemy situation was judged by II Army Corps as follows: The enemy intended to envelop the main battle line, which had been extended to the west by the newly attached infantry divisions; he then intended to reach the Dünaburg–Utena–Kauen road and swing toward Dünaburg from the south or southwest.

At 1000, the order went to the battalion to conduct a road march to Deguziai in the 205th Infantry Division sector with all elements—staff, 2nd Company, and 3rd Company. That required a road march of fifty kilometers on the Dünaburg–Sarasai–Deguziai road in the glaring midday heat. The request to march in the cooler hours of the evening was denied, because the situation was critical and the battalion was urgently needed by the 205th Infantry Division. Toward 1900, the combat elements of the 2nd and 3rd Companies arrived in the sector ordered with a large number of road march breakdowns (motor damage, running gear damage). These were bound to occur as a result of the high temperature and the long march distance. Of the twenty-two "Tigers" that originally participated in the road march, only five "Tigers" from the 2nd Company and three "Tigers" from the 3rd Company were combat ready. The battalion command post was established at 1500 with the 205th Infantry Division at Salakas. With route and combat reconnaissance conducted forward of the right wing of the 205th Infantry Division by elements of the respective reconnaissance platoons, the battalion was committed in the area west and southwest of Salakas.

At 2000 in Salakas, in the presence of the commanding general of the II Army Corps, a discussion of the operation took place at the 205th Infantry Division command post. The following mission was given to the battalion:

> After the road bridge three kilometers southwest of Deguziai was ready, the battalion was to march on to Daugailiai, fifteen kilometers away. The enemy had attacked a regimental group reinforced with assault guns and Flak. This group had established a heavily defended strong point in Pilkoniai. The enemy had encircled it and continued to advance northwest with tanks, mounted infantry, antitank weapons, and individual artillery pieces in approximately regimental strength via Tauragnai to the Dünaburg–Kauen road. It was intended for the battalion to move southwest from Daugailiai, dislodge the enemy at Garniai (two kilometers south of Daugailiai), and establish contact with the Kampfgruppe at Pilkoniai, north of Taranjai. Together with the Kampfgruppe, it would then attack east and capture the isthmus between Lakes Tauragnai and Utenas.

The road bridge three kilometers southwest of Deguziai (iron construction, forty-six-meter span, trusses) only had a load capacity of twenty-four tons. During the night, it was strengthened by a company from the 225th Engineer Battalion, which brought up three cross beams and reinforced the surface to sixty tons.

To repair the tanks that had broken down during the march, the maintenance groups of the company and the maintenance section (ordered to Sarasai) were used. In the course of the night, a few "Tigers" that had broken down rejoined the battalion or were made combat ready again. Toward midnight, the 3rd Company again had nine combat-ready "Tigers."

Successes:	None
Breakdowns:	8 "Tigers" broke down due to mechanical problems

July 10, 1944

To execute the mission, the 3rd Company (Hauptmann Leonhardt) moved at 0100 with nine combat-ready "Tigers" from its assembly area at Deguziai. At 0400, it crossed the reinforced road bridge and reached Daugailiai around 0600. The 2nd Company, which had only five combat-ready "Tigers," remained in Deguziai, secured the road bridge, and worked on the tanks that had broken down the previous day. Using the half-tracks of the scout platoon, the 2nd Company also received the mission to scout for the enemy and conduct route reconnaissance, proceeding west and northwest from Deguziai into the area around Dusetos and Antiliepte. After establishing contact with the 1st Battalion of the 377th Grenadier Regiment (which had the mission in the 225th Infantry Division sector to secure the Dünaburg–Kauen road at Daugailiai), the 3rd Company attacked Garniai as ordered and took Hill 216 two kilometers southwest of it. When the company left Garniai, it received heavy anti-tank, artillery, and mortar fire. A large number of antitank guns and mortars were destroyed. While continuing to advance through restricted terrain laced with individual patches of woods, the company once again became engaged with strong antitank elements and enemy infantry, which offered stubborn resistance using close-combat and other methods. Two tanks were knocked out due to hits on the turret (commander's cupola and the cannon) from antitank cannons firing from the flanks. A further advance of the company would only have resulted in heavy casualties and could not have led to the swift completion of the mission (breakthrough to the encircled regimental group). Without infantry, clearing the patches of woods (which would have been the mission of the infantry battalion that did not support the attack) was out of the question. The company therefore received the order early in the afternoon to break off the fighting at Garniai and establish contact with the 395th Grenadier Regiment at Gateliai, twelve kilometers southwest of Salakas, by swinging wide to the east. Together with this regiment, it was then to advance without delay to Pilkoniai from the northeast.

Shortly before 1300, the battalion received the order for the 2nd Company in Deguziai to advance along the Dünaburg–Kauen road via Daugailiai and then on to Utena. It had to support the attack of an infantry regiment of the 225th Infantry Division. This mission had been ordered by Army Group North for the 225th Infantry Division and was originally supposed to have been executed by the entire 502nd Heavy Panzer Battalion. This mission was not carried out, because a counterorder was received at 1400. The 225th Infantry Division, which had been attacking Utena with its elements since the morning, had broken off the fighting. The division had received the order from Army Group Center (to which it had already been attached for three days without having had contact with it) to get to Wilkomir in the quickest way possible and without getting involved in combat. The 2nd Company, which was already getting ready to attack with seven "Tigers," was stopped and ordered to return to its old position in Deguziai to secure and reinforce the newly formed defensive position of the 205th Infantry Division.

At 1830, after taking on ammunition, the 3rd Company moved southwest from Gateliai (via Brinkliskes) together with the 335th Grenadier Regiment. It had the mission to penetrate to Stugliai and establish contact with the Kampfgruppe in Pilkoniai, from which nothing had been heard since 1000. The bulk of the regiment (1st Battalion) advanced through the woods east of Pilkoniai to engage enemy infantry which had infiltrated and clear the woods. The "Tiger"company had only been coupled with weak infantry forces (eighty men of an alert unit) and two assault guns. The attack proceeded well initially. A number of heavy and medium antitank guns, which the enemy had brought into position south of Brinkliskes, were destroyed. The attack of the company came to a standstill at Hill 188, where the enemy offered renewed heavy resistance with heavy infantry and antitank elements.

Until the onset of darkness, a large number of antitank guns were destroyed, and several artillery pieces were put out of action. Enemy infantry, making a counterattack out of the woods, were successfully engaged. The enemy lost nearly 200 men. When it became dark, the attack had to be stopped at the line reached, because only two "Tigers" out of the original seven operationally ready ones were still capable of fighting. Five vehicles broke down due to the heavy demands placed on the powerplants, the summertime heat, and the long road march on the previous day. The infantry, which had been directed to work with the company (it was poorly led and had only followed the attack hesitantly), was brought into position on Hill 181 with great difficulty (to provide security for the night).

In the course of the night, the Kampfgruppe encircled at Pilkoniai reported that it had already withdrawn from there during the day and had the intention of returning to the main battle line at the 205th Infantry Division sector at the onset of darkness. The continued execution of the attack therefore became unnecessary.

To relieve the 3rd Company and to recover the five "Tigers" that had become disabled on the battlefield due to mechanical problems, the 2nd Company, under the command of Lieutenant Eichhorn, was brought up to Cateliai from Deguziai. Out of these tanks, only two "Tigers" reached their objective shortly after midnight. The remainder broke down on the road march.

Successes:	16 antitank guns destroyed
	15 mortars destroyed
	2-3 infantry companies destroyed
Friendly losses:	8 "Tigers" with mechanical failure
	2 "Tigers" knocked out by hits on the turret
Personnel losses:	2 NCOs slightly wounded

July 11, 1944:

Together with seventy-five infantrymen, Lieutenant Eichhorn and his tanks relieved the 3rd Company around 0200 and took over the security mission on Hill 188.

For July 11, the 205th Infantry Division issued an order to the 335th Grenadier Regiment to withdraw to the line Salakas–Avignosta during the day. This order was issued because the enemy had been attacking with strong infantry forces, individual tanks, and heavy artillery support since the evening of the previous day along the entire front of the 205th Infantry Division. The enemy was attempting to envelop the right flank of the division, and the infantry forces of the division did not suffice to hold the main battle line in the restricted, heavily broken-up, and, in places, heavily wooded terrain.

Hauptmann Leonhardt therefore received the mission to take care of the recovery of his broken-down tanks and return to Deguziai from Cateliai. Four prime movers of the recovery platoon were brought to him at the fork in the road three kilometers north of Cateliai (Uzeniskis). Together with the infantry covering force, which was directed to work with him, Lieutenant Eichhorn received the mission to cover the withdrawal of the 335th Grenadier Regiment. He engaged Russian assembly areas until 0500 and destroyed four antitank guns. Two kilometers west of his position, he observed fourteen Russian tanks and assault guns attempting to break through to the north. They were using skillful exploitation of the terrain west of him in an effort to envelop the right flank of the Grenadier Regiment. It was not possible to engage that armor due to extended patches of woods and depressions as well as Lake Syles lying between them. At 0500, the covering force under the command of Lieutenant Eichhorn, to which the infantry was also assigned, was withdrawn as far as Gateliai, whereby the enemy only attempted to follow with weak reconnaissance patrols. At 0630, he changed positions again, this time to the fork in the road three kilometers north of Gateliai, where he covered the withdrawal of the Grenadier Regiment and its attached weapons (artillery, assault guns, and mortars) until around 1400 (the withdrawal being executed in accordance with the plan). During the time in question, the movement of the enemy along the Lukobiunai–Paberze road increased. It could be determined from the formation of heavy clouds of dust that the enemy was penetrating further to the north with tanks and trucks. At 1330, Eichhorn engaged a two-company strong attack of Russian infantry supported by antitank elements, tanks, and mortars on the fork in the road between both lakes (Uceniskes). In the process, he destroyed more infantry and two antitank guns. One "Tiger" received a hit causing heavy damage on the turret by an antitank gun and had to be sent back to Salakas. At 1400, Eichhorn withdrew along the route to Salakas after blowing up three bridges. At 1500, he crossed the new main battle line, which had been established along the line Avignosta–Salakas between Ligajai and Luodis. By doing that, he completed his mission of covering the withdrawal. He returned to his company with one "Tiger" completely operationally ready and one partially operationally ready.

The recovery of the disabled "Tigers" of 3rd Company and the "Tigers" of the 2nd Company (Lieutenant Eichhorn's group) caused great difficulties due to the extremely poor road conditions, the partially impassable marshy areas, and the weak bridges. Recovery efforts lasted until the afternoon of July 11. All "Tigers" were recovered. A portion of them were even brought up to combat-ready status again on-site by the maintenance squads of the companies. Under the command of Hauptmann Leonhardt, they were assembled in the area around Deguziai.

On July 11 at 0230, the battalion received the order to immediately send one company via Dünaburg to the 215th Infantry Division command post at Tarzeka (fifteen kilometers south of Dünaburg). The Russians, coming from the east via Ryczany and Karasino, had penetrated the main battle line between Lakes Dryswiaty and Rycza in the late afternoon of July 10 with approximately thirty tanks and infantry. During the night, the enemy tanks had smashed substantial elements of the 435th Grenadier Regiment, hitting an attached Lithuanian police battalion especially hard, and rolled over several antitank and Flak positions. Strong infantry forces had advanced along Lake Rycza to the north.

At 0300, Hauptmann von Schiller was sent on the road from Deguziai to Dünaburg with seven operationally ready tanks. From there he continued via Peski to Tarzeka. To do this, he had to cover a distance of sixty-five kilometers. A reduction of the march route from Deguziai or Salakas directly east to the 205th Infantry Division could not be made, because the large number of bridges found along this route had not yet been completely reinforced for "Tigers." A total of five "Tigers" became mechanically disabled on the march to Peski, so that only two operationally ready ones arrived. Together with two tanks brought forward fresh from the repair shop—a total, therefore, of four "Tigers"—von Schiller received the mission to support the counterattack of the 215th Infantry Division. He was to work together with the 2nd Battalion of the 435th Grenadier Regiment to regain the village of Karasino and take back the old main battle line.

At 1515, after artillery preparation, the attack was initiated from Tarzeka via Markinkowicze along the path to Karasino. Weak infantry forces were destroyed at Markinkowicze, and Karasino was taken in a spirited attack against a large number of enemy tanks, assault guns, and antitank elements. Ten enemy tanks (T34s, T60s, and 76.2-mm assault guns) and two heavy antitank guns were destroyed. Our own infantry fought its way forward slowly against strong enemy infantry, which had established itself in the terrain covered with vegetation and small patches of woods. It gained contact with the "Tigers" by late afternoon. A new obstacle line was jointly established at Karasino, and this was held against multiple counterattacks, which the Russians conducted with infantry and artillery support. The enemy suffered high, bloody casualties. During the fighting against the enemy tanks and antitank guns, one "Tiger" was disabled by an antitank gun hit (85 mm) and remained in the main battle line with a thrown track. Two "Tigers" had motor damage. Because a fifth "Tiger" had arrived during the fighting, the defensive fighting in Karasino was continued with a sector facing north and east. The area that had been reached was held. These tanks remained in their covering positions at night to cover the main battle line. The tank that had become immobile was recovered during the night of July 12 and 13.

Successes:	10 tanks (T34s, T60s, and 76.2-mm assault guns) destroyed
	6 antitank guns destroyed
Losses:	2 Panzer VIs with antitank hits on the turret
	6 Panzer VIs disabled due to mechanical failure
Personnel casualties:	2 slightly wounded

July 12, 1944: Situation at the 225th Infantry Division and Employment of the 3rd Company (Hauptmann Leonhardt)

The 225th Infantry Division, which had been attached to Army Group Center until July 10, was attached to the II Army Corps. This was done in light of the situation and the considerable threat to the right wing of Army Group North, which the enemy had been attempting to envelop with armor and infantry. Bordering the 205th Infantry Division, it extended the main battle line west from the lake sector three kilometers west of Deguziai along the Swantoji Creek. On the morning of July 12, the enemy had succeeded in penetrating this new main battle line west of Antiliepte. Individual tanks had been observed advancing north toward Dusetos.

The 3rd Company—at the time still employed in the covering mission at Deguziai—was attached to the 225th Infantry Division and received the mission at 1300 to march to Antiliepte and conduct a counterattack from Antiliepte to the southwest toward Drasinai in conjunction with elements of the 377th Grenadier Regiment. The company arrived in Antiliepte with four "Tigers" and came at just the right time to repulse an armor attack along the Drasinai–Antiliepte road. Two T34s were knocked out. The remaining enemy tanks disappeared in the woods. Assault guns were employed to cover this sector. The 3rd Company attempted to conduct a flank attack via Padustis to Zabiciuniai. The enemy was believed to be conducting an attack to the north there. The company reached Zabiciuniai without enemy resistance. Enemy tanks that had broken through could not be found. At the onset of darkness, the company was pulled back to Antiliepte and, later, to Vensavai on the southern point of Lake Vensavai, six kilometers north of Deguziai. There they performed maintenance on their vehicles.

Successes: T34s destroyed
Losses: None

Situation at the 215th Infantry Division:

On July 11, the former main battle line between Lakes Dryswiaty and Ricu was reestablished only in the southern portion, up to and including Karasino. From there it turned north via Krakino, the lake, and Markinkowicze. In the northern portion of the isthmus, Estonian and Lithuanian police elements were employed. They had the mission of blocking the area up to Lake Ricu. These elements offered little resistance during Russian attacks or even when the signs of Russian attack were imminent. They also left their positions whenever they received minimal artillery fire. That happened three times in the course of July 12. Under the command of Lieutenant Carius, four "Tigers," which had been set up in the patch of woods southeast of Markinkowicze for the purpose of conducting counterattacks, intercepted the withdrawing Lithuanians and Estonians on each occasion and brought them back to their positions by means of small counterattacks.

On July 12, the 1st Company of the 502nd arrived in Dünaburg via rail from the X Army Corps (Idriza). It had ten operationally ready "Tigers" at its disposal. At 1900, after inquiring at II Army Corps, the commanding general, Generallieutenant Hasse, ordered the company to be divided in half. One element with five "Tigers" was to move to Vensavai to reinforce the 3rd Company, which was with the 225th Infantry Division (fifty-five kilometers southwest of Dünaburg). The other element of an additional five "Tigers" was to form a new Kampfgruppe and go to the 81st Infantry Division at the Vazsaliena state farm (twenty kilometers east of Dünaburg). The 81st Infantry Division had recently been inserted between the 215th and the 132nd Infantry Divisions, because the enemy attacks from the east had increased and the 132nd Infantry Division was no longer completely combat ready.

July 13, 1944

The battalion, attached to the II Army Corps as a complete unit after the arrival of the 1st Company, was employed in three Kampfgruppen at the three critical defensive areas of the corps: the 3rd Company (reinforced by half of the 1st Company) with the 225th Infantry Division; the 2nd Company with the 215th Infantry Division; and half of the 1st Company with the 81st Infantry Division.

The 3rd Company (225th Infantry Division) was not employed on July 13, 1944; instead, it remained on call in its assembly area at Vensavai and sent two "Tigers" to Antiliepte to serve as cover. The company conducted route and bridge reconnaissance in the area of the 225th Infantry Division and initiated reconnaissance of the enemy in anticipation of upcoming missions by sending a half-track toward Abeli and points west. An engineer company of the 680th Engineer Construction Battalion was attached to the company and employed to build bridges for "Tigers."

The 2nd Company (215th Infantry Division), under the command of Lieutenant Carius, continued operations with the 380th Grenadier Regiment between Dryswiaty and Lake Ruci. During the night from July 12 to 13, Russian infantry infiltrated through the positions of the Estonian and Lithuanian volunteers along Lake Ricu and attacked the estate in Markinkowicze at 0600. The Lithuanians withdrew to the northwest, a portion to the south. With the assistance of the "Tigers," a new defensive front was established just south of Markinkowicze–Lake Karasino, and the Lithuanian infantry (inasmuch as they were still present) boxed its way forward to Markinkowicze. During the day, the attack of the Russian infantry in the restricted and heavily broken terrain was stopped by reinforcements and the arrival of the Lithuanian and Estonian police in the Markinkowicze–Skabaty sector. In the evening, Lieutenant Carius's "Tigers" were assembled at the command post of the 380th Grenadier Regiment.

The remainder of the 1st Company (81st Infantry Division), consisting of five "Tigers" under the command of Lieutenant Baumann, was assembled by the division near its command post at the estate at Vecsaliela. It was intended to employ it to the east and southeast. The company conducted route and bridge reconnaissance, but it was not employed on July 13.

Successes: Enemy infantry at the 215th Infantry Division
                               location engaged with heavy weapons

July 14, 1944: Situation at the 225th Infantry Division and Employment of the 3rd Company (reinforced by a half company)

By exploiting patches of woods and depressions and by using infantry, the Russians attacked continuously. They attempted to push back the main battle line, which had not yet quite firmed up. As soon as they discovered weak positions in the main battle line, they attempted to push their tanks through individually to exploit the success and continue to penetrate to the northeast.

Toward 0300 on the morning of July 14, a strong infantry assault took place on Antiliepte, supported by the artillery fire of a number of batteries. Supported by the two "Tigers" employed as security at Antiliepte (under the command of Lieutenant Plassmann), this attack was repulsed by the 377th Infantry Regiment. The enemy infantry suffered heavy casualties and lost one heavy antitank gun. During the day, the enemy succeeded in making a penetration three kilometers southeast of Antiliepte at Stossjunai and Hill 175. The enemy crossed the Swantoji Creek and set about establishing a large bridgehead.

In the afternoon, the 3rd Company (reinforced by five "Tigers" of the 1st Company) was ordered to conduct a counterattack in conjunction with the 2nd Battalion of the 377th Grenadier Regiment. All of the tanks were assembled into a Kampfgruppe under the command of Lieutenant Bölter. After a short discussion of the operation at 1800 at the battalion command post in Gaideliai, the counterattack was conducted at 1915 after short preparations concerning coordination with the infantry. It was intended to take the village of Stossjunai by moving via Hill 175. When the Kampfgruppe reached the hill, it was covered with heavy artillery fire. By continuously changing positions, the "Tigers" succeeded in staying on the hill and supporting the advance of the friendly infantry. The tanks received heavy antitank and tank fire from the high ground south of Swantoji Creek. Six enemy tanks were identified in a reverse slope position at a distance of 2,500 meters and were engaged by the combined fire of all of the tanks. They were not successful in eliminating those vehicles, however. A few antitank guns, enemy artillery, and infantry were effectively engaged in the course of the fighting. In the process, six antitank guns and a Stalin organ were destroyed. Because the friendly infantry could not stay on the hill as a result of the increasing artillery fire, the attack was called off. The tanks were then withdrawn to the next depression and assembled toward 2200 in the area of the battalion command post in anticipation of new employment.

Situation at the 215th Infantry Division and Employment of the 2nd Company (Lieutenant Carius):

The main battle line between Lakes Dryswiaty and Ricu could not have been maintained as configured for any length of time because too many infantry forces were required to do that. As a result, a counterattack was planned for the afternoon of July 14 to clean up the penetration north of Karasino and shorten the main battle line.

To do that, a deliberate attack was required to take the village of Bolnorycze (one kilometer north of Karasino) and Hill 175 on the southern tip of Lake Ricu.

Of the original four "Tigers" that were operationally ready, two suffered mechanical damage, so that only two operationally ready tanks could be assembled for the attack. By driving forward to a good position, the two damaged "Tigers" could support the attack. Three Kampfgruppen were formed for the execution of the attack:

The first Kampfgruppe with two "Tigers" and thirty men
The second Kampfgruppe with two assault guns and thirty men
The third Kampfgruppe with two assault guns and thirty men

At 1830, exploiting concentrated artillery fire, the first Kampfgruppe rolled across the main battle line north of Karasino and attacked Dolnorycze. After a short, hard firefight, pockets of resistance and antitank guns in the village, on the high ground, and in the woods were put out of action. While this was occurring, the two damaged "Tigers" provided covering fire from Karasino. Employing skillful exploitation of the terrain (which was laced with vegetation and had impassable patches of marshes in some areas), the two "Tigers" worked their way forward to Hill 173.3 and engaged the withdrawing enemy infantry. Around 2100, the objective had been seized, and the shortest lines of communication to Lake Ricu were established. High, bloody casualties were inflicted on the enemy. He only partially succeeded in escaping the encirclement. The newly won sector was occupied by infantry.

The "Tigers" assembled at their original positions at the regimental command post at Nurwiance. On the way back, in complete darkness, one "Tiger" got stuck in a marsh. The last remaining operationally ready "Tiger" provided help. It also towed two of the assault guns that had become stuck in the course of the battle and could not reach the objective due to the tremendously difficult terrain.

Successes: 8 76.2-mm antitank guns destroyed
                        1 Stalin organ destroyed
                        Horse-drawn columns, mounted infantry, and
                            artillery batteries successfully engaged

> Considerable enemy dead
>
> Bunkers and fighting positions put out of
>   action

No combat activity at the 132nd Infantry Division (Kampfgruppe Baumann). On the afternoon of July 14, Lieutenant Baumann's five tanks were ordered eight kilometers west to an assembly area in the vicinity of the Salonaja Estate.

July 15, 1944

No noteworthy combat activity.

The situation in the II Army Corps sector allowed one to make the assumption that the enemy had called off his attack against Dünaburg from the southwest and south and had probably pulled back in an easterly direction with the bulk of his heavy weapons and armor in order to renew his attack elsewhere.

July 16, 1944 Situation at the 215th Infantry Division and Employment of the 2nd Company (Lieutenant Carius)

The enemy penetrated the main battle line at Marnga (eight kilometers south of Turmont) on the right flank of the 215th Infantry Division in the morning hours of July 16 and then continued north. The "Tiger" Kampfgruppe, under the command of Lieutenant Carius, was initially ordered out of its area of operations with the 380th Infantry Regiment (regimental command post at Furwiance) and moved to Turmont. Starting from an assembly area at Grygance and working with one battalion of the 189th Grenadier Regiment, it was to start an attack to the southwest at 1300. Moving through Margna, its objective was the high ground east of Schablowschtschyana. It was then to continue attacking west toward Awishinka. Further to the west, a second Kampfgruppe (with fresh reinforcements consisting of an assault gun battalion and infantry) was supposed to launch an attack on Schablowschtschyana from Karlischki.

At 1225, before the 2nd Company had begun its attack, the Russians preempted it with an attack from Marnga heading north and west along the entire 189th Grenadier Regiment sector. The Russians reached the high ground north of Marnga. On his own initiative, Lieutenant Carius counterattacked and sealed off the enemy penetration. The start of the friendly attack was moved to 1400. The terrain was ill-suited for armor, because marshy depressions were unexpectedly and continuously encountered among the many small hills. The armor attack was made very difficult by that. The tanks constantly had to seek detours. During the afternoon, Lieutenant Carius reached the hill 300 meters northeast of the first objective (Schablowschtschyana) and engaged heavy and medium antitank guns and heavy infantry forces. He cleaned up the enemy positions during a continuous firefight but did not advance any further because of the obstacles in the terrain. The friendly infantry had not followed the attack. Not until 1730 in the afternoon did they again receive the order to follow the armor attack. A short time later, the Russians attacked again with artillery support, with the result that the friendly infantry again went to ground. Without friendly infantry, Lieutenant Carius held the position until 2100. He then drove back behind the high ground north of Marnga. During the night, he set up in the vicinity of the battalion command post to be ready to defend against new Russian counterattacks.

Successes: 14 47-mm antitank guns and
                              2 76.2-mm antitank guns destroyed;
                              A sizable amount of infantry killed

Situation at the 132nd Infantry Division and Employment of the 1st Company (Kampfgruppe Baumann):

In the previous few days, the situation at the 132nd and 81st Infantry Divisions east of Dünaburg had developed as follows: The former main battle line between Lake Ricu, Lake Snudi and Düna (just west of Troja) had been penetrated by Russian infantry and armor attacks along Lake Snudi. The Russians had succeeded in infiltrating the wooded area southeast of Silene with heavy infantry forces. Initially, we had covered the northern edge of the woods with weak infantry and heavy weapons. We then proceeded to comb the woods from the west to reestablish contact with the troops in the former main battle line south of the woods. The 132nd Infantry Division, which bordered the wooded area with its western flank, intended to conduct an attack along the western edge of Lake Snudi on July 16. To assist in that, Baumann's "Tigers" were sent to the division via the Lielborne–Boloselci Estate by order of II Army Corps. They were to conduct an attack along the Babascki–Borony road in conjunction with the 436th Grenadier Regiment and assault guns. The start of the attack had been ordered for 1600. Baumann started punctually with his "Tigers," overran the forward infantry outposts, and then received surprisingly strong antitank fire from eight heavy antitank guns in the village of Dubinovo (1.5 kilometers south of Babascki). Three vehicles received such damaging hits that they were disabled for the remainder of the fighting. The friendly infantry had not attacked. The assault guns, which were supposed to attack from the west by enveloping Dubinovo, had such heavy losses from the heavy antitank guns that the attack there also bogged down at the very beginning. After the onset of darkness, Baumann's tanks made the return march to their start positions.

Successes:	6 heavy antitank guns and
	4 medium antitank guns destroyed;
	A sizable number of enemy infantry killed
Losses:	3 "Tigers" damaged by heavy antitank guns
Personnel losses:	None

The 3rd Company did not see action on July 16.

July 17, 1944

No activity for the 2nd and 3rd Companies. Under the command of Lieutenant Bölter, one half of the 1st Company (previously attached to the 3rd Company of Hauptmann Leonhardt) was withdrawn from the 225th Infantry Division area of operations during the night of July 16 and 17 and sent by road march via Dünaburg–Vascalina Estate (eighty kilometers) to the 81st Infantry Division. Employing infantry, the enemy had moved to the northwest out of the wooded area southwest of Silene and attacked the covering force on the eastern edge of Silene. At 2030 on the evening of July 17, Bölter was employed with four tanks to cover northwest of Silene. He did not make any contact, however.

July 18, 1944

No combat activity for the 2nd and 3rd Companies.

Situation at the 81st and 132nd Infantry Divisions and Employment of the 1st Company:

During the night of July 17 to 18, the Russians had called off their attacks east and southeast of Silene and withdrawn to the south. For July 18, a local attack using all available motorized weapons and truck-borne infantry was intended to retake the former main battle line between Lake Ricu and Lake Suadi. At the 81st Infantry Division, a Kampfgruppe under the command of Oberst Meyer (commander of the 189th Grenadier Regiment) was formed. It consisted of four "Tigers," five assault guns, ten assault guns with mounted infantry, 2-cm Flak, 88-mm Flak, a Lithuanian

Grenadier Battalion, and accompanying artillery observers. At 1400, this Kampfgruppe moved south from Silene and reached Plauskiety (eight kilometers southeast of Silene) without strong enemy resistance. As they advanced further, the tanks and assault guns ran into a deeply echeloned antitank front. Some of the antitank guns were located away from the road in the woods and were difficult to engage. The "Tigers" destroyed a number of heavy antitank guns and reached the village of Urbany, two kilometers southeast of Plauskiety, at 1730. The infantry had not followed the attack; on the contrary, they went to ground at the first enemy resistance. The southern edge of the wooded area continued to be heavily occupied by enemy infantry. Enemy counterattacks from the west occasionally interrupted the route of advance at Plauskiety and points north.

Due to the heavy threat from the enemy to the flank from the west and increasing enemy pressure (with artillery support), the armored advance elements were withdrawn from Urbany around 2000 by order of the Kampfgruppe commander, Oberst Meyer. It was ordered back to Silene to resupply. The infantry withdrew to the area from the south edge of Lake Ulacz to Domini (four kilometers southeast of Silene) and set up to defend there.

At the 132nd Infantry Division, the pursuit of the enemy withdrawing to the south had already begun at 0730.

With three operationally ready "Tigers," Lieutenant Baumann was directed to work in conjunction with the 436th Grenadier Regiment and two assault guns. He moved south from Babascki along the road and reached Borony, five kilometers to the south, without noticeable enemy resistance. Not until Dzieruki and the edge of the woods south of it did the enemy resistance increase. Antitank and artillery fire brought the attack to a standstill.

The attack was called off in the vicinity of Dzieruki. After darkness had fallen, the "Tigers" were withdrawn to their support base north of Plusy.

Successes:	7 heavy antitank guns destroyed
	Enemy infantry with antitank rifles destroyed
Losses:	1 "Tiger" immobilized due to artillery hit on the running gear
Personnel losses:	1 wounded
	1 loader with gas poisoning

July 19 to 21, 1944

The enemy had stopped his attacks along the entire sector of the II Army Corps and was in the process of withdrawing his forces to the south and west. The 1st Company was pulled out of the 81st Infantry Division operational area and transferred to Saraai in a eighty-kilometer-long road march (thirty kilometers southwest of Dünaburg) as the corps reserve. There, the company had the opportunity to maintain its vehicles.

The 3rd Company, together with the 225th Infantry Division, was attached to the XXXXIII Army Corps on July 19. (See the report on the XXXXIII Army Corps area of operations.)

The 2nd Company remained in the vicinity of Turmont as corps and operational reserve for the 215th Infantry Division. The tanks that came out of the repair shop were assembled in Peski (eight kilometers south of Dünaburg) by Lieutenant Eichhorn. Until the evening of July 21, the situation at II Army Corps remained unchanged.

July 22, 1944

Shortly before 0100, the chief of staff of the II Army Corps alerted the battalion by radio and gave the following orientation on the situation:

On the evening of July 21, strong Russian armored formations had broken through the 290th Infantry Division (employed on the right wing of the I Army Corps) on the northern bank of the Düna and had reached the vicinity of Kraslau. At 1900, they had reached the Kazanova Estate (six kilometers north of Kraslau) and the Kombuli Estate. They then proceeded on toward Izvalta (twenty-eight kilometers east of Dünaburg). The 290th Infantry Division was streaming back and had the mission to form a new line of resistance at Izvalta. It was attached to the II Army Corps. The mission for the 502nd: Cross over to the northern bank of the Düna with all operationally ready "Tigers" and, using the Dünaburg–Izvalta road, reach the 290th Infantry Division command post at Ohmelnickaja as soon as possible. Hold up further enemy armor penetrations in the direction of Dünaburg. Enemy contact along the march route had to be reckoned with.

The 1st and 2nd Companies were alerted by radio. The combat elements were sent along with sufficient supplies to Dünaburg. The company commanders were ordered to proceed ahead of their companies to

the battalion command post in Gorki (two and a half kilometers southwest of the railway line in Dünaburg) to receive the order.

After the orders conference with the company commanders, the battalion command post was moved to the northeast outskirts of Dünaburg
(German military cemetery), where the arrival of the battalion was
expected. Lieutenant Eichhorn, coming from Peski with four "Tigers,"
was dispatched at 0500 on the road to Izvalta to conduct combat reconnaissance and establish contact with the 290th Infantry Division. The 1st
Company (Lieutenant Bölter) followed with six "Tigers" at 0600. The
2nd Company (Lieutenant Carius) reported that it could not arrive until
0800 at the earliest at the battalion collection point. It received the order
to follow the 1st Company. After radio contact had been established with
all elements of the battalion, the commander moved along with the communications section and the route reconnaissance platoon to the 290th
Infantry Division and arrived there around 0900. Lieutenant Eichhorn
did not have any encounters with the enemy along the march to Chmel-
nickaja.

Situation at the 290th Infantry Division:
In the early morning hours, the enemy had attacked against the newly
formed line of resistance Düna–Izvalta–Lielie–Truli (three kilometers
north of Izvalta) and penetrated west with approximately twenty tanks at
Lielie–Truli. The enemy armor was thought to be advancing toward
Vieki (twenty-five kilometers northeast of Dünaburg).

An exact location and route of advance could not be specified. To
engage the enemy armor and to cover the supply route Dünaburg–
Izvalta, the division had employed the rest of an assault gun battalion
around the area Lielie–Truli; it employed two companies of heavy PAK
guns (Model 43s) from the 666th Panzerjäger Battalion in the area of
Izvalta and north of Lipiniski (ten kilometers west of Izvalta). No reconnaissance reports were available at all. The only report had come from
the division trains, and it said that enemy tanks had been seen shortly
before 0900 at Barsuki (twenty kilometers northeast of Dünaburg) just
forward of the Dünaburg–Rossitten Rollbahn. The battalion received
complete operational freedom from the division and directed the 1st
Company, which had arrived at 1000, to attack in the direction of
Leikuni and Lielie-Truli to cut off the Russian armored avenue of
advance. Lieutenant Eichhorn received the mission to drive back along
the Izvalta–Dunaburg road with two "Tigers," conduct reconnaissance to
the north from the train station at Naujene (fifteen kilometers in front

of Dünaburg), and determine the location of the enemy tanks that had been reported at Barsuki. The 2nd Company (Lieutenant Carius) received the order via radio and messenger to drive back to the Dünaburg–Rossitten Rollbahn and advance from there in a northerly direction toward Viski to hold open this important Rollbahn. When the location of the enemy tanks became known, he was to turn to the east and initiate combat.

Shortly before 1100, Lieutenant Bölter attacked Leikuni and encountered the first enemy resistance 500 meters south of the village. The enemy had emplaced approximately eight tanks and a number of antitank guns at Leikuni to protect his southern flank. Six T43s, a number of trucks with towed antitank guns, and antitank guns already in position were engaged and destroyed. While continuing the advance against Leikuni, two "Tigers" were put out of action by enemy fire. The remaining four operationally ready "Tigers" took Leikuni, provided cover until the late afternoon, and sealed off the Russian supply route. Lieutenant Eichhorn, who had advanced north from the train station at Naujene, reached Teltini and the creek north of it. None of the bridges in this sector were capable of supporting "Tigers." However, since one had to count on the enemy armor turning south from Tarsuki, he remained in Teltini until the evening to cover the completely open, deeply exposed flank of the 290th Infantry Division and its supply route. The 2nd Company, which had followed the 1st Company on the Dünaburg–Izvalta road in accordance with its orders, received a new operations order at the train station at Naujene. It turned directly west from there and moved via Krivani towards the Rossitten Rollbahn to advance along that road to Viski. Shortly before 1300, it unexpectedly encountered twenty heavy and superheavy enemy tanks—Josef Stalin and T43 models—at Malinava (four kilometers north of Krivani).

Lieutenant Carius attacked the enemy tanks from the march, moving ahead of his company and followed by Feldwebel Kerscher and Lieutenant Nienstedt. Without any friendly losses, they destroyed seventeen enemy tanks at close and extremely close range with these three "Tigers." Carius himself knocked out ten enemy tanks with his tank. Only three enemy tanks were able to disappear to the east.

Using his company, he then cleared the village of Malinava and established contact with an assault gun company coming from the north. By this action, the Dünaburg–Rossitten Rollbahn, which had been blocked by the Russian tanks since 1000, was once again cleared, and the Russian attack on Dünaburg was brought to a stop.

In a change to its mission, the 2nd Company received orders at 1500 to advance east from Malinava to Barsuki (four kilometers east of Malinava). It was to throw back the additional armor attacks expected there and block the Russian axis of advance, which was now known. The village was reached without any noticeable enemy resistance, and all routes leading north, east, and southeast were blocked.

Due to the intervention of the battalion, especially that of the 2nd Company under the command of Lieutenant Carius, the 290th Infantry Division was given the opportunity to make an unimpeded withdrawal to the west in the evening and establish a new defensive front east of the Dünaburg–Viski Rollbahn. For that purpose, a number of truck-mounted battalions were channeled to the division. These were employed in the defense south of Viski. The battalion received the mission to provide cover in the area Barsuki–Malinava–Bondariski until the new defensive line was occupied. The 2nd Company thus remained in Barsuki. The 1st Company was brought forward on the road to Malinava to provide cover to the north and northeast. Under the command of Hauptmann von Schiller, all tanks in the repair shop that were operationally ready were ordered from Dünaburg to Krivani. They were to act as the ready reserve for operations to the east and northeast.

The trains and the repair company of the battalion, which had previously been in the area north of Dünaburg, were moved to the southern bank of the Düna during the night of July 23. They marched in the direction of Eglaine, and established themselves there. Only the supply elements necessary for the combat troops remained on the northern bank of the Düna.

Successes:	23 tanks knocked out (17 T43s, 6 Josef Stalins)
	6 heavy antitank guns destroyed
	A number of trucks destroyed
Friendly losses:	2 "Tigers" rendered inoperable by antitank gun and tank cannon hits
Personnel losses:	None

July 23, 1944

During the night from July 22 to 23, the 2nd Company, together with weak infantry forces, held the village of Barsuki against enemy attacks with tanks and infantry. Two enemy tanks were knocked out during the night. The covering force could not prevent strong infantry forces and individual tanks from infiltrating into the wooded area east of Malinava and assembling there for the renewed attack west. Shortly before morning (0430), the "Tigers" were pulled back behind the newly formed main battle line. During July 23, using heavy artillery support, the enemy attacked a number of times out of the woods east of Malinava in a northerly direction towards the fork in the Rollbahn five kilometers southwest of Viski. It was beaten back by the assault guns and infantry units there. Because the infantry forces of the 290th Infantry Division did not suffice to completely occupy and hold the main battle line running between the bend in the Düna at Vilusi (twelve kilometers northeast of Dünaburg) and Viski, the enemy attacks south of Viski were increasing, and the staging area of the enemy in the woods east of Malinava gave indications of a renewed attack on Dünaburg, a security line was formed on the northern edge of Malinava in the afternoon. The attempt to establish contact to the north and relieve an encircled Flak unit there was frustrated by the fact that a number of Russian tanks (Josef Stalins) had advanced as far as the Rollbahn at Bandariski through skillful exploitation of the terrain. Two "Tigers" were heavily damaged by fire and immobilized. By order of the 290th Infantry Division, the covering force at Malinava was withdrawn to the Likananka sector at Silacirsi in the evening. The 2nd Company assembled at Krivani.

On the afternoon of July 23, employing forty tanks and strong infantry forces, the enemy succeeded in breaking through the 83rd Infantry Division, which had been inserted between the 205th and 215th Infantry Divisions south and southeast of Sarasai. Because of that, the II Army Corps ordered one company to be pulled out of the sector north of Dünaburg and moved to Sarasai on the same afternoon. Lieutenant Bölter was sent with five "Tigers" at 1900 via Dünaburg to Sarasai.

Successes:	2 tanks (T43) destroyed
	3 heavy antitank guns destroyed
	A large number of enemy dead

July 24, 1944: Situation at the 290th Infantry Division and Employment of the 2nd Company.

North of Malinava, the enemy had advanced further west with heavy infantry and individual tanks via the Dünaburg–Rossitten Rollbahn. He then made the attempt to cross Likananka Creek via the railway bridge (twelve kilometers northeast of Dünaburg) to attack Dünaburg from the north. After this attempt had failed, he again attacked west along the

Likananka Creek. To secure the sector, a covering force with two anti-tank companies (with the Pak 43) and weak infantry was established by the division. Shortly before 1000, the 2nd Company received the mission to move to the villages of Tiltu-Sloboda and Rimsas (twelve kilometers northwest of Dünaburg) via the northern end of Dünaburg. There, it was to block the Likananka Creek sector with four "Tigers" against enveloping attacks against Dünaburg. Lieutenant Carius was sent there with four "Tigers"; the remaining six "Tigers" of the 2nd Company remained under the command of Lieutenant Nienstedt at Krivani. In conjunction with the 503rd Grenadier Regiment, they covered the Dünaburg–Rossitten Rollbahn toward the northeast.

At 1700, Lieutenant Nienstedt received a report that three enemy tanks were located just west of the Rollbahn forward of the Likananka Creek. In order to engage them, he advanced to Silacirsi. At that moment, the enemy moved out of the patch of woods one and a half kilometers east of Silacirsi (approximately twenty tanks and heavy infantry) with the objective of taking the road and penetrating to Dünaburg. They initially succeeded in pushing back the infantry's forward-covering positions. Nienstedt was then able to initiate a firefight between his two "Tigers" and the enemy tanks that had broken through. He was able to knock out seventeen of the twenty attacking tanks, among them two assault guns. He himself knocked out ten enemy tanks with his "Tiger." Using his six "Tigers," he then conducted a counterattack in conjunction with the 44th Engineer Battalion. By evening, the old positions had been regained.

Lieutenant Nienstedt's tanks were pulled back to Krivani at the onset of darkness.

Carius's group was briefed by the battalion in its covering mission at Rimsas and Tiltu-Sloboda and then received the mission from II Army Corps (shortly before 1700) to conduct reconnaissance to the northeast as far as Dublenieki (via Klocki). He was then to assume the mission of temporarily protecting the railroad leading north from Dünaburg for the transport trains still rolling in that area.

In the course of moving forward and directing his tanks, Lieutenant Carius, riding on a motorcycle with sidecar, unexpectedly encountered advanced enemy infantry forces and partisans at the northern outskirts of the village of Kokoniski. He was shot at with machine pistols and guns and severely wounded. Two advancing "Tigers" picked up the heavily wounded Carius and his driver and eliminated the enemy infantry in a rapid advance. At the onset of darkness, the four "Tigers," which were then commanded by Lieutenant Eichhorn, were pulled back as far as the Likananka sector at Tiltu-Sloboda. In the course of the night, one company of infantry was initially brought forward in trucks, followed by an entire battalion. They assumed the mission of covering the sector.

Successes:	17 enemy tanks knocked out
	A large number of infantry killed and heavy weapons destroyed
Personnel losses:	Knight's Cross winner Lieutenant Carius severely wounded
	1 man severely wounded

July 25, 1944: Situation at the 290th Infantry Division and Employment of the 2nd Company.

The enemy had exploited the gap that had come about between the II Army Corps (290th Infantry Division) and the I Army Corps between Malinava and Viski by bringing up new infantry and armor units. By order of the 16th Army, it was intended for an attack to be conducted north by the 290th Infantry Division and south by elements of the I Army Corps from Viski along the Dünaburg–Rossitten Rollbahn. The attack was supposed to close the gap.

In conjunction with assault guns and five "Tigers" under the command of Lieutenant Nienstedt, the 503rd Grenadier Regiment attacked Malinava to achieve that purpose at 1530. Initially, the "Tigers" could only support the attack with fire from the southern bank of the Likananka Creek at Silacirsi, because the road bridge had been demolished two days before. After reconnaissance of a ford located to the west, which was still barely capable of being crossed by "Tigers," Nienstedt accompanied the attack of the grenadier regiment up to the southern edge of the village. He could not advance any further, however, because one of his tanks broke through on a weak bridge. The infantry reached the northern edge of Malinava after heavy fighting and high casualties due to enemy infantry and mortar fire. Indecisive fighting for Malinava took place on the evening of July 25. The Russians conducted a number of counterattacks, which were beaten back for the most part. In the process, Nienstedt destroyed two tanks and three heavy anti-tank guns.

The situation at Lieutenant Eichhorn's location on July 25:

In the course of the night, Russian infantry had advanced via the rail line up to the Düna and occupied the village of Ausgliani, north of the

Likananka. Elements of the security battalion were committed against
them, but they were not able to clear the village. At 1400, loud tank
noises were heard to the north. These led to the assumption that the
enemy wanted to occupy the Likana Estate on the Düna to use the
Dünaburg–Kreuzberg Rollbahn for his further advance (possibly to cross
over the Düna to the west as well).

Lieutenant Eichhorn therefore immediately moved from Tiltu-Sloboda and penetrated through the enemy infantry in Ausgliani. Just east
of the Likana Estate, he encountered an enemy tank unit, which consisted of sixteen heavy tanks (Josef Stalin models) and T43s. Within ten
minutes, all sixteen tanks were knocked out at close range (no more than
300 meters) without any friendly losses. At that point, Lieutenant Eichhorn returned to his original position at Tiltu-Sloboda. During the afternoon, he undertook an advance on the peninsula one kilometer west of
Ausgliani. Two heavy antitank guns of the enemy were destroyed. They
had been firing on the west bank of the Düna and the truck traffic on the
river road.

Successes:	18 tanks (Josef Stalins and T43s) destroyed
	5 antitank guns destroyed
	Enemy infantry engaged
Personnel losses:	1 officer wounded (Lieutenant Nienstedt)
	(stayed with the company)

July 26, 1944

The Russians attacked Malinava a number of times and attempted to
force the friendly cover force back to the Likananka Creek. Lieutenant
Nienstedt's "Tigers" provided cover on the west bank of the Likananka at
Silacirsi and Krivani during the entire day. A ford had been reinforced
west of the demolished road bridge over the Likananka, which enabled
the "Tigers" covering at Silacirsi to be moved 1.2 kilometers north to the
southern edge of Malinava shortly before 1800. Shortly thereafter, the
Russians attacked the northern portion of Malinava with infantry elements in company strength and a few tanks. The attack was repulsed,
with a 12.2-cm assault gun being knocked out. Shortly after 2000, the
"Tigers" at Krivani engaged an infantry assembly area, which had been
identified in a patch of woods north of that village. The attacked
expected from that area did not materialize, however.

Employment of Eichhorn's elements:

Shortly after midnight, the 501st Grenadier Regiment, which had been on the west bank of the Düna as a corps reserve, was transported to the east bank of the Düna by assault boats. By order of Army Group North, it attacked toward the train station at Likana to force the Russian infantry back from the east bank of the Düna and throw them back as far east as the railroad line. That attack was initially conducted without any type of artillery support or heavy weapons. Shortly before morning, the II Army Corps ordered the 501st Grenadier Regiment's attack to be supported by Lieutenant Eichhorn's tanks. At 0600, Lieutenant Eichhorn and his four "Tigers" moved from Tiltu-Sloboda. Once again, he broke through the enemy positions at Ausgliani. They had been considerably reinforced in the meantime by tanks and antitank guns. During the attack, four enemy tanks were knocked out, and a number of antitank guns destroyed. One "Tiger" received a severe antitank gun hit and burned up (total loss). The crew was recovered unharmed. Shortly before 08000, Lieutenant Eichhorn had fought his way through to the 501st Grenadier Regiment and established contact at the road crossing at Waikulani (three kilometers north of Ausgliani). Together with the regiment, he moved east toward the train station at Likana at 0830. He fought his way forward against heavy antitank and tank fire. At that time a second "Tiger" was knocked out by heavy enemy antitank guns and burned up (total loss). Three men in the crew were dead; one man was severely wounded.

Until 1100, the attack advanced slowly as far as Liciji (one kilometer from the train station at Likana). There, however, the infantry stopped in the face of the heavy enemy fire from the railway embankment. The "Tigers" also couldn't attack any further, because the enemy tank and antitank gun fire increased. An additional eight tanks, one rocket launcher, and a number of antitank guns were destroyed. A truck column with mounted infantry, which had been moving in the direction of Ausgliani (south of Liciji), was destroyed. Because the attack no longer promised any success and the grenadier regiment was threatened with being encircled from the south as well as the north by heavy enemy infantry and armor, it was pulled back across the Düna at 1130 by order of the II Army Corps (with the exception of a small bridgehead at Broski and Dimanti).

Lieutenant Eichhorn received the order to fight his way back to his old starting position at Tiltu-Sloboda and conduct resupply. In Ausgliani, in the meantime, the enemy had reinforced himself even more and emplaced a large number of antitank guns. Without initiating a fight with those forces, Lieutenant Eichhorn moved rapidly though Ausgliani with his two "Tigers." In the process, he overran a number of antitank guns and received innumerable tank and antitank gun hits. Approximately forty antitank guns were estimated to have opened fire against the two advancing "Tigers." At 1250, Eichhorn reached his old starting point. Neither of his "Tigers" was capable of further combat.

Starting at 2300, the bridgehead of the 290th Infantry Division north of Dünaburg was pulled back to the south bank of the Düna. This movement took place within the framework of a large withdrawal by the II Army Corps. At 2130, both of the "Tigers" of the 2nd Company, which had been employed on the north bank of the Düna, were pulled back to the south bank over the Dünaburg railway bridge and assembled at the battalion command post in Gorki (2.5 kilometers southwest of the bridge).

The 1st Company, which had been ordered from Dünaburg to Sarasai on July 23 to intercept an expected armor assault there, did not see action up to July 25. On July 25 and 26, it participated in small counterattacks in the 83rd Infantry Division sector southwest of Sarasai and repulsed a number of infantry attacks. No fighting developed against enemy armor to the south and southeast of Sarasai because the enemy tanks which had been reported had called off their attack.

Successes:	12 enemy tanks (T43s) destroyed
	1 122-mm assault gun destroyed
	1 rocket launcher destroyed
	10 antitank guns destroyed
	34 trucks with mounted infantry destroyed
	Enemy infantry engaged
Losses:	2 "Tigers" completely lost
Personnel losses:	3 dead, 1 seriously wounded

July 27, 1944

The new main battle line of the II Army Corps ran along the Lauce Creek, approximately parallel to the Sarasai–Dünaburg Rollbahn, and turned to the northwest along the Düna at Dünaburg. The enemy followed the withdrawal movements of the corps hesitantly. Large-scale fighting did not take place on July 27. The 1st Company was behind the right wing of the corps (87th Infantry Division) at Sarasai and prepared to conduct counterattacks; the staff and the 2nd Company were on standby at Gorki behind the 81st Infantry Division.

Additional withdrawal movements to the northwest were planned for the nights of July 27 to 28 and 28 to 29. It was intended to gain contact with the right wing of the I Army Corps, which was withdrawing to the northwest on the northern bank of the Düna, to make troops available for extending the main battle line to the west (XXXXIII Army Corps sector), and to intercept the enemy who was attacking and exerting heavy pressure to the north in the direction of Riga. In the course of the afternoon, the battalion received the order to pull back as far as the line that was supposed to be reached during the night of July 28 to 29. Starting at 2200, the staff and the 2nd Company moved to a patch of woods behind the Illiuxt Creek four kilometers northwest of Eglaine; the 1st Company moved as far as the Rautensee Estate (ten kilometers south of Eglaine). They had the mission of preparing for further employment with the II Army Corps.

This movement ran according to plan. The 2nd Platoon of the Maintenance Company (previously set up at Eglaine) was moved forty-five kilometers to the northwest in the vicinity of the village of Akniste. Shortly before midnight, the battalion received the order from the 16th Army to move to Abeli in the XXXXIII Army Corps sector (march distance thirty-five kilometers) with its staff, the 1st Company, and the 2nd Company.

SUMMARY AND OBSERVATIONS CONCERNING EMPLOYMENT IN THE AREA AROUND DÜNABURG IN THE II ARMY CORPS SECTOR

The battalion was employed with its staff and two companies (2nd Company and 3rd Company) in the area around Dünaburg in the II Army Corps sector. From July 13 to 20, it had all three companies. On that date, the 3rd Company was detached to the XXXXIII Army Corps. After establishing a new main battle line to secure the open southern flank of Army Group North (the battalion's initial involvement in the operation was to seal off enemy attacks), the battalion was divided into two to four battle groups and used for the following missions within the entire corps sector:

1. Defending against and sealing off enemy armor attacks.
2. Counterattacking in conjunction with infantry support and assault gun units to win back lost villages and sectors of terrain.
3. Conducting temporary covering-force missions in the main battle line.

4. Providing a reaction force to defend against expected enemy attacks.

5. Acting as a covering force for short withdrawal movements.

6. Conducting local combat reconnaissance missions.

All missions were successfully accomplished and garnered the praise of the corps or the divisions for the battalion or the individual companies. The employment of "Tigers" in individual groups (spread over the corps sector and frequently shifted from one division to another) succeeded for the most part in keeping the main battle line of the corps intact until the withdrawal on July 26. Wherever "Tigers" were employed, the Russians called off their attacks or only repeated them with infantry in suitable terrain (woods and the area around lakes). The employment of the "Tigers," just like that of the assault guns, heavy Flak, antitank forces, and artillery, was often rearranged quickly and within a few hours in accordance with the new enemy situation. In order to hold the main battle line or regain it, all available heavy weapons were brought up to the point of penetration. In this process, little attention was paid to the mechanical requirements, especially those of the "Tiger" battalion.

Everything was based on the premise that the main battle line had to be held at all costs—each infantryman was worth more than a "Tiger" (remark of the commanding general of the II Army Corps). The battalion and later the ordnance staff of the 16th Army continuously pointed out the technical problems and made suggestions for employment where the material was put under less demands. This was acknowledged. As a result of the long march distances demanded of the battalion, the "Tigers" had continuous powerplant and running gear damage and were so mechanically overwhelmed that the repair work of the maintenance company and the procurement of replacement parts could no longer keep pace. Details concerning this are available in the technical after-action report. The battalion is of the opinion that one could have achieved the same success if

1. more ground and aerial reconnaissance forward of the main battle line had been conducted in order to obtain a clear picture of enemy strengths and intentions;

2. all heavy weapons ("Tigers," assault guns, 88-mm antitank guns, 88-mm Flak) had been given permanently assigned sectors; and

3. sufficient reserves of heavy weapons had been formed, displaced away from the main battle line, and held in as central an area as possible.

In general, the working relationships with the divisional, regimental, and battalion staffs went well. The attachment relationships were not always uniform. One attempted to avoid attachment below division level; one only wanted to be directed to work in conjunction with regimental and battalion staffs. This was not always achieved. When this occurred, the battalion frequently had to intervene and advise the regiment or battalion on appropriate employment.

Leadership was made difficult by splitting up the battalion into as many as four Kampfgruppen. As far as communications were concerned, medium-wave or ultrashortwave connections could be established to a maximum of three Kampfgruppen using relay stations. Except for the fighting with the 205th Infantry Division from July 10 to 11, the battalion only had influence on the tactical employment of the individual Kampfgruppen inasmuch as the commander was able to participate in the orders conferences for the attack and in the fighting of the individual groups. In addition, the battalion had to be on standby for the corps at all times and available for the commanding general.

The terrain south of Dünaburg could be characterized as at least 80 percent unsuitable for armor employment. The many lakes and creeks (which ran counter to the direction of attack), the isolated marshy areas, and the patches of woods formed terrain obstacles and restrictions, which did not allow deployment, development, and exploitation of the great firing range of the "Tigers." By its very nature, the terrain prohibited the employment of more than company or platoon strength. Most of the missions that were given to the "Tigers" were therefore assault gun missions. It should be noted that the "Tigers" could master these missions better due to their superior armor.

The bridges in the entire area of operations around Dünaburg were extremely bad. It was only due to the attachment of the 680th Engineer Battalion that the "Tigers" got up to the main battle line at all. During the period in question, the battalion reinforced approximately sixty bridges. A number of fords were improved. At least one company of the battalion had to be employed to reinforce each bridge on the roads leading to the maintenance company and the trains in the rear area.

SUCCESSES IN THE PERIOD FROM JULY 4 TO 27, 1944

Day	Battle	Tanks	AGs	A/T	Art.	en. KIA
July 10	Attack south of Daugailiai	-	-	16	-	300
July 11	Attack on Karasino Withdrawal at Salakas	10	-	6	-	-
July 12	Counterattack at Antiliepte	2	-	-	-	-
July 14	Counterattack at Stossjunai	-	-	6	1	-
	Attack north of Karasino	-	-	2	-	200
July 16	Attack at Marnga	-	-	6	-	100
	Counterattack at Babascki	-	-	4	-	-
July 18	Attack south of Silene and south of Babascki	-	-	7	-	150
July 22	Tank battle north of Dünaburg	23	-	6	-	-
July 23	Defense east of Malinava	2	-	3	-	100
July 24	Defense and counterattack at Malinava	17	-	-	-	50
July 25	Tank battle at Likana	16	-	2	-	-
	Defense at Malinava	2	-	3	-	50
July 26	Attack at Likana	12	1	10	1	300
Total successes:		84	1	71	2	1250

OPERATIONALLY READY TANKS AND PERFORMANCE
OF THE MAINTENANCE PERSONNEL

Day	Total in area of operations	Operationally ready	No made ready by maintenance
July 4	33	28	3
July 5	33	28	1
July 6	33	28	3
July 7	33	25	1
July 8	33	25	1
July 9	32	20	1
July 10	32	25	-
July 11	32	13	1
July 12	33	7	-
July 13	45	15	1
July 14	45	15	2
July 15	45	17	4
July 16	45	18	5
July 17	45	20	1
July 18	45	23	5
July 19	45	23	5
July 20	34	17	-
July 21	33	17	2
July 22	33	20	9
July 23	33	13	-
July 24	33	14	1
July 25	33	12	-
July 26	34	10	1
July 27	32	12	1

LOSSES IN THE PERIOD FROM JULY 4 TO 27, 1944

Personnel losses:	Officer	NCOs	EM	Total
KIA	-	-	3	3
MIA	-	-	-	-
WIA (hospital)	1	2	7	10
WIA (at unit)	5	5	8	18
Totals:	6	7	18	-

Material losses:

3 Panzer VIs ("Tiger"):   Complete loss with weapons and equipment

10 Panzer VIs ("Tiger"): Disabled by fire (recovered from the barttlefield and repaired by the maintenance company)

1 motorcycle w/sidecar: Complete loss

AMMUNITION CONSUMPTION IN THE PERIOD FROM JULY 4 TO 27, 1944

88-mm antitank round, model 39	555 rounds
88-mm high-explosive round	876 rounds
MG ammunition	36,000 rounds

Appendix

Beſitzzeugnis

Dem

Otto C a r i u s , Unteroffizier
[Name, Dienſtgrad]

1.Komp./Panzer Regiment 21
[Truppenteil, Dienſtſtelle]

iſt auf Grund

ſeiner am   8. Juli 1941   erlittenen

ein.maligen Verwundung oder Beſchädigung

das

Verwundetenabzeichen

in   S c h w a r z

verliehen worden.

Abt. Gef. Stand, den 2. August 19 41.

[Unterſchrift]

Oberſtleutnant u. Abteilungskommandeur
I. Panzer Regiment 21
[Dienſtgrad und Dienſtſtelle]

Certificate

Otto C a r i u s, Unteroffizier
(Name, Rank)

1st Company, 21st Panzer Regiment
(Organization, Position)

has been awarded the

Wound Badge

in Black

based on his one time wounding or injury

on 8 July, 1941.

Battalion Command Post, 2 August 19 41.

/ signed /

von Gerstorff
(Signature)

Oberstleutnant and Battalion Commander
1st Battalion, 21st Panzer Regiment
(Rank and Position)

Document 7

IM NAMEN DES FÜHRERS
UND
OBERSTEN BEFEHLSHABERS
DER WEHRMACHT
IST DEM

Leutnant Otto   C a r i u s
2. Kompanie/Sehw.Panzer-Abteilung 5o2

AM   2o. 8.   1942

DIE MEDAILLE
WINTERSCHLACHT IM OSTEN
1941/42
(OSTMEDAILLE)
VERLIEHEN WORDEN.

FÜR DIE RICHTIGKEIT:

Major u. Abt.-Kdr.

IN THE NAME OF THE FÜHRER
AND THE
SUPREME COMMANDER
OF THE WEHRMACHT

Leutnant Otto   C a r i u s

2nd Company, 502nd Heavy Panzer Battalion

ON ..20. 8. 1942....

HAS BEEN AWARDED THE
MEDAL
FOR THE
WINTER CAMPAIGN IN THE EAST
1941 / 1942
(EAST MEDAL)

CERTIFIED FOR CORRECTNESS:

Jähde

Major and Battalion Commander

Document 8

Im Namen des Führers
und Obersten Befehlshabers
der Wehrmacht

verleihe ich

dem

Feldwebel C a r i u s , Otto

1o./Panzer – Regiment 21

das
Eiserne Kreuz 2.Klasse

.....Div..Gef..St......, den .15..September19...42

(Dienstsiegel)

Generalmajor und Divisionskommandeur.

(Dienstgrad und Dienststellung)

In the Name of the Führer
and the Supreme Commander
of the Wehrmacht

I award

Feldwebel C a r i u s, Otto
10th Company
21st Panzer Regiment

the

Iron Cross Second Class

Division Command Post, 15 September 19 42

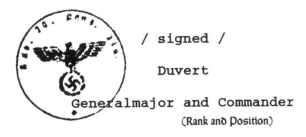

/ signed /

Duvert

Generalmajor and Commander

(Rank and Position)

Document 9

Im Namen des Führers und Oberſten Befehlshabers der Wehrmacht

verleihe ich

dem

Leutnant Otto C a r i u s
2./s.Pz.Abt. 5o2

das

Eiſerne Kreuz 1. Klaſſe.

Div.Gef.Stand ....,den ....23.. Nov. **19**.43

Generalleutnant und Kommandeur
der 29o. Jnfanterie-Division

(Dienſtgrad und Dienſtſtellung)

In the Name of the Führer and the Supreme Commander of the Wehrmacht

I award

```
Leutnant Otto C a r i u s
2nd Company
502 Heavy Panzer Battalion
```

the

Iron Cross First Class

Division Command Post, 23 November 19 43

```
/ signed /

Heinrichs
```

```
Generalleutnant and Commander
290th Infantry Division
```
(Rank and Position)

Document 10

Besitz=Zeugnis

Dem .... Leutnant   C a r i u s ....
(Dienstgrad, Name)

.... 2.Kompanie/Schwere Panzer-abteilung 502 ....
(Truppenteil, Dienststelle)

ist auf Grund seiner am ..8.7.1941.. erlittenen
10.12.1942
2.12.1943

.... drei ....-maligen Verwundung oder Beschädigung

das

Verwundetenabzeichen

in .... Silber .... verliehen worden.

.... O.U. ...., den .... 15. 12. .... 194.3.

Im Auftrage

(Dienstsiegel)

(Unterschrift)

Major u. Abt.-Kdr.
(Dienstgrad und Dienststelle)

Certificate

Leutnant C a r i u s
(Rank, Name)

2nd Company, 502nd Heavy Panzer Battalion
(Organization, Position)

has been awarded the

Wound Badge

in Silver

based on his being wounded or injured 3 *times*

8 July 1941,
on 9 December 1942, *and*
2 December 1943.

Location classified, 15 December 19 43

For the commander:

Jähde

(Signature)

Major and Battalion Commander

(Rank and Position)

Document 11

VORLÄUFIGES BESITZZEUGNIS

DER FÜHRER

HAT DEM

Leutnant C a r i u s
Zugführer 2./s.Pz. Abt. 502

DAS RITTERKREUZ

DES EISERNEN KREUZES

AM 4.5.1944   VERLIEHEN

HQu OKH, DEN 10. Mai 1944

OBERKOMMANDO DES HEERES
I.A.

GENERALLEUTNANT

PRELIMINARY AWARD NOTIFICATION

THE FÜHRER

HAS AWARDED

Leutnant C a r i u s
Platoon Leader, 2nd Company
502 Heavy Panzer Battalion

THE

KNIGHT'S CROSS

OF THE IRON CROSS

ON ....4 May 1944....

HEADQUARTERS, ARMY HIGH COMMAND
10 May 1944

HIGH COMMAND OF THE ARMY
FOR THE COMMANDER:

/ signed /

Burgdorf

GENERALLEUTNANT

Document 12

Der Oberbefehlshaber
der 18. Armee
—

A. H. Qu., den ....6. Mai 1944..............

Herrn

    Leutnant C a r i u s
    Zugfhr.2./s.Pz.Abt.502

    Zur Verleihung des Ritterkreuzes des
Eisernen Kreuzes spreche ich Ihnen meine herz-
lichsten Glückwünsche aus. Auch für die Zukunft
weiterhin alles Gute und reiche Erfolge.

J. V.

Loch

General der Artillerie.
ill.

The Commander-in-Chief
18th Army
—

Army Headquarters, 6 May 1944 ....

Leutnant C a r i u s
Platoon Leader
2nd Company
502nd Heavy Panzer Battalion

I wish to express my heartfelt congratulations to you on being awarded the Knight's Cross
to the Iron Cross. Best wishes for the future and
continued success.

Respectfully yours,

/signed/

Loch

General der Artillerie

Document 13

Paderborn, 2. Juni 1944

Herrn Leutnant Carius
in der schw. Panzer-Abt. 502

Die Panzer-Lehrgänge "Tiger" und die Ersatz- und
Ausbildungs-Abteilung 500 beglückwünschen Sie
zu Ihrer hohen Auszeichnung mit dem Ritterkreuz
des Eisernen Kreuzes und wünschen Ihnen für die
Zukunft viel Soldatenglück und Erfolg.

Heil Hitler!

[Unterschrift]

Major und Kommandeur p.t.

Paderborn, 2 June 1944

Leutnant Otto Carius
502nd Heavy Panzer Battalion

The participants in the "Tiger" courses and the members of the 500th Replacement and Training Battalion congratulate you on your distinguished award of the Knight's Cross of the Iron Cross and wish you continued good luck and success in all military endeavors in the future.

Heil Hitler!

/ signed /

Luder

Major and Commander

Document 14

Der Generalinspekteur
der Panzertruppen

H.Qu.OKH
~~Berlin W 35~~, den 6. Juni 1944

Herrn

Leutnant C a r i u s

Zgfhr.2./s.Pz.Abt.502

    Zu der hohen Auszeichnung, die Ihnen vom
Führer am 4.5.44 verliehen worden ist, spreche ich
Ihnen meine aufrichtigsten Glückwünsche aus.

        Heil Hitler !

Guderian

The Inspector of
Armored Troops

Headquarters
High Command of the Army ...6. June 1944

Leutnant C a r i u s
Platoon Leader
2nd Company
502nd Heavy Panzer Battalion

I wish to express my sincerest congratula-

tions for the distinguished award which was

granted to you by the Führer on 4 May 1944.

Heil Hitler!

/ signed /

Guderian

Document 15

BESITZZEUGNIS

DEM ....L·e·u·t·n·a·n·t........................
(DIENSTGRAD)

........................Otto   C·a·r·i·u·s........................
(VOR- UND FAMILIENNAME)

........2./schwere Panzer-Abteilung 5o2........
(TRUPPENTEIL)

VERLEIHE ICH FÜR TAPFERE TEILNAHME
AN ...25... EINSATZTAGEN

DIE II . STUFE ZUM
PANZERKAMPFABZEICHEN
IN SILBER

........O.U., den 15. Juli 1944........
(ORT UND DATUM)

....
(UNTERSCHRIFT)

Major und Abteilungs-Kommandeur
(DIENSTGRAD UND DIENSTSTELLUNG)

CERTIFICATE
I AWARD

................L e u t n a n t.................
(Rank)

.............Otto C a r i u s.................
(First and Last Name)

.2nd. Company,. 502nd. Heavy. Panzer. Battalion.
(Organization)

THE ..SECOND.. LEVEL OF THE
PANZER ASSAULT BADGE
IN SILVER

FOR COURAGEOUS PARTICIPATION IN

..25. **DAYS OF COMBAT.**

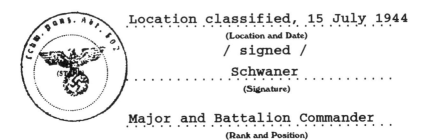

Location classified, 15 July 1944
(Location and Date)

/ signed /

.............Schwaner...........
(Signature)

Major and Battalion Commander..
(Rank and Position)

Document 16

Fernspruch - Fernschreiben - Funkspruch - Blinkspruch

Nacht.-Stelle	Nr.	Befördert				
		an	Tag	Zeit	durch	Rolle
1./N.158	310					
	668/31					
Vermerke:						

Durchgenommen oder aufgenommen

```
++0735/HDAX/FU/668131/BACH/HEGXC+
++0735/HDAX/FU/668131/BACH/HEGXC+
```

Abgang	
Tag: 28.7.	+AN/HERRN/LT/+OTTO/CARIUS///SCHW/+PZ/+ABT/+502//
Zeit: 0120	+AN/HERRN/LT/+OTTO/CARIUS///SCHW/+PZ/+ABT/+502//
Dienststelle	
++FFR++	
++FFR++	F. H. Bur.
	Fernsprech-Anschluß:

```
++DG/+  H D A X / FU  668131//  H D M X C  13386 //
++DG/+  H D A X / FU  668131//  H D M X C  13386 //

W N D F 1859 //  28/+7/+44/0120///
W N D F 1859 //  28/+7/+44/0120///

IN·DANKBARER·WUERDIGUNG·IHRES·HELDENHAFTEN·EINSATZES·IM·
IN·DANKBARER·WUERDIGUNG·IHRES·HELDENHAFTEN·EINSATZES·IM·

KAMPF·FUER·DIE·ZUKUNFT·UNSERES·VOLKES///VERLEIHE·ICH·
KAMPF·FUER·DIE·ZUKUNFT·UNSERES·VOLKES///VERLEIHE·ICH·

IHNEN·ALS· 535/+SOLDATEN·DER·DEUTSCHEN·WEHRMACHT·DAS·
IHNEN·ALS· 535/+SOLDATEN·DER·DEUTSCHEN·WEHRMACHT·DAS·

EICHENLAUB·ZUM·RITTERKREUZ·DES·EISERNEN·KREUZES/+///
EICHENLAUB·ZUM·RITTERKREUZ·DES·EISERNEN·KREUZES/+///

                    +ADOLF·HITLER///F/+H/+QU/+27/+JULI/1944+++
                    +ADOLF·HITLER///F/+H/+QU/+27/+JULI/1944+++
```

F. d. R.

Teletype

TO / LEUTNANT / OTTO / CARIUS ////
502ND / HEAVY / PANZER / BATTALION

IN – THANKFUL – APPRECIATION – OF – YOUR – HEROIC –

ACTIONS – IN – THE – BATTLE – FOR – THE – FUTURE –

OF – OUR – PEOPLE //// I – AWARD – YOU – AS – THE –

535TH – SOLDIER – OF – THE – GERMAN – WEHRMACHT –

THE – OAKLEAVES – TO – THE – KNIGHT'S – CROSS –

OF – THE – IRON – CROSS ////

ADOLF – HITLER //// FÜHRER / HEADQUARTERS / 27 / JULY / 1944

Document 17

Wochenschau der PK-Berichte

Der eherne Schild

Wie die Spitze der Panzerbrigade „Josef Stalin" im Raum von Dünaburg aufgerieben wurde

Von Kriegsberichter Herbert Steinert

PK... Rattern der Panzerketten, Klirren von Stahl, Krachen der Panzerkanonen, das ist die eherne Melodie der Tiger-Panzer, die an den Brennpunkten der Abwehrschlacht im Raum von Dünaburg den schwer kämpfenden Grenadieren die blutige Last der Abwehr von den Schultern nehmen.

Seit dem Tage, an dem das Inferno des an Heftigkeit und Erbitterung immer grausamer sich steigernden Kampfens gegen eine bolschewistische Übermacht dem Kulminationspunkt zuschritt und die zerstörende Macht der Schlacht ihre Furien immer wilder über die seicht im Kampfe stehende Truppe peitschte, stehen die Tiger-Panzer in den Reihen der Grenadiere. Wenn die angreifenden Bolschewisten aus den Wäldern quellen, über Wiesen und durch Sümpfe stürmen, fetzen die Tiger mit Sprenggranaten in die Wellen der erdbraunen Angreifer Wätzen sich aus Mulden und Senken die Massen der sowjetischen Panzer gegen unsere Stellungen, dann zerschlagen Tigerkanonen die stählerne Walze. Treten die Grenadiere zum Gegenstoss an, so fahren die Panzer mit gegen den Feind. Wird ein Tiger abgesetzt, so steht ein Tiger lauernd hinter einem Busch, bis die letzte Gruppe sich vom Feind gelöst hat. Beim Angriff zuerst, beim Absetzen zuletzt, das ist die Losung der Tigerbesatzungen. Und die Grenadiere sind den Männern der Panzer dankbar. Wenn das Klirren der Ketten an ihr Ohr weingt, fühlen sie sich stark und gewappnet im Kampf gegen eine scher erdrückende Übermacht.

Das See-, Sumpf- und Waldgelände im einstimmung zwischen Rede, Gestalt und Auftrag prägten. Unlöschbar von dem Bildnis dieses jungen Offiziers und seiner Welt ist seine Waffe: der Tiger, mit dem er sich im März dieses Jahres für 26 Abschüsse im Nordabschnitt der Ostfront das Ritterkreuz erwarb.

In jeder Lage hat Leutnant C. gewusst und gefühlt, wie er seinen Tiger einzusetzen hat. Er schlug mit ihm den Feind so, dass seine Hiebe überraschten und überrumpelten.

So auch am gestrigen Tage. Da fährt dieser junge Panzerkommandant in Begleitung eines zweiten Tigers über das breite Band einer Rollbahn, um die Strasse gegen überraschende Vorstösse der Sowjets zu sichern. Er weiss nicht, dass zur gleichen Stunde der aus Moskau frisch in den Brennpunkt der Abwehrschlacht im Raum von Dünaburg herangeführte Garde-Panzerbrigade „Josef Stalin" zu einem entscheidenden Vorstoss gegen die Rollbahn angetreten ist. Die Brigade, eine Eliteeinheit der Sowjets, verfügt über die neuesten Panzertypen. Während die Masse der angreifenden Brigade durch unser Abwehrfeuer zersprengt und aufgehalten wird, gelingt der gegnerischen Panzerspitze ein tieferer Einbruch in die Abwehrfront.

Im Glauben an ihre materielle Überlegenheit fühlen sich die Sowjets auf ihrem Marsch sicher. An den wenigen Hütten eines Dorfes, der Rollbahn zum Greifen nahe, verhält die Panzerspitze zur Orientierungspause. Auf kleinstem Raum stehen hier jetzt eng massiert die neuesten sowjetischen Panzertypen. Kommandanten und Führer lungern, Tiger auf. Die Sowjetpanzer schwenken die Türme. Die 17 Eisenklötze rasseln durch ein Kornfeld dem schützenden Waldrand zu. Ihre Kanonen blitzen auf. Abschüsse. Einschläge. Meterhoch spritzt der Dreck um die Tiger. Ihre Motore heulen wild auf. Sie stossen dem Feind nach. Panzerketten. Einschläge reissen tiefe Narben in das Erdreich.

Feuerblitz nach Feuerblitz leckt aus dem wuchtigen Rohr des Panzers von Leutnant C. Wohin er schiesst, da trifft es, und wohin er rollt, da bricht der Widerstand.

Nach 20 Minuten wilder Feuerschläge ist die Spitze der Panzerbrigade „Josef Stalin" zerschlagen und aufgerieben. Die zerfetzten Trümmer der modernsten Panzertypen der Sowjets liegen rauchend, schwelend und brennend zwischen Rollbahn und Wald.

Zehn Abschüsse kann allein Leutnant C. für sich buchen, vier der zweite Tiger. Drei der fliehenden bolschewistischen Panzer wurden von Sturmgeschützen, die den eingebrochenen Panzern nachgestossen waren, zusammengeschossen.

Wo zuvor noch 17 Sowjetpanzer sich über Kartoffeläcker und durch Kornfelder wälzten, da stehen jetzt die schwarzen, ausgebrannten, zerschlagenen Wracks von 17 Stahlkolossen. Nur Schrott und zerbogene Eisenteile liegen an ihrer Stelle. Als ob ein schwerer Hammer Porzellan zerschlagen hätte, so zerrissen die Schlüsse der Tigerkanonen auch die neuesten Typen der sowjetischen Panzerwaffe. Ringsum liegen ihre Trümmer auf der brandigen Erde.

Raum Dünaburg ist unübersichtlich und bietet sich zum Umgehen unserer Kampfgruppen, die an Rollbahn und Engen zwischen Wald, See und Sumpf den Angreifern trotzen, den sowjetischen Massen an. Überraschungen sind hier immer möglich und die Sinne aller, ob am Kartenbrett, im Panzer oder am Gewehr, müssen pausenlos hellwach sein. Oft hat es in diesen Tagen, in denen sich die Schlacht im Rhythmus neu herangeführter sowjetischer Kräfte steigerte, geheissen: «Da können nur noch die Tiger helfen» Dann sahen wir sie über schmale Feldwege rollen, mit donnernden Motoren. Ihre kilirrenden Ketten furchten tiefe Spuren in den zermahlenen Sand und wirbelten ihn hoch auf. Ein, wuchtiges Bild gespeicherter Kraft. Mit hoher Fahrt, in gelbe Staubwolken gehüllt, stiessen die Tiger dorthin, wo bittere Not um unsere Grenadiere war. In einer seltsamen Wiedergeburt schien der Geist des alten Rittertums auferstanden zu sein, jener Geist der Treue und tiefinneren Kameradschaft, deren Gesetz es war, dem Freunde in der Gefahr zu helfen.

Wie einst der Ritter mit seinem gewappneten Ross zu einem kämpferischen Wesen vereint sein musste, so sind die Panzersoldaten in dieser harten und wechselvollen Abwehrschlacht mit ihren stählernen Kampfwagen eins. Denn hier, umlauert von Gefahren und Überraschungen, im Kampf gegen einen an Zahl überlegenen Gegner bedeutet Panzersoldat zu sein mehr, als nur einen Panzer zu fahren und mit seiner Kanone zu schiessen. Beim Zusammenprall mit der masslerten Kraft des Gegners gilt es auch, jenen bedingungslosen Willen zum Siege zu besitzen, der hoch über jeder Masse steht und durch keine Waffe ersetzt werden kann. Hier muss der Soldat des Panzers auch jenen innerlichen Schneid und die Entschlussfreudigkeit besitzen, die seiner schnellen und starken Waffe entspricht.

Einer ist heute herausgetreten aus der Zahl der Tiger-Kommandanten, die im Kampfraum um Dünaburg in einer Abwehrschlacht eingesetzt sind, in der sich die Beispiele für einen höheren als gewöhnlichen Mit von Tag zu Tag, von Stunde zu Stunde wiederholen.

Es ist der Leutnant C. aus Zweibrücken/Westmark. Er ist noch jung, er mag das 23. Lebensjahr eben vollendet haben. Trotz seiner Jugend gehört er zu jenen soldatischen Naturen, deren Wesen und Antlitz sich aus einem harten Frontleben und an den Werkzeugen ihrer Macht in vollkommener Über-

Zigaretten rauchend, über Karten gebeugt, in den Türmen, während einige Panzerschützen auf Raub nach Essbarem durch die Höfe streichen.

Über eine kleine Höhe kommend, prallen

Ritterkreuzträger Otto Carius aus Zweibrücken/Westmark bespricht mit seinem Zugführer einen neuen Einsatzplan
Aufn.: PK Weber

die zwei Tiger des Leutnant C. auf kürzestem Abstand mit den Sowjets zusammen. Dem jungen Panzeroffizier steigt etwas heiss die Kehle hoch. Er zählt:

Insgesamt 17 Sowjetpanzer!
Gegen zwei Tiger!

Die Auseinandersetzung wird hart werden. Wer unterliegt, der stirbt. Ein Zurück gibt es nicht mehr.

Angriff!

Urweltlaft brüllen die Kanonen der zwei

Am Rande des schaurlichen Kampfplatzes steht der Tiger des Leutnant C. Der Leutnant steht im Turm. Oben im Silverschmiesten grauen Hemd, unten die Tarnhose. Es wäre kaum von seinen Männern zu unter-

scheiden, blitzte nicht das Ritterkreuz in der Sommersonne.

Die Rollbahn ist wieder erfüllt von Fahrzeugen. Am Waldrand gehen die Grenadiere in Stellung. Wann wird der nächste Angriff kommen? Drohend sind die Rohre der wuchtigen Tigerkanonen gen Osten gerichtet. Mit ihrem ehernen Schild warten die Grenadiere auf den Augenblick, da im steilen Aufschwung auch hier wieder die Abwehrschlacht im Raum um Dünaburg erneut auf brüllen wird.

Review of War Correspondent Reports

The Bronze Shield

How the Lead Elements of the "Josef Stalin" Tank Brigade were Rubbed Out in the Dünaburg Area

By War Correspondent Herbert Steinert

The rattle of the tank tracks, the clanking of steel, the crash of main guns...that is the brazen melody of the "Tiger" tanks. They have lifted the burden of defense from the shoulders of the heavily-engaged grenadiers in the hot spots of the defensive fighting in the Dünaburg area.

From the day on which the inferno of the increasingly intensive and bitter fighting against bolshevist superior strength moved towards its climax and the destructive power of the battle drove its furies, ever wilder, over the troops who had been fighting for weeks, the "Tiger" tanks had stood among the ranks of the grenadiers. Whenever the Bolsheviks arose out of the woods or stormed across meadows and through swamps, the "Tigers" shredded the waves of the earthbrown attackers with high explosive rounds. Whenever masses of Soviet tanks rolled out of depressions and hollows against our positions, then the cannons of the "Tigers" shattered the steel colossus. Whenever the grenadiers counterattacked, then the tanks also moved with them against the enemy. Whenever the grenadiers are pulled back, then a "Tiger" lurks behind a bush until the last squad has extricated itself from the enemy. Always first in the attack, always last to pull out - that's the motto of the "Tiger" crews. And the grenadiers are grateful to the men of the tanks. Whenever the clanking of the tracks pounds in their ears, they feel strong and well prepared in a battle against an overwhelming superiority.

The lakes, swamps, and wooded terrain in the speech, character, and sense of duty. At one with the portrait of this young officer and his world is his weapon: the "Tiger". In it, he earned the Knight's Cross for himself in March of this year for 26 kills in the northern sector of the Eastern Front.

In each situation, Leutnant Carius has known and felt how he had to employ his "Tiger". He struck the enemy with his tank in such a manner that his thrusts surprised him and caught him unawares.

That was also the case yesterday. Accompanied by a second "Tiger", this young tank commander was moving over the broad expanses of the Rollbahn in order to cover the road against surprise advances by the Soviets. He did not know that at the same moment the "Josef Stalin" Guards Tank Brigade - freshly brought in from Moscow to the critical defensive fighting in the Dünaburg area - had assembled for the decisive advance against the Rollbahn. The brigade, an elite unit of the Soviets, employed the latest models of tanks. While the bulk of the attacking brigade was dispersed and held up, the lead enemy armor elements succeeded in penetrating deeply into the defensive front.

Believing in their material superiority, the Soviets felt secure on their march. Among the few huts of a village - the Rollbahn in arm's reach - the advance guard of the tanks conducted a short break for orientation. The latest types of Soviet tanks were now massed tightly together. Commanders and drivers lounged about - smoking cigarettes, bent over maps, primordial manner. The Soviet tanks swung their turrets. The 17 lumps of iron raced through a grain field to the protective cover of the woods. Their main guns flashed. Muzzle reports. Impacts. The dirt shot up a few meters high around the "Tigers". Their motors howled crazily. They pursued the enemy. Tank tracks. The impacting rounds ripped deep scars into the earth.

One fireball after another followed from the powerful barrel of Leutnant Carius' tank. Whatever he shot at, he hit; wherever he rolled, he broke the resistance.

After 20 minutes of wild firing, the advance guard of the "Josef Stalin" Tank Brigade has been shattered and destroyed. The mangled remains of the latest Soviet tank models lay smoking, smouldering, and burning between the Rollbahn and the woods.

Leutnant Carius can chalk up 10 kills for himself, the second "Tiger" had four. Three of the fleeing bolshevist tanks were destroyed by assault guns which had followed the penetration of the tanks.

Where once 17 Soviet tanks had trundled over potato patches and through fields of grain, there were now only the black, burned out, shattered wreaks of 17 steel colossuses. Only scrap metal and twisted pieces of steel remained in their place. Like a heavy hammer smashing porcelain, the main gun rounds of the "Tigers" also smashed the latest models of the Soviet's armored fleet. Their ruins lay scattered on the scorched earth.

Leutnant Carius' "Tiger" was at the edge of the

Dünaburg area are dense and lend themselves to the Soviet hordes for bypassing our Kampfgruppen which defy the attackers on the Rollbahn and the straights between the woods, lakes, and swamps. Surprises are always possible here and the senses of everyone, whether at the map board, in the tank, or manning a rifle must always remain alert. During these days, in which the fighting intensified to the rhythm of newly introduced Soviet forces, it was often said: "Only the ''Tigers'' can still help us here!" We then saw them rolling over narrow field paths with motors thundering. Their clanking treads burrowed deep tracks in the pulverized sand and swirled it around high in the air. A powerful portrait of stored strength. At high speed, covered in yellow clouds of dust, the ''Tigers'' advanced to wherever our grenadiers were in grave trouble. In a unusual rebirth, the spirit of ancient knighthood appeared to have been resurrected - that spirit of loyalty and deeply internalized comradeship whose code it was to help the friend in danger.

As once the knight with his armed steed must have been unified into one fighting entity, so are the tankers one with their steel fighting vehicle in this hard and ever-changing defensive battle. Because here, surrounded by danger and surprises, in a battle against a numerically superior foe, being a tanker means more than just driving a tank and shooting its cannon. During a collision with the massed strength of the enemy, it is also important to possess that unconditional will towards victory which stands alone high above every crowd and which cannot be replaced by any weapon. It is here that the tank soldier must also possess that internal pluck and aggressive desire to make decisions which correspond to his rapid and powerful weapon.

One was singled out today, one out of the number of ''Tiger'' commanders who have been employed in the defensive fighting around Dünaburg in which examples of a higher than usual courage are repeated from day to day, from hour to hour.

It is Leutnant Carius from Zweibrücken/Westmark. He is still young; perhaps he has just had his 24th birthday. Despite his youth, he has that type of soldierly nature whose being and appearance have been imprinted by a hard life at the front and on the instruments of its power - a perfect synthesis of

in the turrets - while a few tankers strolled though the barnyards on the prowl for something to eat.

Coming over the small rise, Leutnant Carius' two ''Tigers'' collided with the Soviets at the shortest

Knight's Cross winner Otto Carius (from Zweibrücken/Westmark) discusses a new battle plan with his platoon leader.
Photo: War correspondent Weber.

range possible. The young Panzer officer felt his throat get tight. He counted!

A total of 17 Soviet tanks!

Two ''Tigers'' against them!

The fight would be hard. Whoever was defeated would die. But there wasn't any turning back.

Attack!

The main guns of the two ''Tigers'' roared in a

gruesome battlefield. The Leutnant stood in the turret. The oil-smeared gray shirt above, the camouflage pants below. It would be hard to distinguish him from his men if the Knight's Cross didn't gleam in the

summer sun.

The Rollbahn has filled once more with vehicles. At the edge of the woods, grenadiers occupy positions. When will the next attack come? Threateningly, the powerful cannons of the ''Tigers'' are pointed towards the east. With their bronze shield, the grenadiers wait for that moment. Because even here the defensive fighting in the Dünaburg area can roar again at a moment's notice.

Document 18

Fernspruch - Fernschreiben - Funkspruch - Blinkspruch

Nachr.-Stelle	Nr.	Befördert				
		an	Tag	Zeit	durch	Rolle
1.IX.158·	319/ 13957					

Vermerke:

Angenommen oder aufgenommen

+++0733/EINS/BA/HEGXC++ durch
++*0735/EINS/BA/HEGXC++

Abgang			Absendende Stelle
Tag: 29/7.	AN LT/+ CARIUS SCHW/+PZ/+ABT/+502/////		
Zeit: 0200	AN LT/+ CARIUS SCHW/+PZ/+ABT/+502////		16. Armee
Dringlichkeits-Vermerk			Fernsprech-Anschluß:

THUHX/FUE 139 39 29/+7/+0200////
+HQ9X/FUE 139 39 29/+7/+0200////

ZUR VERLEIHUNG DES EICHENLAUBES ZUM RITTERKREUZ DES
ZUR VERLEIHUNG DES EICHENLAUBES ZUM RITTERKREUZ DES

EISERNEN KREUZES AUFRICHTIGE GLUECKWUENSCHE UND MIT
EISERNEN KREUZES AUFRICHTIGE GLUECKWUENSCHE UND MIT

DEM BESTEN WUENSCHEN ZUR BALDIGEN GENESUNG/+////
DEM BESTEN WUENSCHEN ZUR BALDIGEN GENESUNG/+////

L A U X///GENERAL DER INFANTIERIE MIT DER FUEHRUNG
L A U X///GENERAL DER INFANTIERIE MIT DER FUEHRUNG

DER 16/+ARMEE BEAUFTRAGT +
DER 16/+ARMEE BEAUFTRAGT +

F. d. R.

Teletype

TO / LEUTNANT / CARIUS /
502ND / HEAVY / PANZER / BATTALION

HEARTFELT – CONGRATULATIONS – ON – AWARD – OF – THE –

OAKLEAVES – TO – THE – KNIGHT'S – CROSS – OF – THE – IRON –

CROSS – AND – BEST – WISHES – FOR – A – SPEEDY – RECOVERY ////

LAUX //// GENERAL DER INFANTERIE AND

ACTING COMMANDER OF THE 16TH ARMY

Document 19

Fernspruch - Fernschreiben - Funkspruch - Blinkspruch

			Befördert				
Nachr.-Stelle	Nr.	an	Tag	Zeit	durch	Rolle

Vermerke: Durch Kurier !

Angenommen oder aufgenommen			
von	Tag	Zeit	durch

Abgang		Abſendende Stelle
Tag: 30.7.44	**An:**	Okdo.H.Gr.Nord
Zeit:	Leutnant Otto C a r i u s ,	Abt.IIb
Dringlichkeits-Vermerk	schw.Pz.Abt.5o2	
		Fernſprech-Anſchluß :

Herzlichen Glückwunsch zur Verleihung
des Eichenlaubes verbunden mit den
besten Wünschen für baldige Genesung.

Generaloberst
u.Oberbefehlshaber der H.Gr.Nord

Quittung	Fernſpruch Fernſchreiben Funkſpruch Blinkſpruch	Nr.	Von	An	Tag	Zeit	Annehmender Offz. (Uffz.)	
							Name	Dienſtgrad

Cn492

By Courier!

To: Leutnant Otto C a r i u s
502nd Heavy Panzer Battalion

Heartfelt congratulations on the award
of the Oakleaves to the Knight's Cross
of the Iron Cross coupled with best wishes
for a speedy recovery.

/ signed /

Schörner

Generaloberst and
Commander of Army Group North

Document 20

Von der Front

Ritterkreuz u. Eichenlaub für einen tapferen Zweibrücker

Der Führer verlieh einem Sohne unserer Stadt Zweibrücken, dem Leutnant d. R. Otto C a r i u s , Zweibrücken-Bubenhausen, Wattweiler Straße 20, in einem Zeitraume von noch nicht drei Monaten als hohe Tapferkeitsauszeichnungen das Ritterkreuz des Eisernen Kreuzes und das Eichenlaub zum Ritterkreuz des Eisernen Kreuzes.

In den schweren Abwehrkämpfen bei Narwa griff Lt. Carius als Zugführer in einer schweren Panzerabteilung mit 5 Tigern starke bolschewistische Uebermacht an, überrannte durch geschicktes und schneidiges Anfahren sowjetische Pakstellungen, die seinen Gegenstoß hätten flankieren können und vernichtete 5 schwere Pak. Innerhalb weniger Minuten schossen die Tiger 12 schwere und einen schwersten Sowjetpanzer ab. Der Rest der sowjetischen Panzer zog sich in Eile zurück. Obwohl hier immer deutlicher der Schwerpunkt des feindlichen Angriffes lag, verhinderten die paar schweren Panzer den vom Feind mit allen Mitteln erstrebten Durchbruch zum Finnischen Meerbusen. An den beiden nächsten Tagen schoß Lt. Carius weitere 15 Sowjet-Panzer, darunter wieder 12 schwere und einen schwersten ab. Damit hatte er innerhalb von drei Tagen 28 feindliche Panzer vernichtet und erheblich zur Abwehr der starken feindlichen Angriffe westlich Narwa beigetragen. An dem Erfolg, für den die schwere Pan-

zerabteilung am 21. März im Wehrmachtsbericht genannt worden ist, hatte Lt. Carius und sein Zug wesentlichen Anteil. Vom Führer wurde er dafür mit dem Ritterkreuz des Eisernen Kreuzes ausgezeichnet.

Am 22. Juli stand Lt. Carius mit 2 Tigern seiner Kompanie nordöstlich Dünaburg, als die Bolschewisten mit 17 schweren Panzern die vordersten deutschen Linien durchbrachen und sich nun anschickten, Dünaburg anzugreifen. Aus eigenem Entschluß warf er sich den zahlenmäßig vielfach überlegenen Sowjets entgegen. In kurzem heftigen Feuerkampf vernichtete er ohne eigene Verluste den gesamten bolschewistischen Verband, wobei der Abschuß von 10 Panzern allein auf den „Tiger" entfiel, in dem Lt. Carius, weit vorausfahrend, den Angriff führte. Durch diese kühne Tat hat der junge Offizier einen schon fast vollendeten Panzerdurchbruch auf Dünaburg verhindert und die Voraussetzungen für den Aufbau einer neuen Abwehrfront geschaffen. Dafür verlieh ihm der Führer am 27. Juli als 535. Soldaten der deutschen Wehrmacht das Eichenlaub zum Ritterkreuz des Eisernen Kreuzes.

Leutnant Otto Carius ist am 27. Mai 1922 als Sohn des Gewerbeoberlehrers Otto Carius in Zweibrücken geboren. Nachdem er das Gymnasium absolviert hatte, wurde er im Jahre 1940 zur Wehrmacht einberufen. Nach anfänglicher Ausbildung bei der Infanterie trat er zur Panzerwaffe über und wurde 1942 zum Leutnant befördert. Im gleichen Jahre erhielt er das EK II und 1943 das EK I. Außerdem wurde ihm das Panzerabzeichen verliehen und nach viermaliger Verwundung das Silberne Verwundetenabzeichen.

Seine Heimatstadt Zweibrücken ist stolz auf ihren ersten Eichenlaubträger und entbietet dem tapferen Offizier herzlichste Glückwünsche. Der Name Carius bedeutet „der Glückliche" und so möge das Soldatenglück nicht nur unserem Eichenlaubträger, sondern auch seinem jüngeren Bruder und dem Vater der beiden Soldaten, der als Major bei der Wehrmacht steht, treu bleiben.

10

 **From the Front**

Knight's Cross and Oakleaves for a Brave Son of Zweibrücken

In recognition of bravery, the Führer has awarded a son of our city of Zweibrücken, Leutnant der Reserve Otto Carius, Zweibrücken-Bubenhausen, Wattweiler Straße 20, the Knight's Cross of the Iron Cross and the Oakleaves to the Knight's Cross of the Iron Cross within a period of not quite three months.

In the heavy defensive fighting at Narwa, Leutnant Carius, platoon leader in a heavy Panzer battalion, attacked a strongly superior bolshevist force with five "Tigers". By cleverly and boldly approaching Soviet antitank positions which could have flanked his counterattack, he destroyed 5 heavy antitank guns. Within a few minutes, the "Tigers" had knocked out one super-heavy and 12 heavy Soviet tanks. The remainder of the Soviet tanks withdrew in a hurry. Although it became increasingly apparent that the Schwerpunkt of the enemy attack was here, the handful of heavy tanks prevented the breakthrough to the Bay of Finland which the enemy was attempting with all means. In the next two days, Leutnant Carius knocked out an additional 15 Soviet tanks, among them 12 heavy and one superheavy. He had thus destroyed 28 enemy tanks within three days and contributed considerably to the defense against the strong enemy attacks west of Narwa. Leutnant Carius and his platoon played a considerable role in the success for which the heavy Panzer battalion was mentioned in the Wehrmacht report on 21 March. For this he was decorated with the Knight's Cross of the Iron Cross by the Führer.

On 22 July, Leutnant Carius was with 2 "Tigers" of his company northeast of Dünaburg when the Bolsheviks broke through the German lines with 17 heavy tanks and then set about attacking Dünaburg. On his own initiative, he threw himself against the numerically superior Soviets. In a short, intensive fire fight, he destroyed the entire bolshevist unit without any friendly losses. Ten of the kills were due exclusively to the "Tiger" in which Leutnant Carius, far to the front, lead the attack. Due to this bold deed, the young officer prevented a tank breakthrough to Dünaburg and created the prerequisites for the construction of a new defensive front. For this, the Führer awarded him the Oakleaves to the Knight's Cross of the Iron Cross on 27 July as the 535th soldier of the Wehrmacht.

Leutnant Otto Carius was born on 27 May 1922 in Zweibrücken as the son of the trade school instructor Otto Carius. After he had completed college preparatory school, he was called up to the Wehrmacht in the year 1940. After initial training as an infantryman, he transferred to the armor corps and was promoted to Leutnant in 1942. In the same year, he received the Iron Class Second Class. In 1943 he received the Iron Class First Class. In addition, he was awarded the Panzer Assault Badge and, after being wounded four times, the silver Wound Badge.

His home town of Zweibrücken is proud of its first Oakleaves winner and offers the brave officer its sincerest congratulations. The name Carius means "the lucky one" and we hope that fate continues to smile not only on our Oakleaves winner but his younger brother and his father, who serves in the Wehrmacht as a Major.

Document 21

Der Kommandierende General
des XXXXIII. Armeekorps

O. U., den 31. Juli 1944

Herrn

Leutnant Otto C a r i u s ,

s. Panzer-Abteilung 502.

Zur Verleihung des Eichenlaubes zum Ritterkreuz des Eisernen Kreuzes wünsche ich Ihnen herzlich Glück und hoffe, daß Sie sich dieser hohen Auszeichnung bald völlig genesen erfreuen können.

Heil Hitler !

General der Infanterie.

Commanding General
XXXXXIII Army Corps

Leutnant Otto C a r i u s

502nd Heavy Panzer Battalion

On the award of the Oakleaves to the Knight's Cross
of the Iron Cross, I sincerely wish you happiness and hope
that you can soon enjoy your distinguished award in the
best of health.

Heil Hitler!

/ signed /

Lotze

General der Infanterie

Document 22

Paderborn, 4. VIII. 1944

Herrn Leutnant Carius
in der schw. Panzer-Abteilung 502

Die Panzer-Lehrgänge ‚Tiger' und die Ersatz-Abt. 500 beglückwünschen Sie herzlichst zu Ihrer hohen Auszeichnung mit dem **Eichenlaub zum Ritterkreuz des Eisernen Kreuzes** und wünschen Ihnen auch für die Zukunft viel Soldatenglück und Erfolg.

Heil Hitler!

Hoheisel.

Oberstleutnant und Kommandeur

Paderborn, 4 August 1944

Leutnant Otto Carius
502nd Heavy Panzer Battalion

The participants in the "Tiger" courses and the members of the 500th Replacement and Training Battalion congratulate you on your distinguished award of the Oakleaves to the Knight's Cross of the Iron Cross and wish you continued good luck and success in all military endeavors in the future.

Heil Hitler!

/ signed /

Hoheisel
Oberstleutnant and Commander

Document 23

**Der Chef des Generalstabes
des Heeres**

HQu., den 7. August 1944

Herrn
Leutnant C a r i u s
Fhr.Tigerkp.s.Pz.Abt. 502

    Zu der erneuten hohen Auszeichnung, die
Ihnen vom Führer am 27.7.44 verliehen worden ist,
spreche ich Ihnen meine aufrichtigsten Glückwünsche
aus.

            Heil Hitler !

Chief of Staff of the Army   Headquarters, 7 August 1944

Leutnant C a r i u s
Commander
"Tiger" Company
502nd Heavy Panzer Battalion

I wish to express my sincerest congratulations
for the award of another high decoration which was
granted by the Führer on 27 July 1944.

Heil Hitler!

/ signed /

Guderian

Document 24

Heesemann   H.Qu.OKH., den 10.Aug.1944
Oberst und Chef P 5
    OKH / PA

          Lieber C a r i u s !

     Zur Verleihung des Eichenlaubes zum Ritterkreuz des Eiser-
nen Kreuzes durch den Führer darf ich Sie als Chef der Ordensab-
teilung im Oberkommando des Heeres aufrichtig beglückwünschen.

     Damit Sie auf kürzestem Wege in den Besitz Ihrer Auszeich-
nung kommen, bitte ich Sie, nach Wiederherstellung Ihrer Gesundheit
ins H.Qu.OKH zu kommen. Von hier aus erfolgt dann die Meldung beim
Führer. Eine vorherige Rückfrage über den Zeitpunkt der Abreise
nach hier ist jedoch über das stellv. Generalkommando erforderlich.

     Mit den besten Wünschen für Ihre baldige Genesung

          Heil Hitler !

              Ihr

                   Heesemann.

H e e s e m a n n
Oberst and Head of P5
OKH / PA

Headquarters,
Army High Command
10 August 1944

Dear Carius!

As head of the awards department in the High Command of the Army, I would like to take the opportunity to sincerely congratulate you on the award of the Oakleaves to the Knight's Cross of the Iron Cross.

So that you can be presented your award in the quickest way possible, I am asking you to come to the Headquarters of the Army High Command after you have regained your health. From here, you will then report to the Führer. You will need to make arrangements in advance with the district command concerning the time of your departure for here, however.

With best wishes for your rapid recovery,

Heil Hitler!

Heesemann

Document 25

BESITZZEUGNIS

DEM .... Leutnant d.Res. ....
(DIENSTGRAD)

Otto   C a r i u s
(VOR- UND FAMILIENNAME)

2.Komp./schw.Panz.Abt.502
(TRUPPENTEIL)

VERLEIHE ICH FÜR TAPFERE TEILNAHME
AN ..50.. EINSATZTAGEN

DIE ..III..STUFE ZUM
PANZERKAMPFABZEICHEN
IN SILBER

Abt.Gef.Std., 1.9.1944
(ORT UND DATUM)

M.d.F.b.

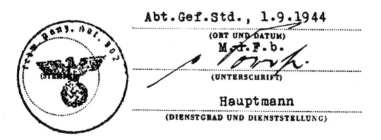

(UNTERSCHRIFT)

Hauptmann
(DIENSTGRAD UND DIENSTSTELLUNG)

CERTIFICATE
I AWARD

Leutnant der Reserve
....
(RANK)

Otto C a r i u s
....
(FIRST AND LAST NAME)

2nd Company, 502nd Heavy Panzer Battalion
....
(ORGANIZATION)

THE .. Third .. LEVEL OF THE
PANZER ASSAULT BADGE
IN SILVER

FOR COURAGEOUS PARTICIPATION IN
.50.. DAYS OF COMBAT.

Battalion Command Post,
1 September 1944
....
(LOCATION AND DATE)

/ signed /

von Foerster
....
(SIGNATURE)

Hauptmann and Acting Commander
....
(RANK AND POSITION)

Document 26

BESITZZEUGNIS

DEM

Leutnant Otto C a r i u s

2./schw.Pz.Abt. 5o2

IST AUF GRUND

SEINER AM 8.7.41, 9.12.42, 2.12.43, 2o.4.44 u. 24.7.44 ERLITTENEN

fünf MALIGEN VERWUNDUNG – BESCHÄDIGUNG

DAS

VERWUNDETENABZEICHEN.

IN G o l d

VERLIEHEN WORDEN.

Lingen/Ems , DEN 11.Sept. 194 4

Reserve-Lazarett Lingen/Ems

Oberfeldarzt u. Chefarzt

CERTIFICATE

Leutnant Otto C a r i u s
(NAME, RANK)

2nd Company, 502nd Heavy Panzer Battalion
(ORGANIZATION, POSITION)

HAS BEEN AWARDED THE

WOUND BADGE

IN ... G o l d ..

based on his being wounded or injured . 5 . times

on 8 July 1941, 9 December 1942, 2 December 1943,
20 April 1944, and 24 July 1944.

Lingen / Ems , 11 September 194 4 .
Reserve Military Hospital Lingen / Ems

/ signed /

Hartmann
(SIGNATURE)

Oberfeldarzt and Commander
(RANK AND POSITION)

Document 27

Schwere Panzer-Abteilung 502   Abt.Gef.Std., 10.9.44.
    - Kommandeur -
_____

An

Leutnant
Otto C a r i u s ,
z.Zt. Res.Laz.
L i n g e n a.d.Ems,
Teillazarett Bonifatius.

Mein lieber C a r i u s !

Als Nachfolger von Herrn Major S c h w a n e r habe
ich lediglich Ihre Spuren bei der s.Pz.Abt.502 wahr-
genommen. Es ist mir aus diesem Grunde ein Bedürfnis,
mich auf diesem Wege Ihnen als Kommandeur Ihrer schö-
nen Abteilung vorzustellen.

Von Ihren hiesigen Kameraden habe ich vernommen,
welch scheußliches Pech Sie bei Ihrem letzten Einsatz
gehabt haben. Ich möchte Ihnen von ganzem Herzen eine
baldige und restlose Genesung wünschen. Die ganze Abteilung schließt sich von ganzem Herzen diesen Wünschen an.

Ich würde mich ganz besonders freuen, wenn Sie auch
Ihren künftigen Aufenthaltsort, sowie Ihre weiteren
Wünsche der Abteilung mitteilen würden, damit Sie die
Abteilung bei Erlangung derselben unterstützen kann.

Gleichzeitig habe ich die Freude, Ihnen die III.Stufe
zum "Panzerkampfabzeichen in Silber" für 50 Angriffe
zu übersenden.

Mit den herzlichen Grüßen und aufrichtigen Wünschen
für baldige Genesung, bin ich Ihr

                        Ihnen ergebener

                        Foorphs.

502nd Heavy Panzer Battalion
  - Commander -
_____

Battalion Command Post,
10 September 1944

To:

Leutnant
Otto C a r i u s,
Reserve Military Hospital
L i n g e n on the Ems,
Bonafatius Hospital

Dear C a r i u s:

As the successor to Major S c h w a n e r, I have come
across your legacy at the 502nd Heavy Panzer Battalion quite
often. For this reason, I feel the need to introduce myself
to you by means of this letter as the commander of this great
battalion.

I found out from your fellow soldiers here what horrible luck
you had during your last operation. From the bottom of my
heart I would like to wish you a speedy and complete recovery. The entire battalion joins me in this heartfelt wish.

It would make me very happy if you would inform the battalion
of your future location as well as any additional wishes, so
that it can support you in realizing them.

I also have the pleasure of sending you the Third Level of
the Panzer Assault Badge in Silver for 50 assaults.

With heartfelt greetings and sincere wishes for a speedy recovery, I remain

Sincerely yours,

von Foerster

Document 28

Oberkommando des Heeres   H.Qu.OKH., den 12.September 1944
__PA/P 5 a 1.Staffel__

           Herrn

           Leutnant C a r i u s ,

           Reservelazarett L i n g e n /Ems
           Teillazarett Bonifatius.

      Da der Führer sich die Aushändigung des Eichenlaubes selbst
vorbehalten hat, ist eine Übersendung der Auszeichnung über das Stellv.
Generalkommando VI.A.K. nicht möglich. Sobald Sie in der Lage sind sich
beim Führer melden zu können, wollen Sie dies dem OKH/PA/P 5 1.Staffel
rechtzeitig mitteilen, damit von hier aus die Meldung veranlasst werden
kann.

Mit den besten Wünschen für baldige Genesung, Heil Hitler !

I.A.

Johanmeyer
Major.

High Command of the Army   Headquarters, OKH,
  PA/P 5 a 1. Section   12 September 1944

Leutnant C a r i u s,

Reserve Military Hospital in L i n g e n / Ems
Bonafatius Hospital

     Because the Führer has reserved the right to present the
Oakleaves, sending the decoration via the VI Army Corps district
command is not possible. As soon as you are in a position to be
able to personally report to the Führer, expeditiously inform
OKH / PA / P 5 1 so that the appropriate report can be generated
here.   ·

For the commander:

 Best wishes for a speedy recovery. Heil Hitler!

Johannmeyer

Major

Document 29

Schwere Panzer-Abteilung 502   Abt.Gef.Std., den 24.9.1944
   - Kommandeur -

     An
     Oberleutnant
     Otto   C a r i u s ,
     z.Zt. Res.Laz.Lingen,
     L i n g e n / Ems
     Teillaz. Bonifatius.

     Mein lieber Carius !

     Ich bin in der erfreulichen Lage, Ihnen Ihre vorzugsweise
Beförderung zum O b e r l e u t n a n t d.Res. in
weiterer Anerkennung Ihrer hervorragenden Einsätze bekannt-
zugeben. Nachfolgend die Durchschrift des heutigen Fern-
schreibens an den Chefarzt des Res.Laz.Lingen/Ems, woraus
Sie RDA und nähere Angaben entnehmen können:

        "Um dienstliche Bekanntgabe der mit Wirkung und RDA.
        vom 1.8.1944 gem.Verfg.OKH/PA Ag P 1/6.Abt.-a3- Az.
        pers.v.31.8.1944 erfolgten vorzugsweisen Beförde-
        rung des Leutnant d.Res.Otto Carius zum Oberleut-
        nant d.Res. wird gebeten."

     Im Namen der ganzen Abteilung und selbstverständlich auch
persönlich wünsche ich Ihnen von ganzem Herzen eine baldige und restlose Genesung, damit Sie bald hier bei uns im
alten Kameradenkreis zu gemeinsamen Einsätzen wieder in
der Lage sind.

     Mit kameradschaftlichen Grüßen bin ich

                            Ihr

                          ergebener

```
502nd Heavy Panzer Battalion                Battalion Command Post,
        - Commander -                          24 September 1944
```

```
        To:
        Leutnant
        Otto  C a r i u s
        Reserve Military Hospital
        L i n g e n  on the Ems
        Bonafatius Hospital
```

Dear Carius:

I am in the fortunate position of being able to inform you of
your advanced promotion to Oberleutnant der Reserve in recognition of your superb actions. What follows is a copy of the
teletype sent today to the chief doctor at the Reserve Military Hospital in Lingen/Ems. You can obtain your date of rank
and additional information from it:

    It is requested that official announcement be made
    of the advanced promotion of Leutnant der Reserve
    Otto Carius to Oberleutnant der Reserve by order
    of OKH / PA Ag P 1/6.Abt.-a3-Az. pers. of 31 AUG 44.
    The promotion was effective 1 AUG 44 with a date of
    rank of the same day.

On behalf of the entire battalion and, it goes without saying, also from me, I sincerely wish you a speedy and complete
recovery so that you are soon in a position to be here among
your old circle of comrades and conducting operations with
them.

With friendly regards I remain

                  Sincerely yours

                    von Foerster

Index

After-action report, 238, 239–47
  on Dünaburg, 238, 260–62,
    275–305
  employment of staff, 238,
    263–74
  on Judennase, 238, 256–59
  on Lembitu, 238, 275–305
  technical, 238, 248–55
Americans, views on, 226–27
Antitank ditch, 122–24, 129,
  131, 133
Antitank guns, 85
  destruction of, 118

Balloons, Russian observation,
  126, 127
Baresch, Karl, 22, 167
Bayerlein, General, 209
Beljajewa, 16
Berlin, 201, 203
Berlin, General, 159
Betzdorf, 211
Biermann, Old Man, 67–68,
  75–76
Biplanes, Russian, 76
Bjeloj, 12–13, 15
Bölter, Oberleutnant, 162–63,
  191

Brittany, 19–20
Bunkers, Russian, 115–16
Bunker Village, 27–28

Carpaneto, Alfredo, 104,
  128–29
Cigarettes, supply of, 79
Clajus, Unteroffizier, 34
Code names, use of, 79, 80
Corduroy roads, 28–29
Croatians, 195

Dehler, August, 3, 5, 15, 16
Delzeit, Oberfeldwebel, 17, 81,
  135, 186–87, 205
Diels, Oberleutnant, 52
Diseases, 77
Dittmar, Feldwebel, 34
Dönitz, Großadmiral, 226
Dortmund, 222
Dünaburg
  arrival at, 153–61
  defensive fighting at, 162–65
  report on, 238, 260–62,
    275–305
Dünaburg-Rossitten Rollbahn,
  162–73
Düna River, 7–8, 162

East Prussia, 204
Eichhorn, Lieutenant, 139, 144, 175, 176, 184, 185, 187, 188
Eitorf, 211
Erlangen, 10
Estonians, 57

Famula, Günther, 109, 130, 133, 135
Fear, handling, 78–79
Feldherrnhalle Division, 85, 86, 95
Film reporter, 154–55
Flak, 88–mm, 10, 105
Friendly fire, 106
Fromme, Hauptmann, 204, 205

Gatschina, 26, 42–43, 44
Gille, General, 200, 201
Göring, Oberfeldwebel, 77, 104, 184, 189
Goruschka, 38
Großdeutschland Panzer Regiment, 100, 113
Gruber, Feldwebel, 87–88, 89, 93, 94, 103, 106, 107
Grünewald, Lieutenant, 27
Gshatsk, 12

Haase, major, 92
Hasso, 97, 137
Held, Oberleutnant, 209
Helmets, use of, 150
Hermann, Commander, 104
Himmler, Heinrich, 191–92, 194–201
Hitler, Adolph, 200, 226
Hungerburg, 61
Hunter/killer teams, 197

Injuries
    description of, 183–86
    recovery in the hospital, 189–93

Jähde, Major, 43, 49–50, 82
Jews, Lithuanian, 6
Johannmeyer, Major, 37, 190
Judennase, 141–150, 238, 256–59
Ju87s, 101

Kamen, 219
Kampfgruppe, 134
Karasino, 153–154
Kassel, 206–207
Kerscher, Feldwebel, 22, 64, 76, 77, 85–86, 89, 92, 93, 94, 103, 130, 154–55, 160, 166, 167, 189
Kienzle, Unteroffizier, 28
Kinderheim, 64, 67, 75, 85, 86, 92
Kirchen, 211
Knight's Cross, 139
Kolpino, 26
Koselsk, 15
Köstler, Unteroffizier, 33, 34, 51
Kramer, Heinz, 40, 70, 85, 133, 189
Küstrin, 204, 205
KV1, 24
KV85, 24

Lake Ladoga, 26, 27
Lake Peipus, 61, 137
Lake Pleskau, 137
Latvians, 57
Lembitu, 63–64, 86
    report on, 238, 275–305

Leningrad front, 25–32

Leonhard, Hauptmann, 143, 205

Leuna synthetic oil facility, 201–2

Linck, 22

Lindemann, commander, 29

Link, Commander, 104, 110–11

Lithuanians, 6, 57

Lokey, 183

Lowez, 40

Lünneker, 172

Lustig, Obergefreiter, 59–60, 148–49, 206, 210

Maintenance crew, 81

Maintenance report, 238, 248–55

Malinava, 165–68, 173

Map, captured, 168–69, 174, 175

Mark IIIs, 16

Mark IVs, 16

Maruga, 155, 160

Marwitz, Stabsgefreiter, 183, 184–85

Mayer, Commander, 104

Mereküla, 95

Meyer, Gert, 11, 43

MG42, 14, 15

Mines

  clearing devices, 103

  German, 146

  Russian, 114, 121–22, 133

Minsk, 7, 152

Model, Feldmarschall, 56–57, 209, 211, 224–25

Moser, Sepp, 207–8

Napoleon, 6

Narwa

  front, developing the, 56–60

  holding, 61–72

  retreat to, 44–52

Narwa-Waiwara-Wesenberg railway line, 61

Naumann, Lieutenant, 143

Nebelwerfer, destruction by, 132–33

Newel, 33–43

Nienstedt, Lieutenant, 139, 166, 167, 175, 188

Oehme, Hauptmann, 18, 27

Olita, 5–6

Operation Sea Lion, 95–96

Operation Strachwitz, 93, 100–108, 120–36

Opolje, 48

Orders, refusal to obey, 153–61

Ostrow, 140

Paderborn, 204, 205

Panzer I, 25–26

Panzer II, 26

Panzer III, 26

Panzer IV, 26, 100, 127

Panzer V, 26

Panzer 38t, 26

Parachute flares, 45

Paris, 20

Personnel losses, statistics on, 308

Pfannstiel, Unteroffizier, 28

Philipp, Oberst, 11

Pirmasens, 185, 186

Pleskau, 137

Ploermel, 19, 25

Ploskaja, 16
Pogostje, 26
Point 312, 120–22, 131, 133,
    134
Polozk, 164
Posen, training at, 1–3
Prisoners, interrogation of,
    113–15
Propaganda, 112–13, 177
Pseidl, Unteroffizier, 70
Pugatschina, 36

Radio, recording of fighting by
    public, 112–113
Radio transmissions, 79–80
Radtke, Hauptmann, 18
Rations, 67, 69–70, 153
Recovery platoons, 42
Reporting of operations, 177
Resistance groups, 192–93
Reval, rest center at, 151–52
Rieger, Sepp, 17, 88, 150, 189
Riehl, Commander, 104
Riga, 139, 178, 179
Riigi, 58–60, 61
Rocket launchers, destruction
    by, 132–33
Rollbahn, 27
    Dünaburg-Riga, 178, 179
    Dünaburg-Rossitten, 162–73
    Gatschina-Wolosowo-Narwa,
        44
    Rossitten-Pleskau, 140
    Welikije-Luki-Newel-Witebsk,
        33–43
Rossitten, 140, 162–65
Ruhr Highway, 216–21
Ruhr pocket, 206–15
Ruppel, Karl, 151–52
Russian campaign, 3–18

calm before fighting, 73–83
Judennase, 141–150, 238,
    256–59
Leningrad front, 25–32
Narwa, holding, 61–72
Narwa, retreat to, 44–60
Newel, battle at, 33–43
Operation Strachwitz, 93,
    100–108, 120–36
Russian attack along bridge-
    head, 84–96
Ruwiedel, Lieutenant, 42, 205

Salzburg, 190, 191, 200, 201
Schäzle, Bernd, 154
Scherr, Hauptmann, 206
Schmidt, Hauptmann, 139, 209
Schober, Hauptmann, 17–18
Schönbeck, Doctor, 138
Schotroff, Funkmeister, 98–99
Schürer, Lieutenant, 139–40
Schwaner, Major, 137, 141, 144,
    172, 180, 186
Sennelager, 205
Serbians, 195
Sieburg, 208–9
Siegen, 211, 212
Sillamä, 78, 87, 88, 96, 98, 115
Sinjawino, 27, 28
Smolensk, 152
Sschinitschie, 15
Ssergeizewo, 37
SS Panzer Corps, IIIrd, 51–52,
    57, 85
SS Panzer Grenadier Division,
    54
SS units, 198–199
Ssytschewka, 12–13
Stalin tanks, 167, 168, 173
Statistics, 306, 307, 308

Stauffenberg, Graf, 192
Strachwitz, Oberst Graf, 96
  Operation Strachwitz, 93,
    100–108, 120–36
Stukas, 101, 109–10
  Operation Strachwitz and,
    124, 127
Surrender, 222–227
Swedish internment camps,
  57–58

Tabun gas, 212
Tanks
  life inside, 76–77
  statistics on, 306, 307, 308
Tigers
  cupola design, problem with,
    133–34
  description of, 21–24, 117–19
  introduction of, 16–17
  Hunting, 206, 207
  at Leningrad front, 27–32
Tirtsu, 89–90
T34s, 10–11, 24, 85–86, 122–23,
  131
T43s, 24

Ulla, 7–8
Unna, 215, 216–21

Vaihingen, 3
Vision blocks, use of, 118
Volkssturm, 214–15, 222
Von Lüttichau, Hauptmann,
  16, 17
Von Schiller, Oberleutnant, 17,
  29, 46, 78, 79, 82, 87, 89,
  90–91, 97–99, 107, 112, 161
  Operation Strachwitz and,
    124–25, 127, 128–29, 135
Von Scholz, Fritz, 54–55
VW Kübels, 169, 180–81

Waldenmeier, Klaus, 11
Weidenau, 213
Wengler, Oberst, 44, 50, 51, 58,
  60, 85
Werl, 215
Wesely, Feldwebel, 49, 104, 110,
  144, 148, 149
Westphalia, hospital in, 203
Wilna, 6, 152
Witebsk, 8, 40, 152
Wolff, Hermann, 181, 185–86
Wolosowo, 44, 48, 50–51

Zwetti, Oberfeldwebel, 38, 39,
  41, 46, 53–54, 59, 77, 80,
  94, 103, 106, 107, 154, 205